C000149982

THE MACROECONOMICS
ANTI-TEXTBOOK

THE MACROECONOMICS
ANTI-TEXTBOOK

A Critical Thinker's Guide

Tony Myatt

BLOOMSBURY ACADEMIC
LONDON • NEW YORK • OXFORD • NEW DELHI • SYDNEY

BLOOMSBURY ACADEMIC
Bloomsbury Publishing Plc
50 Bedford Square, London, WC1B 3DP, UK
1385 Broadway, New York, NY 10018, USA
29 Earlsfort Terrace, Dublin 2, Ireland

BLOOMSBURY, BLOOMSBURY ACADEMIC and the Diana logo are
trademarks of Bloomsbury Publishing Plc

First published in Great Britain 2023

Copyright © Tony Myatt, 2023

Tony Myatt has asserted his right under the Copyright, Designs and Patents Act,
1988, to be identified as Author of this work.

For legal purposes the Acknowledgments on p. xx constitute
an extension of this copyright page.

All rights reserved. No part of this publication may be reproduced or transmitted
in any form or by any means, electronic or mechanical, including photocopying,
recording, or any information storage or retrieval system, without prior permission
in writing from the publishers.

Bloomsbury Publishing Plc does not have any control over, or responsibility for, any
third-party websites referred to or in this book. All internet addresses given in this
book were correct at the time of going to press. The author and publisher regret any
inconvenience caused if addresses have changed or sites have ceased to exist, but can
accept no responsibility for any such changes.

A catalogue record for this book is available from the British Library.

A catalog record for this book is available from the Library of Congress.

ISBN: HB: 978-1-3503-2372-8
PB: 978-1-3503-2371-1
ePDF: 978-1-3503-2374-2
eBook: 978-1-3503-2373-5

Typeset by Newgen KnowledgeWorks Pvt. Ltd., Chennai, India
Printed and bound in Great Britain

To find out more about our authors and books visit www.bloomsbury.com
and sign up for our newsletters.

CONTENTS

PART 3
SHORT-RUN FLUCTUATIONS

8 MONEY AND BANKING: CRONY CAPITALISM AND THE CORRUPTION IT BREEDS

PART 4
CONCLUSION

TABLES AND FIGURES

Tables

Figures

PREFACE: WHAT IS AN ANTI-TEXTBOOK?

Macroeconomics is a vibrant, fascinating, and utterly relevant subject. But why should you read this anti-textbook instead of just a regular textbook? The answer is that standard textbooks are misleading.

In the companion book, *The Microeconomics Anti-Textbook*, Rod Hill and I explain that most economic textbooks are practically clones of one another. They portray economics as a value-free science, with a settled methodology, and a broad consensus among economists about most economic issues. They apply demand and supply ubiquitously and conclude that markets are generally efficient. Government regulations, such as minimum wages or rent control, are undesirable and end up hurting those they are meant to help.

Our aim in the micro anti-text was to critically examine those claims. We show how value judgments pervade economics and economic textbooks. We point out that there are deep divisions within the profession, and that testing hypotheses is full of difficulties that makes reaching firm conclusions over even relatively simple issues (like the effect of minimum wages) rather difficult. We emphasize that the demand-and-supply framework is synonymous with perfect competition, and noncompetitive market structures lead to different conclusions. The key issue is one of model selection.

These themes continue in the macroeconomic anti-textbook. Once again, the ubiquitous use of the perfectly competitive market structure creates (or perhaps reflects) an ideological bias. This is particularly important in two markets: the financial (or loanable funds) market and the aggregate labor market. The fact that the financial market is depicted as efficient, with all participants having perfect information, contributes to the view that the financial system is the source of great wealth creation rather than a source of instability and a center of white-collar crime. When it comes to the labor market, the reflexive application of perfect competition allows mainstream textbooks to parade minimum wages and unions as villains responsible for increasing structural unemployment.

Methodological difficulties associated with model selection are again important. These difficulties have contributed to macroeconomic theory traveling full circle from the classical view that dominated in the 1930s, to Keynesianism that dominated in the 1950s and 1960s, and back to a nearly classical—or neoclassical—view again.

WHY IT MATTERS

As way of explanation, permit me a slight detour back to the absurdity of the Great Depression. For most of the 1930s, unemployment was over 20 percent in the United States—and it was a similar story in Canada and Europe. A lack of jobs meant a lack of income. Low income meant low spending. And since there was not enough spending, there were not enough jobs. Meanwhile, factories stood idle, ready and waiting to produce the goods that people needed. And people wanted the jobs and had the skills required to do them. But the system could not kick-start itself. It was a crazy vicious circle.

The economists of the day—classical economists—had no solution. They believed in the invisible hand, in free markets. They believed that price flexibility guarantees market clearing. The cure for a surplus of oranges is a decrease in the price of oranges. The cure for a surplus of carpenters is a decrease in the wage of carpenters. Similarly, the cure for widespread unemployment is a decrease in wages across the board. But wages did fall—by over 22 percent between 1929 and 1933 in the United States, and the situation just got worse.

Then John Maynard Keynes published "The General Theory" in 1936, and he explained why the system could not kick-start itself, and why falling wages would make the problem worse. He emphasized that it was the government's job to kick-start the economy by injecting new spending into the system.

However, current neoclassical orthodoxy, explained in mainstream macroeconomic textbooks, also blames unemployment on the failure of wages to fall—or fall quickly enough—just like the classical economists. It even has doubts about whether increasing government spending will help kick-start the economy out of a deep recession. Indeed, after the Great Recession of 2008, a vocal group of influential economists claimed statistical evidence showed that *cutting* government spending would stimulate the economy! The fact that such claims were not immediately dismissed as madness illustrates the difficulty of testing hypotheses in macroeconomics. It also illustrates how far current macroeconomics has reverted to the old classical way of thinking. These problems, and in particular the loss of Keynes in mainstream textbooks, is an important motivation for this macroeconomic anti-textbook.

At this point, it would be natural to ask: why bother learning mainstream neoclassical macroeconomics at all?

WHY NOT JUST TEACH THE ALTERNATIVE VIEWS?

This is an important question, and the answer is threefold. First, mainstream economists are neither knaves nor fools. While there are lots of problems with mainstream macroeconomics, it does provide answers to some deep and serious questions and has had some success as a basis for policy.

Second, if you want to understand what is wrong with mainstream theory, and with economic policy based upon that theory, then you need to understand mainstream theory. To be a good critic, one must thoroughly understand what one is critiquing.

Third, since mainstream economics is so dominant in the profession, to progress in economics you are going to have to learn this theory.

What sets this book apart from other books that critique mainstream macroeconomics is that it treats mainstream theory seriously. It does not create "straw man" representations of it to knock them down more easily. Most critiques end up taking a polarized position that rejects the entire neoclassical corpus. The anti-texts (both micro and macro) have a unique role in presenting a clear unbiased presentation of mainstream theory.

The anti-textbook approach is to first present the mainstream textbook material in the first part of each chapter as clearly and succinctly as possible. Then the anti-text material is presented—that is, all the problems, all the unasked questions, all the problematic assumptions, all the problematic statistical evidence. Chapter by chapter we have text, then anti-text. It would be absolutely fine for readers to reject the anti-text, whole or in part, if they find the arguments unconvincing. The idea is to stimulate critical thinking and deeper understanding.

THIS BOOK IS NOT ANTI-MAINSTREAM MACROECONOMICS

It is important to note that this book is not anti-mainstream economics. It engages with the mainstream view and presents it in an unbiased fashion. However, this book *is* anti-textbook economics since the textbooks hide the deep problematic issues. Even more importantly, the mainstream textbooks do not engage with the key challenges we face—climate change, inequality, unemployment, and poverty. Strangely, those issues are barely mentioned in mainstream macroeconomic textbooks. But they *are* covered in this anti-text.

WHO IS THIS BOOK INTENDED FOR?

This book is written for undergraduate students, for the curious layperson, and also for teachers and professors wanting a different approach to the standard macroeconomic principles course. Would a course based upon this anti-textbook be more difficult than one based upon a mainstream text? Since I teach such a course, this is a question I am often asked by students. My response is that a critical perspectives course is enriched. It goes deeper. In that sense it is more difficult. On the other hand, many students have difficulty in mainstream courses because the explanations do not convince them. They feel intuitively that things are being oversimplified or that there are contradictions. For such students, a critical perspectives course might even be easier.

A unique feature of the anti-textbooks is the "questions for your professor" section placed strategically throughout the anti-text portion. These questions will crystallize the anti-textbook arguments in a way that helps students ask their professors key, well-informed questions. These questions might be viewed as being subversive by a mainstream professor wishing to perpetuate the myth of a deep consensus within macroeconomics. They might also be welcomed by professors wishing to encourage critical thinking in their classroom, and who are looking for opportunities to broaden the discussion.

My fundamental aim in this anti-textbook is to show that economics is not dull and dry. Nor is it a science, with a settled body of knowledge, performed by white lab–coated technicians. The interactions between economic theory and the economy make it a fascinating and utterly relevant subject. It needs critical thinkers. May this book whet your appetite for more.

ACKNOWLEDGMENTS

This book has benefited from many helpful comments. In particular, I would like to thank, without implicating, William M. Scarth and Jafar El Armali for extensive feedback on the entire manuscript, and Rod Hill for helpful comments on several chapters. I would particularly like to thank Brian MacLean for many hours of discussions about what a macroeconomic anti-textbook should contain.

ABOUT THE AUTHOR

Tony Myatt received his PhD from McMaster University with distinction in theory and is an award-winning teacher. He has taught at McMaster University, the University of Western Ontario, the University of Toronto, and the University of New Brunswick, where he has been professor of economics since 1992. His research interests have included stabilization policy, the supply-side effects of interest rates, labor market discrimination, unemployment rate disparities, and the methods and content of economic education. He has developed several different introductory courses as vehicles for teaching principles of economics, including "Economics of everyday life," "Economics in the real world," and "Economics through film." None of them have been as successful as the critical perspectives approach embodied in this book. Along with Rod Hill, he is the author of *The Microeconomics Anti-Textbook*.

Part I

INTRODUCTION

Chapter 1

WHAT IS MACROECONOMICS?

Microeconomists are wrong about specific things, while macroeconomists are wrong about things in general.

Yoram Bauman[1]

Within today's standard economic theory, which is commonly called the neoclassical synthesis, the question: "Why is our economy unstable?" is a nonsense question.

Hyman Minsky[2]

1 THE STANDARD TEXT

Economics divides itself into two halves: micro and macro. In contrast to micro (which deals with small chunks of reality) macro is the study of large aggregates. It explains such things as gross domestic product (GDP), booms and recessions, growth in living standards, unemployment and inflation, the exchange rate, and the determination of interest rates. We begin by taking a closer look at how macroeconomics differs from microeconomics.

1.1 Three ways in which macro differs from micro

FIRST: the level of aggregation Whereas microeconomics studies individual choice, production in a single firm, and the markets for single products, macroeconomics focuses on the national (or world) economy.

Both micro and macro involve the tricky process of aggregation. Micro begins with individual choice and aggregates those choices into market demand curves. It aggregates the production decisions of firms into market supply curves, and it puts demand and supply together to determine market prices of particular goods.

Macroeconomics goes further. It aggregates all output produced by the myriad different industries (and services) into one measure of total output called

GDP. It aggregates all the different types of labor—painters and electricians and rocket scientists—into an aggregate called "labor." It aggregates all the different types of machinery—from factories to bulldozers, from electrical power lines to deepwater ports—into an aggregate called "capital." This allows macro to focus on the big picture—the goods market as a whole, the labor market as a whole, and the financial market as a whole.

Macroeconomics seeks to explain variables like overall output and its rate of growth, as well as overall employment and unemployment. Instead of individual market prices, macro is interested in determining the overall price index and its rate of change over time (more commonly known as the inflation rate). We also want to understand what determines the value of a nation's currency (the exchange rate), and the reasons why interest rates change.

SECOND: *the role of the government* Arguably, the point of microeconomics is to investigate how markets succeed so well in allocating limited resources to competing ends—an idea that can be traced back to Adam Smith's "invisible hand" analogy. Micro shows that government intervention usually leaves society as a whole worse off, except where: (1) there are externalities (usually due to missing markets); (2) there is market power; (3) there is asymmetric information. In weighing the potential costs and benefits of government intervention, *market* failure under those three situations has to be weighed against the likelihood of *government* failure (its latent inefficiency). Thus, microeconomics suggests a limited role for the government.

On the other hand, macroeconomics suggests an important new role for the government: managing short-term fluctuations and adverse events in the economy as a whole. This is known as *stabilization policy*.

THIRD: *the assumed resource constraint* Whereas micro focuses on how best to allocate our given resources, macro adds an important new dimension: how best to grow our resources. It asks what factors lead to a higher long-run growth rate? Are there government policies capable of increasing the long-run growth rate?

1.2 The business cycle (and other important concepts)

We have experienced economic growth for several centuries, but this growth has not proceeded in an even fashion. There are booms when output increases quite rapidly, followed by *recessions* where output falls. The short-run alternation between expansion and contraction is known as the *business cycle*. These expansions and contractions around a long-run growth trend are shown in stylized form in Figure 1.1. Perhaps the two most important tasks for macroeconomics are (1) to stabilize output and (2) to grow output. In terms of Figure 1.1, this would entail narrowing the amplitude of the cycle around the trend, and increasing the upward slope of the trend line. The wavy solid line shows the rise and fall of output, and the dotted line illustrates the long-term upward trend of the economy.

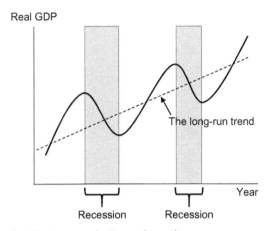

Figure 1.1 The stylized business cycle. Drawn by author

If the most important macroeconomic tasks are to stabilize and grow output, it is because many other important aggregates are driven by output and correlated with it. Falling output generally means decreasing employment and increasing unemployment. Falling output means falling incomes, savings, and investment. Recessions involve the waste of lost output, and high unemployment involves social problems. Finally, there is the worry that a recession might develop into a *depression*, which is a deep and prolonged downturn. Therefore, governments may attempt to reduce the severity of recessions by engaging in *stabilization policies*.[3]

Two important types of *stabilization policy* are monetary and fiscal policy. Monetary policy involves actions by the central bank to change interest rates or to alter the quantity of money circulating in the economy. Fiscal policy involves changes in tax policy or government spending or both. To evaluate the relative merits of these policies we will need to construct an economic model of the macro economy, a model with which we can explain and predict movements in macroeconomic aggregates. Therefore, in closing this subsection, we should be very aware that the depiction in Figure 1.1 of the business cycle as some sort of sine wave—regular and easily predicted—is not true in reality.

To illustrate this, Figure 1.2 plots Canadian output (real GDP) from 1961 to 2016. The upward trend is the dominant feature, but also apparent are three major recessions, one in the early 1980s, another in the early 1990s, and one beginning in 2008 (associated with the global financial meltdown).

The recessions are more obvious in Figure 1.3, which plots the rate of growth of Canadian output over the same period. Also apparent in Figure 1.3 are the irregular changes in the growth rate over time—each business cycle is unique.

1.3 Long-run growth

A central concern of macroeconomics is what determines growth in the standard of living. There are many ways to try to measure "standard of living," from infant

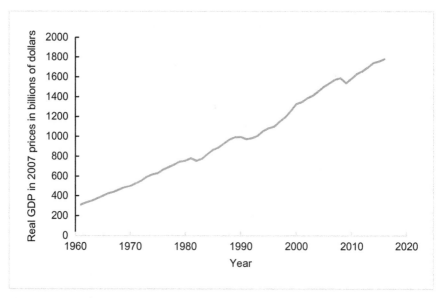

Figure 1.2 Canadian real GDP, 1961–2016
Source: Statistics Canada, Table 380-0106 GDP at 2007 prices, expenditure-based, annual

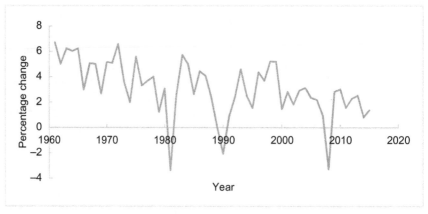

Figure 1.3 The growth rate of Canadian real GDP, 1961–2016. Calculations by author

mortality rates to average life expectancy. However, insofar as our access to health care and our ability to thrive are dependent on our ability to pay, income is a key. Indeed, surveys such as Pew's "Ladder of Life," "The World Values Survey," and the United Nations' "World Happiness Report" suggest that one of the most important components in happiness is real income. Richer countries tend to have higher standards of living, better health care and education, cleaner environments, and more support for families than poorer ones. So, real output per capita is a crucial barometer of standard of living.

While the growth of output is considered in Chapter 3, it is crucial to understand at the outset that *we use different models to analyze growth from those used to analyze the business cycle.* Our growth models abstract from the business cycle. They assume that output is always on its trend growth path—or to rephrase the point, that the economy's resources are always fully employed. On the other hand, the models we use to analyze the business cycle abstract from growth. When analyzing the business cycle, we assume we have given resources and there is no growth.

This separation is best seen as splitting issues up by time. It takes time for growth to occur, for capital to accumulate, for technology to improve. The more time we allow to elapse, the more growth will occur. Therefore, growth is considered a *long-run* issue. On the other hand, the problem in a recession is that some of our current resources—both capital and labor—are unemployed. This is a *short-run* issue, a problem with our current resources. This separation into *short run* and *long run* is known as *analytical time*. There is no close mapping of analytical time onto chronological time; rather, the mapping depends on the skill of the analyst and the particular problem at hand.

Such an approach is justified on two grounds. First, separating growth from the business cycle hugely simplifies our task, allowing us to gain insight into each issue separately. Second, the data presented in Figure 1.2 *do* seem to support this separation of tasks. The three downturns that are so easily visible when looking at Figure 1.3 (those of the early 1980s, the early 1990s, and 2008) are barely perceptible when looking at trend growth over a long period, as in Figure 1.2. Trend growth does seem to be independent of the business cycle.

1.4 Inflation and deflation

Inflation is the term used for a rising aggregate price level. Specifically, the rate of inflation is the annual percent change of the aggregate price level. Price stability means a constant aggregate price level, or at least one that is changing very slowly, while deflation is a falling aggregate price level.

Figure 1.4 plots the rate of change of the most used measure of aggregate prices—the consumer price index—for Canada from 1915 to 2016. We see that since the mid-1990s, inflation has been quite moderate. But it wasn't always like that. There was a period of prolonged high inflation in the 1970s until the mid-1980s. Also, there were short bursts of high inflation, first toward the end of the First World War (peaking at 18 percent in 1917), and second following the Second World War (peaking at 14 percent in 1948). Finally, we notice two periods of quite rapid deflation, first in the early 1920s, and second in the early 1930s.

Overall, however, inflation has dominated and prices have risen considerably over the period. This means that we have to distinguish between *real* and *nominal* values. If we do not correct for higher prices we get a misleading picture. For example, between 1946 and 2001 average wages increased nearly fortyfold. But wage earners were not forty times better off in 2001 compared to 1946, because

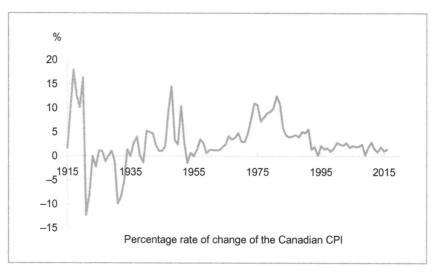

Figure 1.4 Inflation and deflation in Canada, 1915–2016
Source: Statistics Canada, Table 326-0020 Consumer Price Index (CPI), annual (2002=100)

prices also increased (though not as much). After correcting for higher prices, the average worker in 2001 earned about three times as much as in 1946 in *real* terms, or in terms of what they could actually buy with their money. The general point here is any *nominal* magnitude can change either because quantities change or because prices change, or both. But a real magnitude is corrected for price changes, and therefore can only change if quantities change.

1.5 The open economy

A *closed economy* is an economy that does not trade goods, services, or assets with other countries. Since there is no economy like that in the real world, a closed economy is essentially a fiction, useful for simplifying reality. There is one important exception to that last remark: the world economy is a closed economy, at least until we begin intergalactic trade.

Open economy macro studies the effects of the international movements of goods, services, and assets. Most developed economies are very open. We live in an era of globalization, which means two things: first, most countries sell most of what they produce to other countries, and second, capital moves between countries very easily. Capital flows are movements of money (or *financial capital*) across borders. This allows investors to get higher returns than if they were restricted to invest domestically. Further, by allowing access to foreign capital, it permits countries to grow faster than otherwise.

A trade deficit occurs when the value of goods and services bought from foreigners is more than the value we sell to them. Sometimes the media interprets a trade deficit as a bad thing. One concern is that we are losing jobs by importing foreign-made goods. This concern is highlighted when we import more than we export. But a trade deficit is not necessarily a problem.

If the exchange rate is flexible, the international payments to foreigners must equal the receipts from foreigners. This is what the "balance of payments" means. The exchange rate functions as the price of foreign currency, and as in any competitive market, the price will ensure demand equals supply—or in this case, the demand for foreign currency must equal the supply of foreign currency (domestically). Given this balance, a trade deficit is necessarily offset by a corresponding inflow of money—by foreigners buying domestic assets, real or financial. This could be because foreigners want to invest in the domestic economy. Perhaps they are building factories and employing domestic workers. If this inflow of capital is what is driving the deficit on the balance of trade, then it might be a sign of a healthy economy.

On the other hand, a balance of trade deficit might be because our economy is fundamentally uncompetitive—our goods are too expensive, the quality is too poor—and we are borrowing money from foreigners by selling them short-term financial assets to finance the trade deficit. We might also be paying a high rate of interest on these short-term assets to induce foreigners to hold them. In this case, the balance of trade deficit would be a bad sign since living standards will soon drop when the short-term financing dries up. At that point, we will have to live within our means. Therefore, a balance of trade deficit is not necessarily a bad thing, though it could be. The crux of the matter is the causal factors driving it.

Besides addressing questions such as these, open economy macroeconomics also considers whether stabilization policy (monetary and fiscal policy) is helped or hindered by international flows of goods and money.

2 THE ANTI-TEXT

Mainstream macroeconomic textbooks do a good job introducing some important definitions, introducing the student to data, and showing charts of recent economic performance. However, they do not properly address the most important and fundamental question of why we need a separate area of economics called "macroeconomics"! This question is addressed next and the answer developed over the remainder of the chapter. In the process, we delve into some important economic history—that of the Great Depression—and we introduce the student to some of the schools of thought within macroeconomics, and the historical antecedents of those schools.

2.1 Why macroeconomics is necessary: the fallacy of composition

Mainstream texts give a misleading understanding of how macroeconomics differs from microeconomics. Is it really a question of size? It strains credulity to believe that we need an entirely different branch of economics simply because macroeconomics does more aggregation than microeconomics.

In the past, mainstream textbooks gave a different answer as to why macroeconomics is necessary, and a few still do: we need macro because of the *fallacy of composition*. This arises when we assume that what is true for a part (of something) is necessarily true for the whole. Clearly, that is not so. What is true for a part is not necessarily true for the whole.

Consider some everyday examples. Suppose the Fire Marshal wants to ascertain whether there are enough fire exits in a building, and suppose a safe building is one that can be evacuated in under three minutes. Would it be a good idea to test the safety of the building by timing how long it takes one person to exit? It could be argued that if any one person can exit the building in under three minutes, then everyone in the building could. But this is patently false. What about congestion and panic?

Or suppose the government announces a new national program to reduce unemployment by training the unemployed to have better job interview skills. Would this succeed? Certainly, any one person can improve their chances of getting a job by having better interview skills. But if there are not enough jobs to go around, the government's new program will fail.

Consider a third example, the *paradox of thrift*. It is generally considered a good thing for a household to increase its savings. But if all households save more, total spending goes down. A decrease in spending will lead to a decrease in output, and a decrease in employment, which would lead to a decrease in earned incomes. And when earned incomes go down, households cannot afford to save as much, so total savings decrease. This is the paradox of thrift: an attempt by all households to save more leads to a decrease in realized savings! It seems that what is virtuous for one household is harmful for all.

These examples of the fallacy of composition show that the "whole" is not the simple sum of its parts. If not for the fallacy of composition, there would be no need for a separate branch of economics called macro; we could just do micro. Macro is necessary because what is true for a part is not necessarily true for the whole. Therefore, we need to go beyond micro.

Question for your professor: We are told that macroeconomics deals with large aggregates, while microeconomics deals with specific markets. But surely, there's a lot of aggregation involved in getting to market-specific demand and supply curves. So, what really is the difference between micro and macro?

2.2 Why is the fallacy of composition is downplayed in mainstream textbooks?

If the *fallacy of composition* is the reason we need a separate branch of economics called macro, if it is what makes macro essentially different from micro, why don't the mainstream texts emphasize that point? We suggest the only logical answer is that mainstream economics does not consider macro to be inherently different to micro! There are two crucial pieces of evidence for this.

First, at the most advanced level, mainstream economists have been trying to develop *microeconomic underpinnings* to macro since the mid-1970s. Micro-underpinnings (or microfoundations) involve developing decision rules for a *representative agent*—a single individual meant to be representative of all individuals—which we then use as structural equations in the macro model. It is assumed that the decision rule of the single agent coincides with the aggregate choices of myriad heterogeneous individuals in the economy—that what is true for a part is true for the whole. Since this approach is considered valid at the advanced level, it makes sense to downplay the fallacy of composition at the introductory level.

Second, mainstream macroeconomists have come to believe essentially classical conclusions about the macro economy, conclusions that dominated the profession before macroeconomics became a separate branch of economics in its own right, conclusions derived from microeconomics. In particular, mainstream introductory textbooks conclude that the fundamental reason for recessions is price stickiness. If only there were no sticky prices—if only wages and prices were perfectly flexible—there would be no stabilization problem and the economy would always be at full employment.

To understand why this is so problematic, we need to go back to the birth of modern macro and the Great Depression, which is the subject of the next section. But before moving on to this section, it behooves us to say a few more words about the microfoundations research agenda and, in particular, why those foundations are considered necessary by mainstream neoclassical economists. This discussion is of a more advanced nature. It could be omitted without loss of continuity. But the payoff will be a better understanding of the problematic nature of evidence in macroeconomics. *The necessity of microfoundations?* The answer as to why microfoundations were considered necessary requires us to discuss methodology and the limitations of falsifiability.[4] You'll remember that mainstream texts emphasize that the way to determine whether a model is any good is to test the accuracy of its predictions—not to consider the realism of its assumptions. Unfortunately, empirical tests are often not definitive. (Think back to *The Microeconomics Anti-Textbook* and the controversies over the effects of minimum wages and rent controls described in Chapter 2. These controversies were not resolved by an appeal to empirical evidence!)

Therefore, it is argued that some weight must be put on a second criterion for model evaluation: consistency with optimizing underpinnings. After all, we do not want to be basing our conclusions on a model that is internally inconsistent.

Furthermore, there is a problem with the old-fashioned pre-mid-1970s way of deriving macroeconomic structural equations. If we needed a relationship between consumption and income—otherwise known as a consumption function—the old-fashioned way was to estimate a statistical relationship between the variables using *past data*. But in 1976, Robert Lucas showed that the estimated relationship might not be robust to a change in government policy, and if so, it would not be much use predicting the effect of new policy. This result became known as the *Lucas critique*, and it drove an attempt to find structural equations that had parameters that would be invariant to policy changes. Such parameters are called *primitive parameters*, and the commonly held view was that they were to be found in the specification of the underlying utility and production functions. This suggested, once again, going back to the optimization problem of the representative agent, whether that agent be an individual or a firm.

To understand the Lucas critique, we need to know that it coincided with a change in the way economists thought about expectation formation. The old idea was that people formed their expectations of the future based solely on what had happened in the past, a process known as *adaptive expectations*. But why should people restrict themselves to past data? Surely a *rational* person would incorporate all available information, including not only past data but also anticipated government policy changes. It is this change in thinking about expectation formation—the movement toward so-called *rational expectations*—that gives the Lucas critique power. For example, suppose the government announces that it is committed to keeping the unemployment rate below 5 percent. If people believe this announcement, and believe the government has the power to accomplish it, this would likely affect the relationship between consumption and income—there would be less need to save to cover the possibility of becoming unemployed in the event of a recession. This illustrates how a consumption function, based purely on the past relationship between income and consumption, could shift in the event of a change in government policy.

To recap, what drove the micro-underpinnings agenda was twofold: first, the limitations of falsifiability, which led to more emphasis on consistency with optimizing underpinnings; and second, the search for primitive parameters that were immune to the Lucas critique. All mainstream economists strongly supported this micro-underpinnings research agenda, at least up until the great financial meltdown of 2007–8. The strength of the consensus was remarkable for at least two reasons: first, because the microfoundations literature completely ignored the aggregation problem (and hence the fallacy of composition); and second, because the microeconomics used in the micro-underpinnings exercise was not very appealing. We will discuss these in turn.

The first problem concerns the aggregation problem. The aggregation problem refers to the theoretical conditions under which an aggregate of all individuals would behave just like an individual (representative) agent. For example, suppose we derive a representative agent's demand curve for commodity X, and then ask: *under what conditions would the aggregate (or market) demand curve for X have the same characteristics?* Economists have proven that this is possible only when: (1) all consumers have the same preferences; and (2) preferences (across commodities) do not change with income.[5] As Keen (2011: 403) wryly observes, "condition (a) effectively means that there is only one consumer, while condition (b) effectively means there is only one commodity. Aggregation is therefore strictly possible if there is only one consumer and only one commodity. Clearly, this is not aggregation at all." Scarth (2014: 69) summarizes the aggregation literature as follows: "The conclusion of the aggregation literature is that the conditions required for consistent aggregation are so rigid that constrained maximization at the individual level may have very few macroeconomic implications—that is, very few useful insights for aggregative analysis." Again, what is true for a part is not necessarily true for the whole.

The second problem concerns the unappealing nature of the microeconomics used in the micro-underpinnings exercise. As Dorman (2012) explains, "it has three crushing faults, each sufficient by itself to blow a wide hole in a supposedly useful model." First, the optimizing underpinnings are based on a very naïve view of human behavior, one that ignores all the evidence on how humans actually behave: it ignores the insights of behavioral economics, evolutionary biology, neuropsychology, and organization theory. Second, there are no interaction effects to generate multiple equilibria in the microfoundations macro theorists generally use. Third, the optimizing underpinnings all ignore the Sonnenschein–Mantel–Debreu theorem that with many interdependent markets within the economy, there might not exist a unique equilibrium point. In other words, they ignore the possibility of path dependence.

Nevertheless, the microfoundations research agenda is alive and well. The failure of economists to predict the great financial meltdown of 2007–8 did lead some economists to question it, and the advanced macro models derived from them. For example, Paul Krugman (2009) stated, "Most macroeconomics of the past 30 years was spectacularly useless at best, and positively harmful at worst." Willem Buiter (2009) agreed, putting it this way: "The typical graduate macroeconomics training received during the past 30 years may have set back by decades serious investigations of aggregate economic behaviour and economic policy-relevant understanding." Robert Gordon (2009) echoed those sentiments when he said, "We are best served by applying 1978-era macro and forgetting most of the modern macro that has developed since."

But it is important to understand that this triumvirate of critics were not against microfoundations per se. Rather what they wanted was better foundations that incorporate, for example, market failure, agents with limited rationality, financial constraints, and noncompetitive markets—foundations that lead to a model that has predictions consistent with observable reality.

Noah Smith (2012) makes the case for microfoundations this way: we want better models; to get them we should use as much information as possible; incorporating the ways in which economic actors are making their decisions will give us more information; therefore, we should use microfoundations that are based on the way individuals actually behave in practice, as determined by survey data or lab experiments.

Methodologically speaking, the debate about microfoundations and the debate about the representative agent seem to have boiled down to falsifiability again. For example, Scarth (2014: 69) concludes his discussion of the issues by saying,

> Economists should ignore neither aggregation problems [i.e. the fallacy of composition] nor optimizing underpinnings. Yet the current convention is to ignore aggregation issues by building macro models involving no differences between any individuals—the so-called representative-agent model. The only justification for this approach is an empirical one—that the predictions of the macro models, which are based on such a representative agent, are not rejected by the data.

Insofar as one of the main reasons for developing micro-underpinnings involving *the limitations of falsifiability*, we seem to have come full circle!

```
Questions for your professor
#1: How important is the "fallacy of composition"
in macroeconomics?
#2: In macroeconomics, how important is it for a model
to be consistent with "optimizing underpinnings"?
   #3: Aren't optimizing underpinnings always
performed for a "representative agent"? Then aren't
they subject to the "fallacy of composition"?
```

2.3 The birth of modern macro: the Great Depression

The Great Depression was one of the defining moments of the twentieth century. Beginning in 1929 and lasting for over a decade, it affected virtually all the world's market economies—Canada, the United States, Latin America, Europe, Japan, and Australia. If we had to express in as few words as possible the central mission of modern macro, it is to prevent anything like the Great Depression from ever happening again.

What makes the Great Depression unique is not only its depth, duration, and widespread scope but also the economic misery associated with it. At that time, there were hardly any social safety nets—social security or employment insurance. Millions were forced to rely on soup kitchens to eat. Families were evicted from their homes and "shantytowns" arose across North America. Labor strife was pervasive. It was a time of incredible misery.

And in desperate times, people do desperate things. The Great Depression contributed to the rise of fascism in Germany and throughout Europe, partly because economic conditions provided fertile ground.

To begin our study of macroeconomics it is useful to begin right here, with the Great Depression, and ask three questions. Specifically, what caused the depression of 1929? In general, what can cause a depression? And finally, could it ever happen again?

These are complex issues. In his authoritative history of the Great Depression, Charles Kindleberger (1973, chapter 14) argues that there was no single cause. Rather, he emphasizes three forces: panic, contagion, and the absence of a dominant economic power, able and willing to stabilize the international economy. Drawing on Kindleberger's analysis, we can compare economic depressions to forest fires. The metaphor suggests three critical ingredients: dry kindling, a spark, and wind to fan the flames. And even though we may have better fire brigades than in the past, if the kindling is dry enough and deep enough, and the wind is strong enough, once the fire is ignited it can easily get out of control, even today. Let us unpack the metaphor in the context of 1929.

The kindling In 1929, the kindling was provided by some fundamental structural problems in the world economy that made it vulnerable to a downturn. There were three important elements.

First, the Treaty of Versailles (1919) that ended the First World War imposed punitive reparations payments on the defeated nations of Germany, Austria, and Hungary. They made these payments in goods, which were (essentially) free to the victors. This not only crippled the economies of the defeated nations but also weakened the economies of the victors—their industries could not compete against the importation of free goods. Europe was fundamentally vulnerable in the late 1920s.

Second, international monetary imbalances were threatening international trade. Historically, Britain performed the role of the world's banker and sterling (the pound) was the major international currency. In the nineteenth century, Britain's domination of manufacturing export markets led to an enormous influx of foreign currencies, which it recycled back to debtor countries, providing them with the liquidity they needed to keep buying manufactured exports. However, Britain had declined both as a world power and as the world center of international banking. By 1929, it was no longer capable of being the world's banker, but no other country (or group of countries) had yet stepped in to replace her. This left a power vacuum. The result: the world economy was desperately short of liquidity to finance world trade.

Third, there was a huge bubble on the New York stock market waiting to burst. In ten years, the Dow Jones index had risen over 600 percent. Everyone from millionaires to janitors poured their savings into stocks. Then they took out bank loans to invest even more. It was a paper pyramid waiting to topple.

Was there a common component in the three pieces of kindling? The common component was debt. The Treaty of Versailles imposed a debt burden on the losing nations: Germany, Austria, and Hungary. The international monetary imbalance meant that indebted nations were unable to trade. The euphoric stock market bubble in the United States was debt driven.

There is nothing intrinsically wrong with debt—it is simply one side of the ledger with assets on the other. But one aspect is critical: the dollar price of debt is invariably fixed (it is denominated in fixed nominal terms), whereas asset prices are variable. This means that standard measures of financial viability, such as debt-to-asset ratios, vary with changes in asset prices. Such measures may look fine valued at current asset prices. But if the price of those assets should fall, the debt-to-asset ratio could suddenly increase to unacceptable levels.

The spark While the kindling may be complex, the spark is easy to pinpoint. In the last week of October 1929, the US stock market collapsed. In the space of three weeks, the market lost nearly 50 percent of its value. The selling and the declines continued for three straight years. By June 1932, the market had lost 86 percent of its value, still the greatest fall on record.[6] Millions of shares ended up worthless. Those who had bought stocks "on margin" (with borrowed money) could not afford to pay back their bank loans, and the banks themselves began to fail. When banks collapsed, the financial disaster spread. People lost their life savings, and consumer and business confidence collapsed. All this drastically reduced the demand for goods leading to a slump in economic activity, business bankruptcies, and unemployment, which further depressed the demand for goods and worsened the slump. The whole thing spiraled down and spread from one country to another.

By 1932, US industrial output had fallen by 50 percent. Unemployment was over 23 percent. It was a similar story in Canada, and throughout Europe. Output in the Western world did not return to its 1928 level until 1940. Governments felt powerless to do anything about it.

Indeed, the persistence of the Great Depression was mostly because of the incorrect, ill-conceived, and perverse policies followed by governments.

What governments lacked was a clear understanding of the macro economy. They had two main policies: austerity (slashing government spending) and protectionism against foreign imports. Indeed, government policy was the wind that fanned the flames of the forest fire.

The wind Whenever output decreases, governments lose tax revenue, driving their budgets into deficit. In response, governments around the world raise tax rates and slash their spending by cutting programs and enforcing massive reductions in the pay of public sector workers. The idea was not just to balance the budget but also to restore confidence in the nation's finances and the economy in general by following policies that the business class approved of. However, spending cuts and payroll cuts took more money out of the economy, further reduced the demand for goods, and created more unemployment. (Of course, spending cuts and tax increases refer to perverse fiscal policy. It is important to note that by allowing about a third of US banks to fail during the 1929–33 period, monetary policy was also perverse and most certainly fanned the flames!)

Protectionism was a worldwide trend during the 1930s. It had two features. First, governments protected domestic markets by imposing high tariffs on foreign imports. Second, they devalued their currency to make their exports cheaper on world markets. The idea was simple: given a lack of overall demand, the aim was to get more for themselves by shifting demand from their trading partners—a "beggar thy neighbor" policy. And when all countries started doing it, what resulted was a series of competitive currency devaluations. The relative value of currencies became volatile and increasingly uncertain. The combination of high tariffs and uncertain currency values resulted in the collapse of world trade.

These government policies worsened the depression, and hindered recovery. But you cannot really blame the governments: the advice they received was terrible. The economists of the time (referred to as "classical" economists) were followers of Adam Smith and they thought the economy was inherently self-regulating.

2.4 Classical economics and the Keynesian breakthrough

How does the economy regulate itself? Through the invisible hand of the price mechanism. Price flexibility eliminates surpluses and shortages.

Suppose there is a particularly bountiful orange crop and the market is flooded with oranges. The price of oranges would surely fall; otherwise, oranges would rot on the shelves. Next, consider the market for carpenters. Suppose carpenters demand wages of $500 an hour. What would happen? There would be many unemployed carpenters. The remedy? Reduce their wages back to something more reasonable!

Thus, the classical economists reasoned, if prices are left free to adjust, markets will clear. Since this is true for oranges, and true for carpenters, it must be generally true. It must be true for all workers. Therefore, general, large-scale, mass unemployment must be caused by the average wage being too high. The solution is for the average wage to fall.

Yet in the Great Depression wages did fall—average wages fell by over 25 percent in Canada and over 22 percent in the United States—and the unemployment just got worse![7]

The Great Depression led to a feverish effort by economists to understand what had happened, and what could be done. The breakthrough occurred with the 1936 publication of *The General Theory of Employment, Interest, and Money* (usually referred to as *The General Theory*) by John Maynard Keynes—a book that ranks in influence with Adam Smith's *The Wealth of Nations*. Keynes realized that the classical logic that says "what's true for any one type of worker, must be true for all workers" is incorrect: it is a fallacy of composition. Furthermore, it seems intuitively obvious that pushing wages down would *decrease* the demand for goods, and hence would *decrease* the demand for workers. And Keynes built a theoretical model to explain it.

While Keynes started macroeconomics and a school of thought known as Keynesianism, many have argued that his key ideas have been misunderstood or lost in translation. The examination of this claim (that mainstream macroeconomics does not embody Keynes's essential ideas) is one of our themes throughout this book. But for now, we need to make a simple beginning.

Question for your professor: Did the classical economists believe that wage flexibility would bring about full employment? Do modern mainstream economists think the same thing?

2.5 Keynes's General Theory

This section contains an intuitive treatment of Keynes's theory. We begin by noting that GDP is a measure of our collective output, *and* a measure of our collective incomes. As beautifully articulated by Robert Heilbroner (1999: 147), "the central characteristic of an economy is the flow of incomes from hand to hand. With every purchase that we make, we transfer a part of our incomes into someone else's pocket. Similarly every penny of our own incomes, be it wages, salaries, rents, profits, or interest, ultimately derives from money which someone else has spent."

Every dollar we spend provides income to someone else. Every dollar we earn comes from someone else's spending. But the flow of income is not a closed system with the same amount always being passed around. Instead, there are drains where income leaks out, and taps where new income

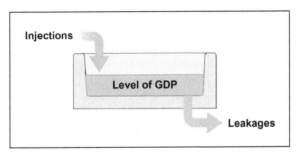

Figure 1.5 The economy as a bathtub. Drawn by author

squirts in. In general, if the leakage of income out exceeds the injection of income in, the amount passed around each time decreases.

Think of the economy as a bathtub. Imagine that the taps are open, but there is no plug in the drain. The level of GDP is the height of water in the bath. Clearly, if the injection of water from the taps exceeds the leakage of water going down the drain, the level of water in the tub (GDP) will increase. But if leakages exceed injections, GDP will decrease. This economy as bathtub metaphor is illustrated in Figure 1.5.

According to Keynes, the leakages are stable and predictable. For example, if we do not spend part of our income but instead save it, then that part is not passed on as income to others.[8] And this propensity to save out of income is remarkably stable and predictable over time. On the other hand, Keynes realized that the injections are much more volatile. The most volatile injection is investment, where "investment" means new spending by firms on capital equipment. Keynes realized that the incentive to accumulate capital was decidedly volatile.

In the twentieth century, there have been several major waves of investment, associated with new technology and opportunities.[9] Each of these has brought with it an investment boom. Each wave of investment drives a boom in GDP, which becomes a self-generating process. An investment boom is like turning up the tap; injections increase and now exceed leakages, leading to expanding GDP, which further stimulates optimism and more investment.

But the reverse can happen too. As investment opportunities dry up, injections decrease, which is like turning down the tap. Injections become less than leakages leading to a decline in GDP, which further deepens the gloom and dampens investor spirits leading to further declines in investment. So, this is how the cycles of boom and bust are generated.

But here is the point: the economy can become stuck. Normally, the cycles are moderate. A nice little boom, followed by a nice little recession. But if the downward swing is intense enough, the economy could be knocked off its kilter, stuck in a gloomy outlook; it could remain in a state of prolonged recession.

This was Keynes's main insight: *The economy can become stuck in a state of profound unemployment. And the root cause of the problem was insufficient investment spending.*

Like Karl Marx, Keynes concluded that capitalism is inherently unstable. Like Marx, Keynes focused on the incentive to accumulate capital—the investment process. But unlike Marx, Keynes does not predict capitalism's inevitable collapse. Instead, he finds a remedy—one implied by the diagnosis. Since slumps are caused by insufficient investment spending by firms, the solution is simple: the government must step in and do the investing itself. The government has a responsibility to stabilize the economy.

Now we say "the government must do the investment spending itself," but it does not much matter on what the government spends. It could invest in education by building schools; it could invest in infrastructure by building roads, railways, and ports. But it also could build useless pyramids. Or it could build tanks and rockets. Obviously, the benefits to the population would be vastly different with each of these options. But the short-term effect on the economy would be the same: the point is to stimulate the economy by injecting new spending into it.

Let us be very clear about Keynes's solution: in a slump, the government is probably already running a deficit. Is Keynes suggesting increasing spending, and worsening the government's budget deficit? Precisely! The Great Depression was eventually ended by massive government spending. But instead of spending on education and infrastructure, they spent on armies, and guns, on fighting the Second World War.

Keynes's solution is as simple as sailing. The government is like the yachtsman on a small boat. When the boat tips to the right, to keep the boat stable the sailor leans to the left.

When incomes are contracting, government spending should be expanding. And when incomes are expanding, government spending should be contracting.

> Question for your professor: Do modern economists
> believe that it is possible for the economy to become
> stuck in a position with profound unemployment?

2.6 Digging deeper into the paradox of thrift

In the previous section, we likened the economy to a bathtub and said that GDP is determined by injections and leakages: when injections are equal to leakages, GDP remains constant. In this last case, we can think of GDP as being in equilibrium—in the sense that (given leakages and injections) it has no tendency to change.

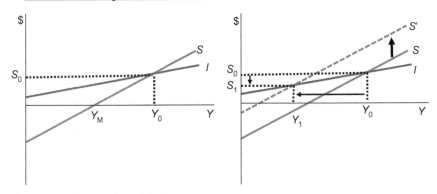

Figure 1.6 The paradox of thrift

We also mentioned that savings are a leakage (a stable one) and investment is an injection (a volatile one). In fact, if we focus on a special case—one where there is no government and no foreign trade—savings become the only leakage, and investment the only injection.[10] This gives us a simple model for determining equilibrium GDP, a model that is sometimes called "The Crude Keynesian Model." It allows us to demonstrate the possibility of the Paradox of Thrift in a very concrete way.

Consider Figure 1.6A. The horizontal axis is output or income, denoted Y. The vertical axis measures the dollar value of savings and investment. Both savings and investment are shown as increasing with income, Y. When income is zero, households spend more than their income—that is, savings are negative. At income level of Y_M households spend all their income, and savings are zero. Beyond Y_M households are able to save a constant proportion of their income. The positive slope of the investment line reflects the *accelerator effect* that postulates improving business confidence as output increases, which leads to increases in investment. Figure 1.6A shows that the equilibrium level of output is Y_0. At Y_0, households choose to save S_0.

Figure 1.6B shows what happens when households desire to save more out of any given level of income. The increased desire to save is shown by an upward shift in the savings function, from S to the dotted line, S'. Unfortunately, the increased leakages cause the equilibrium level of income to fall. As income falls, the desire to invest diminishes, causing the equilibrium level of income to fall even further. Figure 1.6B shows that this process comes to a halt at a much reduced income level of Y_1 where injections once again equal leakages. At Y_1, realized household savings have fallen to S_1, which is *below the level households saved before their desire to save increased*.[11]

Essentially, the paradox of thrift demonstrates the possible harm to the economy of a glut of savings. It leads to a decrease in the demand for goods, and thus a decrease in output and income. In fact, the classical economists were aware of this possibility. The idea was associated with the writings of Thomas Malthus in the early nineteenth century.[12] They knew, for example, that if households saved by stuffing money under their mattresses there would be no way for the money to find its way back into the circular flow. But the possibility was dismissed because they thought such behavior highly unlikely.

Normally households do not stuff money under mattresses. Instead, they deposit their savings in the bank, and maybe the bank lends the money out to someone wanting to borrow it. And when the borrower spends it, the money finds its way back into the circular flow. While there is nothing automatic about this process, it is regulated by a price: the rate of interest. And if prices are free to adjust, markets will clear—or so the classical economists believed.

The role of the rate of interest in ensuring a balance between savings and investment is illustrated in Figure 1.7. The horizontal axis is the quantity of loanable funds, measured in dollars. The vertical axis is the interest rate. Savings are drawn as an upward sloping function of the rate of interest, since a higher rate of interest will likely induce more savings. Investment is drawn as a downward sloping function, since a higher rate of interest raises the cost of borrowing money. Since we know that savings and investment also depend on income (or output), we have held output constant at its full employment level.

An increase in the desire to save is shown as a rightward shift in the savings function, from the solid line to the dotted line labeled S'. At the initial rate of interest, r_1, there is excess savings equal to $Q_3 - Q_1$ dollars. But this savings glut does not cause output to fall; instead, the balance between savings and investment is restored by a decrease in the interest rate to r_2.

Thus, the classical economists reasoned that a price existed that would clear the market for loanable funds. And flexibility in that price (the interest

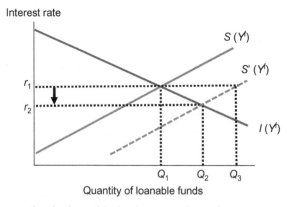

Interest rate

$S(Y)$

$S'(Y)$

r_1

r_2

$I(Y)$

Q_1 Q_2 Q_3

Quantity of loanable funds

Figure 1.7 The market for loanable funds. Drawn by author

rate) was sufficient to eliminate the worry about a glut of savings. The money that was taken out of the circular flow as savings would find its way back into the circular flow as investment. The upshot was that sustained declines in income, or large-scale depression conditions, could not occur in the classical model. But clearly, they did in reality.

In his General Theory, Keynes launched a blistering attack on this classical model. He pointed out that the determination of interest rates shown in Figure 1.7 must be incomplete since savings and investment also depend on output, and output is not necessarily fixed at full employment. He pointed out that, while in normal times people do not save by stuffing money under their mattresses, they may do so in times of great financial uncertainty. In general, people have a desire to hold cash, a desire that he called "liquidity preference." This had to be incorporated into a full model. These interactions were at the heart of Keynes's model. Hopefully, this should help explain why Keynes called his magnum opus *The General Theory of Employment, Interest and Money.*

> Question for your professor: Is it possible there could be a glut of savings? Would you expect that interest rates would adjust to remove it? Or output?

2.7 Schools of thought within macroeconomics

Introductory textbooks convey the impression that there is widespread consensus among macroeconomists. This is far from true. Indeed, the financial crisis of 2007–8 revealed deep fissures between the two dominant schools of thought in macroeconomics: the saltwater school and the freshwater school. This section is designed to provide a roadmap to understanding the ideological position and heritage of most of the major schools of thought in macroeconomics.

At the top of Figure 1.8, we find Karl Marx on the left of the spectrum of economic thought, and Adam Smith on the right. In his 1867 book *Capital*, Marx analyses the capitalist system and finds it to be inherently unstable, prone to crisis, and containing the seeds of its own destruction. And he thought it to be inherently exploitative.

On the other hand, in his book *The Wealth of Nations* (1776) Smith painted a picture of a capitalist system that was inherently stable and self-organizing (the invisible hand idea), in which there was a harmony of interest between economic participants. His belief that flexible prices guarantee market clearing practically defines the classical school. Output according to Smith is determined by the productivity of a nation's factors of production. The role of money is limited to being a means of exchange that facilitate transactions. The tension between Karl Marx on the left and

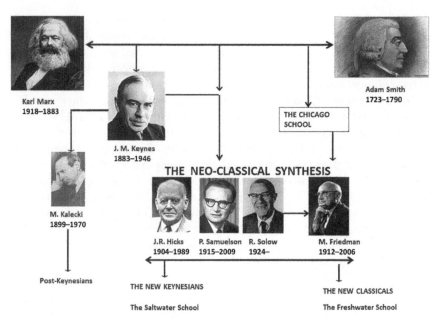

Figure 1.8 The spectrum of economic thought. Drawn by author

Adam Smith on the right defines the extremes of our spectrum of economic thought.

Keynes is shown as descending from this earlier work, closer to Marx than to Smith. Like Marx, he too believed the capitalist system to be inherently unstable, prone to crisis. But unlike Marx, he did not think the problem to be endemic to capitalism. He likened the capitalist system to a car that was fundamentally sound but occasionally broke down because of a problem with its alternator—a problem the government could easily fix.[13]

Most importantly, Keynes did not think the problem of unemployment arose because of a failure of prices to adjust; nor did he think that unemployment could be solved by reducing wages. Indeed, he emphasized that decreases in wages could make things worse. For Keynes, unemployment was caused by a lack of aggregate demand.

The neoclassical synthesis emerged in the early 1950s and was the dominant view until the early 1970s. Arguably, three economists created the core of the neoclassical synthesis: J. R. Hicks, Paul Samuelson, and Robert Solow. (We will discuss Milton Friedman shortly.) Hicks put Keynes's ideas about savings and investment, and money and interest rates, into a mathematical model and created a diagrammatic representation, known as the IS–LM diagram, which is still used in most intermediate macro textbooks. Paul Samuelson dominated the world textbook market and explained the principles of Keynesian economics to generations of students. Robert Solow developed the neoclassical growth model. All three won the Nobel Memorial Prize in Economics, in 1972, 1970, and 1987 respectively.[14]

We situate the neoclassical synthesis (in Figure 1.8) more to the right than Keynes's own thought because it creates a so-called "Keynesian model" that is consistent in the "long run" with the ideas of the classical economists. The neoclassical synthesis is a model of a fundamentally stable economy. Recessions and unemployment can exist in the short run because of wage (or price) stickiness.[15] But given enough time, all prices will adjust, and the economy will eventually return to long-run equilibrium where markets clear and full employment prevails. However, since wages and prices may be slow to adjust, Keynesian stimulus may be necessary to speed up the process of recovery. Thus, the neoclassical synthesis is classical in the "long run" but allows a pseudo-Keynesian world in the "short run."[16]

The fourth figure contributing to the neoclassical synthesis, one who pulls it further to the right, is Milton Friedman (winner of the Nobel Memorial Prize in Economics in 1976). Friedman was an influential member of the Chicago School and as such was a proponent of free markets and deregulation and a fierce critic of the government. Friedman emphasized the importance of monetary policy, and forcefully argued that poor monetary policy decisions were a major factor in causing the Great Depression. More generally, he argued that poor monetary policy contributed to economic instability. Since he distrusted the ability of policymakers, he recommended a very simple monetary growth rate rule.

Friedman is also famous for his contribution to the supply side of the neoclassical synthesis. He argued that the ability of the government to influence output hinged on generating inflation greater than expected. Over time, as expected inflation converges to the actual inflation rate, so actual output converges to its long-run equilibrium level.

Clearly, Friedman defines the right wing of the neoclassical synthesis, and the divisions between the Keynesians on the left and the monetarists on the right were too big to be sustained. In the 1970s, the neoclassical synthesis broke into two opposing schools, known as New Keynesians and New Classicals.

The New Classicals built on Friedman's view of the supply side of the neoclassical model. They argued that expectation formation should be rational, and interpreted this to mean that there should be no systematic errors in expectations. Phrased in this way, expected inflation should only differ from actual inflation by a random error. When incorporated into a model that assumes flexible prices determined by demand and supply, rational expectations predicted that the economy would be at its long-run equilibrium level (save for a random error) *even in the short run!*

But what about the business cycle? Don't we observe long-lasting economic fluctuations around long-run equilibrium, fluctuations known as the business cycle? The New Classical economists argued that our senses deceive us. What we thought were movements around long-run equilibrium were really movements in the long-run equilibrium itself. This view is known as "real business cycle" theory. It regards *stabilization policy* as unnecessary since the economic fluctuations that occur are optimal responses by economic agents: there are no welfare losses involved, so no intervention is needed.

Meanwhile, the New Keynesians fought to defend the existence of a "Keynesian" short run, by insisting that prices are not perfectly flexible in the short run and finding good microeconomic reasons for price stickiness.

What is not shown in Figure 1.8 is the emergence of another synthesis—a so-called "new neoclassical synthesis"—between the New Keynesians and New Classicals. Of course, there remained latent internal dissension within this "new neoclassical synthesis," and this broke to the surface after the 2007–8 financial crash. Recently, new labels for the competing groups have emerged. New Keynesians are nowadays referred to as "Saltwater" economists, since they tend to be located in universities situated on the eastern and western seaboards, while New Classicals are called "Freshwater" economists, since they are located at universities close to the Great Lakes.

The final element of Figure 1.8 is an arrow coming directly from Keynes and descending to Michal Kalecki, whose image is used to represent the post-Keynesian school.[17] Post-Keynesians maintain that Keynes's theory is seriously misunderstood by both wings of the neoclassical synthesis. Crucially, they deny that wage and price flexibility guarantee a return to long-run equilibrium where full employment prevails.

Question for your professor: In 2009, Paul Krugman stated, "most macroeconomics of the past 30 years was spectacularly useless at best and positively harmful at worst." Is there really a consensus in macroeconomics?

2.8 The great moderation

Prior to the financial meltdown of 2007–8, mainstream macroeconomists were proud of their achievements. There appeared to be a new synthesis emerging, a consensus on a new model—one that involved highly sophisticated dynamics, that incorporated random (or stochastic) shocks, and that returned to general equilibrium in the long run. Such models are known as dynamic stochastic general equilibrium models or DSGE models. Emerging from this consensus on the model was a consensus on economic policy: central banks should simply target low inflation, which should be done through interest rate manipulation.

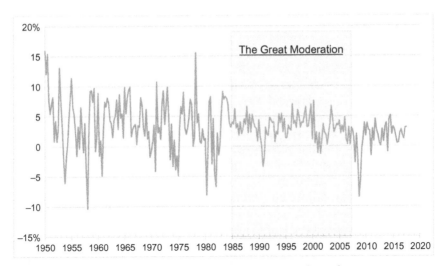

Figure 1.9 US real GDP growth from 1950 to 2017. Drawn by author

Economists believed this new understanding had led to improved economic performance—a period of low inflation, and low volatility of output known as the Great Moderation (1985–2007). Figure 1.9 shows the reduced volatility of output over this twenty-two-year period.[18]

Toward the end of the Great Moderation, mainstream economists believed that they had solved the macroeconomic stability problem. Robert Lucas in his 2003 Presidential Address to the American Economic Association declared that the "central problem of depression-prevention [has] been solved, for all practical purposes." And in September 2007, mainstream economists, blissfully unaware of the impending crisis, debated the causes of the Great Moderation. Was it greater central bank independence? Was it new rules governing monetary policy? Was it deregulation of the financial markets allowing the market to function more smoothly? Then, all hell broke loose.

It is well known that—apart from a couple of exceptions—the economics profession failed to predict the financial crash of 2007–8 and the subsequent Great Recession.[19] Perhaps worse than this was the depth of disagreement on the appropriate policy response. Initially, that response was reasonably good. The banking system was flooded with liquidity. Interest rates were brought down to zero. And fiscal stimulus was provided by most countries in 2008–9. As a result, the world economy narrowly avoided another Great Depression.

But after interest rates hit the zero lower bound in early 2009 and the world economy continued to falter, the profession debated the merits of further fiscal stimulus. Freshwater economists argued fiscal policy had been debunked; that neither a balanced budget expansion nor debt-financed government spending would have any effect. Meanwhile saltwater economists railed against the neglect of what "we thought we knew."

The following year, in 2010, with the worst seemingly avoided, the fiscal stimulus debate was replaced by the fiscal austerity debate as government debt-to-GDP ratios increased. Very influential papers were written, widely cited, and widely discussed, which argued fiscal austerity (cutting spending and/or increasing taxes) would be *expansionary* in a context where high government debt endangered private sector confidence.[20] Paul Krugman likened this view to believing in "confidence fairies" and bemoaned the return of "the dark age of macro."[21]

The prediction failure and subsequent depth of the divisions suggest a subject in disarray. This has precipitated much soul-searching within macro. Many defend the status quo. Some—like Robert Lucas (2009a)— argue that events like the financial crisis are inherently unpredictable. Others, while admitting there was an error, argue it was (mainly) a technical error of monetary policy. For example, Blanchard (2012) argues that monetary policy merely overemphasized inflation targeting and neglected financial prudence. Still others argue that the rot goes very much deeper.

Some—such as Krugman (2009), Buiter (2009), and Gordon (2009)— suggest that macro took a wrong turn in the early 1980s. They believe in the neoclassical synthesis that is mostly the subject of mainstream introductory texts. Their complaint is against the new synthesis that occurred between "New Keynesians" and "New Classicists" and resulted in complex DSGE models. Others—such as the post-Keynesian school—argue that macro took a wrong turn in evolving into the neoclassical synthesis in the 1950s.[22]

2.9 Final remark

We are going to close this introduction to "what is macro" with an extended quote from Hyman Minsky (1986: 99). The beauty of the quote is that it not only pinpoints what is wrong with mainstream theory but also explains why it is important to study it and understand it.

> Economists who offer policy advice are neither fools nor knaves. Knowing instability exists, they nevertheless base their analysis and advice upon a theory that cannot explain instability ... because this theory does provide answers to deep and serious questions and has had some success as a basis for policy. Before abandoning or radically revising neoclassical theory it is necessary to understand the significance of the deep and serious questions that this theory does answer ... and why any alternative economic theory must come to grips with the questions that neoclassical theory addresses.

Chapter 2

MEASUREMENT, MISMEASUREMENT, AND OMISSION

Without data, you're just another person with an opinion.

W. Edwards Deming[1]

I THE STANDARD TEXT

There is no science without measurement. So, like it or not, the nitty-gritty details of accounting and price indices are important topics. We need to measure the key variables on which macroeconomics focuses: output, employment, and unemployment; and prices and inflation.

I.I Measuring output

How do we sum the myriad different things produced? In simple terms, how do we add apples and oranges? Answer: in dollar value terms. However, in a complex economy where many goods are inputs into other goods, we do not count the dollar value of *all* goods. For example, if all steel output is used to make cars, then counting steel output *and* car output would count the value of steel output twice.

There are two ways to avoid "*double counting.*" The most important way is to count only the value of *final goods and services*—goods that are not inputs into other goods. Alternatively, we could subtract the value of intermediate goods from any sector's output, to construct that sector's "value-added," and then sum the value-added of *every sector* in the economy. The value-added measure is useful since it tells us the relative importance of different sectors to the economy and provides a check on the *final goods* methodology.

A country's output is known as GDP, or gross domestic product. It is useful to categorize final goods and services into five basic groups. They are represented by symbols as follows: consumption (C), investment (I), government purchases (G), exports (X), and imports (IM). The five groups combine to form total GDP (often represented by Y).

$$Y \equiv C + I + G + X - IM \tag{2.1}$$

This breakdown of final goods into five basic groups is an identity. All macroeconomic models make use of this GDP accounting identity, so it needs to be memorized and understood. Consider the elements on the right-hand side of the identity.

The first group of final goods is consumption goods, C. This is the largest category, usually around 60 percent of the total. Of the four major components of GDP employed by macroeconomists, consumption is the easiest for the typical person to understand. Every one of us is engaged in consumption on a daily basis and there is nothing mysterious or misleading about it.

Second, we have gross private investment, I. This is *not* financial investments, such as buying bonds or shares. Rather, it is spending on plant and equipment by both residents and nonresidents. It is quite a broad category, including spending on railways, ports, office buildings, and shopping malls. It also includes all investment in housing. The most surprising aspect of investment spending is that it includes *changes in inventories*. Businesses need inventories to operate, and since inventories are costly, it is correct to count them as an investment. Further, we want to measure the economy's output, but since not all output will be immediately sold, we need to include changes in inventories.

The third category is government spending on final goods, G. This includes things like roads, parks, defense, or judiciary. It does not include transfer payments such as pensions or employment (or unemployment) insurance. Transfer payments are not final goods but are spent by the recipients on the final goods of their choosing.

Fourth, the goods and services we produce but sell abroad are categorized as exports, X. Finally, we import some goods and services from abroad, IM. Since we did not produce them, they must be subtracted from the total.

All the output produced by the economy generates incomes in the economy. The value of all the incomes must equal the value of output. All the money received by firms is used to pay for the factors of production it uses, or becomes profits. Thus, we get a third measurement of GDP by summing wages, rents, interest, equipment maintenance (*depreciation spending*), and profits. To get the market value of production we need to add sales taxes to this sum.

In summary, nominal GDP can be measured in three ways. First, we can sum expenditures on *final* goods and services. Second, we can sum the value-added of *all* sectors of the economy. Third, we can sum all incomes paid to factors of production. When building macroeconomic models, the term "Y" can be described as either "output" or "income." They are equivalent.

GDP versus GNP Finally, you may be wondering about another term, GNP, or gross national product. How does this relate to GDP? GDP measures output produced *domestically*, in a particular country; GNP measures output produced by residents (or *nationals*) of a country. Since GDP is a better indicator of economic activity within national boundaries, this is the measure economists use when estimating their models.

So, for example, income earned in Canada by non-Canadians would be included in Canadian GDP, but excluded from Canadian GNP. Similarly, the wages of Canadian consultants who are working temporarily in China would be excluded from Canadian GDP, but included in Canadian GNP. In countries where there is a lot of foreign ownership of industry, we would expect more factor income to flow out (as repatriated profits) than to flow in—so we would expect GNP to be smaller than GDP for those countries.

For most countries, there is very little difference between GDP and GNP. For example, in 2018 Canada's GNP was about 1½ percent smaller than its GDP, reflecting the impact of some foreign ownership of Canadian industries. Where there is a very large proportion of foreign ownership of domestic industries, GNP can be substantially smaller than GDP. For example, in Ireland, US multinationals directly employ a quarter of the private sector labor force and create 57 percent of nonfarm private sector value-added. As a result, in 2016 the Irish GNP was only 70 percent of its GDP.

1.2 Measuring real output

Our solution for the problem of how to sum the myriad different things produced in an economy was to use market prices and add the dollar values of things produced. But over time the dollar value can change for two reasons: there can be a change in quantities or there can be a change in prices. Since we want a measure of output, we need to separate price changes from quantity changes. The most direct way to do this is to use *base year prices* to get the constant dollar value of output—otherwise known as real GDP.

To illustrate this, suppose the economy only produces apples and oranges. Table 2.1 shows prices and quantities (in kilos) in this fruit economy.

Between 2018 and 2019, nominal GDP rose from $9,800 to $11,950. This is nearly a 22 percent increase! But we note that while output of both apples and oranges did increase slightly, prices also rose. To separate price changes from quantity changes, we calculate the value of output using base year prices. The choice of base year is entirely arbitrary. Using 2018 prices, 2018 output will be unaltered. But 2019 output becomes $7 × 1,050 + $4 × 710 = $10,190. This suggests a much smaller real rate of growth of output of nearly 4 percent.

Table 2.1 Output and prices in the fruit economy

	2018			2019		
	Price	**Quantity**	**Value**	**Price**	**Quantity**	**Value**
Apples	$7	1,000	$7,000	$8	1,050	$8,400
Oranges	$4	700	$2,800	$5	710	$3,550
	Nominal GDP in 2018 = $9,800			Nominal GDP in 2019 = $11,950		

So, calculating real GDP is simple: we just sum expenditures on final goods and services using base year prices! This keeps prices constant. And clearly, real GDP will equal nominal GDP in the base year.

1.3 Real GDP, measurement issues, and economic well-being

Real GDP is supposed to measure economic activity—an economy's production of goods and services. How accurately does it do this? There are two well-known problems.

First, unpaid work is not included. Thus, if a woman marries her gardener, GDP would fall—assuming she no longer pays him for gardening. Only services for pay are counted as part of GDP. The value of household work, performed mainly by women, is not counted as "productive activity."[2] It has been estimated that, on average, the value of unpaid household production is equal to at least 70 percent of the household's money (or market) income after taxes, making housework the most important "missing piece of the economic pie" (Becker and Becker 1997).

If only services for pay are counted as part of GDP, what happens when you buy the house you previously rented? Does GDP go down? The answer here is "no." GDP contains an imputation for the value of owner-occupied housing. Statisticians estimate what you would have paid had you rented your current accommodation. For the purposes of the statistics, it's as if you were renting your dwelling from yourself.

The second problem with real GDP as a measure of economic activity is that it does not include any work that is not declared. This could be work that is bartered (I will fix your tractor, if you repair my roof), or it could be legal work that is hidden from authorities to avoid paying taxes, or it could be part of the illegal economy. Interestingly, cannabis was legalized in Canada on October 17, 2018, but use of cannabis was widespread before that. The fact that the production of cannabis was not counted before legalization, but will be counted afterward, should give measured real GDP a temporary high (so to speak).

So, real GDP is a good, but not perfect, measure of an economy's production of goods and services. Dividing by the size of the population gives us a good, but not perfect, measure of the *average standard of living*, called "real GDP per capita." How well does real GDP per capita measure economic well-being?

Even if real GDP were a perfect measure of *economic activity*, real GDP per capita would still be an imperfect measure of *average well-being*. There are four problem areas: first, the distribution of income; second, the treatment of leisure; third, the treatment of the environment; and fourth, more subtle issues around the quality of life and the nature of the goods actually produced. We will consider them in turn.

The distribution of income What if real GDP per capita was high, but all the income was going to a few wealthy families, while most of the population lived in abject poverty? Clearly, in this case, real GDP per capita would give a very misleading idea of average well-being.

The treatment of leisure Real GDP per capita does not include leisure. It is possible that GDP per capita could be high, despite productivity being low, because the entire population over the age of five is working eighty hours a week. In this case, average well-being would be low because the population is getting insufficient leisure. On the other hand, suppose machines displace workers, and while GDP per capita remains high, most people have too much undesired leisure and suffer depression, angst, and loss of meaning. Leisure is tricky: desired leisure improves well-being; undesired leisure reduces it.

The treatment of the environment Destruction of the environment is ignored when calculating real GDP per capita. Well-being can be adversely affected by air and water pollution, or lack of green spaces.

More subtle issues Suppose real GDP per capita were high, but most of the goods produced (for whatever reason) were military goods. Or more generally, suppose that productivity is high, but that very few consumer goods were produced. Instead, crime and sickness are so prevalent that a large proportion of the workforce is working as police or in hospitals. In these cases, average well-being could be low despite high real GDP per capita.

Despite these problems, real GDP per capita remains the single most useful measure of changes in the standard of living. Indeed, its usefulness is enhanced by an awareness of its limitations.

1.4 Price indices and the inflation rate

The consumer price index or CPI is the most common measure of the overall price level. First, the statistical agency surveys households to determine what the average household buys. If the average household spends 20 percent of its budget on food, then food will be given a weight of 20 percent. These surveys determine the "basket" of goods and services, the cost of which is tracked. Second, each month representatives of the statistical agency go out to grocery stores, department stores, and so on, to check on the prices of the items in the basket. The current value of the CPI is the current cost of purchasing this basket, relative to the cost of purchasing it in a base year, multiplied by 100.

$$\text{CPI} = \left(\frac{\text{Current cost of purchasing the basket of goods and services}}{\text{Cost of purchasing the basket in the base year}} \right) \times 100$$

For example, suppose that households buy nothing but fruit, and the basket of fruit comprises forty oranges, fifty grapefruit, and a hundred bananas. Table 2.2 details the construction of the CPI for this fruit economy.

Table 2.2 shows that the cost of the basket of goods in the fruit economy was $63 in 2018 and $73.50 in 2019. If we use 2018 as the base year, the CPI in that year is necessarily 100. The last column shows that the CPI had risen to 116.7 by

Table 2.2 Construction of the CPI for the fruit economy

	2018	2019
Price of an orange	$0.20	$0.40
Price of a grapefruit	$0.60	$0.65
Price of a banana	$0.25	$0.25
Cost of the market basket (40 oranges, 50 grapefruit, 100 bananas)	(40 × $0.20) + (50 × $0.60) + (100 × $0.25) = **$63**	(40 × $0.40) + (50 × $0.65) + (100 × $0.25) = **$73.50**
CPI using 2018 as the base year	$\text{CPI} = \left(\dfrac{\$63}{\$63}\right) \times 100 = 100$	$\text{CPI} = \left(\dfrac{\$73.5}{\$63}\right) \times 100 = 116.7$

2019. The rate of increase in consumer prices is known as the *rate of inflation*. It is calculated as the rate of change in the CPI as shown below.

$$\text{Rate of inflation in year } t = \left(\frac{\text{CPI}_t - \text{CPI}_{t-1}}{\text{CPI}_{t-1}}\right) \times 100$$

Applying the formula to the fruit economy, we find that the rate of inflation in 2019 was 16.7 percent.

It is instructive to consider an alternative way of doing the calculation. The alternative is to construct a price index for each commodity, by dividing the current price by the base year price and multiplying by 100. Then create a weighted average of the price indices, where the weights are the relative importance of each commodity in total expenditure in the base year.

In our example, in 2018 the average household spent $63 on fruit. Of that $8 was spent on oranges ($0.20 × 40), $30 was spent on grapefruit ($0.60 × 50), and $25 was spent on bananas ($0.25 × 100). Thus, the weights used to sum the individual price indices are 0.127 for oranges (=8/63), 0.476 for grapefruit (=30/63), and 0.397 for bananas (=25/63). Table 2.3 shows that this method yields precisely the same answer as before.

If one thinks about the methodology of constructing the CPI, and hence deriving the rate of inflation, one realizes there is a tension. On the one hand, the goods and services in the basket, and the weights given to them, must stay constant in order for the relative *cost* of the basket to be an index of *prices*. But on the other hand, both the goods and services included, and the weights assigned to them, must be updated periodically in order to stay relevant. The existence of this tension leads all statistical agencies to revise, periodically, the basket of goods and the weights assigned to them. For example, the Bureau of Labor Statistics (BLS) in the United States has historically updated its basket, and the weights, approximately every ten years.

This fixed weight aspect of the CPI is the most important reason why it overestimates the inflation rate. In our construction of the CPI in the fruit

Table 2.3 Alternative construction of the CPI for the fruit economy

	2018	2019	2019 index per item	Weight	Weighted index per item
Price of an orange	$0.20	$0.40	(0.40/0.20) × 100 = 200	0.127	25.4
Price of a grapefruit	$0.60	$0.65	(0.65/0.60) × 100 = 108.3	0.476	51.6
Price of a banana	$0.25	$0.25	(0.25/0.25) × 100 = 100	0.397	39.7
Overall fruit index in 2019 = 25.4 + 51.6 + 39.7 = 116.7					

economy, after the price of oranges doubles, in reality people will buy fewer oranges. People substitute toward cheaper goods. By keeping the basket unchanged, the CPI overestimates true inflation, the true increase in the cost of living. This problem is called *substitution bias*.

A second problem is *unmeasured quality change*—government statisticians do not adequately adjust the CPI for changes in the quality of goods. If a new personal computer has 20 percent more memory, processor speed, and data storage than last year's model, while its price increases by only 5 percent, then has the price really increased or decreased? In a sense, the situation is the same as paying 5 percent more for a pizza that is 20 percent bigger.

For these reasons, the CPI overstates the true inflation rate and overstates the true increase in the cost of living. Consequently, government expenditures that are linked to the CPI, such as public pensions, face automatic growth that is greater than if the CPI provided a "true" measure of the change in the cost of living.

Total CPI versus core CPI In attempting to control inflation, we need to be able to separate short-term blips from long-term changes. The core CPI attempts to do that by excluding from the basket of goods those with the most volatile prices. The goods in this "volatile" category are fruits, vegetables, gasoline, fuel oil, mortgage interest cost, natural gas, intercity transportation, and tobacco. The core CPI also removes the effect of changes in sales taxes on the remaining items. Figure 2.1 plots the annual inflation rate using both core CPI and the complete CPI for Canada, over the twenty-four-year period 1985–2019.

It is apparent that the core CPI inflation rate is less volatile. One measure of volatility is the standard deviation, and the core inflation rate has a standard deviation of 0.95, compared to a standard deviation of 1.3 for the CPI inflation rate.

The GDP deflator One other price index deserves mention: the GDP deflator. This is an index of prices for all goods produced domestically and is useful because it provides us with an alternative way of calculating real GDP. First, we calculate a price index for each good; then we aggregate them using weights determined by the relative value of production of each good.

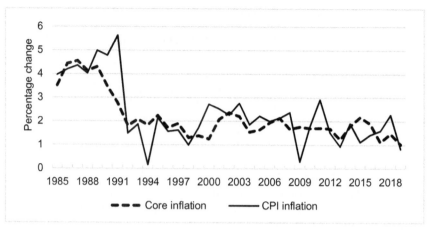

Figure 2.1 CPI inflation and core inflation in Canada, 1985–2019

$$\text{Weights used in the GDP deflator} = \frac{\text{Value of production of good "} i \text{"}}{\text{Value of total productoin}}$$

Once we have the GDP deflator, we can use it to convert nominal GDP to real GDP.

$$\text{Real GDP} = \frac{\text{Nominal GDP}}{\text{GDP deflator}} \times 100$$

Other real magnitudes Just as we can deflate nominal output to get real output, so we can deflate nominal wages to get real wages. The nominal wage is the money payment. The real wage is what that money can buy in terms of goods and services. For example, in the United States, nominal wages increased more than eightfold between 1964 and 2019, but real wages only increased slightly more than 13 percent.[3]

We can also calculate the real rate of interest, not by dividing the nominal rate of interest by an index of prices but by subtracting the rate of inflation. So, if a bond yields 10 percent in nominal interest, but prices increase by 3 percent, the real yield of the bond is 7 percent. In symbols, if "r" represents the real interest rate, "i" the nominal interest rate, and "π" the rate of inflation, we have the expression: $r = i - \pi$.

1.5 The unemployment rate

Labor force data are obtained by a monthly survey of households. In Canada, the sample size for the Labor Force Survey is about 56,000 households, or about one in 240 Canadian households. In the United States, the equivalent survey is called the Current Population Survey, and its sample size is about 60,000 households. With a national population ten times greater, this is a proportionately smaller survey, representing about one in 2,000 households.

The population of working age (which for most high-income countries is either 15+ or 16+) is divided into two large groups—those not in the labor force and those in the labor force. The participation rate is the percent of the population of working age that is in the labor force.

Those in the labor force are in turn divided into two groups—the employed and the unemployed. The unemployment rate is the percent of the labor force that is unemployed.

People are counted as employed if they did any paid work during the period covered by the survey. Even if the person worked for just a brief period, they are counted as employed. In most countries, even one day would be enough to count someone as being employed. So, some of the employed are fully employed, others are not.

People are counted as unemployed if they did not do any paid work, *and* they made an effort to find paid work during the period covered by the survey. If someone is not working, but is available for work and actively seeking work, that person is counted as unemployed. If someone is *not* working, but did *not* actively seek work, that person is *not* counted as unemployed—they are counted as not in the labor force.

There is an important reason why the measured unemployment rate may *overstate* the true unemployment rate: it includes those who are voluntarily out of work and not looking for work, even though they say they are looking. Such people may be happy receiving benefits from the state (called *employment insurance payments*, in Canada) and want to remain unemployed as long as those benefits last.

There are also reasons why the measured unemployment rate may *understate* the true unemployment rate. First, if there is no work, some may become discouraged and give up looking for work. These so-called "discouraged workers" are not counted as unemployed, nor as being in the labor force. Second, some people are involuntarily working "part-time" but are counted as "employed." Some of them may have part-time jobs but want full-time jobs; others may have full-time jobs but are working reduced hours.

Most statistical agencies collect data on discouraged workers and on those who are working part-time for economic reasons (no full-time jobs available). For example, these workers are counted as unemployed in the measure of unemployment called "U6" published by the US BLS.[4] Figure 2.2 plots "U6" along with the official unemployment rate, from January 1, 1994, to April 1, 2019.

We can see from Figure 2.2 that including discouraged workers and involuntary part-timers raises the measured unemployment rate quite substantially, especially in recessions. During the Great Recession of 2009–14, the official unemployment rate reached a high of nearly 10 percent, whereas U6 was nearly 17 percent! Nevertheless, it is also apparent that the movements in the two series are nearly identical—the official unemployment rate mirrors the movements of U6 almost exactly. We conclude that the official rate is useful as an *indicator* of labor market conditions, not as a literal measure of the number of people unable to find jobs.

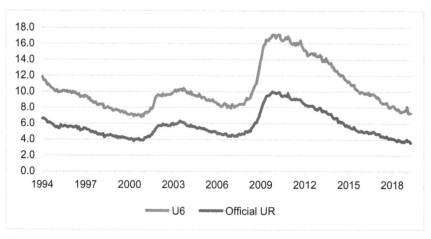

Figure 2.2 Unemployment rates in the United States, 1994–2019

The natural unemployment rate High unemployment, such as occurred in 2010, has high costs—both to society and to the individuals unemployed. It results in lost incomes and human capital, as well as lost production. The income losses can be devastating for the people who bear them, and prolonged unemployment can permanently damage people's job prospects. The economic losses during periods of high unemployment are the greatest documented wastes in a modern economy. They are many times larger than the microeconomic inefficiencies caused by monopoly. But what do we mean by high unemployment? Can we expect zero unemployment at full employment?

In fact, there will always be some unemployment, even at full employment, for *frictional* and *structural* reasons. The economy is constantly churning—some people enter the workforce while others leave; some jobs are created while others are destroyed. Some unemployment, even at so-called "full employment," is to be expected.

Moreover, some unemployment is even desirable. The optimal amount of time to spend searching for a new job is not zero—at least not in a world where workers and jobs are heterogeneous. Since workers have different preferences and abilities, and jobs have different attributes and requirements, it makes sense for both workers and firms to spend time searching for the best match.

That is why the full employment level of unemployment is called the *natural rate of unemployment*—because some unemployment is both *inevitable* and *desirable*. The word "*natural*" does not mean that it is determined by *nature*. The natural rate of unemployment *can* be changed by human decisions; it is determined by institutions and policies, such as union strength, minimum wages, and unemployment benefits. But the natural rate of unemployment *cannot* be lowered by expansionary macroeconomic policies without triggering an increase in the rate of inflation, possibly leading to inflation spiraling out of control. We will deal further with the natural rate of unemployment again in Chapter 10.

2 THE ANTI-TEXT

2.1 Introduction: conspiracy theories and fake news

We live in strange times. Conspiracy theories are rife, and maybe some of them are even true! What information should we trust? Should we trust official government statistics about the economy? Well, that might depend on where you live. Apparently, the official Chinese government statistics on its economic growth cannot be trusted. Indeed, the current (2019) prime minister of China, Li Keqiang, famously said in 2007 that he did not trust the official numbers himself! Instead, he looked at railway shipments, electricity generation, and bank loans to get an idea of economic activity.[5] And in Argentina, the government now admits that inflation data were officially manipulated between 2007 and 2015.[6] So, should we trust government-collected economic data in rich developed countries?

According to a recent opinion poll, more than 40 percent of Americans distrust official government economic statistics, such as CPI or GDP data.[7] There is a popular website called "Shadowstats.com" where, for an annual fee, you can get what they claim are *the real numbers*. These show (as you might expect) that inflation and unemployment are higher, and economic growth is lower, than the official figures. "Shadowstats.com" is run by John Williams who claims that the *"gimmicks"* built into the official inflation numbers to make them lower are *"effectively criminal."*[8]

Even mainstream liberal media, such as Harper's Magazine, ran a piece in 2008 claiming that "Washington has *gulled* its citizens and creditors by *debasing* official statistics" and that *"corruption has tainted* the very measures that most shape public perception of the economy" [emphasis added]. And in the run-up to the 2016 presidential election, when the official US unemployment rate was 5 percent, Donald Trump described this as "totally fiction," "complete fraud," and "such a phony number" and claimed that *real unemployment* in the United States could be as high as 42 percent.[9]

This part of the chapter will dig into these worries and investigate these claims. Evidence-based policy requires trustworthy data. Without it, everyone has their own facts, and informed discussion and policy debate break down. The focus is on the accuracy of the official measures of inflation, unemployment, and GDP.

2.2 The measurement of inflation

Do the official statistics on the CPI understate inflation as Shadowstats. com asserts? Or does the CPI overstate inflation as the mainstream textbooks argue?

A key point is that the CPI measures the cost of a basket of goods purchased by the *average* household. Some of those goods will be increasing in price quite rapidly; others may be decreasing in price. The weight put on each good is determined by the spending patterns of the average household—the average household with 1¾ children and 2½ automobiles. For any real household, the CPI will underestimate the inflation rate if its spending is more heavily weighted on items that are increasing in price faster than average.

For example, poorer families spend a higher proportion of their income on food than the average household does. If food prices increase more than the average price (as they have done recently), the CPI will underestimate the inflation rate for poorer families. Similarly, students spend a very high proportion of their income on education and books. In Canada, this category only has a 3 percent weight in the CPI, whereas it might comprise (say) 40 percent of the budget for students. So, if the cost of education and books increases faster than other items (as they have recently!), students will likely face a higher rate of inflation than the official inflation rate.

But none of this is hidden. All statistical agencies publish the weights they put on each item. Moreover, they publish separately the price indices for every group that comprises the basket of goods. Everyone is perfectly able to use their own expenditure weights to calculate their own CPI and, from there, calculate their own personalized rate of inflation.

So, even though many people can rightfully claim that the inflation they experience is higher than the official rate, this does *not* validate the claims of Shadowstats.com and other bloggers and magazine writers. For those claims to be valid, the CPI must systematically understate inflation *even for the average household*.

John Williams of Shadowstats.com claims that the BLS changed its methodology in the 1980s and 1990s, and if they were using their original methodology, the level of inflation would be much higher. He claims that BLS now puts in "substitution factors" and adds "hedonic adjustments" that deliberately bias the reported numbers in a downward direction. However, as Greenlees and McClelland (2008) explain, the changes made in the 1980s and 1990s were very minor. For example, it is true that some substitution away from expensive goods and toward cheaper goods is now "factored in"—but the substitution in question is not from apples to bananas, or steak to hamburger, but away from apples whose prices have increased more, to other apples in the same city whose prices have increased less. As for the "hedonic adjustments," this allows for improvements in quality of a very limited set of goods—goods whose quality was demonstrably improving. The adjustments were previously confined to housing and apparel but in the 1990s were expanded to include goods such as computers, televisions, and refrigerators. These changes employ methods recommended by the International Monetary Fund and approved by the Statistical Office of the European Communities.[10]

There are two further points to make. First, in 2008 John Williams of Shadowstats.com admitted that he does no calculations in preparing his alternative measure of inflation—he just jacks up the official inflation rate by 2 percentage points.[11] Second, checking official data is important, and constructing alternate measures of inflation is worthwhile. In fact, academic researchers at MIT have done exactly this with their Billion Prices Project (BPP).

The BPP started with the idea of creating "software robots" that could monitor daily price fluctuations of millions of items sold online. It is a glimpse of how it is now possible to use Big Data to produce a real-time mapping of the economy. Half a million prices were collected every day in the United States from June 1, 2008, until August 1, 2015. (By comparison, the BLS collects approximately 80,000 prices on a monthly or bimonthly basis.) The data were aggregated into price indices using expenditure weights, just like the official CPI data. But there were no "gimmicks"—no "substitution factors" or "hedonic adjustments"—just the raw aggregated data, and lots of it. And since they make their data publicly available, I have used it to check the official inflation numbers. Figure 2.3 compares the official inflation rate calculated from the CPI with the inflation rate calculated from the BPP aggregate price index.[12]

Comparing the two series in Figure 2.3, there is no evidence that the official inflation rate understates inflation. The two series move together, sometimes one is higher, sometimes the other. The average inflation rate over the period is practically identical in both cases: it is 1.37 percent using the official CPI numbers and 1.35 percent using the BPP numbers.

Having disposed of the conspiracy theories concerning the official inflation numbers, what can we say about the mainstream textbook treatment of the CPI? The textbooks complain that it does not sufficiently allow for substitution toward cheaper goods, nor for quality improvements,

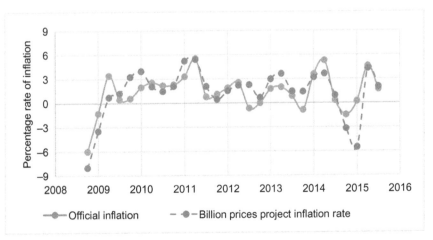

Figure 2.3 Quarterly inflation in the United States, official CPI versus BPP

and hence it has a tendency to overstate inflation. This is a long-standing claim, with a somewhat tortured history, which actually helps to explain the views of people like John Williams.

In the 1990s, many right-wing US politicians sought ways to cut government programs, and in 1996, the US Senate established the Boskin Commission to recommend changes to CPI measurement. The idea was that reducing the official inflation rate would help reduce the growth of expenditures on CPI-indexed programs, most notably social security. It would also reduce the growth of union wages indexed to the CPI.

The Boskin Commission consisted of economists who viewed CPI measurement through the lens of neoclassical micro theory, where the true change in the cost of living is the change in income that keeps an individual on the same "utility curve." They concluded that the CPI overstated the true inflation rate by as much as 1 or 2 percentage points a year. Had their recommended changes been implemented (they weren't), senior citizens would have lost billions in social security payments. And interestingly, John Williams may have been correct to jack up the official inflation numbers by 2 percentage points to get the real inflation rate.

So much for the history of the argument; what about the argument itself? Since the CPI allows for almost no substitution between goods (just between high-priced apples and low-priced apples, for example), and insufficiently allows for quality improvements over time, does it overestimate the true increase in the cost of living, as the mainstream textbooks emphasize? The answer to that is not clear.

First, consider quality adjustments. As discussed, government statisticians already make minor adjustments for quality changes. Their caution is justified. Adjusting for quality is tricky, and it is just as possible to adjust too much as too little. How do we compare "breathable fabric" to regular cotton? Is that a quality improvement? Even when there is an obvious cardinal scale, such as computer speed, it is unclear whether a 20 percent increase in processor speed will have any benefit for the typical user. Moreover, any quality adjustment that is made must apply to both the CPI *and to the measure of output, GDP.* If one country starts making much larger adjustments than other countries, then the relative growth performance of that country would appear to improve. Clearly, it is important that statistical agencies in different countries follow common procedures to maintain the comparability of statistics across countries.

Second, it is not possible to deal with the substitution question in aggregate. We know for certain only two things. First, the CPI measures the cost over time of buying *the same goods*; second, we know that cost-conscious consumers will substitute away from expensive goods to cheaper ones. But we do not know, nor can we know, whether the substitution that occurs is subjectively painful or not. And since we do not know that, we cannot know how much extra income would be necessary to compensate for this subjective pain. (In neoclassical theory, the extra income required to remove the subjective pain—to keep someone on the same "utility curve"—is the measure of the true increase in the cost of living.) We do not know an individual's preferences, let alone the entire population's preferences. So, the calculation of a true cost of living index is simply impossible.

Since it is not possible to construct a true index of the cost of living, it seems a bit beside the point to criticize the CPI for not being that true index. The CPI does what it was designed to do—to measure how the cost of buying the same goods changes over time. And we have seen that it does that quite well.

One final remark on the measure of core inflation: you will remember that this is the measure that excludes volatile elements. Kevin Phillips (2008), among others, has described core inflation as "inflation ex-inflation"—that is, inflation after the inflation has been removed. Comparing the two series in Figure 2.1, there are more times when the CPI inflation rate is above the core rate than when it is below. As a result, the average inflation rate over the thirty-five-year period, as measured by the CPI, is 2.3 percent, but only 2.17 percent as measured by the core. This does not seem like much, but over the thirty-five years of our dataset, the cumulative rate of price increase is 122 percent when measured by the CPI, but only 111 percent when measured by the core.

So, in a way, core inflation *is* "inflation ex-a-tiny-bit-of-inflation." But this could actually be a good thing. The core measure is only used by central banks to determine their monetary policy. And if core inflation is biased in a downward direction, then they will be slightly less likely to stamp on the brakes (by increasing interest rates), and bring economic growth to a standstill, for fear that inflation is getting too high. We will have more to say about that in a later chapter.

```
Questions for your professor
#1: Given what's been going on in labor markets,
is it appropriate to use the perfectly competitive
framework   when   talking   about   employment   in
macroeconomic models?
#2: The textbook teaches that the CPI inflation rate
overstates the true increase in the cost of living.
But is it possible to calculate the true inflation
rate for an aggregate of people? Doesn't the CPI do
what it was intended: measure the increase in cost
of a constant basket of goods?
```

2.3 The measurement of unemployment

It was in September 2015 that Donald Trump called the official unemployment rate of 5 percent a "joke" and a "phony" number. At that time, "U6" was 10.3 percent. So, where did Trump come up with an unemployment rate of 42 percent? Louis Jacobson (2015) of Politifact.com traced the source to a blog by David Stockman, ex budget director for President Ronald Reagan, who now runs his own website called "Contra Corner." He thinks of himself as someone who "refutes mainstream delusions."

Stockman created his own estimate of the unemployment rate for the year 2014. He began with "a plausible measure of the potential workforce," which he thinks is the entire civilian (and noninstitutionalized) population between the ages of sixteen and sixty-eight, or 210 million Americans. Then he assumes everyone wants a full-time job for forty hours a week, fifty weeks a year. This amounts to 420 billion potential working hours. However, only 240 billion working hours were recorded by the BLS in 2014, implying 180 billion hours of "unemployment." Dividing by the potential workforce of 420 billion hours, we get his unemployment rate of 42.8 percent.

Of course, Stockman's assumptions are extreme, and Jacobson (2015) had no trouble demolishing his estimate. Not everyone of working age either can work (perhaps they are sick or disabled) or wants to work. And many of those working part-time do not want full-time jobs.

Nevertheless, Stockman's method is provocative. Even the more inclusive measure of unemployment, U6, does not include people who have not looked for work for over a year; nor does it count those who either retire early or return to education *because* they cannot find a job. So, perhaps we *should* forget the *measured* labor force and instead base the unemployment rate on the "potential labor force."

Indeed, a recent high-profile paper in the *Brookings Papers on Economic Activity* takes precisely that view. Austin, Glaeser, and Summers (2018) say, "We take the view that the distinction [between 'unemployed' and 'not in the labour force'] is relatively arbitrary since almost all of the not working would presumably work if the price was right" (p. 162). Rather than focus on the unemployment rate, they focus on the "not-working rate," which is the officially unemployed plus those "not in the labour force" as a proportion of the population.[13] And in particular, they focus on the not-working rate of prime-aged men (those aged between twenty-five and fifty-four), which is shown in Figure 2.4.[14]

$$\text{The "Not} - \text{Working" Rate} = \frac{\text{Unemployed} + \text{Not in the Labor Force}}{\text{Population}}$$

It is apparent that the not-working rate of prime-aged men is highly cyclical—there was a massive increase in the slump of 2010, for example—and has a strong upward trend. As recently as 1968, the not-working rate of

Figure 2.4 The "not-working rate" of prime-aged men

prime-aged men was only 5.3 percent. But with the economy (supposedly) at or close to full employment in 2018, it was as high as 13.8 percent.

The plight of prime-aged men has been described as "America's invisible crisis" by Eberstadt (2016). At the stage of life when people are normally at their most productive, these men are spending around 5½ hours a day watching TV, isolated, and mostly depressed. The numbers involved are massive, and yet invisible—at least in terms of the unemployment rate.

To get a sense of how the plight of "not-working males" is affecting the US economy, we can modify the unemployment rate to include them. But rather than assume that everyone of working age can work and wants to work full-time, as Stockman assumed, we can better estimate the "potential labor force" by assuming that civilian men have (or would like to have) the same rate of participation in the labor force as they had on average between 1948 and 1954, a rate of 86 percent. Figure 2.5 shows this modified unemployment rate and compares it to the official rate.

As one would expect, the modified unemployment rate contains the same cyclical "ups and downs" as the official rate but diverges further from it as time progresses. It seems the official unemployment rate is increasingly failing as an indicator of true labor market conditions because a large section of the labor force has simply dropped out because there are no jobs.

Discouraged workers and the rise of the "not-working" is one aspect of the changing nature of the job market. The other aspect is the increase in involuntary part-time workers. Some commentators view this as the more serious problem.

Jim Edwards (2019), writing about the UK labor market, says, "Mass unemployment—the historic kind, with dole queues, unemployment benefits, and idle workers on street corners—has been replaced by

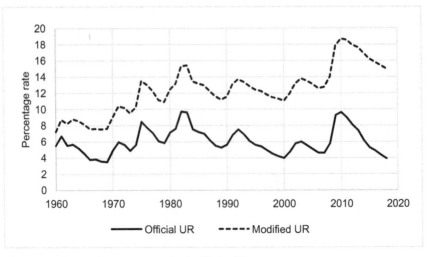

Figure 2.5 Unemployment rates in the United States

low-paid, part-time, 'gig economy' or 'zero-hours' contract work." "Zero hours," or casual contracts, allow firms to hire staff and keep them on standby. They are counted as employed but have no guarantee of *any* work or pay. Sometimes shifts can be as short as a few hours, and workers will be called in without advance notice. In 2015, more than half a million people in the UK were employed on "zero hours" contracts. Companies like Uber, Amazon, Just Eat, and Deliveroo switch their demand for labor on and off, on a minute-by-minute basis.

Figure 2.6 shows the rise of involuntary part-time employment as a percentage of total employment in Canada and the UK.[15] In both countries there seems to be a secular (or long run) increase in the incidence of involuntary part-time work. Since these workers are counted as "employed," this indicates an increase in the extent to which the official unemployment rate is increasingly failing as an indicator of true labor market conditions.

The final piece of evidence that the official unemployment rate is failing to reflect accurately true labor market conditions is perhaps the most contentious. It is the observation—in many countries around the world—that as unemployment rates fall below consensus estimates of the "natural unemployment rate," wages are not tending to increase. That is unexpected, because a tight labor market usually drives up wages. The literature describes this phenomenon as a "flattening of the Phillips curve" and searches for explanations as diverse as lower union density, greater international competition, or inflation expectations anchored at or below zero. However, certainly the simplest and most direct explanation for the phenomenon is that there is a lot of unemployment that is now hidden— either as "discouraged workers" drop out of the labor force or as workers are forced into the part-time "gig" economy.

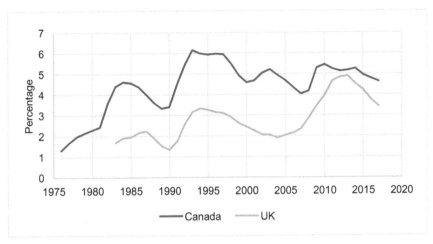

Figure 2.6 Involuntary part-timers as a percent of total employment

In conclusion, the mainstream macro textbooks maintain that, despite its problems, the official unemployment rate is a useful *indicator* of labor market conditions. This section has pointed to increasing evidence that the official unemployment rate and even broader measures such as "U6" are failing in that task.

```
Questions for your professor
#1: Do measures of discouraged workers include all
the people who dropped out of the labor force because
they could not find jobs, or only some of them?
#2: How is the rise of the "gig" economy affecting
the incidence of involuntary part-time work?
```

2.4 The significance of unemployment

The mainstream texts do not adequately convey the adverse consequences to individuals and society of high unemployment, and partly because of this, they do not adequately explain the case for full employment as a macro goal. The better textbooks contain a couple of sentences paying lip service to the cost of unemployment in terms of lost incomes, lost production, and the deterioration of human capital. But this barely hints at the full corrosive effect of high unemployment. The worst textbooks claim that unemployment is voluntary as a result of the optimal decisions of a representative household!

Tcherneva (2017) likens unemployment to a disease, and suggests a job guarantee program as "disease intervention." The disease afflicts some communities harder than others; some communities suffer depression-era unemployment rates on an ongoing basis.[16] Austin, Glaeser, and Summers (2018) link this to declining geographic mobility, which is itself caused by lack of affordable housing in high-income areas. They propose geographically targeted employment policies.

Evidence links unemployment to illness, depression, anxiety, higher rates of alcoholism, and mortality. This is true around the world.[17] Higher unemployment rates are also strongly linked to higher suicide rates.[18]

Unemployment does not just affect the unemployed; it also harms their children and families both physically in terms of malnutrition and emotionally in terms of mental health.[19] Children's educational attainment, labor market outcomes, and social mobility are negatively affected.[20]

But the effects of unemployment go further, beyond the unemployed and their families. It can cause urban blight and elevated crime rates.[21] There is a strong correlation between youth unemployment, crime, and social unrest.[22] Finally, the social exclusion produced by unemployment exacerbates interracial and interethnic tensions, and antisocial and criminal behavior.[23]

So, why do mainstream textbooks minimize the adverse consequences of unemployment? Why do they not adequately make the case for full employment as a macroeconomic goal? It was not always thus, and so some historical background is in order.

After the Second World War, policymakers in Western industrialized countries embraced the idea that full employment should be a government objective. The arguments were eloquently stated by William Beveridge in his 1944 book, *"Full Employment in a Free Society."* He begins with the thesis that since individual employers are not capable of creating full employment, it must be the responsibility of the state.

Throughout the 1950s and into the early 1970s, the UK embraced the full employment goal. Unemployment averaged 2 percent between 1950 and 1973, reaching a postwar low in July 1955 of a mere 1 percent. In the United States, the objective was signed into law in 1946 with the passing of the Employment Act that decreed it was the federal government's responsibility to "promote maximum employment."

But in the 1970s, the experience of stagflation deeply affected mainstream macro thinking. The theory evolved that any attempt to hold the unemployment rate below the "natural rate" would cause accelerating inflation. And further, if unemployment were held *above* the "natural rate" there would be accelerating *deflation*. This "accelerationist hypothesis," coupled with the realization that it was very difficult to know precisely what was the natural rate, led to the death of the full employment goal. This was facilitated by the then accepted belief that the economy was stable, and would tend toward full employment on its own anyway.

By the 1980s, mainstream macro had convinced policymakers to focus on controlling inflation. In the 1990s, inflation control became even more focused. The mainstream position was to target inflation, typically at 2 to 3 percent, and to forget completely about any employment goal. This is where the mainstream macro stands today. And it is this position that underpins the tendency of the mainstream textbooks to downplay the costs and significance of high unemployment and to attribute it to microeconomic causes.

2.5 The measurement of value-added

Textbooks suggest that it is relatively easy to determine the value-added of any sector of the economy: simply subtract the value of intermediate inputs from final sale price. But increasingly goods are produced by vertically integrated multinational corporations operating in a global economy. Products move repeatedly across borders, typically in an unfinished state: a shirt without buttons, a car without a transmission, or a computer wafer without a chip. If we do not know what these items are worth—and there is no market and therefore no price for such unfinished goods—it is difficult to determine *where* the value-added takes place. Instead of market-determined prices for unfinished goods, companies establish their own "transfer pricing." This is problematic since different jurisdictions have different tax rates and companies claim that most of the value-added occurs in jurisdictions with the lowest tax rates.

Recently, Apple (and the Irish government) achieved notoriety for abuse of transfer pricing. They struck a deal that Apple would pay a tax rate of 5/1,000th of a percentage point on its global profits to Ireland, and then claimed that a few hundred people working in Ireland produced all the value-added for the company.[24] In 2016, an EU Commission declared this illegal, not because it had any problem with the claim that all the value-added occurred in Ireland but because the tax rate was so low it was effectively *state aid* to a single company. It gets funnier. After the Commission ordered Apple to pay €20 billion in unpaid Irish taxes from 2004 to 2014, the Irish government appealed the ruling. It did not want revenue that amounted to about 10 percent of its GDP!

The Apple case is the tip of the iceberg. The growing role of intellectual property makes matters even worse, because ownership claims can be easily moved around the world. As Stiglitz (2019) explains, that's why the United States long ago abandoned using the transfer price system within its country, in favor of a formula that attributes companies' total profits to each state in proportion to its share of sales, employment, and capital.

Clearly, we need new rules for the global system. Countries are losing their ability to raise tax revenue and becoming dependent on corporate charitable donations for infrastructure, and social spending. Consider that Microsoft recently pledged $500 million to expand the availability of affordable housing in Seattle, which would generally be the job of public agencies.[25]

Even in the area of creating new international regulations, multinationals are acting while nation-states are stuck in inertia. For example, in the face of threats of foreign interference in elections, and lacking an agreed international framework to govern the process, Google and Facebook have announced their own policies.

At the end of the day, taking back sovereignty from multinationals will require international cooperation, which has been sorely lacking in recent years.[26]

It is disappointing that mainstream textbooks do not mention this important issue in the measurement chapter. The fact that it is difficult to establish where value-added takes place happens to have far-reaching consequences.

Finally, the arbitrariness involved in the measurement of value-added implies there is arbitrariness to the measure of GDP. But what about the other two measures: the final goods approach and the income approach? To be consistent, they too must be affected. And they are. If a multinational corporation shifts some value-added to a low-tax jurisdiction through manipulating its internal pricing, then the value of imports would increase. The final goods approach to measuring GDP *subtracts* imports. And of course, the income approach would register less income earned in the domestic economy.

> Question for your professor: Do vertically integrated multinational companies use internal "transfer pricing" to establish where their value-added takes place? What are the ramifications of that?

2.6 GDP as a measure of well-being

Mainstream textbooks point out that real GDP per capita contains many flaws as a measure of economic well-being.[27] While this is true, GDP was never intended to be a measure of well-being. It was designed to be a measure of economic activity—a job it does quite well. Furthermore, the mainstream textbook discussion of these "flaws" distracts us from the real issue: what are the appropriate goals for macroeconomic policy?

Standard macro textbooks are oriented toward the goals of growth (increasing real GDP per capita) and low inflation. How to challenge this narrow conception of the goals of macroeconomic policy? Good question!

One way has been to propose *composite indices of socioeconomic performance*. The most famous of these is probably the Human Development

Index promoted by the United Nations. This combines indicators from three domains: real GDP per capita, a health indicator, and an education indicator. Other composite indicators have been proposed that combine a wider range of measures.

Composite indices draw attention to a range of meritorious goals, and measure progress in them. This allows more transparency and debate. For example, the index compiled by the Canadian Centre for the Study of Living Standards includes indicators for the value of government services, the net accumulation of stocks of productive resources, the distribution of income, and economic security.

However, there are two drawbacks with composite indices. First, changes in the indices depend on the weights assigned to the components, and there is no objective way to assign weights. (As a result, equal weights are usually assigned. Since the component indices are publicly available, others can choose different weights if they so choose.) Second, changes in the composite index are generally impossible to understand without detailed examination.

Therefore, some progressives advocate instead for the use of multiple indicators without any attempt to form a composite. For example, the main macroeconomic goals might be to maintain growth in real GDP per capita above 2.5 percent, unemployment below 5 percent, inflation below 4 percent, while reducing carbon dioxide emissions by 2 percent per year.

A major advantage of using multiple indicators is greater transparency. The goals themselves can be the subject of political debate and democratic decision-making. It might turn out that many "so-called" important issues aren't really important. This is the position taken by Krugman (1994), who suggests that the real economic issues relevant to the quality of people's lives are productivity growth, income distribution, employment, and unemployment. On the other hand, inflation, the budget deficit, international competitiveness, and the state of financial markets only have "an indirect bearing on the nation's well-being" (p. 11).

Stanford (2015: 372) provides an excellent example of how multiple indicators can be used to evaluate the relative performance of different countries. He uses a table containing four countries and fifteen indicators. Despite the large number of indicators and multiple countries, the comparison is easy to follow. Finally, the direct measurement of happiness has gained widespread acceptance. A discussion of this approach is contained in Chapter 4.

2.7 The measurement of investment

The textbooks imply there is a clear distinction between investment (I) and government spending (G). They fail to emphasize that part of government spending is also investment: public sector investment.

For example, would a new airport be part of "*I*" or part of "*G*"? The answer depends on who pays for it. If it were built by the private sector, it would be part of "*I*." If it were built by the government, it would be part of "*G*."

Now, there is a good reason to treat private sector investment and public sector investment as distinct categories in the context of stabilization policy—private sector investment is volatile, determined by *expectations* of profit, which can swing from overexuberance to overly pessimistic, whereas public sector investment is policy determined, and (as Keynes recommended) can take up the slack when private sector investment is too low.

But from the point of view of growth theory, it is total investment that matters because that is what drives productivity growth. Yet, textbooks continue to call "*I*" "investment" as if it were the whole of investment, and emphasize how an increase in "*G*" can crowd out "*I*"—ignoring that public sector "*I*" is part of "*G*"!

It leads to the mistaken impression that only the private sector engages in investment. The textbook presentation is associated with a probusiness, antigovernment bias.

Question for your professor: Is investment spending only undertaken by firms, or is any household spending categorized as investment? (Answer: yes, household spending on housing.) Is any government spending categorized as investment? (Answer: no, it is not.)

2.8 Conclusion

Without measurement, there are no facts, and without trustworthy facts, everything is just a matter of opinion.

The anti-text has evaluated the trustworthiness of official measures of inflation and unemployment. We conclude that the official measure of inflation is okay. It does a good job of measuring inflation as it affects the average family, though it may understate inflation for important subgroups such as the poor (when things like food are increasing in price faster than average). The mainstream textbook criticism of the CPI is because the textbooks view price measurement through a very thick neoclassical lens. But it is not possible to construct an aggregate price index that jives with neoclassical micro theory.

On the other hand, official measures of unemployment are not okay. The better mainstream texts will compare the official unemployment rate to wider measures (such as "U6") that include "marginally attached" workers. They conclude that the official unemployment rate is useful as an *indicator* of labor market conditions but not as a literal measure of the number of people unable to find jobs. This conclusion is wrong. Even wider measures that include marginally attached workers fail to account adequately for discouraged workers. A partial solution for that problem would be the use of "not-working" rates. It is only a partial solution because even not-working rates are downwardly biased by involuntary part-time work, and there is evidence that involuntary part-time work is becoming a more important phenomenon in some countries. What is needed is better data, and abandonment of the idea that any one measure can adequately summarize labor market conditions.

With regard to measuring GDP, mainstream textbooks miss an opportunity to discuss the difficulties in determining where value-added takes place in a globalized economy. Multinationals use "transfer prices" to determine where value-added takes place, but this allows them to divert profits to the lowest tax jurisdiction. This has far-reaching ramifications, even to the point of undermining the viability of the state itself.

While on the subject of GDP measurement, the textbook focus on the difficulties of using real GDP per capita as a measure of economic well-being is misplaced. GDP was never intended to be such a measure. It is like complaining that a camel is not a horse. Further, it distracts attention from the key issue: what should be the goals of macroeconomic policy?

Turning to the components of GDP, there is no justification for mainstream textbooks' overly simplistic definitions of investment versus government spending. The student is left with the view that only private sector investment will improve long-run productivity, and government spending is all for beer and balloons. Apparently, there is no public sector investment worth mentioning. This is a probusiness, antigovernment bias.

Finally, the mainstream texts do not adequately convey the adverse consequences to individuals and society of high unemployment, and partly because of this, they do not adequately explain the case for full employment as a macro goal.

Part 2

LONG-RUN ECONOMIC GROWTH

Chapter 3

GROWTH: WHAT WE KNOW AND WHAT WE DON'T

Humanity is conducting an unintended, uncontrolled, globally-pervasive experiment whose ultimate consequences could be second only to a global nuclear war. The earth's atmosphere is being changed at an unprecedented rate.

> The world meteorological conference on "The Changing Atmosphere" (1988)[1]

I THE STANDARD TEXT

1.1 Introduction

In the developing countries, close to a billion people lack sufficient food to eat and clean water to drink. Roughly one-quarter of the world's children suffer from malnutrition. Meanwhile, among the rich industrialized countries the most pressing health problems are those caused by excessive food and drink. Yet, for centuries, European peoples existed close to subsistence levels, with periodic famines, as many in less developed countries do today.

Why are people in the rich industrialized countries so much better off than a century ago? Why are people still so desperately poor in developing countries today? The answer to both questions is that some countries have been successful at achieving long-run economic growth, while others have not.

To understand how important growth is for our standard of living, consider the mathematical approximation called the "Rule of 70." The number of years it takes any variable to double is seventy divided by its average annual growth rate.[2] For example, suppose real GDP per capita rose on average 2.2 percent per year over the last century (which it did in Canada). Applying the Rule of 70 implies that it took approximately thirty-two years ($70 \div 2.2 \approx 32$) for real GDP per capita to double; sixty-four years to double again; and ninety-six years to double three times for an eightfold increase ($2 \times 2 \times 2 = 8$). Canadian real GDP per capita actually rose 798 percent during the one hundred years of the twentieth century, confirming that the Rule of 70 is a good approximation.

The point is that small changes in GDP per capita (2.2 percent is not very much) have big implications over a long period. So, the currently rich countries got that way *a little bit at a time, over a long period of time.*

But this does not explain growth. We need to know, what are the sources of growth? What policies promote it? Why have some countries grown while others have not? As the 1995 Economics Nobel Prize winner Robert Lucas observed, these questions are so compelling that "once one starts to think about them, it is hard to think about anything else" (1988).

1.2 The crucial importance of productivity

Long-run economic growth depends on one essential ingredient—increasing *output per worker-hour* (*Y/L* or *labor productivity*)—and there are three ways to achieve it. First, increase the amount of physical capital (machinery and equipment) per worker. Second, improve the education and skills (or *human capital*) possessed by the average worker. Third, and most important, improve the level of technology. We can express this in terms of an aggregate production function for the economy as a whole depicting output per worker, *Y/L*, as a function of its main determinants: physical capital per worker, *K/L*; human capital per worker, *H/L*; and the state of technology, *t*. (We note that technology, *t*, is sometimes referred to as "total factor productivity" and should not be confused with labor productivity, *Y/L*.) This is shown below as equation (3.1).

$$Y/L = f(K/L, H/L, t) \tag{3.1}$$

What can we make of this? Clearly, having physical capital makes workers more productive: a construction worker is more productive with a backhoe than a shovel; an accountant is more productive with a computer than a pencil and paper. But the law of diminishing returns tells us that as we increase any one input, *holding all other inputs constant*, the gains in output will eventually diminish. So, eventually this process of capital deepening runs out of steam. When the capital-to-labor ratio (*K/L*) gets high enough, the returns from further increases in capital are too small to be worth it. This is illustrated in Figure 3.1.

In Figure 3.1, everything is measured in constant dollar terms. As we move from point A to B, *K/L* increases by $2,000, and labor productivity (output per worker) doubles from $1,000 to $2,000. Moving from point B to C, we see that another increase in *K/L* of $2,000 has a much smaller effect on productivity, only producing a $500 increase in output per worker. Thus, as capital deepening progresses, it has a diminishing impact on productivity. However, the change in productivity never becomes negative.

Returning to the aggregate production function (equation 3.1), *H/L* refers to the skills and knowledge embodied in the workforce. Clearly, it is not enough to have good equipment—workers must also know how to operate it. Diminishing returns also apply to human capital deepening. More skills per unit of labor (*H/L*), holding all other inputs constant, will produce diminishing gains in output.

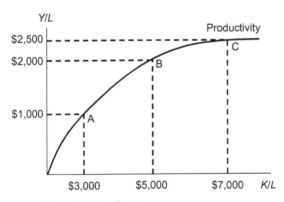

Figure 3.1 The aggregate production function

On the other hand, diminishing returns *may or may not* apply to technology, *t*. It mostly depends on how "technology" is defined: the narrower the focus, the more likely are diminishing returns. For example, the returns to a faster and faster computer chip *are* likely to be diminishing. On the other hand, it is unclear whether there are diminishing returns to *knowledge as a whole*. Furthermore, since the nature of technological change is to change the way things are done, measuring its effect *holding all other factors constant* is problematic. It is this aspect of technological change—it potentially defies the law of diminishing returns—that makes it the most important element in improving our standard of living.

1.3 The production function and growth accounting

When we fit an aggregate production function to the data, we get estimates of the productiveness of an extra unit of physical capital per worker (K/L), and an extra unit of human capital per worker (H/L). Then we multiply these numbers by the increase in each component over time. The sum of these gives us the increase in productivity accounted for by *total capital deepening* (increases in both K/L and H/L). We estimate the effect of technological change as the unexplained residual after everything else has been accounted for.

For example, suppose that physical capital per worker grows 0.75 percent a year, and that estimates of the production function suggest that each 1 percent increase in physical capital per worker raises output per worker by 0.33 of a percentage point (holding human capital and technology constant). That implies the growth of physical capital per worker is responsible for 0.75 × 0.33 ≈ 0.25 percent growth in annual productivity.

Following a similar procedure, suppose human capital per worker grows at 0.5 percent a year, and that each 1 percent increase in human capital raises output per worker by 0.67 of a percentage point (holding physical capital and technology constant). Then growth in human capital per worker is responsible for 0.5 × 0.67 ≈ 0.34 percent growth in annual productivity.

The effect of total capital deepening (both human and physical) is the sum of these amounts, or 0.59 (=0.25+0.34) percent a year. If the average annual growth rate of average labor productivity (Y/L) was 4.7 percent a year, then technological change must be responsible for the remaining 4.1 percent a year.

We could express this in terms of the relative importance of technical change. In this example, total capital deepening accounted for 12 percent [≈(0.58/4.7)×100] of the growth in productivity, while technical change accounted for the remaining 88 percent.

Robert Solow (1957) was the first to perform this exercise. He used US data from 1909 to 1949, a period when gross output per worker-hour doubled. He found that only 12.5 percent of the growth in productivity was due to capital deepening. The remaining 87.5 percent was attributable to technical change.

1.4 What about natural resources?

Up to this point, we have ignored natural resources, such as fertile land or mineral deposits. To illustrate its effect, we could have added another term (N/L) to the production function to indicate natural resources per capita. Then it would be clear that holding other factors of production (K/L, H/L, and t) constant, the more natural resources per capita (N/L), the higher will be the level of output per capita.

While important historically, natural resources are a less important determinant of living standards in the modern world. Yes, there *are* a few examples of countries whose wealth depends almost entirely on their natural resources (oil-rich countries such as Kuwait, for example). However, there are many more examples of rich countries with very limited natural resources (such as Japan, Taiwan, or South Korea).

1.5 Public policy: savings and investment

We have seen that workers are more productive when there is more capital equipment. Since capital is a produced factor of production, society can change the amount of capital it has by producing more. However, an economy can only produce more capital goods if it produces less consumption goods. There is no free lunch: *society needs to refrain from consuming today so that it can save and invest and be more productive tomorrow.*

Think of an agrarian society: farmers have a choice—they can consume all their seeds today, or they can save some to plant next year. Assuming away the Paradox of Thrift from our long-run analysis, more savings means more investment. (Remember, growth analysis assumes full employment. Therefore, by assumption there is no possibility of the Paradox of Thrift occurring.) So, how can the government encourage savings and facilitate its transformation into investment?

The most necessary ingredient is a sound well-functioning financial system. If households do not trust their banks, they will not deposit their savings with them. A financial system starved of cash will be unable to channel funds to firms. Not only is appropriate government regulation necessary, but so too is responsible monetary policy: excessive inflation erodes the value of financial assets and discourages savings.

Later in the book (in Chapter 5), we will analyze in much greater detail how financial markets channel savings into investment spending. For now, the key point is that investment must be paid for either out of domestic (national) savings or out of foreign savings. Domestic savings come from domestic households and the government when it runs a budget surplus. Government budget deficits absorb savings that would otherwise have gone to finance investment and growth—they *"crowd out"* investment. Foreign savings come from other countries. A country can *import* foreign savings by allowing foreign investment. If a country finances its investment using foreign savings, it is borrowing from abroad.

Of course, the use of foreign savings is not free. Investors want a return on their investment and this return will be repatriated abroad. Nevertheless, the increase in real GDP generated by foreign investment will be greater than the amount paid to foreigners. Therefore, foreign investment is beneficial overall.

Often there is an additional payoff to foreign investment: foreigners may bring new technology that diffuses through the domestic economy, raising productivity in many sectors. For these reasons, economists advocate that governments should remove restrictions on foreign ownership of capital.

1.6 Two implications of diminishing returns

Suppose the government succeeds in increasing total savings: what benefit can we expect? If capital is subject to diminishing returns—as we think it is—an increase in the savings rate only leads to a *temporarily* higher growth rate. As more capital is accumulated and the capital-to-labor ratio increases, the benefits from *additional* capital become smaller, and growth slows down. The higher saving rate leads to a higher *level* of productivity and higher income per capita, but not to a permanently higher *growth* rate in those variables.

Another implication of diminishing returns to capital is that (all other things equal) it is easier for a country to grow fast if it starts out relatively poor. Poverty is associated with a low capital-to-labor ratio, implying a high marginal product of additional capital. Where workers lack rudimentary tools, even a small amount of additional capital raises productivity substantially; but where workers already have sophisticated equipment, additional capital has only a small effect on productivity. This effect of initial conditions on subsequent growth is called *the catch-up effect*. It implies that living standards around the world should *converge*.

This *convergence hypothesis* has been extensively tested. Considering only countries that are currently wealthy, the convergence hypothesis does well empirically. For example, it seems to explain why South Korea grew faster than the United States (6 percent average growth versus 2 percent) between 1960 and 1990 despite a similar share of GDP to investment. However, when we compare the growth rates of countries that are still poor with those of now advanced economies, the evidence for convergence disappears. This is not so surprising given that convergence is conditional on other things being equal— things like education, infrastructure, and the rule of law—and in Africa and parts of Latin America these conditions do not obtain.

1.7 Other public policy measures to stimulate growth

Education The second term in the aggregate production function (equation 3.1) is human capital per worker. Most human capital is the result of government spending on education. The quality of education critically affects a country's ability to innovate.

Research and development Scientific advances are usually a necessary prerequisite for technological improvements. However, translating science into useful products and processes requires R&D spending. This can be encouraged by government subsidies and granting of temporary monopoly power in the form of patent protection.

Infrastructure Roads, railways, power lines, ports, and communication networks provide the foundation for economic activity. The government's role is either to provide this infrastructure directly or to regulate and support its private provision. Without it, there is no foundation for economic activity. Lack of infrastructure is a major problem in many poor countries.

Property rights and political stability A necessary condition for a market economy is the enforcement of contracts and protection of property rights. Failure to protect property rights, or to prevent widespread bribery and corruption, impedes the coordinating power of markets. It also discourages domestic saving and investment from abroad. One threat to property rights is political instability. The possibility that physical capital could be confiscated clearly reduces the incentive to invest. A country with an efficient court system, honest government officials, and a stable constitution will enjoy a higher economic standard of living than a country with a poor court system, corrupt officials, and frequent revolutions and coups.

Free trade One of the most important insights in economics is that there are gains from trade. The principle of comparative advantage shows that even less efficient nations benefit from trading with more efficient nations. No nation can afford to give up the gains from trade. Restricting trade leads to a loss of income, and therefore lost savings and investment, and hence slower growth.

The only economically sound argument for protecting an industry against foreign competition is the *infant industry* argument. Whenever an industry has large economies of scale, costs will fall as the industry grows. In such cases, the country first in the field has a cost advantage. Theoretically, a temporary trade restriction is necessary to allow an infant industry to mature into a strong industry with an acquired, but real, comparative advantage. If it were not protected, it would be driven out of business and its comparative advantage might never develop.

The trouble is that some infant industries never grow up but continue to rely on tariff protection for their existence. Furthermore, it is very hard to tell which infants will be successful and which will not. In the 1950s, many Latin American countries imposed tariffs and import quotas on manufactured goods in an effort to nurture domestic industries. Most of the resulting industries remained inefficient, high-cost producers dependent on subsidies and tariff protection. So, while the infant industry argument is theoretically valid, in practice *trying to pick winners* is inadvisable.

1.8 Is world population growth sustainable?

Worries about overpopulation have been around for a long time. In 1798, Thomas Malthus predicted that the pressure of population growth on a fixed supply of land would lead to diminishing food output per worker over time. His conclusion that humanity is doomed to live on the edge of starvation gained economics the epithet "the dismal science."[3] Any technological progress or capital deepening would only relieve the situation temporarily since it would permit further increases in population.

Of course, Malthus's predictions have proven wildly wrong. Population has increased from around 800 million in 1798 to over 7 billion today, and average incomes have increased as well. Interestingly, England *was* running out of a key resource in Malthus's day—not land but wood. A shortage of wood led to efforts to mine coal, which led to the development of canals and railways to transport it. In short, it was one of the causes of the English Industrial Revolution in the eighteenth century! Clearly, Malthus seriously underestimated the possibilities of technological progress.

While it is true that famines have occurred from time to time, Amartya Sen (1981 and 1993) has shown they are rarely caused by a lack of food. They mostly occur when a vulnerable segment of the population loses its ability to buy food—often through loss of work (caused by local floods, for example). More recently, massive famines have occurred in places like South Sudan, and in Yemen, as a result of war and insurgency, not through overpopulation.

While worries about population *size* seem to be misplaced, a fast population *growth rate* may have negative implications for growth. For any given savings rate, faster population growth makes it harder to increase (or even maintain) the capital-to-labor ratio (K/L), leading to lower productivity and lower GDP per worker. In addition, faster population growth implies larger cohorts of school-age children, burdening the educational system. Educational attainment (and human capital per worker, H/L) tends to be low in countries with high population growth.

In many poor African countries, population is growing around 3 percent a year, which implies a doubling every twenty-three years (70/3 ≈23). Can incentives be used to control population growth? Between 1979 and 2016, China allowed only one child per family, and couples who violated this rule were subject to substantial fines. According to the Chinese government, about 400 million births were prevented. Other countries have attempted to reduce population growth by increasing awareness about, and availability of, contraception. However, there are economic incentives that make large families attractive, and until these change attempts at voluntary birth control programs will fail. As countries grow and become wealthier, children change from being net economic assets to net economic liabilities, and this drives "the demographic transition" toward low birth rates and low population growth.

1.9 Resources and the environment

Resource constraints The fear that we might run out of resources came to prominence in 1972 with the publication of *The Limits to Growth* by a think tank of scientists known as "The Club of Rome." This report was an extremely detailed look at a host of essential resources, comparing rates of use with available supplies. Famously, they predicted severe shortages within a couple of decades, bringing growth to a grinding halt. Since then we have witnessed the prices of these natural resources fall to unprecedentedly low levels and world growth continue unabated. It is instructive to consider where they went wrong.

A major problem was they assumed *constant* input/output ratios, which amounts to assuming away market forces. In fact, if the relative price of a nonrenewable resource goes up, we economize on its use, substitute other things in its place, and find it worthwhile to recycle it. Furthermore, "available supplies" of a resource is a very elastic concept. What we consider a viable deposit depends upon the selling price of the resource. In short, the approach of comparing rates of use with "available supplies" is entirely naïve.

However, the *fundamental problem* with the Club of Rome's report was—once again—its underestimate of the potential for technological progress. When they predicted shortages of tin and copper, tin was used for food containers and copper to make telephone wire; now food comes in plastic, and most phone calls are transmitted wirelessly.

Arguably, the key resource—underlying all others—is the human intellect. Coal and uranium were just lumps of useless rock in the ground until mixed with human intellect. Moreover, human intellect is an always-renewable resource. In 1981, Julian Simon pushed this argument to its logical conclusion by claiming that since the amount of human intellect is increasing (quantitatively through population growth and qualitatively through education) the supply of resources will grow faster than demand and push resource prices down![4] The environmental activist Paul Ehrlich famously bet Julian Simon that between 1980 and 1990, scarcity would drive resource prices up. Simon easily won the bet. There is very little talk about how we are running out of energy or important minerals nowadays. A lot of that is because of the work of Julian Simon.

Environmental constraints Critics of growth say industrialization pollutes the air we breathe and the water we drink. It results in climate change, ozone depletion, and general environmental collapse. The more rapid our growth, the more waste the environment must absorb. In an already wealthy society, further growth usually means satisfying increasingly trivial wants at the cost of mounting threats to the ecological system.

The classic work on growth and the environment was published in the mid-1990s by Grossman and Krueger (1995). They found that as GDP per capita increases, pollution increases initially but eventually falls, forming an inverted "U." The reason for the shape is that clean water and clean air are "normal goods," the demand for which increases as incomes rise.

Furthermore, growth does not necessarily cause pollution. It does not have to be associated with more stuff. It could be used to buy more education, health care, research, leisure, and better working conditions. Pollution and environmental decay are caused by the wrong kinds of growth, involving "dirty" industries that produce negative externalities. But negative externalities can be corrected using regulatory legislation, specific taxes ("effluent charges"), or other market-based incentives such as tradable emissions permits.

1.10 Conclusion

A country's standard of living depends on the productivity of its workers. To encourage growth in productivity, policymakers must encourage the accumulation of both physical and human capital, and promote a fertile environment for technological progress. Since savings make investment possible, savings must be encouraged: first, by maintaining a sound, well-functioning, banking system; second, by avoiding public sector deficits (that drive up interest rates and crowd out investment); and third, by removing restrictions on foreign inflows of capital.

The government must avoid creating inefficiencies by interfering in the market mechanism. Rather, it should support the invisible hand by maintaining property rights and political stability.

Free trade allows a nation to maximize the benefits from specialization and comparative advantage. On the other hand, trade restrictions lead to a loss of income, and therefore lost savings and investment, and hence slower growth. More controversial is whether the government should target and subsidize specific industries that might be especially important for technological progress. Protecting infant industries is good in theory but can be bad in practice.

Finally, environmental problems are caused by negative externalities, which can be corrected. In general, economists view resource scarcity as a problem that the price mechanism handles quite well. It is not a fundamental limit to long-run growth. Since the most important resource is the human intellect, limitless growth is possible.

2 THE ANTI-TEXT

2.1 The extent of our ignorance

In Section 1.3, we discussed the production function and growth accounting. There we explained how the production function yields estimates of the contributions to growth provided by each factor of production. The effect of technical change is calculated as a residual. We mentioned how Robert Solow (1957) was the first to perform this exercise using US data from 1909 to 1949. He found that only 12.5 percent of the growth in productivity was due to *capital deepening*—the effect of more capital per unit of labor and more human capital per unit of labor. The remaining 87.5 percent was attributable to technical change. While the exact percentage contribution of productivity growth varies between countries and time periods, it remains true that it is generally the most important source of growth.

The key point is that economists understand the process of capital deepening quite well but are ignorant as to the causes of technical change.[5] Using Solow's original estimate, one could say that economists are $87\frac{1}{2}$ percent ignorant of the causes of productivity growth!

> Question for your professor: Easily the most important source of growth is technological progress. Do economists know what causes it? If not, how can they claim any expertise in recommending policies to promote growth?

2.2 Debunking the aggregate production function

The core of neoclassical macroeconomics—including growth theory, real business cycle theory, and short-run models of unemployment—relies on the aggregate production function. Unfortunately, there are a number of severe methodological problems associated with it. In particular, there are the problems posed by both the Cambridge capital controversy (that started in the 1950s and lasted well into the 1970s) and what may be generically termed "aggregation problems" found in the somewhat broader aggregation literature.

Consider the neoclassical story about the determination of r (the return to capital). Given an aggregate production function with capital as one input (among others), we determine the marginal product of capital, which determines its rate of return, r. But how do we add up all the different kinds of capital—all the different tools, machines, and structures—to get one measure of capital to put into the production function? The answer is that we must add everything in value terms. But the value of capital depends on its return, r. Therefore, in order to be able to aggregate capital in value terms we require that the price of capital, r, be known *before* we determine the marginal product of capital, which is then supposed to determine the return on capital, r. So, there is a circularity issue.

Now, there are many examples of simultaneous mutual dependence in economics that can be routinely solved. For example, in our short-run macro models (considered in Chapter 6), consumption depends on income, and income depends on consumption. But this does not prevent us from uniquely solving for both income and consumption.

Unfortunately, when it comes to the valuation of capital, things are not so easy. During the "Cambridge capital controversy," it was shown there might be *no unique equilibrium solution*: no necessary inverse monotonic relationship between r (the rate of return on capital) and K/L (the capital-to-labor ratio). The marginal productivity of capital might fall for a while as K/L increases but then may suddenly increase. So, the return on capital might be lower when it is "more scarce." And this means that diminishing returns doesn't hold, the determination of growth contributions doesn't hold, and the convergence hypothesis doesn't hold. Indeed, it strikes at the very heart of the mainstream story that determines the distribution of income, and the productivity of factors, in a purely technical way.

The neoclassical economists responded with two arguments. First, they argued the aggregate production function is not the intellectually respectable version of their theory, so showing it to be false did not damage their core theory. The intellectually respectable version is the extremely disaggregated (and complex) *general equilibrium theory.* In this theory, each disaggregated factor—each type of capital—earns a reward equal to its marginal product. Unfortunately, general equilibrium theory is itself plagued by difficulties in showing uniqueness and stability (see Ackerman 2002, and Hill and Myatt, chapter 6 addendum). More importantly, it provides no support for a "relative scarcity theory of income distribution." One cannot assert that, *ceteris paribus*, an increase in the supply of "capital" causes the return on "capital" to fall; nor can one assert that, *ceteris paribus*, an increase in the supply of labor causes real wages to fall.

Their second argument was to acknowledge the logical problems with the aggregate production function, but to defend it as an extremely useful simplifying device that is supported empirically. They pointed out that econometricians have successfully estimated countless aggregate production functions, which must mean that the practical relevance of the capital controversy is extremely limited. Unfortunately, this argument was blown apart by a stunning article by Anwar Shaikh.

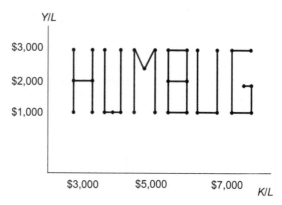

Figure 3.2 The HUMBUG production function

In 1974, Shaikh showed that the empirical success of the aggregate production function is based on a tautology. Econometricians mistakenly identified a *key accounting identity* for a production function! (That accounting identity is "the value of goods is identically equal to labour-cost plus capital-cost.") To grab the reader's attention, Shaikh created data that spelled out the word "HUMBUG" when plotted in a diagram with output per unit of labor on the vertical axis, and capital per unit of labor on the horizontal axis. In other words, the word "HUMBUG" appeared where we would expect the normal concave production function to be. This is illustrated in Figure 3.2.

Obviously, a HUMBUG production function is quite absurd. It is pure humbug. There are no diminishing returns here! But since Shaikh's data exhibited constant income shares between labor and capital, an aggregate production function fitted the data perfectly. All the deviations between the HUMBUG data and the normal-shaped production function were categorized as "technological change." This certainly made the pattern of technological change quite random and strange, but economists have no presumptions about how technological change should behave, or what it should look like. And therefore, the humbug data worked just fine.

Further, Shaikh showed that an aggregate production function could be derived mathematically from the key accounting identity, with just a few manipulations, as long as income shares were constant. So, Shaikh had shown both theoretically and empirically that aggregate production functions perform well because of an underlying accounting identity: the value of goods equals labor cost plus capital cost.

Shaikh's point has been updated and generalized in a recent book by Felipe and McCombie (2013) entitled *The Aggregate Production Function and the Measurement of Technical Change: Not Even Wrong*. The title emphasizes that the aggregate production function is not capable of being statistically refuted. In that sense, it is "not even wrong."

For mainstream economists, this critique must be (and has been) resisted at all costs. Acceptance of it would be destructive of huge swaths of modern work in mainstream neoclassical economics.

```
Question for your professor: [Take a deep breath!]
We need to know the value of capital, so that we can
aggregate all the different types of capital into
one measure of "capital," which we can then insert
into the production function to determine the value
of capital. Isn't there a problem here?
```

2.3 Critical evaluation of textbook policies to promote growth

It is noteworthy that the textbooks recommend a generic set of policies to promote growth—a "one size fits all" approach. But there are many different countries, with different problems and endowments, in different stages of development. With so much heterogeneity, why should we presume that one set of policies is appropriate?

The set of policies that mainstream textbooks propose dates back to the early 1980s when there was a right-wing shift in the UK (with the election of Margaret Thatcher in 1979) and in the United States (with the election of President Ronald Reagan in 1981), and neoliberalism first emerged. It was forcefully championed by Milton Friedman and the Chicago School. The view that such policies were appropriate to all countries was adopted by the IMF, the World Bank, and the US Treasury, and since they are all based in Washington, DC, this became known as the Washington Consensus.

Neoliberalism and the Washington Consensus The neoliberal agenda has two main goals: removing restraints on the private sector and shrinking the public sector—and if possible remaking what remains of it in the private sector's image.

The removal of restraints on the private sector involves deregulation, trade liberalization, and unimpeded international movement of capital.

Shrinking the public sector is achieved in two ways: directly, through privatization of publicly owned assets; and indirectly, through tax cuts coupled with deficit and debt hysteria—a method known as "starving the beast." The indirect method eventually forces spending cuts, as debt and debt hysteria mount. All this—the neoliberal agenda—is sold as increasing "efficiency" and "competition." The public sector is painted as bloated, bureaucratic, and inefficient.

Loans from the IMF and World Bank were (and still often are) conditional on accepting an imposition of the neoliberal agenda under the guise of "stabilization" or "structural adjustment" programs. Often these programs have led to riots in the recipient country.

However, neoliberalism is no longer unquestioned truth within international institutions like the IMF and World Bank—especially their research divisions. Nevertheless, neoliberal policies continue to be adopted worldwide. This is empirically shown by three top IMF economists writing in the IMF's flagship publication. In a 2016 paper (entitled "Neoliberalism: Oversold?") Ostry and his coauthors construct a composite index showing that neoliberal policies are continuing to gain ground and continue to have adverse impacts.

International capital mobility In arguing that neoliberalism has been "oversold," Ostry and his coauthors are particularly critical of unimpeded international movements of short-term capital (or foreign indirect investment). They link this with increased speculation, economic volatility, and risk of financial crisis, with no offsetting benefits. They note that between 1980 and 2016, there were 150 episodes of surges in capital inflows into more than fifty emerging market economies; about 20 percent of the time, these episodes ended in a financial crisis, many of which were associated with large output declines. As Dani Rodrik (1998) observes, "boom and bust cycles are hardly a sideshow or a minor blemish in international capital flows; they are the main story."

Besides increasing the risks of a financial crash, Furceri and Loungani (2016) argue that "footloose capital" has appreciably raised inequality and reduced labor's share of GDP. They discuss three channels through which the effect occurs. First, internationally mobile capital lowers the bargaining power of workers and hence their share of income; second, foreign capital flows are a source of volatility and crisis, which disproportionately hurt lower income groups; third, the benefits from foreign capital flows accrue largely to higher income groups.

The adverse effects of short-term international capital movements have been noted for a very long time. Back in 1972, James Tobin (who won the Nobel Memorial Prize in Economics nine years later) proposed a small tax on international currency transactions to "throw sand in the wheels" of short-term capital mobility.[6] While this *Tobin Tax* has been discussed extensively, and has been backed by different countries at different times, it has never been implemented by a major developed economy.[7] Why? Evidently, the lobbying power of the financial sector overrides sensible policy implementation.

As far as international movements of *direct capital* are concerned, the consensus opinion is that it has helped increase growth in developing countries, and hence income convergence between developing and advanced economies over the last three decades. One common term used to describe the movement of *direct* capital (basically factories relocating abroad) is "outsourcing." Mainstream theory predicts this will increase total world income but is silent on how the gains will be shared between participants. There is only a small literature arguing that outsourcing could produce net economic losses in advanced economies (see Gomory and Baumol 2001; Samuelson 2004).

In supporting unimpeded movement of capital, mainstream textbooks implicitly defend the view that outsourcing does not disturb the "result" that capital mobility is beneficial to all. Yet, this view has no empirical backing. Meanwhile, back in the real world, outsourcing has helped fuel the populist sentiment against globalization because it can seem so patently unfair. This is especially the case when outsourcing is motivated to avoid legal restraints in advanced economies, such as environmental regulations, or collective bargaining laws (see Rodrik 2016).

> Question for your professor: Is outsourcing jobs to low-wage countries in the best interest of high-wage countries? Is there any evidence on this?

Free trade As a policy to promote growth, recommending trade liberalization seems out of touch with both economic history and with current events—since "free trade" agreements nowadays are less about liberalizing trade flows and more about ensuring the mobility of capital, enshrining corporate rights, and limiting the sovereignty of governments.

In terms of economic history, countries like the United States, Canada, and Germany all erected high tariff walls in the nineteenth and early twentieth centuries, to protect their fledgling industries against British competition.[8] In the twentieth century, many East Asian countries have used the same model, notably Japan, South Korea, Taiwan, and Singapore. More recently, China has become the world's second largest economy with little or no regard for the rules of "free trade." Rather, the Chinese government has used currency controls, impeded the inward flow of capital, protected its domestic markets against foreign competition, and subsidized its own exports (see Mishrafeb 2018). In addition, the Chinese government also maintains strong, profitable, and important State-owned enterprises, especially in what they consider "strategic" industries.

> Question for your professor: Most currently rich countries developed behind high tariff walls. So, what evidence is there that "free trade" is good for growth?

Promote savings Efforts to promote savings only make sense in the strict confines of a "long-run" model, where savings equals investment by assumption. But a short-run model better approximates the real world, where the paradox of thrift can occur, or where trillions of dollars of savings can be kept in idle cash reserves, and not invested. Policies to promote domestic savings look foolish in that context. As Keynes (1923) says, the "long run is a misleading guide to current affairs. In the long run we are all dead."

Put succinctly, the long run is to macro what perfect competition is to micro. In micro, perfect competition is used as a handy reference model to get one's intuition straight, a useful enough first approximation. As such, it is completely misleading, as argued in Hill and Myatt (2021). In macro, "long-run equilibrium" serves the same role, and is just as misleading.

Furthermore, the idea that government deficits crowd out investment is based on the (implicit) assumption that government spending is for consumption purposes. If the government spends on investment, the crowding out argument collapses. Investment by government-owned enterprises—in water or electrical utilities, railways, or ports—should not be classified automatically as consumption just because government does the spending.

The proportion of government spending that can be categorized as "investment" can be expanded by recognizing that spending on public health measures—such as disease control and clean water—is crucial public infrastructure. More pointedly, the private sector does not invest in basic scientific research because private markets are unable to appropriate the returns. So, government spending on education—especially scientific education—can easily be categorized as "investment." Government *investment* spending can be expanded further by recognizing that natural, civic, and social capital are also important to growth.

Mainstream textbooks seem to take the way things are measured in the National Accounts as representing "truth" and, as a result, they consider only the accumulation of physical capital as "investment."

Question for your professor: Currently corporations have trillions in idle cash reserves. Then how can it make sense to promote even more savings?

Industrial policies This is an omitted topic from most mainstream textbooks, and the few that do discuss it have an ambivalent attitude toward it (citing the difficulty of "picking winners"). The neoliberal agenda of shrinking the size of the public sector does not resonate with an actively engaged government investing in the economy. Yet, successful economies have always relied on an active government sector—investing, owning, and directing, as well as protecting and regulating.

This is obvious and well known in the case of China. But even in the United States, the government has played a crucial role in developing innovation. As Mariana Mazzucato (2015) explains in her book *The Entrepreneurial State*, if asked to think of a private sector innovating icon, Apple comes readily to mind. But all the crucial technological developments that make the iPhone so smart were publicly funded, including GPS, touchscreen display, and even SIRI (the voice-activated system). Similarly, most of the breakthrough drugs were not developed by pharmaceutical companies but were developed by nonprofit academic medical centers or at the National Institutes of Health (see Angell 2004). Two more examples: the algorithm behind Google was funded with an NSF (National Science Foundation) grant, and the internet grew out of a Defense Department project initiated in 1969.

Certainly, there are examples of bad industrial policy, where politicians make poor choices and pour public money down a bottomless drain. An oft-cited example is the import substitution strategy followed by many Latin American countries from the 1950s to the 1980s. This leads Rodrik (2010) to emphasize that the key to successful industrial policy is not the government's ability to pick winners but rather its capacity to let the losers go—which he views as a much less demanding requirement.

For Mazzucato (2015), the real problem with the mainstream view about industrial policy is twofold: first, the role of the government is not acknowledged; and second, the public sector takes most of the risks in the modern innovation process but gets little of the reward. Taxing the companies that successfully commercialize a product—like Apple and the iPhone—is not enough. There are too many ways for companies to avoid taxation in the modern globalized world. She has various recommendations for how governments can receive a return on their investments. One suggestion is that governments receive an equity stake in companies that use its intellectual property. In Finland (and Scandinavia generally) this already happens.[9]

The fact that the role of the government is not acknowledged has implications for our next topics, sustainability and the fight to stave off environmental collapse.

Question for your professor: I read that the crucial technology that makes the iPhone so smart was publicly funded. And most of the breakthrough drugs were developed by academic medical centers or at the National Institutes of Health. Why doesn't the text discuss the government role in making these breakthroughs?

2.4 Is world population growth sustainable?

Over fifty years ago, Paul Ehrlich (1968) compared population growth to a bomb that would lead to the collapse of civilization. He claimed that the world's optimal population is less than 2 billion people. If starvation doesn't get us, "toxification" will. Figure 3.3 shows the world population from AD1 to 2019. We see that exponential growth really begins around 1750, and currently looks like a moonshot. Optimists point to the decrease in the population growth rate, which peaked at 2.1 percent in 1962, and has since fallen to around 1.2 percent currently. Nevertheless, even the most optimistic projections have world population growth continuing until around 2100, when human numbers will be close to 40 percent more than today, at more than 11 billion. Can the world really sustain that many people? And since population growth rates in rich industrialized countries have already fallen to fractions of a percent, and in some countries are negative, this seems like a "third world" problem.[10] "They" need to get their populations under control!

But a different picture emerges when we reflect on the fact that 20 percent of the world's population living in rich industrialized countries are consuming 75 percent of the world's resources. As far as CO_2 emissions are concerned, Hans Rosling (2014) invites us to forget about countries, and think only in terms of income. Half the world's emissions are by the world's richest billion. Nearly all the CO_2 emissions, 87½ percent, are by the richest 3 billion. The poorest 4 billion emit only 12½ percent. When we think of it this way, it is clear the population issue is intimately bound up with distributional questions.

And did you know that if the entire world's population were living as densely concentrated per square mile as people happily live today in Paris, the entire world's population would fit into the state of Montana? Or if they preferred they could fill up just 55 percent of the state of Texas. The entire rest of the world would be entirely empty of people. It could be just a giant nature and animal reserve.[11]

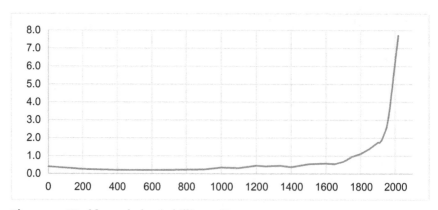

Figure 3.3 World population in billions, AD1–2019

Of course, that last calculation is entirely misleading. It omits all the land in the periphery, outside the giant city, that would be required to grow food and mine resources, and provide the city with water, and dispose of the city's waste. A city's ecological footprint is many times its physical footprint. And if everyone in this giant city were living like the average North American, we would need about $5\frac{1}{2}$ worlds to service such a city.[12]

So, the question of whether world population is sustainable *is* intimately bound up with who gets what, and with whether we can change the way we do things. But the way things are currently done, we can answer a categorical "no." World population growth is not sustainable, but is one factor among many driving ecological collapse. Let us investigate further.

2.5 Sustainability: the doomsters versus the growth men

The mainstream textbooks argue that negative externalities are correctable using market-based solutions, and resource scarcity will be solved by allowing the market to allocate scarce resources and by human ingenuity. Further, as economic development proceeds, environmental pollution follows an inverted U-shape: it initially gets worse, but reaches a peak, beyond which richer countries enjoy cleaner environments.

But we are currently faced with the collapse of the living world. And this is occurring in the context of extreme inequality, where democratic governments are captured by billionaires and their lobbyists, where scientists are distrusted and muzzled, and where a confused populace looks to demagogues for easy solutions. It is not a pretty picture.

Reflect on what you consider to be the five most severe environmental problems facing humanity today. No, really do it. Make a list.

Was it hard to narrow it down? Perhaps top of your list was climate change. But after that, there is so much choice!

There is the loss of biodiversity and mass extinctions of species. The rate of extinction of species is today between 1,000 and 10,000 times greater than "normal." The current geological age is denoted "Anthropocene" to indicate the massive (and adverse) impacts humans are having on the Earth's ecosystems.

There is the proliferation of plastic that is killing life in the oceans, getting into even the remotest corners of the world, broken down into the tiniest particles entering our bloodstreams, mixed with the salt we put on our food, inside the flesh of the fish we eat, but never ever disappearing. You recycle you say? Well, it turns out there is no magical land of recycling.[13] Did that make your list?

There is deforestation especially in the tropics, to make way for cattle or agriculture. Not only do natural forests act as biodiversity reserves, they are also carbon sinks—which are disappearing.[14]

There is soil degradation and declining cropland. In weight, we are losing 25 billion tons of fertile topsoil each year. In area, we are losing 168,000 square miles of productive agricultural land to degradation yearly (that's about the size of Arizona). Fierce competitive pressures in agriculture force farmers to cut costs as much as possible. As a result, soil conservation suffers.

There are water shortages due mainly to the irrigation requirements of agriculture but exacerbated by climate change. Not to mention the depletion of fish stocks, partly due to overfishing and again exacerbated by climate change.

The mainstream textbook treatment dramatically underestimates the severity of the environmental problems we face. The first thing missing is recognition that many of the problems in our list are created by the very market forces the textbooks rely upon to efficiently allocate scarce resources.

The second thing missing is more fundamental: the textbooks lack a structure for thinking about how a sustainable economic system can even be visualized. We need a worldview where there are limits to the rate at which we turn natural wealth into "output," and there are limits to the amount of waste that can be absorbed by the environment without causing its collapse.[15] And the distribution of output needs to matter, with human happiness the goal—not growth for growth's sake. We take up this issue in the next chapter.

But let us return to climate change. This is the challenge of our lives. It is associated with increased frequency and intensity of tropical storms, and longer and more intense heat waves; increased droughts, floods, and forest fires; and rising sea levels. The increased acidification of the sea, its rising temperature, and its loss of oxygen are threatening the death of the seas. Climate change literally poses an existential threat, and therefore it should and must be discussed in macroeconomics textbooks.

2.6 The climate emergency

The problem of climate change is linked to economic growth: the larger the economy, the more homes, factories, and vehicles to be powered. At present, world energy consumption is overwhelmingly dependent upon fossil fuels (at around 81 percent of the total).

Given this reality, it is astonishing that only one mainstream macroeconomics textbook says anything about climate change.[16] The remainder treat climate change purely as a microeconomic topic, as an externality like any other, capable of being solved with a carbon tax (or tradable emissions permits). But is it true? Since climate change is a huge topic, we are going to concentrate on explaining only three things: first, that the situation is dire; second, what should be done; and third, why it is not being done.

The situation is dire   Figure 3.4 shows world temperatures, 1850–2018. The solid line shows a five-year moving average of air temperatures over

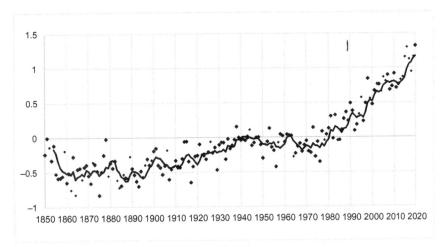

Figure 3.4 Global temperatures (differences from 1961 to 1990 average) in degrees Celsius

Source: Climatic Research Institute, University of East Anglia

land, in degree Celsius (depicted as the difference from the 1961–90 average).[17] The original data points (the dots) are also shown. The data points themselves are averages from over 4,800 readings from around the globe. Notice how the five-year average is starting to rise at an increasing rate, and how three of the four most recent readings (2015 to 2017) lie above the five-year moving average line. Notice how close we are already to 1.5 degree Celsius increase in average temperature. This is significant because the IPCC (the UN Intergovernmental Panel on Climate Change) report of 2018 clarified that even 1.5 degrees of warming was extremely dangerous, and 2 degrees of warming might trigger tipping points (or amplifying feedbacks) leading to an unstoppable climate catastrophe. So, we are already pretty close to a level of warming considered extremely dangerous.

An interesting way to understand the amount of excess energy that the world's current level of warming represents is to compare it to the energy released by a nuclear bomb. As of 2012, that excess energy was the equivalent of four Hiroshima-sized atom bombs exploding every second—or nearly 400,000 bombs per day. And that was *then*.[18]

Rising temperatures are related to the *density of greenhouse gases* (GHGs) in the earth's atmosphere, and human emissions are driving this increase in density. By far the most important GHG, at about 80 percent of the total, is carbon dioxide. The solid line in Figure 3.5 shows world emissions of CO_2 against the left-hand scale. Notice that neither the Rio meeting in 1992, nor the Kyoto Protocol in 1997, nor the Paris Agreement of 2015, had any long-term effect on slowing *the rate of increase* of emissions.[19]

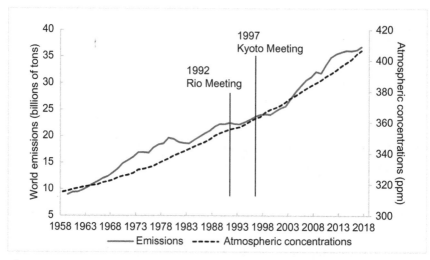

Figure 3.5 World CO$_2$ emissions and atmospheric CO$_2$ concentrations

While emissions are a flow per year, atmospheric concentrations are a stock, shown in Figure 3.5 as the dotted line measured against the right-hand axis.[20] Current concentration levels (as of June 2019) are 415 parts per million (ppm). According to James Hansen, the NASA physicist and father of climate change awareness, the CO$_2$ density at which the earth's energy is in balance, and the climate is stabilized, is 350 ppm.[21]

This difference between stocks and flows is important. While stabilizing emission levels would be a welcome development, the stock of atmospheric concentrations will continue to increase unless emissions are cut drastically. *Indeed, to stabilize atmospheric concentrations at current levels, annual emissions would need to be cut to around half their current levels.*

Furthermore, even if we could wave a magic wand and suddenly cut emissions by half today, the more than 400 ppm of CO$_2$ already in the atmosphere will keep warming the planet for centuries, until the Earth's atmosphere-ocean ecosystem reaches an equilibrium temperature. The analogy is to imagine you have just jumped into bed on a cold night, under a thick layer of blankets. It will take quite a while to warm up, with no increase in blankets. The thickness of the blankets, in this analogy, is the atmospheric CO$_2$ concentration.

The bottom line is this: using reasonable estimates of climate sensitivity to atmospheric CO$_2$ concentrations, we are already virtually certain to shoot past the 1.5 degree Celsius threshold. The planet has warmed more than 1 degree to date. Given today's atmospheric CO$_2$ concentrations, at least another 0.6 degrees of warming and perhaps as much as 0.9 degrees is guaranteed before the climate reaches equilibrium.[22] This is why Homer-Dixon (2015) wonders why the signatories to the Paris Agreement felt the need to "peddle fantasies with unreachable targets." How can we possibly imagine that humanity can keep warming below 2 degrees, let alone 1.5 degrees?

The answer lies in the fine print of the climate studies used to support arguments that it is still possible to cap warming at these levels. All these projections have two things in common: first, the longer it takes to begin to reduce emissions, the quicker we must reduce them later; and second, *every pathway currently available to us requires enormous "negative emissions" later in the century*. The trouble is that we do not know how to do that yet.[23] And the amount that will have to be extracted is beyond breathtaking. As Homer-Dixon (2015) notes, the 1.5 degree Celsius target requires about a half-trillion tons of CO_2 to be removed from the atmosphere between 2050 and 2100. This would be, by far, the largest industrial project that human beings have ever undertaken and would probably absorb a substantial fraction of global GDP.[24]

Is this dire enough yet? If not, consider where we are likely headed. Emissions are showing no sign of being reduced; indeed, they are increasing every year. If global emissions continue growing as they have in the past—a business as usual scenario—the temperature increase would be 5 or 6 degree Celsius by 2100. And if we managed to cap emissions by 2040, and hold them there, the temperature increase would be around 4 degree Celsius. If emissions peaked in 2040, and fell gradually to zero by 2100, the temperature increase would be around 3 degree Celsius.

Furthermore, as the IPCC report of 2018 emphasized, it is not even clear that 2 degrees of warming is safe. Certainly, humanity does not seem to be grasping the fact that the changes we are initiating are potentially irreversible. Climate change may not be gradual; rather there exist several *"doomsday tipping points."* One of the most feared involves melting permafrost.

A vast expanse of permafrost in Siberia and Alaska has started to thaw for the first time since it formed 11,000 years ago.[25] The cause is the higher than 3 degree Celsius rise in local temperature over the past forty years. Peat bogs cover an area of a million square miles (or almost a quarter of the earth's land surface) to a depth of twenty-five meters. They store at least two trillion tons of CO_2 worldwide. This is equivalent to a century of emissions from fossil fuels. This melting is an irreversible ecological landslide—a vicious circular feedback becoming stronger and stronger, and is doing so more quickly with every passing summer.

What should be done? It is clear what needs to be done. The 2018 IPCC report calls for the world to cut emissions in half by 2030, and get to net zero by 2050. The real question is "how?"

The almost universal answer from the economics profession is through some sort of carbon pricing.[26] This was underlined recently by the award of the 2018 Nobel Memorial Prize in Economics to William Nordhaus, a long-time proponent of carbon taxation as a way to reduce GHG emissions.

The argument is simple enough. In a situation of global warming, carbon emissions are a pollutant, and the polluter should pay—that is how we *internalize* the *externality*. We need to "decarbonize" our economy in the most efficient way possible, and it is always more efficient to use the price system, the market mechanism. It gives people "freedom and choice" when responding to the price signal. Economists argue that "standards" and "regulation" are inefficient because they impose the same standards on all firms. But since some firms can reduce emissions more easily, an efficient system would utilize this fact! Those that can reduce emissions easily should do so and avoid the carbon tax. For those that cannot, it is cheaper to pay the tax. But the tax remains as an incentive to reduce emissions.

What this universal answer is missing is any sense of urgency, or sense of scale, or sense of political acceptability. As far as urgency is concerned, many political and environmental activists are now talking of the need to *fight a war* on climate change. But wars were not won using the market mechanism. We need to throw everything we have at the problem. We need massive mobilization, reminiscent of the wholesale industrial retooling that took place during the Second World War. And this requires an active government coordinating the effort on many fronts.

Further, reliance on the price mechanism will fail because of the scale of change required, and the political opposition that the necessary scale will generate. Yes, carbon taxes do work. But tiny carbon taxes produce tiny changes. We need massive change, and therefore we need massive carbon taxes. But massive carbon taxes are unlikely to be politically acceptable.

For example, in Canada the Federal government imposed a carbon tax of just C\$20 per ton in 2019, with the intention of raising it annually until it reaches C\$50 by 2022. Every C\$20 per ton tax implies an increase in gasoline prices of 4.6 cents per liter, which in Canada's case means around a 4 percent price increase in 2019. Despite the fact that 90 percent of the money raised from the tax is given back to households, provincial leaders have been elected in four provinces who have vowed to scrap the tax. These provinces are now challenging in the Supreme Court the Federal government's right to impose a carbon tax in their provinces.

The situation was much worse in France. They began taxing carbon in 2018 at a price of nearly C\$67 a ton, implying an increase of 15 cents a liter of gasoline (a 6½ percent price increase). But at the prospect of the carbon tax going up to C\$82 a ton in January 2019 (implying a further increase of 3 cents per liter), mass demonstrations and riots broke out across France. The so-called "jaune-gillets" (or yellow vest) movement forced the postponement of the 2019 increase.

In Canada's case, the carbon tax is much too small. In order to achieve Canada's Paris Agreement (2015) commitment of a 30 percent cut in its 2005 level of emissions by 2030, most commentators agree that the tax must be at least double—it should have started at C$40 and gone to C$100 by 2022.[27] An even higher tax would be necessary to reach the IPCC 2018 target of a 50 percent cut by 2030. In the case of France, it seems their projected carbon prices are in line to meet the Paris target of a 30 percent cut by 2030, but not the new IPCC 2018 target of a 50 percent cut.[28]

Now, we could debate how to "frame" carbon taxes to make them more politically acceptable, including the crucial question of what happens to the revenues raised.[29] But surely such a discussion is rendered moot by contemplating the size of the taxes necessary to get to net zero emissions by 2050. The IPCC 2018 report gives a range for the necessary carbon taxes since there is substantial variation "across models and scenarios." They state that the minimum price in 2030 would have to be close to C$180 with a maximum to the range equal to C$8,000 a ton. The range of necessary prices nearly doubles by 2050 and continues increasing through 2100. At that point, the minimum price would be just over C$900 with a maximum close to C$40,000 a ton.[30]

So, if the universal answer of economists—carbon pricing—is lacking a sense of urgency, scale, or recognition of the opposition it will engender, what should be done?

The answer is "as much as possible"—and that *certainly includes as much carbon pricing as electorates will permit*. What we need is *massive* investment by the state, a proverbial "green new deal." Subsidies rather than taxes will be more politically acceptable as a way of changing behavior—to electrify vehicles, to green the production of electricity, and to upgrade/insulate buildings.

And how will this be paid for? Not through raising taxes—unless we can finally get some taxes put on the super rich (see Chapter 4) and the multinational corporations that currently pay practically nothing (see Section 2.5, Chapter 2). Rather, I advocate deficit financing, including financing it through printing money. "But increasing debt will impose a burden on future generations," you might say, and "printing money will generate inflation." Well, friends, unless we fix this there will be a future we do not want, where future generations will have to deal with the mess. And future inflation is the very least of our problems. (We will discuss more fully the possibility of money-financed fiscal policy in Chapter 9.)

Why is it not being done? There are three main reasons it is not being done. First, there is the classic free rider problem, all wrapped around questions of distribution and equity. Second, there is the power of "vested interest" that deliberately cultivates climate change denial using a disinformation campaign and a political system in the United States that is vulnerable to being bought. And third, there is the influence of economists, and in particular lauded experts like William Nordhaus, who for years have preached that our priority is to grow the economy and it is better to do very little until the price of action falls. Let us expand on these themes.

First reason: free rider and equity The equity issue works like this: "I may be the world's biggest emitter today, but you have been emitting for years, and it's your fault that atmospheric concentrations are as high as they are today." Who says this?—the developing countries: China and India in particular. The free rider effect works like this: "I don't need to cut down my emissions if everyone else cuts down theirs." Or, it can work like this: "What is the point of me cutting down my emissions if you are just going to increase yours." Who says this?—the developed countries: the United States and Canada in particular. Both the equity issue and the free rider effect have figured prominently in the difficulty of finding a global solution to a problem without borders.

The validity of the equity issue was recognized in the 1997 Kyoto Protocol in the form of *the principle of common but differentiated responsibilities*: since the currently rich developed countries have historically put most of the GHGs in the atmosphere, they were obliged to reduce their future emissions. On the other hand, most developing countries (China and India) were given a delayed timeline to reduce emissions.

While the Kyoto Protocol did seem promising in its day—192 parties (national governments and supranational governments) agreed to a legally binding international treaty to fight climate change—it floundered on the free rider problem: the United States never ratified it and Canada withdrew, mostly because of the delayed timelines given to less developed countries. And in fact, reductions in Europe were swamped by increases in China and India.[31]

Second reason: the power of "vested interest" The amount of CO_2 the world can emit while still having a chance of limiting global warming is known as our *carbon budget*. This is just a tiny fraction of known fossil fuel reserves. This means that the vast majority of known reserves cannot be burnt. Yet, the full extent of those fossil fuel reserves is booked as assets by the companies that own them. Recognizing that these reserves are "stranded assets" would reduce the market value of oil and gas companies to a small fraction of their current levels.

Big Oil has known for decades about climate change and the role that burning fossil fuel plays.[32] But they decided to follow the model used by tobacco companies in resisting tougher smoking regulations and health lawsuits: they focused on sowing doubt over the science. They have funded a "climate change denial" industry, and funded political candidates that espouse such views.[33] (In 2013, Robert Brulle estimated that the total funding given to the "climate change denial industry" was nearly a billion dollars a year in the United States.[34]) Their official lobby groups—the Global Climate Coalition, the International Emissions Trading Association, and the World Business Council for Sustainable Development—have sent more than 6,400 delegates to climate talks since 1995 working to undermine scientific consensus and slow policy progress.[35]

In addition, the "vested interest" of Big Carbon interacts with competing national interests. No country wants to leave its "valuable" carbon assets in the ground.[36]

With regard to political systems that are vulnerable to being bought, the United States is perhaps currently the most dysfunctional of any. And perhaps the most important factor in creating that dysfunctionality was the 2010 "Citizens United" decision of the Supreme Court that allowed corporations (and unions) to spend unlimited amounts of money to influence elections.[37] In the UK, the most important factor seems to be the ownership of newspapers and satellite TV stations that propagate misinformation and/or ignore the climate change problem.[38]

Third reason: the influence of economists William Nordhaus won the 2018 Nobel Memorial Prize in Economics for his work creating "integrated assessment models" where economic growth affects CO_2 emissions, while climate change in turn affects economic growth. The basic mechanisms that Nordhaus described continue to inform the models that the IPCC uses today.

A key element of these models is the "discount rate," which is how economists value the present compared to the future. A discount rate of zero means future generations are valued equal to the present; a high discount rate means that future generations are valued less, or are "discounted," compared to the present. A high discount rate makes it harder to make the case for climate mitigation.

Nordhaus prefers a high discount rate. This allows him to argue that we shouldn't reduce emissions too quickly, because the economic cost to people today will be higher than the benefit of protecting people in the future. Instead, we should focus on GDP growth now. The justification is that future generations will then be much richer than we are, and therefore better able to manage the problem. Basically, the argument is wait until the relative cost of action is lower.

Using this logic, Nordhaus has long claimed that from the standpoint of "economic rationality" it is "optimal" to keep warming the planet to about 3.5 degree Celsius over preindustrial levels. But how can such extreme temperatures be okay? The explanation involves, first, understanding the *unfair* way in which economists value life and, second, understanding the *insane* way in which economists value agriculture.

Economists value people's lives according to their lifetime income. If you were injured, and could not work, and it was someone else's fault, you could sue for loss of lifetime earnings. Clearly, the amount that a high earner is worth is much more than a low earner. It is this that I am claiming is unfair: it gives most to those that have the most. So, if climate breakdown ends up starving and displacing a few hundred million impoverished Africans and Asians, that will register as only a tiny blip in world GDP. Poor people do not add much "value" to the global economy.

As far as agriculture goes, it is valued the same as any other sector, by its contribution to global GDP. The sectors most vulnerable to global warming—agriculture, forestry, and fishing—contribute relatively little to global GDP, only about 4 percent. So even if the entire global agricultural system collapses in the future, the costs, in terms of world GDP, would be minimal. Yet, it is absurd to believe that the global economy would just keep rolling along despite a collapse in the world's food supply—it is this that I call insane.

This is why climate scientists and ecologists have a very different opinion of Nordhaus' legacy. As Hickel (2018) quips, "Nordhaus received the Nobel prize for climate catastrophe."

2.7 SUMMARY

Growth in productivity is the most important driver of increases in the standard of living. Economists are $87\frac{1}{2}$ percent ignorant of the causes of productivity growth. Huge swaths of neoclassical theory—including growth theory—are based on the HUMBUG aggregate production function.

Despite their ignorance, textbooks confidently recommend a generic set of neoliberal laissez-faire policies to promote growth. The important role played by government is ignored. The historical growth experience of European countries in the nineteenth century, and East Asian countries including China in the twentieth century, is ignored.

We have exceeded the environmental ceiling in many dimensions. There is a climate emergency and we're headed for climate catastrophe, yet the rate of global emissions continues to *climb*. We know there are irreversible tipping points.

Big Oil has known about climate change since the 1970s. They continue to fund fake think tanks, fake grassroots movements, and political parties (the US Republican Party) that deny the problem. Governments continue to subsidize Big Oil.

In talking about our slim chances of holding global warming to "substantially less that 2°C" as endorsed in the Paris Agreement, Homer-Dixon (2015) says this:

> To this point, climate skeptics have generally been the ones living in fantasy land. They've told themselves warming isn't happening, that humans aren't causing it, that it won't cause much harm, or that we'll eventually invent a neat technology to solve the problem. Anything to avoid facing the truth. Now, when the skeptics are in retreat and the world finally sees climate change for the appalling crisis it is, those of us who have been working for action shouldn't be peddling new fantasies.

Upon reading this chapter you may conclude that we are doomed. But we cannot stop trying. Noam Chomsky describes himself as a pessimist by force of logic but an optimist by force of will. Or, as I like to say, we're in a car hurtling toward a cliff edge, and our chances of avoiding the edge are disappearing by the minute. But I know I will be in the back seat shouting "BRAKE!" What will you be doing?

Chapter 4

GROWTH: HAPPINESS AND INEQUALITY

Instead of economies that need to grow, whether or not they make us thrive, we need economies that make us thrive, whether or not they grow.

Kate Raworth[1]

Like slavery and apartheid, poverty is not natural. It is man-made and it can be overcome and eradicated by the actions of human beings ... Overcoming poverty is not a gesture of charity. It is an act of justice.

Nelson Mandela[2]

I THE STANDARD TEXT

The two main topics covered by macroeconomics are long-run growth and short-run business cycles. It seems that mainstream macroeconomics textbook authors believe that inequality is irrelevant for these two topics. And while the ultimate aim of economic policy is to increase well-being (or happiness), mainstream economics remains focused on their two main topics (reducing business cycles and growing GDP) as the best ways to achieve it. Unbelievably, there is no standard text that considers whether this is true.

2 THE ANTI-TEXT

What the text does not do, the anti-text must. We begin with the relationship between growth in real income per capita and happiness. Then we consider the effects of inequality on growth, and on well-being. Finally, we look at the extent to which inequality has increased, and consider its causes.

2.1 Does more income make us happier?

The Easterlin Paradox All economic textbooks assume that growth in GDP per capita will lead to rising well-being, welfare, or happiness. But is it true? In 1974, Richard Easterlin famously used measures of "subjective wellbeing" gathered by sociologists and psychologists, but long ignored by economists. He concluded that economic growth in real GDP per capita does not lead to increased human happiness!

He made three types of comparisons. First, he compared the average happiness of people living in rich countries with that of people living in poorer countries at a point in time, and found *no evidence that average happiness was higher in richer countries than in poorer countries.* Second, *as countries got richer over time he found no evidence that average happiness increased.* Third, and this is the paradoxical result, he compared income groups in a single country at a point in time and found that higher income groups *were clearly happier* than lower income groups, and the effects were large. These three results form the "Easterlin Paradox."

Easterlin suggested that the Paradox could be resolved by recognizing the importance of relative income, status, and social norms. If happiness depends on relative income, then the rich will be happier, in any given country at any given time, because they are better able to meet wants that are largely socially constructed. But when everyone's income rises, the relevant frames of reference shift. And because relative income is largely unaffected, people feel no better off than before. Thus, average happiness is no higher in rich nations than in poor nations, and rich nations do not get happier over time as they get richer.

If the Easterlin Paradox were true, it would undermine the view that economic growth is one of the most important policy objectives. But the idea that the level of absolute income is completely irrelevant to human happiness—as the Easterlin Paradox asserts—seems implausible. Could it be that the great achievements of the rich countries in lifting themselves out of extreme poverty over the last two hundred years—longer lives, reduced infant mortality, better nutrition, and education—count for nought in terms of human happiness?

Sure enough, as more data accumulated, the strong form of the Easterlin Paradox began to crumble. By the 1990s, the accepted view had morphed into a consensus that increases in real GDP per capita produce quite big increases in happiness when there are still basic needs to be met. *But beyond a certain income threshold, relative income becomes the dominant factor.* This finding was widely supported.[3] Layard (2003, 2005) put the threshold at a GDP per capita between $15,000 and $20,000.

The concepts refined This remained the consensus until Daniel Kahneman—recipient of the Nobel Memorial Prize in Economics in 2002—started asking rather profound questions, such as: *Do we know what we mean by "happiness"?* And further: *Was the word well understood by survey respondents?* Kahneman (2010) convincingly argues that we don't and it wasn't. He argues the root of the problem is confusion between the *experiencing self* and the *reflective self.* It is the experiencing self that replies when the doctor asks, "Does it hurt *now* when I touch you *here?*" But it is the reflective self that replies when the doctor asks, "How have you been feeling *lately?*" Kahneman points out that these are two very different entities, which correspond to two very different notions of happiness.

The experiencing self resonates to real-time happiness, such as spending time with people we like, being smiled at, or treated with respect. This type of happiness is referred to as "emotional wellbeing." The reflective self equates happiness to the satisfaction she feels when thinking about her life. Education and money are much more important to the reflective self than they are to the experiencing self. This type of happiness is best referred to as "life satisfaction." Kahneman points out that there is only a 0.5 correlation between the two.

If there are two quite different conceptions of happiness, which conception of happiness is most important? The answer to that is not clear.[4] Ask yourself, would you rather be happy *in your life,* or *about your life?* Most people would surely want both. The point is to be clear about what we are asking people. Fortunately, in recent years people like Kahneman have helped design the questions for the Gallup Organization World Poll that covers more than half a million people.

Besides the clarification of what we mean by "happiness," the appropriate measure of income has also been clarified. Real GDP per capita was always measured in constant dollar terms. But according to Kahneman and Krueger (2006) this is a mistake. A basic fact of perception known as Weber's Law states that the smallest perceptible change in a stimulus— the intensity of light or sound, for example—will be a constant percentage of the stimulus, as the stimulus changes, not an absolute amount. In the context of income, a $100 raise does not have the same significance for an executive as for someone earning the minimum wage; but a doubling of their respective incomes might have a similar impact on both. Plotting income on a log scale means that a horizontal movement of 0.01 (say) corresponds to a 1 percent change at any point in the figure, and thus respects Weber's Law. Thus, we should relate the logarithm of income to our measure of happiness.

What effect have these clarifications had? One group of researchers (clustered around Justin Wolfers) used them to mount a fierce critique of the Easterlin Paradox. For them, "there is no paradox and never was." They attribute the appearance of a paradox to insufficient data, or failing to take the logarithm of income, or mismeasurement of happiness over time.[5] Despite these attacks, the Easterlin Paradox lives on.

The emerging new consensus The alert reader has probably noticed that all the analysis thus far has focused on only two variables, a measure of income and a measure of happiness, and researchers have simply correlated them. The reader may have wondered about all the other things that influence happiness—things like age, gender, health, education, marital status, employment status, and so on. Unfortunately, the datasets available in the past did not include such variables. But that is gradually changing, and so the debate about the relationship between income and happiness is still very much alive. To give a flavor of the ongoing debate, we will mention two more studies—both of which use very large datasets.

First, Kahneman and Deaton (2010) report an analysis of more than 450,000 responses to a daily survey of 1,000 US residents conducted by the Gallup Organization during 2008 and 2009. They controlled for fifteen variables that could influence happiness besides income.[6] They found that "life satisfaction" rose steadily with log income, but while "emotional wellbeing" also increased with log income, there was a satiation point around an annual income of $75,000.[7]

Second, Jebb et al. (2018) used data from over 1.7 million people from 164 countries—a dataset that approximates a worldwide representative sample of adults—collected during the years 2005–16. Controlling for demographic factors, they found evidence of satiation for both "life satisfaction" and "emotional wellbeing." Satiation occurs at $95,000 for "life satisfaction" and $60,000 to $75,000 for "emotional wellbeing." However, there is substantial variation across world regions, with satiation occurring later in wealthier regions. They conjecture that this is due to relative income and social comparison effects. Higher incomes within regions extend the satiation point because the standards of social comparison are higher.[8] They also find that in certain parts of the world, incomes beyond satiation are associated with lower "life satisfaction."

Conclusion There are several important points. First, while research on the relationship between well-being and income has been ongoing since the 1970s, it is finally reaching maturity. More and more data are being carefully collected and we can expect increasingly refined results. What we know so far is that the pure form of the Easterlin Paradox does not hold: absolute income matters. On the other hand, absolute income is not all-important. There is now a consensus that "emotional wellbeing" has a satiation point, and emerging evidence that "life satisfaction" has one. The importance of relative income and social norms is supported.

Second, measures of subjective well-being are at least as accurate as other data. Much supposedly "hard objective" data are obtained from "fluffy" surveys and questionnaires, just like the happiness data. As Wolfers (2011) explains, "Scratch the surface of our objective statistics and you will find them built upon fluffy value-laden questionnaires. Where does the unemployment rate come from? Asking people ... What about GDP? Much of our GDP data is built on surveys." Furthermore, as Layard (2010) explains, subjective well-being data are well correlated with at least four relevant sets of corroborating variables: the reports of friends, the plausible causes of well-being, physical functioning, and measures of brain activity.[9]

Third, policymakers need to move away from a fixation on growth of GDP and focus more on well-being.[10] In thinking about average well-being, the distribution of income is important. For example, in the United States between 1972 and 2002, average well-being did not increase despite real GDP per capita nearly doubling! The explanation is that most of these income gains went to a tiny fraction of the population: the very rich (see Stevenson and Wolfers 2008). Recognizing the importance of income distribution for well-being makes a nice segue to our next section.

One final comment before moving on: it is surprising that none of the "happiness" research (of which we are aware) mentions sustainability. This gap is astonishing. In order to be happy now, we need a sense that our lives will not be significantly worse in the future, that there will be a world where our children can flourish. There is already evidence that concern over climate change is linked to a decline in well-being, depression, and anxiety (see, e.g., Helm et al. 2018).

Question for your professor: If your income went up by \$100, while everyone else's income increased by \$1,000, would you feel better off? If not, why do the textbooks deny this and focus only on growth of GDP?

2.2 The effects of inequality on growth

> We have reached a tipping point. Inequality can no longer be treated as an afterthought.
>
> OECD Secretary General, 2015

Not only is inequality not mentioned in the mainstream textbook growth chapters, it is not mentioned anywhere in the macro textbooks. Yet, inequality is not only bad for well-being (discussed in the next section); it is also bad for growth itself.

Macroeconomics did not always ignore inequality. The classical economists of the nineteenth century, such as David Ricardo and Karl Marx, put issues of income distribution front and center. Their focus was the "functional" distribution of income, which classifies people according to their function (or role) in production, determined by the resources they own. For Marx, there was a clear distinction between capitalists who own capital and receive profits, and workers who receive wages, and the struggle over income shares was intimately bound up with the prospects for growth or stagnation.

The omission of inequality from mainstream macro textbooks *need not* reflect political bias; it *could* stem purely from a belief that it is not theoretically important. After all, neoclassical economists have tended to downplay behavioral differences between people—a tendency exacerbated by the rise of the representative agent model described in Chapter 1. If people are identical (in terms of tastes and risk tolerance) then a change in the distribution of income will have no effect on any economic aggregate (such consumption, savings, or employment).

On the other hand, consider the following quote by one of the most influential mainstream economists, Robert Lucas (recipient of the Nobel Memorial Prize in Economics in 1995):

> Of the tendencies that are harmful to sound economics, the most seductive, and in my opinion, the most poisonous, is to focus on questions of distribution ... The potential for improving the lives of poor people by finding different ways of distributing current production is *nothing* compared to the apparently limitless potential of increasing production. (Lucas 2004)

In the above quote, Lucas advocates ignoring the distribution of income. The justification he offers sounds a lot like "trickle-down" economics: ignore inequality; growth itself will cure poverty. Of course, pure trickle-down economics goes even further to argue for tax cuts to the rich, since they are the ones that save and invest. According to that view, inequality is good for growth. But is it true?

The introductory chapters of most mainstream textbooks emphasize a trade-off between equity and efficiency encapsulated by the leaky bucket metaphor: redistributing income is like carrying water from the rich to the poor using a leaky bucket—the result may be more equitable but is inevitably wasteful. Combined with trickle-down economics, this forms a powerful argument saying that inequality is good for growth. It is often referenced by right-wing politicians wanting to give tax cuts that benefit primarily the rich. So, it is important to note that the idea that inequality is good for growth is not supported by the evidence—quite the contrary, in fact.

Empirical studies have looked at the relationship between inequality and growth from various perspectives: comparative country analysis over the short term and the long term; the effect on trend growth and the effect on growth spells; they have used different ways of measuring inequality; and have used different control variables. No matter what perspective they have taken, they have found that more inequality is associated with slower and less durable growth.[11]

More recently, since the Financial Crisis of 2007–8, economists have increasingly focused on the links between rising inequality and the fragility of the financial system, and the role of political economy factors (especially the influence of the rich) in allowing financial excess to balloon ahead of the crisis. As Raghuram Rajan points out in his book *Fault Lines* (2010), a dysfunctional political culture prevented a distributional response to rising American inequality. Instead, it led to the deliberately encouraged palliative of risky credit extension to lower income groups and the explosion of subprime lending, which contributed to the financial crisis.

What about the effects of redistribution itself? Do we know whether efforts to redistribute income using taxes and transfers really are a "leaky bucket"? In an interesting paper published by the IMF, Ostry, Berg, and Tsangarides (2014: 4) explain, "Inequality may impede growth at least in part because it calls forth efforts to redistribute that themselves undercut growth. In such a situation, even if inequality is bad for growth, taxes and transfers may be precisely the wrong remedy." However, they decisively reject this possibility.[12] They have two main findings. First, lower net inequality is robustly correlated with faster and more durable growth, for any given level of redistribution. And second, redistribution appears generally benign in terms of its impact on growth. It appears the leaky bucket is not so leaky after all.

What are the mechanisms that make inequality harmful to growth? The evidence suggests that inequality undermines progress in health and education. Of particular importance, it reduces the opportunities available to the most disadvantaged groups. Other effects include investment-reducing political and economic instability, loss of social cohesion, and weakening of the financial system.[13] Given that we are highly confident of the negative impact, do we know how big it is?

According to OECD research, over the past two decades up to the Great Recession the cumulative growth rate would have been 6 to 9 percentage points higher had income disparities not widened in Italy, the UK, and the United States (see Cingano 2014). To get a handle on this number, consider the UK as an example. Between 1987 and 2007, its cumulative growth rate was 52 percentage points. An increase of between 6 and 9 percentage points is certainly quantitatively important. Since UK GDP in 2007 was around US$3 trillion, an increase of 6 percentage points would represent a gain of US$180 billion.

Question for your professor: The textbooks emphasize a trade-off between equity and growth. Can we see some evidence evaluating that please?

2.3 The effects of inequality on well-being

In their book *The Spirit Level* (2009), Wilkinson and Pickett compare indices of health and social development in twenty-three of the world's richest nations (and in the individual US states). For almost any quality-of-life indicator you can imagine[14]—from life expectancy to rates of obesity, levels of community trust to rates of imprisonment, teenage pregnancy to drug abuse—they find that *in every case* outcomes are *significantly worse* in countries where there is more inequality.[15] Outcomes are unrelated to whether those countries are rich or poor. The societies that do best for their citizens are those with the narrowest income differentials—such as Japan and the Nordic countries. The most unequal—the United States as a whole, the UK, and Portugal—do worst.[16]

As one would expect, *The Spirit Level* has been subject to a barrage of criticism from right-wing think tanks. For example, Wilkinson and Pickett have been accused of cherry-picking their data (not true), of fudging their data (also not true), and of mistaking correlation with causation (partially true: *The Spirit Level* only shows correlations not causal relations, but the authors are quite aware of this).[17]

However, one criticism that does hit its mark concerns the (perhaps overly) ambitious aim of *The Spirit Level* project. That aim is to show that *equality is better for everyone—even the rich!* To be clear, they want to show that whatever a person's educational level, social class, or income group, that person is likely to enjoy worse health and suffer more social problems than people in the same socioeconomic category in more equal societies. Wilkinson and Pickett liken income inequality to a general social pollutant because of its detrimental effects on health that spread across all income groups, even the high-income groups. It is this claim that David Runciman (2009) explores.

Runciman points out that most of the graphs in *The Spirit Level* show average measures. It is certainly true that *average measures* of obesity, incarceration rates, teenage pregnancies, educational attainment, and so on are worse in societies that are more unequal. But this could be because the bottom 20 percent does so badly that it brings down the average for society as a whole. If so, it doesn't follow that almost everyone is worse off, as Wilkinson and Pickett would have us believe. The rich (or even the middle class) might be untouched by the problems caused by inequality. (Of course, in the limit, if the problems faced by those at the bottom of the income distribution turn into some form of widespread social unrest, then everybody loses.)

Runciman acknowledges that this criticism does not apply to all the data in *The Spirit Level*. For example, Figure 4.1 compares infant mortality rates for England and Wales with those of Sweden, dividing the data into six segments according to the father's social class (and a seventh segment for single mothers).[18] It shows that infant mortality is higher in England and Wales for every single social group than it is in Sweden. Another

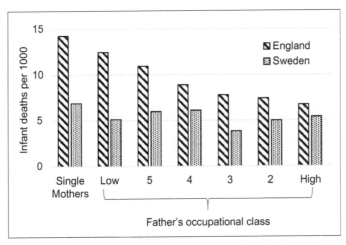

Figure 4.1 Infant mortality by class—Sweden compared to England and Wales

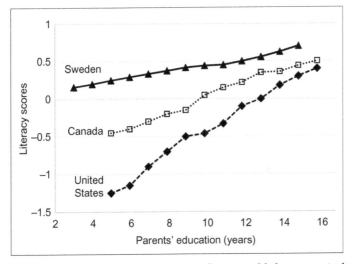

Figure 4.2 Literacy scores of sixteen- to twenty-five-year-olds by parents' education

example is shown in Figure 4.2.[19] This time we see that literacy scores are better in societies that are more egalitarian. Yes, the benefits of living in a more egalitarian society are largest in the lowest categories, but there are benefits for every social class.

Apart from these examples, there are many cases where only population averages are presented, but it is possible to demonstrate that the adverse consequences of inequality are too big to be borne only by the bottom 20 percent. For example, the United States is more prone to obesity than countries that are more egalitarian, but it cannot be only the poor

20 percent that are affected since roughly 69 percent of all US adults are overweight or obese.[20] Similar calculations can be made for other issues, such as the variations between countries in the feeling that others are trustworthy, or the prevalence of mental illness.[21] Nevertheless, technically Runciman is right. These kinds of calculations do not show that the adverse consequences extend all the way up the income distribution. For some issues *The Spirit Level* fails to show that even the rich are better off in a more egalitarian society.

Despite this, it is impossible to read *The Spirit Level*, and not be persuaded by the benefits of greater equality. Perhaps its most important contribution is to show that a myriad of seemingly disparate social problems have a single systemic cause: inequality. As Wilkinson and Pickett explain,

> We pay doctors and nurses to treat ill-health, police and prisons to deal with crime, remedial teachers and educational psychologists to tackle educational problems, and social workers, drug rehabilitation units, psychiatric services and health promotion experts to deal with a host of other problems ... And even when the various services are successful in stopping someone reoffending, in curing a cancer, getting someone off drugs or dealing with educational failure, we know that our societies are endlessly re-creating these problems in each new generation. Meanwhile, all these problems are most common in the most deprived areas of our society and are many times more common in more unequal societies.

2.4 Increasing inequality and its causes

After the Second World War, inequality was on a downward trajectory in the rich developed countries. But in the early 1980s, the trend reversed. Income inequality has now reached historic highs in most OECD countries and is still rising. Figure 4.3 shows a measure of inequality—the Gini coefficient—for five developed countries from 1983 to 2015.[22] The Gini coefficient ranges from zero (where everybody has identical incomes) to unity (where one person has all the income). The key point: the lower a country's Gini coefficient, the more equal is its income distribution.

There are two key features of Figure 4.3, each of which could inform different lines of enquiry. The first feature—that inequality has increased in all countries over the twenty-two-year period—could send us off in search of factors affecting all countries. Two possible culprits spring to mind: globalization and technological change. The second feature— that not only are there significant differences in inequality between the five countries, but also inequality has increased more in some countries than others—suggests that we look at differences between countries. And since all those countries are high-income capitalist countries with similar technology, the explanation must be found in institutional and policy differences between them.

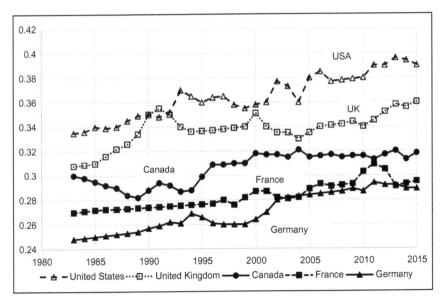

Figure 4.3 Gini coefficients, 1983–2015

Explanations that focused on globalization and technological change were attractive to economists, perhaps because they were essentially *technical explanations*, not requiring any political economy. But they have now gone out of favor because they failed to explain a host of observed trends.[23] Most importantly, it was gradually realized that rising inequality is being driven by an increasing concentration of income at the extreme top of the income distribution—and that is not a prediction of either globalization or technological change.

Figure 4.4 shows the increase in the income share (out of total GDP) of the top 1 percent for five developed countries between 1980 and 2014. We see that the very rich are becoming very much richer in all five countries. In the most extreme case, the United States, the income share of the top 1 percent nearly doubled from 10.6 percent in 1980 to over 20 percent in 2014.[24] Over the 1980 to 2014 period, while the bottom 50 percent in the United States had virtually no income growth at all, the top 1 percent enjoyed pretax income growth of 205 percent. Indeed, the richer the group we consider, the faster was their income growth. For example, the richest 1 percent of the 1 percent group experienced income growth over 400 percent.

Faced with this evidence, some Chicago-type economists have turned to yet another "technical" explanation: the rise of "winner-take-all markets."

Winner-take-all markets A winner-take-all market is one where the best (or most popular) performers capture most of the rewards. The spread of

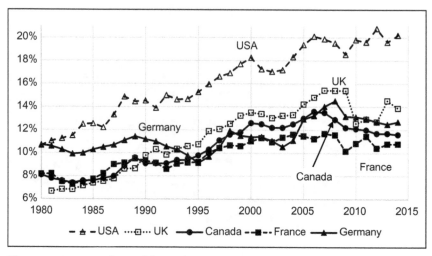

Figure 4.4 Income share of the top 1 percent, 1980–2014

such markets is associated with mass communications technology and globalization. The best examples are in sports, music, and film. The best tennis player wins the tournament. The rock superstar earns millions, while the local band struggles to survive. The increasing proliferation of winner-take-all markets is associated with rising inequality since fewer people take more of the money—most of it in fact.

The trouble with this explanation is that the logic of winner-take-all markets only applies when performance (or popularity) is easy to measure—you win the tournament, or you don't. But *most of the earnings elite* are *super-salaried executives* whose performance is very hard to assess. They have many varied tasks to perform and the results of their decisions may not become apparent for several years.

Instead, there is a much more straightforward explanation for the dramatic increases in executive pay that have occurred everywhere in recent years. (Figure 4.5 shows data for the United States where we see a dramatic increase in the ratio of CEO-to-worker compensation ratio beginning in the 1985–95 period, the period that gave birth to neoliberalism.[25]) That more straightforward explanation is that CEOs have power, and since the mid-1980s, they have greater incentives to use it.[26]

CEOs have power because, as Baker (2016) explains, corporate governance is subject to serious collective action problems that prevent shareholders (the owners) asserting true control. In practice, CEO pay is constrained by social norms, not market discipline, and these social norms have clearly changed. Krugman (2014) argues that falling tax rates for the rich have emboldened the earnings elite. He explains, "When a CEO could keep only a small fraction of a higher income obtained by flouting the social norm, he might decide that the opprobrium wasn't worth it. Cut his

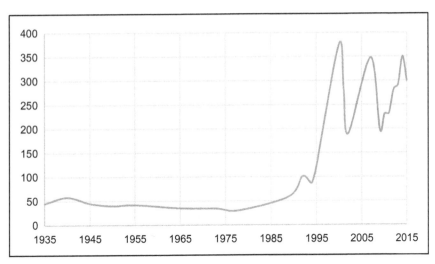

Figure 4.5 CEO-to-worker compensation ratio, United States

marginal tax rate drastically, and he may behave differently. And as more and more of the super-salaried flout the norms, the norms themselves will change."

Here we see the role that policy differences play in explaining differences in inequality between countries. While many countries have cut top tax rates in recent decades, the depth of these cuts has varied considerably. For example, the top tax rate in France in 2010 was only 10 percentage points lower than in 1950, whereas the top tax rate in the United States was less than half. And while the CEO compensation ratio was 354 in the United States in 2014, it was only 100 in France. Figure 4.6 shows the variability among countries with regard to the CEO-to-worker compensation ratio.[27]

Further evidence that changes in top tax rates motivated increases in self-awarded CEO pay is provided by Alvaredo et al. (2013). They plot the change in top marginal income tax rates (since the early 1960s) against the change in the top 1 percent income shares, for eighteen high-income countries (shown as Figure 4.7).[28] It shows that there is a strong correlation between reductions in top tax rates and increases in pretax income shares. In particular, note that countries such as Germany, Spain, or Switzerland, which did not experience any significant top-rate tax cut, did not show increases in the top 1 percent income share. Hence, the evolution of top tax rates is strongly negatively correlated with changes in pretax income concentration.

The falling share of labor Accompanying increased income inequality is increased wealth inequality. In 2015, the richest 1 percent owned 50 percent of global wealth, up from 44 percent in 2010. It is estimated that if present trends continue, they will own 64 percent of the world's wealth by 2030.[29] Since

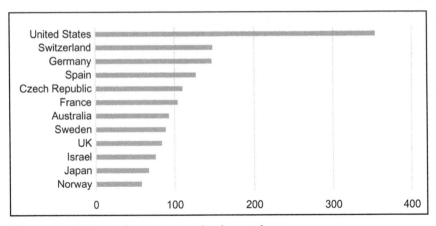

Figure 4.6 CEO-to-worker compensation in 2014 by country

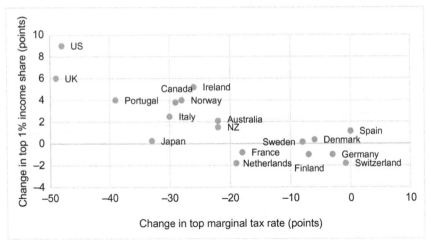

Figure 4.7 Changes in top income shares and top marginal tax rates since 1960

it is the rich who own most of the wealth in society, it is the rich who receive most of the earnings from capital. And recently, the earnings from capital as a share of GDP have been increasing. This produces a double-whammy effect: ownership of capital is increasingly concentrated in the hands of the rich, while capital is earning an increasing share of GDP. Piketty (2014) estimates that *increased inequality of capital income accounts for about a third of the overall rise in US inequality. The other two-thirds is the rise of super salaries.*

The increasing income share of capital in GDP means a falling labor share. To get a sense of its trajectory over time, Figure 4.8 shows the labor share of GDP in the United States from 1947 to 2017.[30] This fall in labor share, while quite common, was not universal across developed

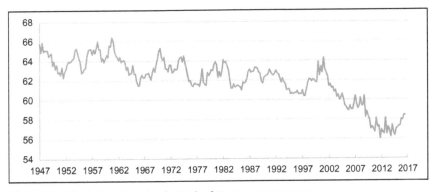

Figure 4.8 The labor share in the United States, 1947–2017

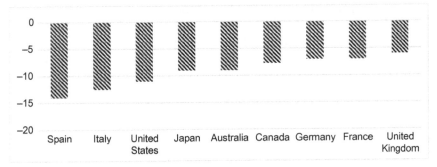

Figure 4.9 The change in labor share in advanced economies, 1970–2014

economies.[31] It fell quite sharply in some advanced countries but very little in others, as shown in Figure 4.9.[32]

Institutional and policy differences between countries We have already mentioned differences in progressive taxation, and its importance in not only moderating after-tax income differences but also helping to maintain social norms with respect to CEO pay. Another important policy difference concerns minimum wages. In the United States, the minimum wage has fallen by a third in real terms since the 1970s, whereas in France it has risen fourfold.

Of particular interest are differences in "union density" (the share of workers affiliated to a union) between countries. Researchers at the IMF, Jaumotte and Buitron (2015) focus on the experience of twenty advanced economies over the 1980–2010 period.[33] While controlling for other determinants of inequality—such as technology, globalization, financial liberalization, top marginal personal income tax rates, and common global trends—they discover a strong negative relationship between unionization and top earners' income shares.[34]

The magnitude of the effect is also significant; the decline in union density explains about 40 percent of the average increase in the income share of the top 10 percent. Another key result is that the decline in union density has been strongly associated with less income redistribution, likely through unions' reduced influence on public policy. Historically, unions have played an important role in the introduction of fundamental social and labor rights. It is noteworthy that in Sweden and Germany, trade unions are represented in corporate governance bodies, taking part in strategic decision-making.

Conclusion While all high-income countries have been similarly impacted by globalization and technological change, inequality has soared in some but been relatively stable in others. This suggests that institutional and policy differences must play a key role in explaining changing inequality.

The comparison between the United States and Western Europe is particularly instructive. In 1980, both blocs had similar inequality. By 2017, while little had changed in Europe, inequality soared in the United States.[35] Why is Europe so much better at keeping inequality in check? The key reasons seem to be: higher top tax rates, more redistribution, higher minimum wages, and greater union density. These factors seems to be at the root of the two proximate drivers of inequality: the lower labor share of output and the rise of super-salaried executives.

Question for your professor: Inequality has increased massively in some OECD countries (like the United States), but very little in others (like France). What institutional and policy differences account for this difference?

2.5 Inequality and the dynamics of capitalism: Piketty's analysis

We have noted that capital's share in GDP has been increasing, and this worsens inequality since the ownership of capital is itself so unequal. This rise in capital's share could be policy related, caused by falling minimum wages (in real terms), declining union membership, deregulation, and so on. The advantage of such explanations is that policy differences could explain differences in the extent to which capital's share has increased. On the other hand, perhaps there is something deeper going on, something inextricably tied to the evolution of capitalism.

In his 2014 book *Capital in the 21st Century*, Piketty investigates the intrinsic dynamics of capitalism. He asks, "Do the dynamics of private capital accumulation inevitably lead to the concentration of wealth in ever fewer hands, as Karl Marx believed in the nineteenth century?" In his fascinating book, Piketty uses mainstream neoclassical growth theory to analyze this question. And because the economics is interesting, and involves just simple algebra, it is worth your while to consider a few equations. Think of it as simple symbolic logic.

To begin, define r as the rate of return on capital. Since the quantity of capital is K, then total capital income must be rK, and capital's share in GDP is rK/Y.

$$\text{Capital's share of income} = \frac{rK}{Y} \qquad (4.1)$$

If we assume that r is constant for the moment, then capital's share of income depends on the capital-to-output ratio, K/Y. Piketty's data show that this ratio has been increasing in the UK, United States, and France since the 1950s as shown in Figure 4.10.[36] He predicts this increase to continue because the rate of growth of output will slow down, while the rate of savings will not. The next few lines explain precisely how this works.

The neoclassical model assumes that all savings are invested, or $S = I$. Suppose for simplicity that a constant proportion of income is saved, so that $S = sY$, where s is that proportion. Further, suppose (for simplicity) the depreciation rate of capital is zero, so all investment adds to the size of the capital stock, $I = \Delta K$ (where the "Δ" symbol means "the change in"). Now equating savings to investment implies $sY = \Delta K$.

$$\text{Savings} = \text{Investment} \Rightarrow sY = \Delta K \qquad (4.2)$$

Dividing both left- and right-hand sides of (4.2) by K yields:

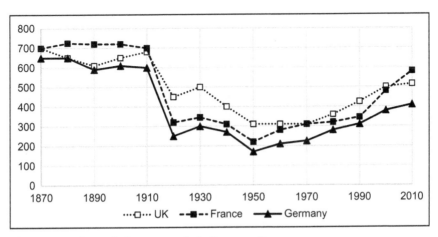

Figure 4.10 The capital-output ratio in Europe, 1870–2010

$$\frac{sY}{K} = \frac{\Delta K}{K} \tag{4.3}$$

In long-run equilibrium, the capital-output ratio, K/Y, will be constant. This implies that capital must eventually grow at the same rate as output. Let's call that growth rate, g.

$$\frac{\Delta K}{K} = \frac{\Delta Y}{Y} = g \tag{4.4}$$

Finally, we focus on equation (4.3), replacing $\Delta K/K$ with g, dividing both sides by s, and inverting. We get:

$$\frac{K}{Y} = \frac{s}{g} \tag{4.5}$$

Eureka! We have found the determinants of the long-run equilibrium capital-output ratio. Piketty predicts the capital-output ratio will increase because g is likely to decrease. World growth will fall because it is the sum of productivity growth and population growth, both of which are expected to decline.

For example, suppose the savings rate, s, stays constant at 10 percent, but the long-run rate of growth falls from 3 to $1\frac{1}{2}$ percent. This implies the long-run capital-output ratio will increase from 3.3 (= 10/3) to 7 (= 10/1.5). Holding r (the return on capital) constant, the increase in the capital-output ratio will increase capital's share of income (equation 4.1).

The increase in capital's share of GDP worsens inequality, since the ownership of capital is itself so unequal. But once the economy reaches its new long-run equilibrium, the capital-output ratio stops increasing, and the increase in inequality will stop—at least from this source. Unfortunately, the rise in the capital-output ratio was just the left jab. Next comes the blow to the chin.

Once the capital-output ratio has stabilized, wage earners can expect their incomes to rise as fast as productivity increases through technological progress. (This will be a little less than the overall growth rate, g, which is the sum of technological progress and the rate of population growth.)

On the other hand, someone whose income comes entirely from accumulated wealth will earn r percent a year. People who are very wealthy are likely to consume only a small fraction of their income. The rest is saved and accumulated, and their wealth will increase by almost r percent each year, and so will their income.

Piketty's main point is that as long as $r > g$, as long as the rate of return exceeds the rate of growth, the wealth of the rich, and the income from it, will grow faster than income from work. If $r > g$, inequality will continue to increase without limit. It is a dystopic vision of the future of capitalism. It is a vision where society will inexorably become dominated by inherited wealth concentrated in the hands of a tiny minority.

The future involves a return to the past, to levels of inequality last seen in the nineteenth century—the so-called Belle Époque in France—when the great bulk of wealth, around 90 percent, was inherited rather than saved out of earned income. And the bulk of this inherited wealth was owned by a tiny minority. In 1910, the richest 1 percent controlled 60 percent of the wealth in France; in Britain, 70 percent. As Krugman (2014) remarks, "No wonder nineteenth-century novelists were obsessed with inheritance."

Piketty's suggested solution is for an annual progressive tax on wealth. While such a tax would generate revenue (for redistribution or social spending), revenue generation is not the main goal. The point is to reduce the after-tax return on capital, so that r is brought down below g, or at least reduces the gap. While Piketty discusses in some detail how such a tax might be made operational, he is not optimistic about the likelihood of it being adopted. He observes, "The experience of France in the Belle Époque proves, if proof were needed, that no hypocrisy is too great when economic and financial elites are obliged to defend their interest" (Piketty 2014: 514).

Piketty's book has received praise from such luminaries as Nobel Prize winners, Paul Krugman and Robert Solow. Krugman (2014) compares Piketty to Einstein in saying the book has provided "a unified field theory of inequality," which has "transformed our economic discourse." Solow (2014) entitles his book review, "Piketty Is Right." Needless to say, not everyone feels the same. Let us consider some of the criticisms of Piketty's analysis.

The dependence of r on K/Y In neoclassical theory, the rate of return on capital is determined by capital's marginal product, which will fall as capital accumulates (see Section 1.6 of this chapter). How much it falls depends on a specific property of the production function known as the *elasticity of substitution*. If this elasticity were unity, r would fall just enough that, as K/Y increases, capital's income share would stay constant. However, if the elasticity were greater than unity, capital's income share would increase as K/Y increases.

Since capital's income share was approximately constant for many decades, economists believed the elasticity of substitution was indeed unity. Since Piketty predicts an increasing capital share, he could be interpreted as saying the elasticity of substitution must now be greater than 1. Then the question arises as to why a technical feature of the production function should suddenly change.

But Piketty makes no statement about the elasticity of substitution. Indeed, he makes no gesture toward recognizing that r (the return on capital) is determined within the model that he uses. Instead, he relies on historical data going back hundreds of years to show the rate of return has remained remarkably steady at 5 percent. This is why he believes slower growth will widen the gap between r and g. For some mainstream neoclassical economists, this failure to determine r within the model is a serious weakness of Piketty's analysis.

Does Piketty have it backward? Piketty uses "wealth" and "capital" interchangeably. In fact, the numerator in his estimates of capital-output ratios is the *market value of wealth*. So, his measure of capital is not physical but financial. There are two problems here. First, many assets are part of wealth but not part of K: art, hoards of precious metals, land, and housing (for example). Second, measures of financial wealth can fluctuate wildly even though the stock of productive capital may not have changed. Stock market values, the financial counterpart of productive capital, are subject to bubbles and crashes.

Solow (2014) notes the problem but dismisses it saying, "as long as we stick to longer-run trends, as Piketty generally does, then arguably, this difficulty can be disregarded." On the other hand, James Galbraith (2014) regards it as a source of terrible confusion. Naidu (2017), Baker (2014), and Galbraith all agree that it leads to Piketty getting the causality backward: it is not the increase in the capital-output ratio that prompts capital's share to rise—it's the rise in capital's share that increases the financial value of capital and, hence, the measured capital-output ratio. The point is that the value of any asset is determined by its expected future earnings, not by the amount of savings and investment it took to create it.

Labor's share of GDP will fall if wages do not keep up with productivity growth. So, anything that weakens labor's bargaining position will increase capital's share in GDP. Higher expected future profits increase the price of corporate shares, which increases Piketty's K. Therefore, lower minimum wages, weaker unions, more "flexible" labor contracts, increasing monopoly power—all will increase capital's share, driving up the measured capital-output ratio.

Conclusion We do not agree with Solow: the confusion between "wealth" and "capital" cannot be disregarded, even when sticking to longer-run trends. As Galbraith (2014) explains, the longer-run trends identified by Piketty in Figure 4.16 are best explained by events that changed the profitability of capital and, hence, its valuation. For example, the dramatic fall in the capital-output ratio of all three countries after 1910 was not due to the destruction of capital in the First World War, since there was almost no physical destruction in Britain or Germany during that war. Rather it was largely due to much higher output, produced by wartime mobilization. Similarly, the fall in capital-output ratios after 1930 was caused by the collapse of asset values during the Great Depression: it wasn't physical capital that disintegrated, only its market value.

If you believe Piketty's account, then practically the only remedy for increasing inequality is a progressive wealth tax. But if you believe that capital's share rises as a result of capitalists getting the upper hand in the perpetual battle over the distribution of income, then many more solutions become plausible.

> Question for your professor: Thomas Piketty predicts
> that inequality will increase everywhere, and with
> no limit! Is he right? What could be done about it?

2.6 Conclusion

Money won't buy you happiness, an old adage says. But actually it will, at least up to a point. Beyond that point, the adage is correct: more money will not make us happier. This suggests we should *not* be striving for unlimited growth of incomes.

It was refreshing to see the world's first "well-being" budget introduced in New Zealand in May 2019 that will focus on poverty reduction and mental health. Why? Because it is well established that inequality is not only bad for well-being; it is also bad for growth itself. If inequality had not increased in the UK between 1987 and 2007, GDP in the UK in 2007 would have been higher by about $180 billion. That would have bought a lot of NHS (National Health Service) improvements.

For almost any quality-of-life indicator you can imagine—from life expectancy to rates of obesity, levels of community trust to rates of imprisonment, teenage pregnancy to drug abuse—average outcomes are significantly worse in countries where there is more inequality. For some issues, more egalitarian societies produce better outcomes for every social class, even the rich. There is some truth to the idea that inequality can be regarded as a general social pollutant that makes everyone worse off.

As for the causes of inequality, economists have favored technical explanations such as globalization or technological change, though they are now mostly abandoned. Thomas Piketty recently suggested another technical explanation using the key equations from neoclassical growth theory. He predicts the share of GDP going to capital will continue to increase because the rate of growth of output will slow down. Further, if the real rate of interest exceeds the long-run growth rate (which historically it usually does), inequality will continue to increase without limit. Piketty's suggested solution is an annual progressive tax on wealth, though he is not optimistic about the likelihood of it being adopted.

Critics of Piketty suggest he has the causality backward. Capital's share of GDP is increasing because the balance of power has shifted toward capital as a result of the implementation of neoliberal policies—in particular, lower minimum wages, lower top tax rates, and lower union densities. Lower top tax rates are implicated in the rise of CEO pay.

While all high-income countries have been similarly impacted by globalization, technological change, and slowing growth of output, inequality has soared in some but been relatively stable in others. This suggests that institutional and policy differences must play a key role in explaining changing inequality.

Chapter 5

THE FINANCIAL SYSTEM: THE BELLY OF THE BEAST

> It stands as an impressive discursive achievement
> of big finance to have evaded responsibility for the
> crisis and shifted the blame to the state.
>
> Stephen McBride[1]

I THE STANDARD TEXT

1.1 Introduction

A sound, well-functioning financial system is the most important ingredient
to encourage savings and facilitate its transformation into investment. This
chapter begins by describing what the financial system is and what it does.
We describe the most common financial assets, stocks and bonds, and the
mechanics of how they are priced. Along the way, we consider an extremely
influential hypothesis, the *efficient market hypothesis* (EMH), which suggests
that asset prices in financial markets are priced appropriately. In other words,
financial markets are efficient.

Next, we discuss financial institutions and their three key functions: to
reduce transaction costs, reduce risk, and increase liquidity.

Finally, we discuss how savings and investment can be modeled as the supply
and demand for loanable funds, and how this determines long-run interest rates.
In a modern open economy, total savings is the sum of private, government, and
foreign savings. An important application raises concerns about government
deficits, since they crowd out investment and impose long-run costs on the
economy.

1.2 Financial markets

The most important financial markets are the stock and bond markets. Both
facilitate transformation of saving into investment.

The basics of stocks and bonds A stock is a share in the ownership of a
corporation. The holder of the stock may benefit through the receipt of

dividends and/or through share price appreciation (capital gain). However, in the event of bankruptcy, creditors of the corporation have no legal claim on the shareholders: the shareholders enjoy "limited liability."

Why might the original owners of the corporation wish to sell shares in their company? It is one way to obtain additional funds for investment. Diluting ownership also allows the original owners to diversify. If the owners of the company do not want to dilute their ownership, they can instead obtain additional funds by issuing corporate bonds. These bonds are then traded—bought and sold—on bond markets.

Bonds are promises to repay the amount borrowed, the "principal," at some date in the future, and to pay a fixed amount (called a "coupon") at regular intervals as interest. Bonds are categorized by maturity length. If the redemption date of the bond is fifteen years after the issue date, the bond is said to be a fifteen-year bond. If the bond has no maturity date—it pays its coupon forever—it is called a "perpetuity."

From the standpoint of savers, bonds are less risky than shares because—in the event of bankruptcy—bondholders get paid before shareholders from the sale of the corporation's assets. Because they are less risky, bonds usually generate lower returns.

The mechanics of bond price determination What is a bond worth? What is its fundamental value? A bond entitles its holder to regular coupon payments, and eventual repayment of principal. The fundamental value of the bond is the *present value* of this stream of payments.

Present value is a way of taking time into account when valuing money. A dollar next year is *not* the same as a dollar today. A dollar invested today will be worth $\$1(1+i)$ next year, where "i" is the annual rate of interest. Now ask yourself, how much must you invest today in order to receive $1 at the end of the year? It is $\$1/(1+i)$. The proof is simple: if we invest an amount $[\$1/(1+i)]$, after one year it will be worth $\left[\$1/(1+i)\right](1+i)=\$1$.

Similarly, the present value of $1 realized two years from now is equal to: $\$1/(1+i)^2$.

That is what you must invest today in order to have $1 in two years. Again, the proof is simple: after two years, the amount $[\$1/(1+i)^2]$ will be worth $[\$1/(1+i)^2](1+i)^2$.

We can apply the concept of present value to determine the value of a bond. For example, assume a perpetuity pays a coupon of $A at the end of every year. The price of this bond, P, should equal its present value.

$$P = \frac{\$A}{(1+i)} + \frac{\$A}{(1+i)^2} + \frac{\$A}{(1+i)^3} + \cdots + \frac{\$A}{(1+i)^n}$$

This is an infinite sum, but the solution is easily obtained once we recognize that the expression on the right-hand side is a geometric progression—easily and routinely solved in mathematics. We show the solution in the appendix of this chapter. However, it is already clear that if the interest rate increases, the price of the bond must fall. This follows since the interest rate divides every term on the right-hand side of the expression. So, bond prices move inversely to the interest rate. In this example, we prove in the appendix that the value of the bond is simply $A divided by the interest rate, i.

$$P = \frac{\$A}{i}$$

This is an important general result: bond prices move inversely to interest rates—if interest rates increase, bond prices decrease.

The mechanics of stock price determination What is a stock worth? What is its fundamental value? A stock entitles the holder to a share of the earnings. So, a share is worth the present value of the expected stream of future earnings per share.

For example, in New Brunswick, Canada, the provincial government has a monopoly on the sales of alcoholic beverages (beer, wine, and liquor) through a crown corporation called "NB Liquor." Since New Brunswickers are steady drinkers, this corporation furnishes steady profits. These profits have been around $160 million a year for over a decade. So, if NB Liquor were privatized (sold to a private company), how much would it be worth?

The NB Liquor franchise clearly has some risk associated with it—New Brunswickers might suddenly all become teetotal. But if we ignore this risk, and any other risk you might think of, then we could treat NB Liquor as an infinitely long-lived bond that pays a coupon of $160 million a year. We have just solved the problem of how to value such a bond. The value is the coupon payment divided by the rate of interest. If the interest rate were 5 percent, the value of such a bond would be $160 m ÷ 0.05 = $3,200 million. If 100 million shares were issued, each share should be worth $32. This would be the fundamental value of a share in the newly privatized company.

1.3 The efficient market hypothesis

This hypothesis says that the actual price of a stock always equals its fundamental value. In other words, the asset market is efficient.

The EMH view originated in the mid-1960s, propounded by the Chicago School, and associated with Eugene Fama (1965 and 1970 with Burton Malkiel). It was dominant until the 2008 Financial Crash, but is still very influential today.

Proponents of EMH believe in deregulating financial markets for two reasons. First, they believe that unhindered competition is the best way to discipline financial market behavior. And second, they believe that inefficient government regulations prevent financial markets creating wealth. Needless to say, EMH played an important role in the deregulation of the financial sector that began in the 1980s.

EMH does *not* require *all* investors to be rational and fully informed. What it does require is that at least *some* investors are rational and fully informed. If at least some investors use all available information, and make accurate calculations, then asset prices should trade at their fundamental value. If they did not, there would be an opportunity to make profit by trading the stock. Smart investors would sell when an asset is overpriced, and buy when it is underpriced.

The key to understanding the evidence that supports EMH is the idea that asset prices will reflect all available information. From this follows the implication that asset prices will change only in response to *new* information. But new information is inherently unpredictable, otherwise it would not be *new* information. Therefore, future asset prices should be inherently unpredictable. Therefore, any given stock price should follow a random walk—its next movement is just as likely to be up, as down.

The random walk prediction has been very hard to refute. The prediction became the title of a best-selling book by Burton Malkiel, called *A Random Walk Down Wall Street*, which has (as of 2020) gone through twelve editions and sold over 1.5 million copies.

A second testable prediction of EMH is derived from the idea that future movements of stock prices are random. It implies that it is not possible to be a better money manager than anyone else. In particular, any given mutual fund may outperform others in any given year, but this is purely due to chance. Next year, today's best performer will be randomly located in the pack of mutual funds. Again, this conclusion has been supported by numerous studies.[2]

1.4 Financial institutions

Financial institutions are also called financial intermediaries. Their role is to gather funds from savers and channel them to borrowers to finance investment. They do this by accepting deposits and making loans. They earn profits if the interest they earn (from loans) is greater than the interest they pay (on deposits).

Banks are the most important financial institutions measured in terms of the amount of money they channel. But lots of other financial intermediaries also accept deposits and make loans. These are called "*nonbank financial intermediaries*." Since their role is so similar to banks, and because they are often less regulated and more opaque, they are also called "*shadow banks*." In particular, a list of shadow banks would include: pension funds, insurance companies, investment banks, private investment firms, mutual funds, and hedge funds. They all accept deposits and make loans.

How does the financial system facilitate the transformation of saving into investment? It does so by performing three tasks: reducing transaction costs, reducing risk, and increasing liquidity.

Reduce transaction costs Transaction costs include: search and information gathering costs, bargaining costs, and policing and enforcement costs. Suppose a corporation wishes to raise $100 million for investment spending. One way would be to negotiate loans from thousands of individuals. The other way would be to deal with only one lender: a financial intermediary. Businesses and households know and trust the financial intermediary, and this trust relationship reduces transaction costs.

Reduce risk A business owner can reduce risk by incorporating and selling shares of the company to others. If things go well, everyone benefits. If not, no-one is financially destroyed. Similarly, an individual investor can reduce risk by diversifying, by holding many different stocks and asset classes. The aim of diversifying is to make the possibility of losses independent events. The existence of asset markets facilitates the reduction of risk.

Increase liquidity Lenders often want to lend short term—they want to have the option to withdraw their money should they need it. Whereas borrowers prefer to borrow longer term—they want the security that the loan will not be suddenly withdrawn. This problem is technically called *maturity mismatch*. It causes less money to flow from lenders to borrowers than is available.

Bridging maturity mismatch is accomplished by both financial markets and financial institutions. In an efficient financial market, bonds and shares can be easily traded, which increases liquidity. Liquid assets can be quickly converted into cash; illiquid assets cannot. Financial institutions clearly bridge maturity mismatch, since they borrow money very short term, and lend the money longer term. This ability to increase liquidity is sometimes referred to as *maturity transformation*.

1.5 Savings and investment in a closed economy

This section deals with how investment spending is financed. We can easily show that savings and investment are identically equal in a realized sense. This is a simple fact of accounting. But the accounting identity is useful because it shows us the sources of savings. Consider the GDP accounting identity introduced in Chapter 2 (using "Y" to denote real GDP):

$$Y \equiv C + I + G + (X - IM) \tag{5.1}$$

To begin, we will simplify and assume a closed economy where there is no external trade, allowing us to drop the last term $(X - IM)$. We will return to include the foreign sector in a later section. Rearranging the now simpler identity, putting the key term "investment" on the left-hand side, we get:

$$I \equiv Y - C - G \tag{5.2}$$

We will call the total savings generated within the economy, *national savings*. It is the sum of *private savings* (from households) and *public savings* (from the government sector).

Governments spend on goods and services, G, collect revenues, and distribute transfers such as public pensions. The term for taxes minus government transfers is *net taxes, T.* Government saving is the difference between its net tax revenues, *T,* and its spending on goods and services, *G.*

$$S_{Public} \equiv T - G \tag{5.3}$$

Households save whatever disposable income is not consumed. Noting that disposable income is gross income, *Y,* minus net taxes, *T,* we can write:

$$S_{Private} \equiv (Y - T) - C \tag{5.4}$$

Summing the two components gives us national savings, $S_{National}$, where:

$$S_{National} = S_{Private} + S_{Public} \tag{5.5}$$

Substituting (5.3) and (5.4) into (5.5) yields:

$$S_{National} \equiv (Y - T - C) + (T - G) \tag{5.6}$$

Notice that we can cancel out the net tax term, *T.* This yields:

$$S_{National} \equiv Y - C - G \tag{5.7}$$

Comparing (5.7) with (5.2) we see that in a closed economy investment spending is identically equal to national savings. Any decrease in total savings leads to a fall in investment. As noted in Chapter 3, reduced total investment will lead to slower growth in GDP per capita, and hence lower standards of living.

When government spending exceeds its net tax revenue, it runs a deficit. But a deficit constitutes negative public savings, and all else equal, this reduces total savings. This implies that government deficits are a cause for concern. In the next section, we show that not only do increased government budget deficits decrease total investment, they also lead to higher interest rates.

1.6 The market for loanable funds in a closed economy

The interest rate is the cost of borrowing and the reward for lending: it is the price of loanable funds, determined by the supply and demand for loanable funds.

Of course, in reality there are many different interest rates that reflect different assets (stocks or bonds), different terms to maturity (short term versus long term), and different risk factors (high risk versus low risk). We simplify by assuming only one interest rate, which can be regarded as the benchmark interest rate.

The supply of loanable funds is national savings, the sum of private savings by households and public savings by government. It is an upward sloping line, since households will provide more funds at higher interest rates.

The demand for loanable funds comes from firms eager to add to their capital equipment—borrowing and investing are the same thing. To determine whether to go ahead with a project, they compare the rate of return with the cost of borrowing money. The lower the cost of borrowing money, the more projects will be undertaken throughout the economy, and the greater the demand for loanable funds.

What factors would cause the demand and supply curves for loanable funds to shift?

Suppose households decide they want to leave larger bequests to their children. This would increase the quantity of savings for any given interest rate, shifting the supply of loanable funds to the right. Alternatively, rising home prices might make homeowners feel richer, reducing their need to save for retirement. This would shift the supply of loanable funds to the left.

On the demand side, suppose firms become less optimistic about the future. They decrease their estimates of the profitability of new investment projects, and decrease the quantity of loanable funds they want to borrow at any given interest rate. This would shift the demand curve for loanable funds to the left.

In a nutshell, the loanable funds model is just an application of the familiar demand and supply framework, where the "good" is loanable funds, and the "price" is the interest rate. As such, the quality of the equilibrium is efficient. It maximizes the gains from trade (between lenders and borrowers) since there are no unsatisfied borrowers or lenders at the equilibrium interest rate. The only offers not accepted are from lenders who demand an interest rate higher than the equilibrium rate. Further, it efficiently allocates savings to investment projects. Only projects that are profitable at the equilibrium interest rate are funded. In this way, a well-functioning financial system increases the long-run growth rate.

1.7 Using the loanable funds model to evaluate public policy

What policy should the government pursue to increase savings and investment? In answering this question, we need to avoid the pitfall of increasing private savings at the expense of lower public savings. For example, the government might encourage more private savings by reducing taxes. But this will decrease tax revenue, which will reduce public savings. Indeed, in equation (5.6) taxes cancel out of the equation for national savings. So, tax changes may not increase national savings.[3]

Another possibility is for the government itself to save more. But as we have just seen, trying to increase its savings by increasing its taxes will not work. The way that works is by decreasing its purchases of goods and services, G.

However, suppose the government does the opposite. Suppose it is election year and the government decides to increase its spending to the point where it is running a deficit. What effect does this have?

Figure 5.1 uses the loanable funds model to illustrate the effect of the deficit. The initial equilibrium (before the increase in government spending) is E_1 where private demand for loanable funds, D_1, equals the supply. The new equilibrium at E_2 occurs after the increase in government spending. The newly created deficit needs to be financed somehow. If the government finances it through borrowing,

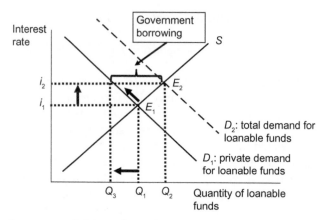

Figure 5.1 Government deficits and crowding out

the total demand for loanable funds increases to D_2. This drives up interest rates leading to the new equilibrium at E_2. While the higher interest rate does induce more savings in total, a good chunk of it is absorbed by the government. The quantity of loanable funds left over for the private sector falls from Q_1 to Q_3. In effect, the government budget deficit has *crowded out* investment spending, leading to lower growth and lower living standards over time.[4]

However, this result is derived for a closed economy, and no economy in the modern world is a closed economy. In open economies, firms can borrow on international markets at the world interest rate. We need to expand the model, and the accounting identities, to address this.

1.8 Savings and investment in an open economy

The symbol "Y" represents output *and* income, and there are only three things households can do with their income: spend it, save it, or give it to the government as net taxes.

$$Y \equiv C + S_{Private} + T \tag{5.8}$$

If we replace "Y" with "$C + S_{Private} + T$" in the national income accounting identity (equation 5.1) we get:

$$C + S_{Private} + T \equiv C + I + G + (X - IM) \tag{5.9}$$

The consumption term cancels out, leaving:

$$S_{Private} + T \equiv I + G + (X - IM) \tag{5.10}$$

Rearranging terms, and putting investment on the right-hand side, we get:

$$I \equiv S_{Private} + (T - G) + (IM - X) \tag{5.11}$$

In words, this identity says that

$$I \equiv S_{\text{Private}} + S_{\text{Public}} + S_{\text{Foreign}} \tag{5.12}$$

In moving from (5.11) to (5.12), we already know that public savings are the same as the government budget surplus "$T - G$." What is new in equation (5.12) is that we have replaced the balance of trade deficit "$IM - X$" with foreign savings, "S_{Foreign}." A country that spends more on imports than it earns from exports must borrow the difference from foreigners. A trade deficit represents a capital inflow from abroad, or foreign savings.

How does this capital inflow—the inflow of foreign savings—manifest? A country imports foreign savings by allowing foreign investment. But this can take several different forms: *foreign direct investment* occurs when a foreign company builds and operates a factory domestically; *foreign portfolio investment* occurs when foreigners buy stocks or bonds. If those are issued by private companies, then foreigners are providing resources for domestic companies to build new physical plant. If the bonds are issued by the government, then foreigners are supplementing public savings.

Of course, the use of foreign savings is not free. Investors want a return on their investment and this return will be repatriated abroad. Nevertheless, the increase in real GDP generated by foreign investment will be greater than the amount paid to foreigners. Therefore, foreign investment is beneficial overall.

It is helpful to think back to the definitions of GDP and GNP: gross *domestic* product is the income earned *domestically*, within a country, by both residents and nonresidents; whereas gross *national* product is the income earned by the "*nationals*" of a country (wherever they may be). Foreign investment increases the domestic capital stock, and therefore increases labor productivity, domestic wages, and domestic output. But since it implies profits and interest income flowing abroad to "non-nationals," GDP will increase *more* than GNP.

Before we move on to consider how the open economy affects the loanable funds model and the crowding out result, we will use our accounting identities to discuss the Twin Deficit Hypothesis.

The twin deficit hypothesis If we rearrange identity (5.11) to leave the trade deficit on the right-hand side, we get:

$$(I - S_{\text{Private}}) + (G - T) \equiv (IM - X) \tag{5.13}$$

First, suppose there is perfect mobility of financial capital around the world, and domestic interest rates are fixed at the world rate. Second, remember that the loanable funds model is a long-run model where we are always at full employment, which implies income is fixed. Third, since both income and interest rates are fixed, both household savings, S_{Private}, and investment, "I," are fixed. Now if we consider changes, we can put a change operator "Δ" through the above identity and drop the $(I - S_{\text{Private}})$ term (since both terms are fixed).

$$\Delta(G - T) \equiv \Delta(IM - X) \qquad\qquad (5.14)$$

Equation (5.14) tells us that an increase in the government budget deficit is one-for-one related to an increase in the trade deficit. Somebody should have told President Trump![5] On the one hand, he waged trade wars on Canada, Mexico, and China, imposing punitive tariffs on imports, and blamed the US balance of trade deficit on unfair trade deals; on the other hand, he passed massive tax cuts (benefiting mainly the rich), leading to trillion-dollar budget deficits! Talk about inconsistent policies!

1.9 The market for loanable funds in an open economy

Nowadays, financial capital moves across international boundaries with ease. Firms and governments can borrow internationally at world interest rates. How does this affect the "crowding out" conclusion?

The situation is depicted in Figure 5.2. The increased government spending causes a deficit and the government decides to finance it by borrowing in the loanable funds market. This shifts the demand for loanable funds from D_1 to D_2. But since the economy is small enough that the extra borrowing does not affect the world interest rate, there is no increase in interest rates, and there is no crowding out—no reduction of domestic investment. Instead, the government deficit is financed by foreign savings.

While there is no effect on investment, nor long-run growth of GDP, interest payments on the accumulated foreign debt must be paid out of domestically produced output. This drives a wedge between output and income, or more technically between GDP and GNP. *What is crowded out is domestic ownership of*

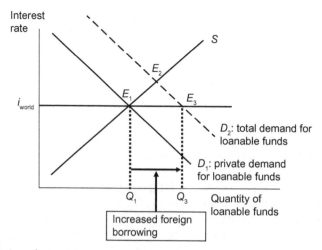

Figure 5.2 Crowding out in an open economy

the capital stock. And this will lead to a reduction in the growth rate of consumption (and hence standards of living). So, there is still a crowding out effect.

1.10 Inflation and interest rates

Anything that affects the supply or demand for loanable funds will impact interest rates.

However, perhaps the single most important factor is expectations about future inflation. This variable simultaneously shifts both the supply and demand for loanable funds. The fact that expectations of inflation are so much lower now than they were in the late 1970s and early 1980s is the major reason why interest rates are much lower now than earlier.

While most loan contracts specify a nominal interest rate, what matters for both lenders and borrowers is the implied real interest rate. Remember, in Chapter 2 we distinguished between real and nominal interest rates: the nominal interest rate, i, equals the real interest rate, r, plus the rate of inflation, π.

$$i = r + \pi \tag{5.15}$$

If we begin with a situation where there is no inflation, no difference between nominal and real rates of interest, then the demand and supply of loanable funds will determine both the real and nominal interest rates. For example, in Figure 5.3, both the real and nominal interest rates are 4 percent in the initial equilibrium labeled E_1.

Now what happens if there is positive inflation? We might think that the nominal rate of interest would increase one-for-one with the inflation rate. But when the deal is made, we do not know what the future inflation rate will be during the course of the loan. The best we can do is estimate it. So, the nominal interest rate will increase one-for-one with expected future inflation, as shown in equation (5.16), where π^e indicates the expected inflation rate.

$$i = r - \pi^e \tag{5.16}$$

This argument that nominal interest rates should increase one-for-one with expected inflation was propounded by Irving Fisher (1896), and as a result, it is known as the *Fisher Effect*. Of course, it is apparent that should something else shift the demand or supply for loanable funds—something other than expected inflation—then nominal interest rates would not move one-for-one with expected inflation. The Fisher Effect is only strictly true in a situation where the real rate of interest is constant.

Figure 5.4 plots interest rates and inflation for Canada from 1960 to 2018.[6] We see that the two series do not move one-for-one. But when inflation is high, so too are interest rates; and when inflation is low, so too are interest rates. We also see that except for brief periods, interest rates exceed inflation, indicating that the ex post real rate of interest was generally positive—indeed, it averaged 2¼

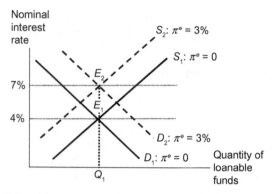

Figure 5.3 The Fisher Effect

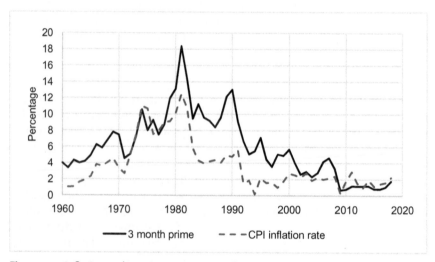

Figure 5.4 Inflation and interest rates in Canada

percent over the entire fifty-eight-year period. However, from 1973 to 1975, and again from 2010 to 2018, inflation exceeded the nominal interest rate, implying a negative real rate of interest. In the earlier period, in the early 1970s, the cause was a rapid and unexpected acceleration in inflation. (Only expected inflation causes nominal interest rates to react.) In the later period, from 2010 to 2018, the cause was extremely low nominal interest rates. These were engineered by the Bank of Canada in order to stimulate the economy (see Chapter 9).

1.11 Summary

The job of the financial sector is to channel savings into investment. Financial institutions facilitate the process by reducing transaction costs, reducing risk, and increasing liquidity.

Savings are identically equal to investment and there are three sources of savings: private, public, and foreign. The cost of using foreign savings is repatriated returns. Nevertheless, the increase in real GDP generated by foreign investment will be greater than the amount paid to foreigners. Therefore, foreign investment is beneficial overall.

In the long run, the loanable funds model determines interest rates and the quantity of funds lent and borrowed. We used this model to show that government deficits increase interest rates in a closed economy, and crowd out investment. In an open economy funds flow in from abroad, which prevents interest rates from increasing. While total investment is not crowded out, domestically owned investment *is* crowded out. In both open and closed economies, the long-run burden of persistent government deficits is lower future growth of income and consumption.

The loanable funds model depicts an efficient market. The EMH pushes the notion of efficient asset markets even further by presenting evidence that asset prices trade at their fundamental values. The fundamental value for a stock is the present value of the expected future stream of earnings per share.

The *twin deficit hypothesis* links government budget deficits with trade deficits, and the *Fisher Effect* says that if real interest rates are constant, nominal interest rates will move one-for-one with expected inflation.

2 THE ANI-TEXT

2.1 Introduction

The financial industry has a key role in the functioning of the economy. It needs to do all the things the texts claim it actually does well. But there is serious doubt whether the claim is true. The texts ignore the debate that has erupted within the economics profession about the problematic nature of the financial system in many capitalist economies. Nor do they construct a serious critique of EMH. Finally, they do a generally poor job of conveying the details of saving and investment, which implies that they draw misleading policy conclusions from the loanable funds model.

2.2 Macroeconomic instability and the financial system

The spark that caused the Great Depression was the stock market collapse of October 1929, which then triggered a banking crisis. The root cause of the Great Financial Meltdown of 2007–8 was reckless lending of the financial sector that fed a house price bubble. When it burst, the value of a complex web of financial assets (ultimately dependent on house prices) plunged. This triggered the Great Recession. In the intervening eighty years—between the Great Depression and the Great Financial Crash—financial institutions lobbied for and gradually eroded the regulations put in place by President Roosevelt in the 1930s to prevent anything like the Great Depression from ever happening again.

The crises of 1929 and 2008 dominate the economic landscape of the last one hundred years like towering behemoths. But there were many other crises. In the nineteenth century, financial crises occurred on average about every ten years. And there have been plenty in the twentieth century. The latter half of the twentieth century alone has seen the Latin American debt crisis (1970s), the Japanese asset price bubble (1986–92), the Savings and Loan crisis in the United States (1986–95), the Asian financial crisis (1997), and many others.

These crises are not exceptions As Hyman Minsky (1986) put it, "We need a theory that makes instability a normal result in our economy, and gives us handles to control it." That is precisely what Minsky sought to provide with his *financial instability hypothesis* (FIH).

2.3 Minsky's financial instability hypothesis

Minsky's FIH can be succinctly expressed by two slogans. First, *success breeds excess, and excess breeds failure*. And second, *markets have an incredible ability to forget*. The first slogan is what drives Minsky's "basic-cycle"—a financial cycle that is present in every business cycle. The second slogan is what drives Minsky's "super-cycle"—a slow tectonic shift toward ever more reckless behavior.

The basic-cycle It begins with people becoming progressively more optimistic about the value of their assets and their future revenue streams. The optimism affects both borrowers and lenders, eroding market discipline. An increased willingness to take on more risk leads to increases in *leverage ratios, collateral ratios*, and a *leverage cycle*.

Leverage is essentially amplification. You can amplify the gains of the underlying financial asset by buying it using borrowed money—the more borrowed money, the greater the leverage. For example, suppose you buy a $100 million financial asset by borrowing $95 million and using $5 million of your own capital. The leverage ratio is the ratio of assets to capital, which in this case is $100 \div 5 = 20$.

Now suppose the value of the financial asset increases by a modest 5 percent, from $100 million to $105 million. Since the value of debt has not changed—it is still $95 million—your capital is now worth $10 million. That is a 100 percent increase. The leverage ratio of 20 has amplified the gain of 5 percent to become 100 percent.

High leverage is necessarily risky because it amplifies not only gains but also losses. If asset values fall by more than 5 percent, capital falls by more than 100 percent. In effect, the value of the asset is now worth less than the debt, and the business is technically insolvent.

Incentives exist within financial institutions for leverage ratios to be too high, which worsens instability. In particular, traders working at banks and other financial intermediaries are gambling using "other people's money." If the gamble pays off, they receive hefty bonuses and become very rich. If not, no big deal. At worst, they may need to find another job.

Collateral ratios determine the amount banks are prepared to lend relative to the value of the collateral. A rise in collateral ratios permits borrowers to borrow more for any given collateral, which allows them to increase their leverage. In an upswing, this increases demand for assets, generating further asset price increases, increasing the value of collateral, permitting a further increase in bank lending. This process is called the leverage cycle.

The three phases Like the first slogan says, the three phases are *success*, *excess*, and *failure*. It begins with a *tranquil phase* associated with success. Everything seems reasonable. Finance engages only in "hedge finance," where expected revenues can repay both the interest and the principal. But the success of this stage leads inevitably to the second, the *fragile phase*, associated with excess. This is where the financial sector engages in "speculative finance," where expected revenues only cover the interest owing but not repayment of principal.

Finally, excess gives way to failure in the third stage. This is the *bust phase*, where "speculative finance" gives way to "Ponzi finance" and borrowers rely on capital gains to meet their obligations. But capital gains only occur in the upswing. And unfortunately, what cannot go up forever must eventually decline. All the mutually reinforcing feedback loops work just as well, or perhaps even better, in reverse. Capital preservation necessitates selling quickly. The automatic sell rules built into computer programs further accelerate the speed of decline.

The super-cycle The super-cycle has two dimensions, illustrated in Figure 5.5. *Regulatory relaxation* is the slow erosion of the "thwarting institutions" critical for stability of capitalist economies. First, regulatory capture occurs as a result of lobbying efforts and the revolving door—where executives from the industry being regulated are hired to the regulatory body because clearly "we need someone who understands the industry inside-out." And when those executives lose their jobs on the regulatory body, they are rehired by the industry they were regulating. For example, ex-Goldman-Sachs executives fill the top positions in the Federal Reserve, Securities Exchange Commission, and the Treasury. Next is regulatory "relapse," when regulators forget past crises and weaken regulations. They become convinced by claims that the industry can regulate itself, and that government regulations are inefficient, preventing the industry creating as much wealth as it could. This leads to "regulatory escape," where regulations are repealed.

While this process is unfolding on the one hand, there is increased risk-taking on the other. Partly, this is achieved through financial

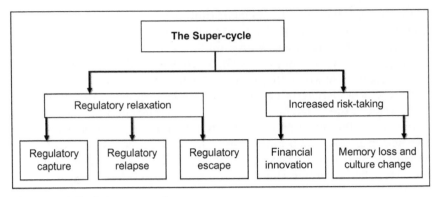

Figure 5.5 Minsky's super-cycle

innovation—the creation of new financial products not previously conceived, and therefore not regulated. The end of a super-cycle is a full-scale crisis, after which the thwarting institutions are renewed, and the process begins again.

> Question for your professor: Are we going to consider any theories that explain the mechanisms behind the evolution of financial crises? Or, are we going to view them as rare events that are not worth studying?

2.4 Minsky's super-cycle in the United States

The recent history of the United States follows the pattern of a Minsky super-cycle. The story begins after the Great Depression when President Roosevelt enacted three pieces of financial regulation to prevent anything like the Great Depression from ever happening again. This is where the thwarting institutions are renewed.

First, the Glass–Steagall Act (1933) prevented commercial banks (that take deposits and grant loans) from acting as investment banks (that issue stocks and shares, and organize huge business deals such as mergers). Investment banking is inherently more risky than commercial banking, and the Glass–Steagall Act kept the two types separate.

Second, the Federal Housing Administration Act (1934) regulated the terms of mortgages and insured them against default. It established interest rate ceilings on mortgages (making them more affordable) and minimum down payment requirements (making them less risky since borrowers were less leveraged).

Third, the Federal National Mortgage Association (known as Fannie Mae) was created in 1938. This purchased the now federally insured mortgages from banks and other financial lenders. Fannie Mae would resell these mortgages to investors needing safe assets. The process funneled cash into the banks, allowing them to make more mortgages. The system worked well for about fifty years. It took a long time to forget the Great Depression. But beginning in the early 1980s, Roosevelt's reforms began to be dismantled.

The process of regulatory escape Mortgage interest rate ceilings were lifted in 1980, and the terms and conditions of mortgages were deregulated in 1982.[7]

These changes opened the door for small consumer finance companies to move into the mortgage business and begin peddling exotic, high-interest loans.[8] In 1977, these little consumer finance companies owned a mere 0.5 percent of the home equity loan market. But by the end of the 1980s, they had 32 percent. Their exotic "alternative" mortgages included negative-amortization loans (whereby borrowers do not pay off the principal) and balloon mortgages (which oblige borrowers to make a large payment at the end of the loan's maturity in exchange for lower monthly charges). These alternative mortgages figure prominently in the subprime crisis, either through predatory lending, or poor risk controls, or hidden punitive charges that tipped people into foreclosure.

In 1999, the Glass–Steagall Act was repealed.[9] The consolidation of commercial and investment banks was supposed to allow the resulting "full-service" banks to better compete and enjoy economies of scale. Instead, it enhanced the scope for conflicts of interest and perverse incentives. Because full-service banks make most of their money selling equities and bonds, and arranging "deals," the creditworthiness of the companies to whom they extended loans became secondary. For example, we now know that major full-service banks continued to give loans to Enron even as it approached bankruptcy because of the lure of mega-profits from new deals, if it avoided bankruptcy.

Stiglitz (2003: 143–4) says, "The bubble—and the bad behaviour—were reinforcing: the stronger the bubble, the stronger the incentives to take the actions to keep it going. The banks must surely have known that when the bubble burst, many of the loans they had made would fail. Thus, the banks' loan portfolios depended on keeping the stock market bubble going." The bubble Stiglitz is referring to is the stock market bubble of the late 1990s—the one that burst in August 2000. But the same set of incentives was at work in generating the real estate and stock market bubble that burst seven years later.

The process of financial innovation One of the most important innovations was securitization of riskier mortgages, mortgages that were not federally insured, not backstopped by the US government. Financial institutions repackaged huge batches of mortgages into an alphabet soup of investment vehicles (SIVs, CDOs, ABCP, and more) and sold them on to unsuspecting investors.[10]

These new investment vehicles were riskier and more profitable. Because of the higher risk, big investors sought reassurance. This was met in part by credit rating agencies assigning grades to securitized bundles. But it was also met by the development of *credit default swaps (CDSs)*— ways of insuring the investment vehicles against default by the ultimate borrowers, the homeowners. The value of these CDSs was estimated in 2008 to be around $62 trillion and involved complex interrelationships between financial institutions.

The financial institutions that insured the mortgage-backed securities against default thought that the risk of any one householder defaulting was independent of any other householder defaulting. So, by issuing huge numbers of CDSs, they were "diversifying." But this reasoning ignores the possibility of a systemic event—like a real estate bubble bursting—creating huge swaths of mortgage defaults.

It is noteworthy that the unsupervised growth in the credit default swap market was due to another piece of deregulation—the Commodity Futures Modernization Act (CFMA) of 2000. This legislation guaranteed that CDSs would not be regulated like other "futures contracts." It also whacked the Securities and Exchange Commission's budget when they asked for more funding to oversee all these new types of deals.[11]

The meltdown The reckless behavior of the financial sector fueled the biggest home price boom in US history. Beginning around 2002, house prices nearly doubled before they hit a peak as early as June 2006. Beyond that date, the decline in house prices gathered steam, leading to an accelerating increase in mortgage defaults. The financial institutions that issued the CDSs faced a catastrophic liability. But since it was not clear which financial institutions were at risk, by July 2007 banks were increasingly reluctant to lend to each other. This drying up of interbank lending began the credit crunch. Bear Stearns (the largest investment bank in the United States) collapsed in March 2008 but was bailed out by the US Federal Reserve. Lehman Brothers was allowed to go bankrupt on September 3, 2008.

The wisdom of letting Lehman Brothers go bankrupt has since been questioned. The point was to send a disciplinary message to the financial system. But the effect was to spread panic throughout the world banking system. It was an experiment that was not repeated. Subsequently, on September 16, 2008, AIG was bailed out with $182 billion of US taxpayer money. The banking crisis, in the United States at least, was very gradually stabilized over the next two years by the Troubled Asset Relief Program (TARP) (passed into law on October 8, 2008), which authorized $700 billion to buy toxic assets from financial institutions.

Renewal of the thwarting institutions The Dodd–Frank Act was enacted in July 2010. President Barack Obama called it a "sweeping overhaul of the US financial regulatory system, a transformation on a scale not seen since the reforms that followed the Great Depression."

Among other things, it established a bureau to protect consumers against financial abuses, a financial oversight council, and gave the Federal Reserve new powers to regulate systemically important institutions. It also tried to handle the "too big to fail" issue by creating an "authority" to handle the liquidation of large companies.

But Wall Street was lobbying against Dodd–Frank before the ink was even dry. In early 2017, President Trump passed an executive order to roll back some of the regulatory provisions within Dodd–Frank. The renewal of the "thwarting institutions" has lasted less than seven years. The process of regulatory escape has already begun. So, if anyone asks "could it happen again?" the correct answer is, "it is not a question of *if* but *when*."

Question for your professor: Prof, in your opinion, why did the Great Financial Meltdown of 2007–8 occur? Were the authorities correct in letting Lehman Brothers go bankrupt?

2.5 A critique of the EMH

EMH asserts that asset prices are always at their fundamental values. Even if this were possible as a long-run equilibrium situation, what about the costs and time required to gather information? What about the out-of-long-run-equilibrium trades where those with newly acquired information bid the price up (or down) to its fundamental value? As Grossman and Stiglitz (1980) note, to assume that asset prices always reflect all available information gives rise to a paradox: *if true, no-one would have any incentive to incur the costs of gathering information, which implies the information would not be collected.* Neat as it is, the so-called Grossman-Stiglitz paradox did not discernably impact belief in EMH. Perhaps it was regarded as a trivial limiting case.[12]

Is there evidence that asset markets are not efficient? For starters, there is the micro evidence produced by behavioral economists showing that individuals make systematic errors.[13] But as long as there are people who don't make errors—the über-rational who can capitalize on the mistakes of others—the market as a whole could still be efficient.

Therefore, behavioral economists searched for anomalies in the *market as a whole*. And while this effort has been moderately successful in finding anomalies for specific products, at specific times, it misses the bigger

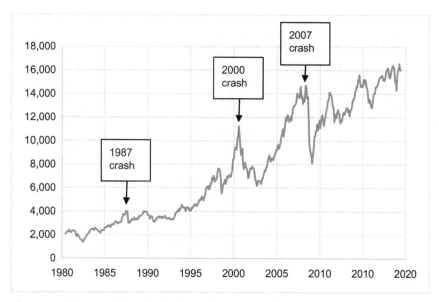

Figure 5.6 Boom and bust in the Toronto stock market

point.[14] Surely, the big problem with EMH is the mammoth bubbles and crashes that occur in aggregate stock price indices. For example, Figure 5.6 shows three market crashes in the TSX composite index for the Canadian stock market between 1980 and 2019.

However, the huge swings in aggregate stock price indices do not (by themselves) prove anything. As we saw in Section 1.3, the fundamental value of a stock is determined by its discounted stream of *expected future earnings* per share. A bad recession (that was not previously expected) would lower the entire stream of expected future earnings, having a dramatic impact on the fundamental value of all stocks.

So, the question of causality is key. Is a previously unexpected recession causing a fall in the discounted stream of expected future earnings, and hence in asset prices? Or, is the collapse of asset prices causing the recession?

In the case of the Great Recession (2008–14), we know the causality because of the timing. The house price bubble started to collapse as early as June 2006. The stock market collapse began on October 1, 2007. And in the United States, two successive quarters of negative real GDP growth (signaling the beginning of the Great Recession) began in the second quarter of 2008. The timing makes clear that it was the bursting of the housing bubble that caused the banking crisis, and the banking crisis that then caused the Great Recession. This is not disputed by anyone.[15]

But is this true more generally? In fact, there is evidence that confirms causality running from financial instability to real macroeconomic instability.

First, Akerlof and Shiller (2009) emphasize with one detailed historical example after another that it is not changes in our expectations of future earnings that determine the bubbles and crashes in asset prices, but rather it is changes in our "animal spirits"—the swings from irrational exuberance to irrational pessimism. When prices are rising we forget about the last bubble, and we get caught up in the current story, the current myth, in the frenzy of making money.[16]

Second, if stock market fluctuations are just reflecting changes in the real economy, then those fluctuations should be explained by variations in expected future dividend streams. But numerous papers have shown that fluctuations in expected future dividends are much too small—they can account for only a small part of the variance in stock prices.[17]

Third, we have the evidence of first-hand experience. The 1987 crash— like the 1929 crash—was swift (occurring in one day), large (wiping out 23 percent of equity values), and international in scope (it affected stock markets worldwide). But unlike the 1929 crash, there were no obvious fundamental reasons for it. It defies explanation. Completely by chance, Robert Shiller—recipient of the Nobel Memorial Prize in Economics (2013)—happened to be surveying traders while the stock market was crashing in 1987. Traders told him they were selling simply because other people were selling. It was mob psychology, not the working of an efficient market.

How does this evidence compare with that which supports EMH? Section 1.3 noted that the random walk prediction has been very hard to refute. And numerous studies have supported the prediction that today's best performing mutual fund will be randomly located in the pack of mutual funds next year. So, which evidence wins in this battle of the evidence?

The key point is that the evidence supporting EMH *does not concern itself with the overall level of asset prices*. It concerns itself only with the movement of individual asset prices, and one asset price compared to the next. Larry Summers (1985) makes this point in withering fashion by comparing proponents of EMH to practitioners of "ketchup economics": "They have shown that two quart bottles of ketchup invariably sell for twice as much as one quart bottles of ketchup ... Indeed, most ketchup economists regard the efficiency of the ketchup market as the best established fact in empirical economics" (p. 634).

Finally, we need to understand why the determination of the overall level of asset prices can be inefficient and prone to huge swings, even while the determination of individual asset prices is efficient. How can EMH be right on a micro level and wrong on a macro level? There are three fundamental points here.

First, the fallacy of composition explicitly warns us that something that is true for a part (micro) might not be true for the whole (macro)!

Second, what something is worth depends not just on its fundamental value but also *on what everyone expects everyone else will be willing to pay for it*. The inherent uncertainty over the future of the economy interacts with uncertainty about other people's expectations about the likely actions of other investors! As Keynes (1936: 156) says, a good trader practices "the third degree" of abstraction in trying to anticipate what average opinion expects average opinion to be, with some practicing even higher degrees of abstraction.[18]

Third, the über-rational traders are unable to profit from the irrational trades of others when the whole market is irrational and stays that way for a long period. Shorting a stock too early can bring bankruptcy. Holding a stock while its price is plunging does the same, even though it may make no sense to sell in terms of fundamentals. As a result, the smart money is forced out of the market. In a nutshell, *the market can stay irrational longer than the rational can stay solvent.*

Question for your professor: I have heard it said that the stock market is "micro efficient, but macro inefficient." What does this mean? Does it help to explain financial instability?

2.6 The loanable funds market: information and efficiency

From our study of microeconomics, we know that the demand and supply framework is shorthand for a perfectly competitive market, and that such markets are efficient: the right quantity is produced, at the lowest possible cost, and is distributed to those who value it most. In applying this framework to the *loanable funds market*, the textbooks suggest (sometimes explicitly) that credit markets in modern industrial economies are also efficient—the right people save and lend, the right investments are financed, and at the lowest possible interest rates.[19]

But these conclusions are simply made-up by textbooks, and are not even supported by sound neoclassical theory. In particular, the conclusions of the competitive model cannot be applied to situations where there is imperfect and asymmetric information, which is routinely involved in credit markets—which the textbooks call the *market for loanable funds*.[20] Consider all the reasons why imperfect and asymmetric information characterizes credit markets.

First, banks cannot know everything relevant to a customer's creditworthiness—people have an incentive not to divulge damaging information about their past; and their future ability to repay loans depends on a host of uncertain elements (usually) better understood by the individuals themselves. Second, those who deposit their money in banks cannot know everything about the solvency and risk profile of any given bank. Third, the same is true of shareholders of banks. Fourth, borrowers cannot know everything about how honestly the terms, conditions, and fees associated with loans may be presented to them by either banks or credit brokers (as was apparent with subprime loans).

Crucially, asymmetric information gives rise to a cluster of well-known problems: *the principal-agent problem, the moral hazard problem, and the adverse selection problem.* Competitive markets cannot function efficiently when these problems are present: government regulation is required. So, how do these problems manifest in credit markets? Let's use the Great Financial Crash of 2007–8 as our example.

The principal-agent problem This is where "agents" benefit at the expense of the "principals" they are supposed to serve. This played its part in the global financial meltdown when the management of banks focused on maximizing their own short-term reward by, for example, inflating short-term profits to maximize the value of their stock options. Managers ignored the long-run interest of their shareholders. It was involved when financial institutions gave predatory loans to individuals who had little chance of paying them back—the infamous NINJA (no income, no job, and no assets) mortgages. It was involved when those same financial institutions repackaged these loans into an alphabet soup of investment vehicles and sold them on to unsuspecting investors.

Moral hazard This is where incentives are changed by certain kinds of contracts, which leads to a change in behavior that is hard to monitor. This played its part in the meltdown for at least four reasons. First, because the banks didn't hold the mortgages they extended but sold them on to other investors, they had little interest in the real creditworthiness of the borrowers. So, the normal incentive of banks to vet the creditworthiness of its customers was short-circuited (or distorted) by the creation of the new investment vehicles. Second, the agencies that assigned credit ratings to the investment vehicles were compromised by the fact that their fees depended on the quantity of ratings they gave. (The better the ratings they gave, the more business they would be given.) Third, the investors that purchased the "alphabet soup" of investment vehicles did not sufficiently care about their ultimate riskiness because they insured against the possibility of default (or at least they thought they did) by buying CDSs from huge insurance companies like AIG. Fourth, depositors at the banks didn't have to worry about the risk of bank collapse since their deposits were insured by the government-owned Federal Deposit Insurance Corporation.

Adverse selection This is where particular contracts disproportionately attract undesirable customers. This is always involved in credit markets, since experience suggests that those who are dishonest, desperate, or overly optimistic are much less likely than others to drop out of the loan market as interest rates rise. This makes the business of extending loans more risky as interest rates rise.

So, the problems associated with asymmetric information certainly manifest themselves in credit markets, and were certainly crucially involved in the global financial meltdown.

The textbook claim that the loanable funds market is efficient is somewhat bizarre.

There is a further problem with the textbook use of the demand and supply framework to depict equilibrium in the loanable funds market: it cannot depict a credit crunch. If we try to do so by shifting the supply curve of loanable funds to the left, the equilibrium interest rate will increase. But interest rates may be very low in a meltdown as the central bank floods financial markets with liquidity. Financial institutions themselves are not only short of liquidity but also short of capital. As asset values fell, many of them in 2007–8 had liabilities far exceeding the (now reduced) value of their assets. They were effectively insolvent—hence the call for massive government bailouts.

With banks in such dire state, even sound borrowers—businesses like General Electric, for example—were unable to find the funding they required. This is what is meant by a "credit crunch." *Interest rates may be low (even approaching zero), but loans are difficult to obtain.* This is a classic case of how the demand and supply model is inadequate to explain the credit market in a financial bust.

Question for your professor: Can markets function efficiently when there is imperfect and asymmetric information? Then why does our textbook suggest that the loanable funds market is efficient?

2.7 The financial industry is too big

We know that trading assets is a major activity of the financial sector, one that provides huge private returns. But is all that trading activity socially productive? Or is it possible that there are too many resources devoted to trading activities?

In 1957, Paul Samuelson noted the perverse rewards to getting information just slightly before everyone else. He says, "Imagine someone who consistently received crucial information one second before everyone else. The social value of that extra second would be minimal; but the private rewards could be huge." So, to the extent that the rewards of the financial sector are geared to a socially unproductive activity—getting information milliseconds before others—its rewards will far exceed its social productivity.

The second reason to think the financial sector is too big is that it receives an implicit subsidy. When things go wrong, as they periodically do, the financial sector is bailed out by the public sector. This occurs because financial institutions are viewed as too important. They are too big to be allowed to fail. This creates asymmetry on the outcomes—heads I win a lot, tails you lose.

The bailouts are an implicit subsidy to financial markets. Subsidies are what economists recommend when the private provision of a good is less than the socially desired outcome. Since there is no reason to think that is true in the case of financial markets, the subsidy has no justification, leading to an industry that is too big.

If you have any doubt that the history of public bailouts is an implicit subsidy, imagine you own a Formula 1 car racing team, and every time you crash a car, the government fixes it for you at no cost. The government may not give you an upfront subsidy, or a subsidy based on the number of races you enter, but nevertheless, not having to pay for repairs represents a massive dollar gain. Plus, it creates an incentive to drive more recklessly than otherwise.

```
Question for your professor: Getting information
milliseconds before others would be privately
rewarding but not socially productive. Isn't that a
lot of what the financial sector does?
```

2.8 The truth about savings

The textbook story has savings flowing from households to firms to finance their investment.[21] But the texts do not show any data on the components of savings, nor the components of investment. Corporate saving is not mentioned.

Corporate savings In fact, in some countries household saving is just a small portion of total saving. And in many modern capitalist economies, the corporate sector is a net lender to the rest of the economy, implying that the total funds the corporate sector saves exceed the total funds it invests. There are two reasons for this.

First, corporate after-tax profits have tended to be high outside of recessionary periods, partly due to a trend toward lower taxation of corporate profits. And second, corporate investment levels have tended to be low.

In 2005, *The Economist* observed, "For the past three years, while profits have surged around the globe, capital spending has remained relatively weak. As a result, companies in aggregate have become net savers on a huge scale."[22] In 2012, *The Economist* summarized a study of fifty-one countries. It found "companies' share of private saving rose in aggregate by 20 percentage points, 1975–2007."[23] It noted that worldwide cash stockpiles had continued to grow following the global recession.

Many mainstream textbooks (and right-wing think tanks) suggest giving tax breaks to rich households so that they will save more; or giving tax cuts to corporations to stimulate investment. But the basic facts do not support these policy proposals. Indeed, in 2012 Bank of Canada governor, Mark Carney, chastised Canadian corporations for their buildup of cash, calling it "dead money." The Canadian Labour Congress followed up with a report in January 2013 that the quantity of this "dead money" had reached $500 billion. It concluded, "Rather than investing the windfall from their tax cuts to create jobs, Canada's largest non-financial corporations are hoarding cash and paying fat compensation to their CEOs."

Government savings The texts show "crowding out" when government borrowing increases. What they don't explain is that if the government's budget was balanced in a "structural sense"—meaning revenues would just equal spending when the economy is at long-run equilibrium—the government budget would automatically go into deficit in a recession, and this would be a good thing! In fact, it is so good it has a special name: *an automatic stabilizer.*

An automatic stabilizer is anything that causes spending to move inversely to GDP. For example, in a slump government spending automatically increases because spending on unemployment benefits and welfare spending increases. In addition, since the government's tax revenue depends on GDP, in a slump tax revenue automatically falls.

So, the government budget automatically goes into deficit as the economy goes into a slump. But this will not crowd out investment! Indeed, by preventing output from falling as much as it otherwise would, it is supporting the conditions for profitable investment.

The lesson here is never assume shifts in government savings occur as a result of deliberate policy; they may well be automatic responses.

However, there is a more subtle point going on here. We are criticizing the "crowding out" result by using examples where the economy is not in long-run equilibrium, whereas the "crowding out" argument is only valid in long-run equilibrium. The modern trend in macroeconomics textbooks has been to start with long-run issues. They discuss growth first, then finance, all assuming that the economy is in long-run equilibrium. This assumes away the economic problem.

Keynes says in *A Tract on Monetary Reform* (1923), "But this long run is a misleading guide to current affairs. In the long run we are all dead." This has been misinterpreted to mean that Keynes did not care about the future. But he goes on to say, "Economists set themselves too easy, too useless a task, if in tempestuous seasons they can only tell us, that when the storm is long past, the ocean is flat again." Keynes is not arguing that we should recklessly enjoy the present and let the future go hang. Rather, he is exasperated with the mainstream view that the "long run" should be a guide policy.

The emphasis in the early chapters of macro textbooks on long-run issues is analogous to the emphasis in the early chapters of micro textbooks on perfect competition. Both give an aura of efficiency to the free market economy. Put succinctly, *the long run is to macro what perfect competition is to micro.*

```
Question for your professor: Don't corporations
currently have stockpiles of idle cash? Does that
mean the crowding out result is not relevant
right now?
```

2.9 The truth about investment

Mainstream texts create the impression that all investment is private sector investment, while government spending seems to be for "beer and balloons." It seems to be wasted, or at least have no positive impact on productivity growth. But governments do a lot of investment spending, whether it be on infrastructure, or human capital development, or even preserving environmental capital. Since this has already been mentioned in Chapter 2 we do not need to dwell on this point again here.

But there is another issue obscured by the textbooks: a good chunk of investment spending is the construction of residential structures. For example, in Canada in 2014, this amounted to nearly 30 percent of business gross fixed capital formation. The bulk of this consists of building owner-occupied homes. This is incongruous with the textbook emphasis on the importance of investment for productivity growth.

From the household's point of view, it makes sense to regard the purchase of a house as an investment. But a house is not "capital" like plant and equipment. It does not raise the productivity of labor. A house is an expensive consumer durable, like the family car.

This raises the question of why new owner-occupied homes are included as "investment" in the national accounts. The answer is to maintain equivalence between the treatment of owner-occupied and rented housing. But why do the texts downplay this component of private sector investment? It would seem that there is both an ideological reason and a theoretical one.

The ideological reason is this. Savings are supposed to augment the capital-to-labor ratio and increase productivity to deliver growth in real GDP per capita. If savings are being used to build more and bigger houses, the importance of savings is undermined. In the worst case, such investment could be Donald Trump adding yet another mansion to his list of personal homes.

The theoretical reason is that the standard texts rely upon neoclassical micro theory to think about concepts such as capital and investment. In this theory, any long-lived durable good is capital. So there is no basis within neoclassical economics to distinguish between different types of capital and investment. Another factory, another mansion—it's all the same. Furthermore, in neoclassical theory efficiency is achieved when the expected returns on different forms of investment are equalized across sectors. And efficient use of capital supposedly maximizes growth. But it would be hard to convince readers of an introductory textbook of this line of reasoning. So the textbook authors who believe it just sweep it under the rug.

Question for your professor: If the rich get richer, and inequality worsens, the rich may channel savings into second or third mansions. Wouldn't this be treated as investment in the national accounts? But would it be good for growth?

2.10 Concluding remarks

Reading the mainstream textbooks one would be forgiven for thinking that the financial sector is the "jewel in the crown" of modern capitalist economies. It is thanks to this sector that economies grow and thrive. The anti-text argues that such a view is the heart of the problem. It obscures the real and serious ongoing problems caused by a financial sector that is too big and the source of major instability.

Minsky's FIH advances a two-part explanation for financial instability in modern capitalist economies. The basic-cycle relies on psychological factors, while the super-cycle advances a political economy explanation. Interestingly, the evolution of the Great Financial Crash can easily be seen in terms of a Minsky super-cycle. Indeed, when it occurred in 2008, many writers in the financial press dubbed it a "Minsky moment." However, this terminology indicates they clearly did not understand Minsky. It did not happen in a "moment." The seeds had been growing over many years.

If Minsky has it right, then EMH must be wrong. Our explanation for why it is wrong involves fundamental uncertainty and the necessity to preserve capital in the face of a hurricane of irrational trades.

Up to that point, we had not examined any structural problems in the world of finance. However, our critique of the textbook treatment of the loanable funds model rectifies this. We emphasize the problem of imperfect and asymmetric information that gives rise to a cluster of well-known problems—problems that require government regulation to fix. We document the presence of these problems in the Great Financial meltdown.

Finally, the textbook treatment of the components of savings and investment obscures several awkward features. For example, corporations are not net borrowers but net lenders who are sitting on trillions of idle cash. It is laughable that, in the face of this idle cash, the textbooks continue to argue that government deficit financing can crowd out investment spending.

APPENDIX: THE VALUE OF A PERPETUITY

In Section 1.2 of the text, we give the value of a perpetuity that pays $A at the end of every period as:

$$P = \frac{\$A}{(1+i)} + \frac{\$A}{(1+i)^2} + \frac{\$A}{(1+i)^3} + \cdots + \frac{\$A}{(1+i)^{n-1}} \frac{\$A}{(1+i)^n}$$

To solve it, divide both the left-hand side and each term on the right-hand side by $(1+i)$.

$$\frac{P}{(1+i)} = \frac{\$A}{(1+i)^2} + \frac{\$A}{(1+i)^3} + \frac{\$A}{(1+i)^4} + \cdots + \frac{\$A}{(1+i)^n} + \frac{\$A}{(1+i)^{n+1}}$$

Now subtract the second expression from the first!

$$P - \frac{P}{(1+i)} = \frac{\$A}{(1+i)} - \frac{\$A}{(1+i)^{n+1}}$$

Note there are now just two terms on the right-hand side, just one from the expression for "P," and one from the expression for $P/(1+i)$. All others cancel out. Since there are an equal number of terms in both expressions, if we have one leftover from the expression for "P," we must have one leftover from the expression for $P/(1+i)$.

Next, we note that as n tends to infinity, the term $(1+i)^{n+1}$ tends to infinity, and A divided by $(1+i)^{n+1}$ tends to zero. This eliminates the last term, leaving us with only one term on the right-hand side. Putting the left-hand side over the common denominator we get:

$$\frac{P(1+i) - P}{(1+i)} = \frac{\$A}{(1+i)}$$

Multiplying by sides by $(1 + i)$, and simplifying the numerator of the left-hand side, we get

$$P + Pi - P = Pi = \$A \text{ or } P = \$A / i$$

An alternative approach is to use the formula for the sum of geometric expression. That formula is:

$$a + ar + ar^2 + ar^3 + \cdots + ar^n \rightarrow \frac{a}{1-r} \quad \left(\text{as } n \rightarrow \infty\right)$$

In our case, the first term "a" is $\$A/(1 + i)$. And the common ratio "$r$" is $1/(1 + i)$. Substituting these into the formula we get:

$$P = \frac{\dfrac{A}{1+i}}{1-\dfrac{1}{1+i}} = \frac{\dfrac{A}{1+i}}{\dfrac{1+i-1}{1+i}} = \frac{A}{i}$$

Part 3

SHORT-RUN FLUCTUATIONS

Chapter 6

SHORT-RUN MACRO MODELS: A REVOLUTION THAT MISFIRED

The New [Neoclassical] Synthesis, like the Old Synthesis of fifty years ago, postulates that the economy behaves like a <u>stable</u> general equilibrium system whose equilibrating properties are somewhat hampered by frictions … The syntheses, old and new, I believe are wrong … The genuine instabilities of the modern economy have to be faced.

Axel Leijonhufvud (2009)[1]

Axel Leijonhufvud, made a distinction in his 1966 book, on "Keynesian Economics and the Economics of Keynes," between Keynes and the Keynesians. He meant that orthodox Keynesian interpretations of the General Theory … got it all wrong.

Roger Farmer (2009)[2]

I THE STANDARD TEXT

1.1 Introduction

The focus of this chapter is the business cycle—the short-run fluctuations in economic activity—the seemingly inevitable ebb and flow from boom to recession and back again. We present two models: first, the Aggregate Expenditure Model, and second, the Aggregate Demand and Aggregate Supply (AD–AS) Model.

The aggregate expenditure (AE) model focuses exclusively on the determinants of aggregate demand (AD). If aggregate supply (AS) were horizontal, knowing the position of AD would be enough to determine output. So, we can regard the AE model as implicitly assuming a horizontal AS. That is, it assumes constant prices.

Within this simplified framework, we can focus on two important aspects: first, how AD is derived and what shifts it; second, how and why the economy moves toward short-run equilibrium.

The AE model is interesting in its own right, since in the very short run, when prices *are* constant, it is all we need to determine output. This initial focus on the AE model makes sense given that most recessions are caused by negative AD shocks. But supply shocks are important too. To explain their impact, we need to develop the AD–AS model.

The 1970s was the decade when the importance of supply shocks became fully appreciated. Following the Arab-Israeli War of 1973, the world price of crude oil more than quadrupled. Another dramatic increase occurred in the aftermath of the Iranian Revolution of 1979. As a result of these events, the world oil price rose from about $2 a barrel in early 1973 to more than $30 a barrel in 1980. This dramatic increase in the price of energy caused a slump across the industrialized world. But this slump was different: it was accompanied by higher inflation. The combination of recession *and* inflation came to be known as "stagflation."

As we will see, governments can influence AD through their spending or taxation policies. But it is much more difficult to influence AS. This creates a policy dilemma. When facing stagflation, is it better to fight the slump by expanding AD and worsen inflation? Or is it better to fight inflation by decreasing AD and worsen the slump? In any event, we clearly need a model that will distinguish between negative AD shocks like in the Great Depression, and negative AS shocks like those of the 1970s.

1.2 The AE model

We will develop the model in seven steps.

Step 1: The GDP accounting identity
From our study of the GDP accounts (in Chapter 2), we know that GDP (denoted "Y") is identically equal to the sum of consumption (C), investment (I), government purchases of final goods (G), and exports (X) minus imports (IM).

$$Y \equiv C + I + G + (X - IM) \tag{6.1}$$

Step 2: Planned AE
Define "AE" as planned aggregate expenditure. Just like GDP, this can be broken down into its component parts, but we put a "P" superscript to indicate planned magnitudes. These plans are not mere wishes or dreams. They are realistic intentions based on budget constraints.

$$AE \equiv C^P + I^P + G^P + (X^P - IM^P) \tag{6.2}$$

Step 3: The equilibrium condition
The next equation is not true at all times; it is only true in equilibrium! In equilibrium, output equals planned spending.

$$\text{In equilibrium: } Y = AE \tag{6.3}$$

Step 4: Planned spending and actual spending

Consider next the relationship between actual and planned spending, and ask ourselves, why should they ever be different? For example, if our consumption plans are realistic, based on our actual budget constraint, why should we not consume what we planned? This line of thinking suggests some simplifying assumptions. We will assume that actual spending always equals planned spending for four of the five categories: consumption, government spending, exports, and imports. These assumptions are stated as in equation (6.4A).

$$C=C^P, G=G^P, X=X^P, IM=IM^P \tag{6.4A}$$

The realism of the assumptions stated above depends upon the availability of sufficiently large inventories. Normally, in market economies this is the case. Only on the rarest of occasions, such the release of a new iPhone, does the frenzy to have the latest and greatest lead to long lineups and frustrated consumers at the end of the day.

However, it is important to realize that keeping stock of inventories is an investment. And this explains why investment is the only category of spending not included in the set of assumptions labeled (6.4A). If planned spending were to increase suddenly, the stock of inventories would decrease unexpectedly, causing investment to be less than planned.

As far as investment is concerned, we assume that actual investment is the sum of planned and unplanned investment. Just like in life, what actually happens to you is the sum total of what you plan and what you don't plan! The final wrinkle is to identify unplanned investment as *unintended changes in inventories*, "ΔV." This investment equation is labeled (6.4B):

$$I = I^P + \Delta V \tag{6.4B}$$

Next, simplify planned AE, equation (6.2), using the set of assumptions labeled (6.4A). We will call the result equation (6.5):

$$AE \equiv C + I^P + G + (X - IM) \tag{6.5}$$

To complete step 4, subtract equation (6.5) from equation (6.1), noting from equation (6.4B) that the difference between actual and planned investment is unintended changes in inventories.

$$Y - AE = I - I^P = \Delta V \tag{6.6}$$

Equation (6.6) is extremely useful. It will be central to our analysis of equilibrium and stability in steps 6 and 7.

Step 5: Planned spending increases with income

Another entirely reasonable assumption is that planned AE increases with actual income, Y. Suppose this relationship is a straight line, with an intercept and a slope. Denote the intercept as alpha (α), and the slope as beta (β).

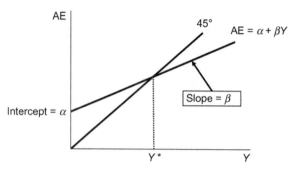

Figure 6.1 Equilibrium output

$$AE = \alpha + \beta Y \qquad\qquad\qquad (6.7)$$

Clearly, many things could influence planned AE besides income. This list of things could include wealth, or employment prospects, or business outlook, or taxes, and many others. For now, all of these will be grouped into the intercept term. If any of those things change, the intercept will be affected.

Step 6: The 45-degree line
We plot AE on the vertical axis and Y on the horizontal axis, ensuring the same units of measurement.

We now draw a line that begins at the origin and ascends at a 45-degree angle. This is a locus of points that are equidistant from both axes. At every point on this line, Y = AE. This line is equation (6.3), the equilibrium condition!

Step 7: Equilibrium and stability
Figure 6.1 plots both the AE line, equation (6.7), and the 45-degree line. The point where AE intersects the 45-degree line is the equilibrium level of output, Y^*. We can check this conclusion using equation (6.6). At Y^*, Y = AE. This implies that I = IP and that ΔV = 0.

   If there are no unintended changes in inventories, firms are selling what they planned to sell, and they have no reason to change their production. In short, Y^* is the equilibrium level of output. Given the position of the AE line, output has no tendency to change at Y^*.

   But suppose output is not at Y^*. What happens then?
Suppose output is above equilibrium, at Y_1 in Figure 6.2. At this point, output is greater than AE ($Y_1 > AE_1$). From equation (6.5), we see that since $Y >$ AE, then $I > I^P$, which implies that $\Delta V > 0$. In other words, unintended changes in inventories are positive, or there are *unintended accumulations of inventory*. Therefore, firms will cut production and output will fall.

   We can easily consider the opposite case, where output is below equilibrium, without a diagram. Since we know that Y = AE in equilibrium, if output were below equilibrium, then Y would be less than AE. This implies that $I < I^P$, which

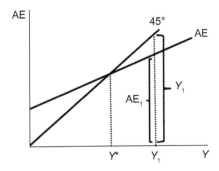

Figure 6.2 Stability

implies that $\Delta V < 0$. In words, unintended changes in inventories are negative, or there are *unintended depletions of inventory*. Therefore, firms will increase production and output will rise.

We have demonstrated that whenever output is above equilibrium, output will fall; and when output is below equilibrium, output will rise. So, wherever we start, output will move toward the equilibrium point. In other words, *the equilibrium is stable.*

1.3 Understanding stability

Using a minimum number of assumptions, we have just demonstrated that the economy is stable. Isn't that grand? Isn't it nice to know the economy is stable!

The right answer is "not really." For one thing, we must not confuse a model of the economy with the actual economy. For another, the equilibrium output level in the AE model might be very undesirable. Remember, experience during the Great Depression suggests that the economy could become stuck in an "underemployment equilibrium," and the equilibrium level of output in the AE model has been defined without any reference to full employment. It could be, for example, that Y_1 in Figure 6.2 is full employment output. If so, the difference between Y_1 and Y^* would be *the recessionary gap*. Since the economy is stable, it will not budge from Y^*. There is only one way to eliminate the recessionary gap, and that is to increase AE. One way to do this is to increase government spending.

At the introductory level of macroeconomics we always assume that government spending is exogenous—it does not change as Y changes. If so, changes in "G" will only affect the intercept of the AE line, not its slope. Figure 6.3 shows that a change in G can shift up the AE line just enough to achieve full employment at Y^f. It should be apparent that the resulting change in Y is much greater than the change in G that caused it. Using symbols, we can say that $\Delta Y/\Delta G > 1$. This is our first glimpse of *the income-expenditure multiplier*: the increase in G has a multiplied effect on Y.

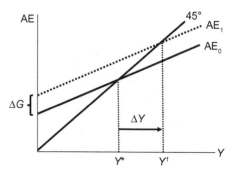

Figure 6.3 Moving to full employment equilibrium

1.4 Understanding equilibrium

Question: Why are we interested in the equilibrium position? The usual student answer is that the equilibrium position is the optimal position. But there are two distinct interpretations of equilibrium: first, equilibrium as a position of rest; and second, equilibrium as an optimal or efficient position. The two interpretations of equilibrium overlap. Optimal points *are* points of rest since no-one has any incentive to change their behavior. But points of rest *are not necessarily* optimal points.

In the AE model, the equilibrium is a point of rest. There is no suggestion that the equilibrium is optimal. People's planned spending may be too low.

1.5 Unpacking planned AE

Our next task is to study the components of AE. We begin with consumption. At about 60 percent of GDP in OECD countries, consumption is the biggest component of AE.

Consumption The most important determinant of real consumption spending is real disposable income, "*YD*." We will frame the relationship between *C* and *YD* as a "*consumption function*," shown in Figure 6.4.

Many other variables could influence consumption. For example, real wealth is an influence. If people feel wealthier, they increase consumption even if their disposable income does not change. Or if interest rates decrease, people might increase consumption even with no change in their disposable income. All these other influences on consumption are treated as shift variables: they shift the relationship between *C* and *YD*. It is the relationship between consumption and income that creates the multiplier that we noted in Section 1.2.

What else do we know about the relationship between *C* and *YD*? First, as long as consumers have any savings to draw down, or credit available, consumption will still be positive even if disposable income is zero. This implies the consumption function will have a positive intercept, which we will call

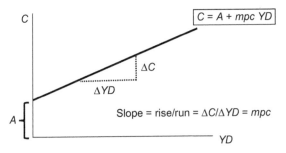

Figure 6.4 The consumption function

"autonomous consumption" and denote as "*A.*" Second, if disposable income increases, both consumption and savings will increase. That implies that the change in consumption is less than the change in disposable income, which means the slope of the consumption function is less than one. The slope of the consumption function is called the *marginal propensity to consume* or *mpc*. As we will see, *mpc* is a very important parameter!

Planned investment Planned investment depends negatively on interest rates and taxes, and positively on expected future output and business confidence. However, investment is extremely volatile. This is because business confidence is the most important factor, and this depends on future expectations, which are subject to abrupt shifts. Figure 6.5 compares year-to-year fluctuations in consumption spending with fluctuations in investment spending in Canada, from 1965 to 2017.[3] It is apparent that consumption is relatively stable, whereas investment is highly volatile. In particular, gross investment turns very negative in recessions, as in 1981, 1990, 2000, and 2007.

Government Government spending is treated as exogenous (or determined outside of the model). We define net tax revenue as total tax revenue received by the government minus total transfer payments made by the government, and we denote it as "*T.*" (For the remainder of this chapter, the term "taxes" means "net taxes" unless stated otherwise.) We assume that net tax revenue rises with income, and assume the simplest possible linear functional form, where
$\bar{T}$ is the intercept, and *t* the slope, of the tax function:

$$T = \bar{T} + tY$$

Net exports There are four important determinants of our net exports: our own income, foreign income, relative prices, and exchange rates. However, the AE model assumes *constant prices*. Recognizing that the exchange rate is a price—the price of foreign exchange—and that foreign incomes are exogenous, we are left with one variable: our own income. The higher is domestic income,

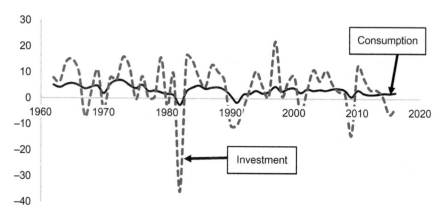

Figure 6.5 Annual fluctuations in consumption and investment spending in Canada, 1965–2016

the greater is the demand for imports, and hence the smaller is net exports. Thus, we can express the net export function as a linear relationship with an intercept, $\overline{X}$, and a negative slope, "*m*."

$$X - IM = \overline{X} - mY$$

1.6 The multiplier effect in a simplified model

The simplest possible model assumes no taxation, and assumes both planned investment and net exports (*NX*) are exogenous. In this case, the model boils down to three equations:

$$Y = AE \text{ in equilibrium}$$

$$AE = C + \overline{I} + \overline{G} + \overline{NX}$$

$$C = A + mpc\,Y$$

Substituting everything into the equilibrium condition yields:

$$Y = A + mpc\,Y + \overline{I} + \overline{G} + \overline{NX}$$

Bringing the *Y* terms over to the left-hand side, we have:

$$Y(1 - mpc) = A + \overline{I} + \overline{G} + \overline{NX}$$

Finally, dividing both sides by (1 − *mpc*), the solution for the equilibrium value of *Y* is:

$$Y = \frac{1}{(1-mpc)} \left[A + \overline{I} + \overline{G} + \overline{NX} \right] \qquad (6.8)$$

We learn a great deal from equation (6.8). First, since all the spending categories are summed on the right-hand side, we know that each dollar of autonomous spending—whether it be from investment spending, government spending, net exports, or autonomous consumption—has the same impact on output. Regardless of where the dollar of autonomous spending comes from, every dollar has the same impact on output.

Second, every dollar of spending has a multiplied effect on output. To determine the effect on output, every dollar of spending is multiplied by the ratio: $1/(1-mpc)$. Since mpc is a fraction, $(1-mpc)$ is also a fraction, and hence the ratio $[1/(1-mpc)]$ must be a number greater than one.

For example, suppose mpc were 0.8 (implying we spend 80 percent of any increase in income we receive). Then the ratio $1/(1-mpc)$ would be equal to 5. That is to say, any increase in exogenous spending, no matter where it originates, would have a fivefold effect on output.

Suppose there is an increase in government spending, $\overline{G}$. With every other component of spending constant, the effect on output would be: $\Delta Y = [1/(1 - mpc)] \times \Delta\overline{G}$. We can state this as the effect on output per dollar of government spending:

$$\frac{\Delta Y}{\Delta\overline{G}} = \frac{1}{(1-mpc)}$$

Or, suppose there is an increase in investment spending, $\overline{I}$. With every other component of spending constant, the effect on output would be: $\Delta Y = [1/(1 - mpc)] \times \Delta\overline{I}$. Stating this as the effect on output per dollar of investment spending:

$$\frac{\Delta Y}{\Delta\overline{I}} = \frac{1}{(1-mpc)}$$

Since every dollar of spending has the same multiplier effect, we can simply write down the multiplier (in this simplified model) on its own:

$$\text{The Simple Multiplier} = \frac{1}{(1-mpc)}$$

What is the intuition for the existence of the multiplier? Suppose investment increases by 100. Initially, this increases output and incomes by 100. But if the marginal propensity to consume is 0.8, the extra income of 100 leads to a second round increase in consumption of 80, and this further increases output and

Table 6.1 The multiplier and induced increases in consumption

	Increase in real GDP	Total effect on real GDP
First round	100	100
Second round	80	180
Third round	64	244
Fourth round	51.2	295.2
Fifth round	40.96	336.16
...		
Final round	$\rightarrow 0$	500

incomes by 80. Since incomes have again increased by 80, there will be a third round induced increase in consumption of 0.8 × 80 = 64. Clearly, this is not the end of the matter. Table 6.1 takes the process further into the fifth round and beyond.

While Table 6.1 only goes as far as the fifth round, it is clear that subsequent increases in consumption are getting smaller and the process will converge. Indeed, we know that the total increase in Y will be 500 from the multiplier formula, assuming *mpc* is 0.8.

It is important to note that the multiplier formula is model specific: the formula depends on the assumptions we make and we have simplified a great deal. In particular, we have assumed that *all prices* are constant, including the price of goods, the price of labor (the wage rate), the price of money (the interest rate), and the price of foreign exchange (the exchange rate). In developing our simple model, we also simplified by assuming no taxes, and no marginal propensity to import. Allowing for taxes and a positive marginal propensity to import would reduce the multiplier, since less of any increase in income is spent on domestic goods: some income would be diverted to the government (in taxation revenue) and some to foreigners (when we buy imported goods).

Next we develop the AD–AS model that allows prices to be *endogenously* determined by the model. We begin by developing AD.

1.7 Aggregate demand

The AD curve is a downward sloping line in price-output space. It looks just like a regular "micro" demand curve, but it is not. A regular micro demand curve slopes down for two reasons. First, a lower price level makes the good cheaper relative to other goods, and therefore people buy more of it. This cannot be the case for an AD curve because it describes the demand for aggregate output. Second, a lower price level has a small positive income effect, allowing people to buy more goods. Again, this cannot be the case for the AD curve because we are not holding constant the dollar value of national income as the price level changes. So, why does it slope down?

AD is derived by noting how the position of the AE line shifts in response to price changes. It shifts because a lower price level increases desired consumption, desired investment, and net exports, which shifts the AE line up. We'll discuss each effect in turn.

The price level and consumption: the wealth effect We are confident that as households' wealth increases, their consumption will increase at every level of income. There are all kinds of empirical evidence supporting this effect. However, besides the relationship between wealth and consumption, *we need an additional relationship*: an inverse relationship between the aggregate price level (P) and the real value of wealth (W). Why should the real value of wealth change when the price level changes? Most components of wealth—real estate (houses), art, stores of precious metals, productive machinery, infrastructure, and so on—would change in price along with the aggregate price index. If so, *the real value* of these items wouldn't change. Therefore, we need to find an asset *with a fixed nominal value, so its real value will increase when aggregate prices fall.*

There is one such asset: money. Money has a fixed nominal value, so the *real value of money rises as the price level falls*. For example, suppose you have $4,000 in a bank account. If the price level falls by 25 percent, that $4,000 can buy as much as $5,000 would have bought previously. With that gain in wealth, you increase consumption.

How big is this effect? Let's take the Canadian economy as an example. In 2018, Canadians held about $1,600 billion worth of deposits and currency.[4] Each 1 percent fall in prices adds about $16 billion to wealth, worth about nearly 1 percent of GDP. So, it is not negligible.

The price level and investment: the interest rate effect We have mentioned that the price of money is the interest rate. Logically, if the interest rate is set by the demand and supply of money, an excess supply of money would normally cause the interest rate to fall. We will develop this model more fully in Chapter 9, but at the moment, we just need the basic idea. Further, we have just established that a fall in the price level increases the real value of money—in other words it increases the real money supply. So, a fall in the aggregate price level creates an excess supply of money, which should cause the interest rate to fall.

How does this occur? In effect, after the fall in prices, people are holding more money balances than they want, given the interest rate. Therefore, they try to decrease their money holdings by buying other financial assets such as bonds. This drives up bond prices and drives down nominal interest rates (interest rates and bond prices move inversely to one another), bringing the money market back into equilibrium.

The fall in interest rates should stimulate spending, in particular, investment spending. Once again, we have a link between a fall in the price level and an upward shift of the AE line, and hence an increase in the equilibrium level of output demanded.

The net export effect A lower price level makes Canadian goods cheaper relative to foreign goods. Therefore, not only will foreigners buy more Canadian goods,

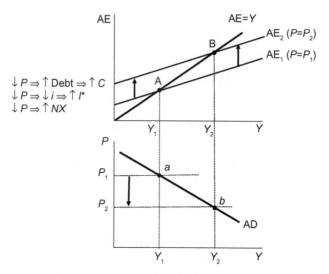

Figure 6.6 Deriving the AD curve: the effect of a decrease in prices

but also Canadians will buy less foreign-made goods. In sum, net exports will increase.

These three effects, and the derivation of the AD curve, are illustrated in Figure 6.6. We begin with the price level at P_1 and output at Y_1, at point "A" in the upper diagram. This combination gives us point "a" on the AD line marked in the lower diagram. Then we postulate that the price level falls to P_2, which shifts up the AE line in the upper diagram, increasing the equilibrium output demanded to Y_2. We move to point "B" in the upper diagram and point "b" in the lower diagram. We complete the derivation of the AD line by joining points "a" and "b."

Having derived the slope of the AD curve, we next consider what could cause the curve to shift *while holding the price level constant*. We will focus on what could shift AD to the right—that is, cause it to increase.

First, long-term expectations might improve. Consumers may become more optimistic about their expected future disposable income, and therefore increase consumption. Or, firms may become more optimistic about expected future sales, and therefore increase investment spending.

Second, the government could increase its spending or decrease taxes.

Third, the central bank could lower interest rates. This could stimulate both consumption and investment spending.

Clearly, the AD line will shift down and to the left if we put the underlying causes into reverse. That is to say, if expectations become more pessimistic, if the government decreases spending or increases taxes, or if the central bank increases interest rates, the AE line will shift down for any given price level, causing the AD line to shift down and to the left.

1.8 Short-run aggregate supply

The short-run aggregate supply (SRAS) line tells us how much output will be supplied at any given price assuming constant: wages and other input prices, the capital stock, and the state of technology. Holding those factors constant, there is normally a positive relationship between output supplied and the price level. Why? A higher price level, with given wages and other input costs, leads to higher profits and increased output in the short run.

So, what determines the slope of SRAS?—The slope of underlying marginal cost curves. And what determines that? Fundamentally, the steepness of the underlying marginal cost curves is determined by the extent of diminishing returns.

With so much being assumed constant, is the SRAS a useful construct?— Yes, since we know the capital stock and technology are relatively slow to change. And in practice nominal wages are sticky in the short run. Often there are wage contracts that last several years. Even without contracts, firms are reluctant to reduce wages in bad times since workers resent it. But this reluctance is eroded the greater the length and severity of the downturn. Similarly, firms are reluctant to increase wages in good times for fear of encouraging further wage increases. So nominal wages are "sticky"—slow to fall and slow to rise.

A leftward (or upward) shift in SRAS can be caused by increased wages, or increased commodity prices (raw materials, or oil prices), or by decreased productivity. They lower profits and reduce short-run output. Alternatively, a rightward (or downward) shift in SRAS is caused by decreases in nominal wages, decreases in commodity prices, or increases in productivity. They increase producers' profits and shift the SRAS down and to the right. Figure 6.7 illustrates an increase in SRAS.

1.9 Long-run aggregate supply

We define the long-run aggregate supply (LRAS) line as potential output, Y_p. Consider the determinants of potential output, Y_p. The familiar answer is that the most important determinants of Y_p are: the size of the labor force and the human capital embodied in it (its skills and education); and the size of the capital stock and the level of technology embodied in it. It is crucial to note that a change in the aggregate price level does *nothing* to affect Y_p. Therefore, LRAS is a vertical line in P, Y space, situated at Y_p as shown in Figure 6.8.

We define the "long run" as a period long enough that all prices (including wages) are fully flexible. As explained in the next section, long-run equilibrium occurs on the LRAS at Y_p, at a point where AD and SRAS intersect. Two such points are shown in Figure 6.8. If the SRAS were $SRAS_1$ and AD were AD_1, then the economy would be in long-run equilibrium at E_1. Alternatively, if the SRAS were $SRAS_2$ and AD were AD_2, then the economy would be in long-run equilibrium at E_3.

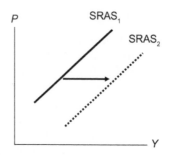

Figure 6.7 An increase in SRAS

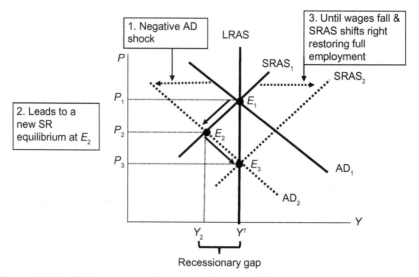

Figure 6.8 Equilibrium and stability in the AD–AS model

1.10 Equilibrium and stability in the AD–AS model

Suppose the economy is initially in long-run equilibrium at E_1 in Figure 6.8. Now suppose there is a negative AD shock. Perhaps there is a stock market collapse, causing a decrease in wealth that will decrease consumption. Or perhaps there is bad political news—turmoil in the Middle East—that adversely affects long-term expectations and causing a decrease in investment spending.

While many events can cause a negative AD shock, the impacts on the economy are the same. The AD line shifts from AD_1 to AD_2, leading to an excess supply of goods at the initial price level, P_1. This causes prices to fall, and as they fall, the economy moves down the initial SRAS line, $SRAS_1$. The new short-run equilibrium is at E_2, where the new lower AD line, AD_2, intersects the original SRAS line, $SRAS_1$. Since wages are sticky and slow to change, output comes to rest at Y_2 and the economy suffers a recessionary gap.

In response to the recession, the government has two options: it could expand AD through fiscal and/or monetary policy moving the economy up $SRAS_1$ and back to the original LR equilibrium, E_1. Or, the government could decide to take no action and wait for the economy to fix itself. The latter option relies on the automatic adjustment properties of the economy. In particular, when the economy is in a slump, jobs will be scarce and workers seeking jobs will be plentiful, and the bargaining power of unions will be weak. As a result, wages will gradually fall, and as they do, the SRAS will shift down and to the right, moving the short-run equilibrium position from E_2 to E_3. The process stops when output is back to Y^f.

Evaluating the options Which of the two options is better? Should the government actively expand AD or passively allow the economy to self-correct? The answer depends on the depth of the recession and its expected duration. If the recession is minor and expected to be short-lived, governments may prefer to do nothing. Perhaps AD will bounce back on its own. On the other hand, if the recession is deep and expected to be long-lived, governments may prefer to actively offset it.

There are two key points from this analysis. *First, in the long run, the economy is self-correcting. Second, Keynesians believe the self-correcting process is slow.*[5]

1.11 Supply shocks pose a policy dilemma

In the short run, there are two policy objectives: output stability and price stability, where price stability means stable prices (or low inflation). When the shock comes from the demand side, there is no conflict between these objectives. If the government acts to stabilize output, it also stabilizes prices. But this is not the case for supply shocks.

Figure 6.9 depicts an original long-run equilibrium at E_1. We then suppose that a negative supply shock occurs—perhaps OPEC decides to reduce the supply of oil, causing oil prices to rise. This shifts the SRAS line up to $SRAS_2$, moving the short-run equilibrium to E_2. While output has *fallen* to Y_2, prices have *risen* to P_2. If the government decides to engage in active policy, it can either try to stabilize prices by reducing AD to AD_3 (which reduces output to Y_3, making the output gap worse!), or it can try to stabilize output by increasing AD to AD_2, which would further increase prices to P_3.

Of course, since the economy is fundamentally stable, the option of doing nothing is always available. Given enough time, the recessionary gap will cause wages to fall, and the SRAS line will shift back to its original position.

1.12 Conclusion

The basis of the AD curve is the AE model. There are three reasons why AE shifts up when prices fall: the wealth effect, the interest rate effect, and the net export effect. These generate the downward slope of the AD line.

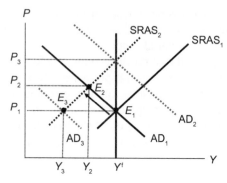

Figure 6.9 Supply shocks pose a policy dilemma

There are two AS curves—the SRAS assumes wages are constant, while the LRAS assumes that all wages and prices are flexible. The LRAS line is vertical and situated at full employment output, Y^f.

In the full AD–AS model, the economy is fundamentally stable. It automatically returns to full employment output, Y^f, given enough time. But mainstream Keynesians believe this process is slow.

The slow speed of adjustment means there is a role for active government policy. The government can speed up the process of recovery from a recession by expanding fiscal policy (increasing spending or reducing taxes) or the central bank can reduce interest rates to stimulate consumption and investment spending.

While the government has the ability to offset demand shocks, supply shocks create a policy dilemma: either stabilize prices or stabilize output. The fundamental cause of recessions is wage stickiness. If wages adjusted more quickly, the process of recovery would be quicker.

2 THE ANTI-TEXT

2.1 Is mainstream macro any different to classical economics?

In Chapter 1 we argued that the persistence of the Great Depression was mostly because of the incorrect and ill-conceived policies followed by governments, policies recommended by the economists of the time—the so-called Classical economists. They thought the economy was inherently self-regulating. If wages were free to adjust, labor markets would clear. For the Classical economists a lack of AD—caused by a glut of savings for example—was not normally a worry because the interest rate could adjust, keeping the supply of loanable funds in balance with the demand. However, they were aware that if there were a crisis of confidence then people might hoard their savings and spending could fall. This partly explains why governments followed policies of "sound finance" to restore confidence, where "sound finance" meant balanced budgets. In the context of the Great

Depression, this meant slashing government spending, which made the Great Depression worse.

In contrast, in the General Theory, Keynes argued that capitalist economies can get stuck in an undesirable equilibrium characterized by high unemployment. There is no automatic adjustment mechanism to restore full employment. Furthermore, any attempt to reduce wages to cure unemployment could make the problem worse, not better. Keynes believed the source of the problem to be insufficient spending, particularly investment spending (since this is the most volatile component). Therefore, he recommended that governments increase their spending to restore full employment. Governments should focus on stabilizing the economy, not balancing their budget. It might be helpful to put Keynes's essential message in point form.

• Capitalist economies have no automatic adjustment mechanism that restores full employment.
• Attempts to reduce wages to cure unemployment could make the problem worse.
• The source of the problem is insufficient spending, particularly investment spending.
• Governments must adjust their spending to maintain full employment, not to balance their budget.

Now, where does the mainstream neoclassical model fit in? Is it closer to the old-fashioned Classical model? Or is it closer to Keynes's views?

The mainstream textbooks present two models: the AE model that assumes constant prices and underpins the AD line; and the AD–AS model that is the main neoclassical model. Let us take them in turn.

In the AE model, equilibrium can occur below full employment, and the problem is caused by insufficient spending. Unless something causes spending to increase, the unemployment will persist indefinitely. Since the government spending multiplier is just as powerful as the investment spending multiplier (indeed, they are all equal), the government has the ability to correct the problem by increasing its spending. However, since the AE model assumes constant prices, it is not equipped to analyze the effect of falling wages or prices. And since it is unclear how any deficit would be financed, it is not equipped to analyze whether increasing government debt could be a problem. In brief, there is nothing about the AE model that is contrary to Keynes, and it is certainly closer to Keynes than to the Classical model.

How well does the AD–AS model do? This model says that the economy automatically returns to full employment, and that recessions are temporary. It also says that wage stickiness is the fundamental cause of recessions. Eliminating wage stickiness would improve economic performance. Clearly, this conflicts with Keynes's essential message in several important respects and hardly differs from the Classical model: they both blame unemployment persistence on the failure of wages to fall.[6]

So, where does the mainstream model go wrong? We do not need to reinvent the wheel here. As long ago as 1968, Leijonhufvud published his treatise "*On Keynesian Economics and the Economics of Keynes*" exploring this issue. And there is a whole school of thought, post-Keynesian economics—which we discussed in Section 2.7 of Chapter 1—committed to developing macroeconomic theory true to the vision of Keynes's essential message. So, it is helpful to evaluate this question from a post-Keynesian perspective.

From a post-Keynesian perspective, the big problem with the mainstream model arises when it derives a downwardly sloped AD line from the AE model. In particular, post-Keynesians deny that falling prices will shift the AE line up. And this means that the AD line is unlikely to be downward sloping.

What about the rest of the AD–AS model? Are there any problems arising from the supply side? In fact, post-Keynesians have no problem with the notion of SRAS, though they might prefer it to be flat up to Y_p. And instead of assuming competitive markets lurking in the background, they would prefer to assume oligopolistic markets, where prices are marked up over costs.

Nor do post-Keynesians have a big problem with the notion of potential output, Y_p, though they would prefer to make Y_p path dependent: that is, to introduce *hysteresis*.

As far as the AE model is concerned, post-Keynesians do not like every feature. They would prefer to incorporate distribution effects where consumption depends not just on aggregate disposable income but also on its distribution across households. And they would prefer to acknowledge that in reality, most savings come from profit recipients—not the average household. But while those aspects can be important in certain circumstances, mostly the AE model works fine.

The key point is that post-Keynesians deny that falling prices will shift the AE line up, implying that the AD line is unlikely to be downward sloping. Let us return to that derivation to see why.

Question for your professor: The Classical model of the 1930s blamed unemployment on failure of wages to adjust. How does the textbook model differ from this? Are we saying deflation is good?

2.2 Probing the slope of the AD line

The mainstream texts emphasize three reasons why the AD line slopes down, three reasons why a decrease in the aggregate price level will increase aggregate spending. We will take each in turn, beginning with the wealth effect.

The wealth effect This focuses on money, since it is the only asset that has a fixed nominal value. The texts imply that this effect could be big. Yet, in all countries, currency in circulation is relatively small. Only by including bank deposits do we get a more significant number. For example, Canadians held about $90 billion in currency in 2018, about 4 percent of nominal GDP, but about $1.6 trillion worth of bank deposits (M2), which is about 75 percent of nominal GDP.[7] So, the key question is: are bank deposits really *net* assets?

To introduce this topic, first ask yourself, which is safer: "currency" or "bank deposits"?

It is clear that currency is safer. Bank can go broke. So, right away we know there is a big difference between currency and bank deposits.

In monetary economics, currency is referred to as *"outside money."* It is a liability of no-one else.[8] Therefore, it is a *net* asset. Bank deposits are referred to as *"inside money"* because the deposits are a liability for the banks. This liability is offset by bank assets, which are loans, and these loans are liabilities of households. The way in which bank-created money cancels out with bank-created liabilities is illustrated in Table 6.2.

Table 6.2 Inside money is not a *net* asset

Banks		Households	
Assets	Liabilities	Assets	Liabilities
Loans to households	Deposits of households	Bank deposits	Bank loans

Table 6.2 contains simplified "T-accounts" for banks and households. (For the purposes of this discussion, we use the term "households" to include both households and firms.) Each "T-account" shows assets on the left and liabilities on the right, and these must be equal (otherwise someone is going to jail!). Bank deposits are a liability of the banking sector because they are owned by households, and banks are obliged to give this money back on demand. This liability is offset by the assets that banks own. Their assets are primarily the loans they have made. Banks are in the loan business. They give out car loans and mortgages, and since this money must be paid back to banks with interest, these loans constitute bank assets.

On the other hand, from the point of view of households the bank loans are their liabilities. Households must pay those loans back. And clearly, the money that households have in their bank accounts constitutes household assets. Considering Table 6.2 as a whole, it is clear that *the assets of banks are the liabilities of households, and the liabilities of banks are the assets of households.* They cancel each other out.

When prices fall, those to whom the banks owe money (owners of bank deposits) are made better off in real terms. On the other hand, those who owe money to the banks (the recipients of bank loans) are made worse off in real terms. These two effects cancel each other out, and *net* wealth does not increase. There is no net wealth effect from inside money.

There is, however, a *redistribution effect*. The price fall redistributes wealth from debtors to creditors via the intermediary of the banks. Some households will have more bank deposits than bank loans, and these net creditors will be made better off. Other households will have more bank loans than bank deposits, and these net debtors will be made worse off.

A key question now arises: can we expect there to be different wealth effects for debtors versus creditors? It seems reasonable to suppose that they would behave differently. Debtors may have a higher propensity to consume than creditors. If so, this redistribution of wealth will lower overall consumption.

Moreover, debtors may be made so worse off by the increase in the real value of their debts that they may be driven into bankruptcy. If they cannot pay back their loans, both creditor and debtor are worse off! When debtors default, some inside wealth is destroyed. This too reduces consumption. The effect of prices on wealth and its impact on consumption are summarized in Table 6.3.

Table 6.3 Deflation and the wealth effect

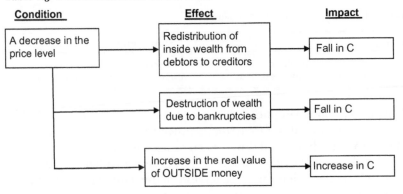

Table 6.3 shows that the two biggest effects of a price decrease—the redistribution of inside wealth and the destruction of wealth due to bankruptcies—operate to reduce consumption. Only the third effect, the effect of a price decrease on outside money, operates to increase consumption. This last effect is likely very small, as even very quick "back-of-the-envelope" calculations show. For example, in Canada in 2018, currency was about 5 percent of total money assets (as measured by M2). Each 1 percent fall in prices would add less than $1 billion to wealth (0.01 × $90 billion = $0.9 billion), which amounts to about 4/100 of a percentage point of GDP. The effect is miniscule.

The interest rate effect Since this effect operates rather circuitously, let us begin by reviewing the causal links, shown in symbolic form where the symbol "⇒" should be read as "implies" and represents a causal link. Clearly the "implies" symbol appears four times, indicating four causal links. If any one of the four breaks down, the interest rate effect will not work. What could possibly go wrong?

$$\downarrow P \Rightarrow \uparrow(M/P) \Rightarrow \downarrow i \Rightarrow \downarrow r \Rightarrow \uparrow I$$

The first causal link is between a fall in the price level and an increase in the real money supply $[\downarrow P \Rightarrow \uparrow(M/P)]$. This link would be unassailable if we treated the nominal money supply, M, as fixed. But as we have seen in the previous section, the banking sector is responsible for creating most of the money supply in circulation. And when the price level falls, the real value of household debt (including their bank loans) increases.

If households respond to this increase in debt by withdrawing money from their bank deposits to repay debt, the money supply would fall. In addition, in a bad deflation, if the debt effect drives households into bankruptcy, banks themselves could fail, again causing M to fall.

The second causal link is between an increase in the real money supply and a decrease in nominal interest rates $[\uparrow(M/P) \Rightarrow \downarrow i]$. The argument is that the increase in the real money supply creates an excess supply of money. Therefore, households reallocate their assets. They try to decrease their money holdings by buying other financial assets such as bonds. This drives up bond prices and drives down nominal interest rates.

Now, if there is a lower limit to nominal interest rates, and interest rates are already hitting this floor, this will not work. One lower limit is zero.[9] It does not make sense for banks to pay households to borrow money from them! And since there must be a margin between the interest banks pay on savings deposits, and the interest they charge on loans, the lower limit must be some level above zero (rather than zero itself).

The third causal link is between a decrease in the nominal interest rate and a decrease in the real interest rate $[\downarrow i \Rightarrow \downarrow r]$. According to the Fisher Effect (see Section 1.10, Chapter 5) the difference between the two interest rates involves the expected rate of inflation. The real rate equals the nominal interest rate minus the expected rate of inflation.

$$r = i - \pi^e \quad [\text{Real interest rate = nominal rate – expected inflation}]$$

The problem with the third link is now apparent. A fall in prices might lead to a decrease in expected inflation. If both "i" and "π^e" are falling, the effect on "r" is unclear.

Before moving onto the fourth causal link, it is worth mentioning a more direct way in which the first three causal links may fail. Those first three links provide an argument that a decrease in the price level will cause a reduction in the real rate of interest. We have invoked (1) reduced deposits to repay loans, (2) possible bank failures, (3) lower limits to nominal interest rates, and (4) offsetting decreases in expected inflation. These effects broke the link between a fall in P and the fall in r. But there is a more direct route.

Suppose the central bank successfully targets inflation, such that expected inflation, π^e, is constant. Further suppose that the nominal interest rate, i, is at the lower bound. In this case, i cannot fall any more, and r cannot fall anymore. The link between a decrease in "P" and a decrease in "r" is broken.

The fourth causal link—between a decrease in the real interest rate and an increase in investment spending ($\downarrow r \Rightarrow \uparrow I$)—is perhaps the weakest of them all. Think about a firm making investment decisions in the midst of a deep recession. In that context, firms will have a lot of idle (or underutilized) capital equipment and laid off workers. *Why would they build new capacity when they already have too much?* Furthermore, in a bad recession, expectations have likely turned pessimistic since prospects for future sales will seem dim. Again, *why would firms build new capacity to make products they will not be able to sell, just because the interest cost of borrowing is a little lower?* Idle equipment, dim prospects for sales, widespread uncertainty all mean that investment will not be interest sensitive. So, the final causal link, at the end of this extremely tenuous linkage, is likely to be the weakest of all.

The net export effect A lower price level makes Canadian goods cheaper relative to foreign goods. Therefore, foreigners will buy more Canadian exports, and Canadians will buy less foreign-made imports. Thus, a fall in the aggregate price level increases net exports, which increases AE. The anti-text has two points here. First, this wouldn't work if foreigners were also experiencing price decreases. Second, foreigners could simply devalue their currency to recover their competitive position.

The point here is that the net export effect works at the expense of foreigners: as a result of our deflation, they export less and import more. They are worse off. If it works, the domestic economy has "exported" its unemployment. This is a type of "beggar thy neighbor" policy. It ignores a key lesson of the 1930s: *lack of world demand cannot be fixed by redistributing demand from one country to another.*

In conclusion, the mainstream texts give three reasons for the AD line to be downward sloping. It is this slope that gives rise to the automatic stability properties of the neoclassical model. It implies that falling wages shift the SRAS curve down and along the AD line, and increase output. It implies that the fundamental cause of recessions is wage stickiness. Yet, this crucial component of the model is as fragile as thin soaking-wet paper.

```
Question for your professor: In a recession, firms
have idle equipment and poor sales outlook. Would
a fall in the real cost of borrowing really induce
them to build more capacity in those circumstances?
```

2.3 An upward sloping AD line and the self-correcting economy

Falling prices (or deflation) have many complex ramifications throughout the economy. As discussed in the previous section:

- The wealth effect may reduce consumption by redistributing wealth from debtors (90 percent of population) to creditors (the rich). If creditors have a lower marginal propensity to consume than debtors, spending will fall. It may also destroy wealth through bankruptcies, which will further reduce spending.
- The interest rate effect may not work for many reasons. It may fail to increase the money supply; it may fail to reduce real interest rates; and it may fail to increase investment even if real interest rates are reduced.
- Finally, the net export effect may invoke retaliatory measures from our trading partners, leading to a dislocation of trade.

Given the overwhelming importance of inside money and household debt, we should consider the possibility that a falling price level could shift the AE line down. As shown in Figure 6.10, this implies an upward sloping AD line!

In Figure 6.10, we begin with a price level of P_1 and output at Y_1. The combination gives us point "A" in the upper diagram, and one point on the AD line labeled "a." Then consider the effect of a fall in the price level to P_2. If debt effects dominate, consumption falls and the AE line shifts down, giving us a new equilibrium at Y_2. The combination of P_2 and Y_2 gives us point "b" in the lower diagram, and another point on the AD line. Joining points "a" and "b" gives us an upward sloping AD line.[10]

The negative consequences of a rising debt burden were first analyzed by Irving Fisher (1933) during the deflation of the Great Depression. He was struck by the devastation—loan defaults, bankruptcies, property seizures—caused by rising real debt. These consequences were felt by households, corporations, and farmers. As a result of his writing, this effect is now generally referred to as "*the Fisher debt-effect.*"

It is instructive to consider the effect of a negative demand shock in the context of an upward sloping AD line. Before we do so, we must be confident of how an upward sloping AD line would shift when AE falls. We do not need a new diagram for this exercise. Figure 6.10 will do nicely. We need to imagine that prices are constant, and an exogenous fall in investment spending (say) causes the AE line to shift down from AE_1 to AE_2. Clearly, output will fall from Y_1 to Y_2. Since prices are fixed (by assumption) at P_1, the new AD line must pass through point "F" in the lower diagram. In other words, no matter the slope of the AD, a decrease in spending will shift the line to the left.

Now consider Figure 6.11, which shows the effect of a negative AD shock in the context of the full AD–AS model when the AD line is upward sloping. We begin in full equilibrium at E_1 when a negative AD shock occurs, moving the AD line to the left. The new short-run equilibrium occurs at E_2 (where

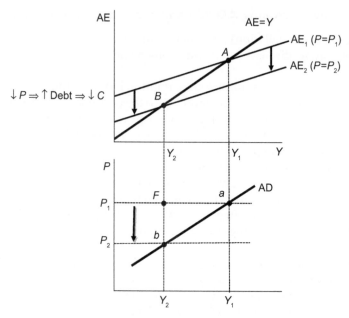

Figure 6.10 The AD line when debt dominates

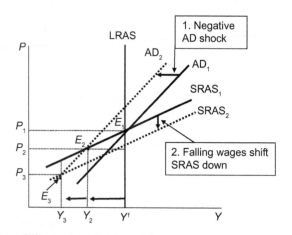

Figure 6.11 Instability in the AD–AS model

AD$_2$ and SRAS$_1$ intersect). The negative AD shock causes output to fall to Y$_2$. If the government does nothing, the recessionary gap will lead to lower wages, causing the SRAS line to shift down.

Now here is the key point: *as wages (and prices) fall, the economy moves even deeper into recession.* The upward sloping AD line has broken the economy's self-correcting mechanism. Government intervention is necessary to prevent it slipping ever deeper into recession.

Incorporating a Fisher debt-effect, and making the AD line upward sloping, is a simple way to make the AD–AS model consistent with Keynes's own views. Indeed, in the context of this model we can clearly see why *Keynes recommended wage rigidity as a policy prescription*. Consider the following quote from the General Theory (1936, chapter 19, section III):

> I am now of the opinion that the maintenance of a stable general level of money-wages is, on a balance of considerations, the most advisable policy for a closed system; whilst the same conclusion will hold good for an open system, provided that equilibrium with the rest of the world can be secured by means of fluctuating exchanges. There are advantages in some degree of flexibility in the wages of particular industries ... But the money-wage level as a whole should be maintained as stable as possible, at any rate in the short period.

The above quote shows quite clearly that Keynes favored stable money wages *as a policy prescription*. That is to say, the economy performs better with stable money wages. This idea is incomprehensible in the mainstream AD–AS model where unemployment exists only because money wages are sticky, and flexibility in the money wage restores unemployment.

```
Question for your professor: Sometimes the text
recognizes that deflation is something to be
avoided. But when discussing the self-corrective
properties of the AD-AS model, it treats deflation
as a good thing. How do we reconcile this conflicting
treatment?
```

2.4 Corridors of stability

While the upward sloping AD line provides an interesting variant of the AD–AS model, its instability is a mixed blessing. On the plus side, it explains why government intervention is necessary in the context of a very bad recession, and it explains why Keynes viewed wage stability as desirable. On the negative side, it is hard to believe that modern capitalist economies are *always* unstable. In fact, for the most part they seem able to weather minor shocks fairly well. It is just the occasional major shock that can push them off-balance and into an ever-descending spiral.

This observation led Leijonhufvud (1973a) to propose the idea of "corridors of stability." Inside this corridor, when output is near enough to full employment output, the economic system can easily handle small shocks. But if there is a big shock, which pushes the economy outside the stable corridor, then an ever-worsening contraction could occur. Combining local stability and global instability allows us to explain both the general robustness of the system most of the time (to small shocks) and its occasional peculiar vulnerability to severe recession (when there are large shocks).

The corridor exists (according to Leijonhufvud) because the economy possesses various dampeners or buffers. For example, if a negative AD shock is small and expected to be temporary, firms may not cut back production and lay off workers. They may be afraid of losing their experienced workforce. They may be content to allow output to accumulate as unsold inventories—for a time. Furthermore, if workers are laid off, but they expect to be back at work soon, they can borrow or run down their savings so as to maintain their consumption. For these reasons, the multiplier effect of the negative shock is muted.

However, if the shock is beyond a certain size, these cushions are insufficient. And since such large shocks are relatively rare events, economic agents will not have well-developed norms and expectations about what to expect. They are likely to hunker down and prepare for the worst. Firms will curtail production and lay off workers to reduce costs as much as possible; while consumers will decrease their spending to protect their liquid assets. As Leijonhufvud (1973a: 27) put it, "the relation between the magnitude of the shock to which the system is exposed and the size of the 'buffer-stocks'—particularly of liquid assets, and most particularly of money—that transactors maintain is critical to whether effective demand failures of major consequence will emerge or not."

2.5 Conclusion

The mainstream textbooks tell a pretty twisted tale. They begin in the early chapters talking about the Great Depression and the failure of the Classical Economists to properly handle the crisis, with how they incorrectly applied the thinking of Adam Smith and believed that wage and price flexibility would restore market clearing. Then (after some intervening chapters) they present the AD–AS model that embodies exactly the same conclusions: the fundamental cause of unemployment is wage stickiness; if wages were perfectly flexible, output would never diverge from full employment equilibrium; the more wages are flexible, the better.

The source of the inconsistency is the AD curve. To get a negative slope, the AE curve must be shifted *up* by a decrease in the price level. That is to say, deflation increases AE. This chapter has unpacked the logic lying behind this reasoning and suggests that a more interesting and relevant model would be the exact reverse: one where the AE curve would be shifted *down* by a decrease in the price level. This produces a model where the economy is not self-correcting, one where government intervention is required to stabilize the system, and where falling wages makes the problem worse.

Chapter 7

FISCAL POLICY: WHY DEFICITS AND DEBT MIGHT NOT MATTER

A well-timed and well-designed fiscal retrenchment can sometimes be expansionary. In fact, a cursory look at the data [suggests] this has been the case in Austria, Denmark, and Ireland in the 1980s, as well as in Spain, Canada, and Sweden in the 1990s.

Kenneth Rogoff (2019)[1]

What the expansionary austerity types are claiming is that the indirect effect of austerity on confidence will outweigh the large direct depressing effect of cutting government spending now. That's a very tall order.

Paul Krugman (2012)[2]

I THE STANDARD TEXT

1.1 Introduction

The aim *of stabilization policy* is to keep economy as close as possible to full employment, without generating inflation. To do this, the government has two kinds of policy at its disposal: monetary and fiscal. While this chapter focuses on fiscal policy, we also explain the current preference for monetary policy.

Fiscal policy involves the spending and taxation decisions of the government. When discussing short-run macro models in Chapter 6, we emphasized that each dollar of autonomous spending—whether it be government spending, investment spending, or consumption spending—has the same impact on output. And further, each dollar of spending has a multiplied effect on output. In the scaled-down model of Chapter 6, the *simple multiplier* was the inverse of one minus the marginal propensity to consume.

In this chapter, we develop more realistic multiplier formulas allowing for both taxes and imports. Importantly, we show that the tax multiplier (in absolute terms) is smaller than the government spending multiplier. This means that an increase in government spending financed by an equal increase in taxes would still have a positive effect on output. In other words, *the balanced budget multiplier* is greater than zero.

We also show that since real-world tax revenues increase with income, the size of the autonomous spending multiplier is less than the simple multiplier developed in Chapter 6. However, this is not entirely bad news since the dependence of tax revenue on income implies that the government budget automatically moves toward a deficit position in a recession. This gives the economy more stability in the face of autonomous changes in aggregate expenditure (AE). This feature is called as an *automatic stabilizer*.

Next, we move on to consider problems with fiscal policy. First, there are several reasons why the impact of fiscal policy may be much smaller than previously acknowledged. Second, even if fiscal policy has a significant impact on output, there are reasons to believe that the impact may not occur when it is needed. Finally, we consider the long-run relationship between deficits and debt, and the sustainability of government debt.

Before we begin this journey, it is useful to have an idea of the relative size of the government sector across countries. Compared with the situation a century or more ago, governments play a large role in the economy. Two key indicators of the scale of a government's role are its revenues relative to GDP and its expenditures relative to GDP.[3] Figure 7.1 shows both these indicators for the G7 countries in 2017.[4] We see that the United States has the smallest government sector of the G7 countries, and that in 2017 every G7 country except Germany was running a deficit.

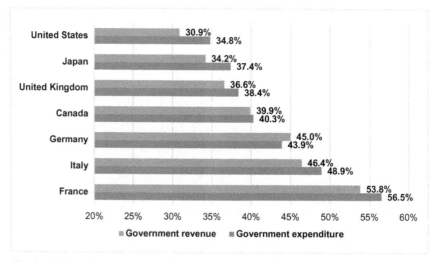

Figure 7.1 Government revenues and expenditures as a proportion of GDP, 2017

The data in Figure 7.1 are for all levels of government combined—the aggregate government sector. In a federal state such as Canada, this includes municipal, provincial, and federal governments. On what does a typical government spend? In developed countries with public health care the four big items are health, education, social services (transfer payments), and protection of persons and property (police, prisons, and the justice system). These four items can easily comprise over 80 percent of program spending (total spending ignoring debt service charges).

1.2 Income-expenditure multipliers allowing for taxes and imports

While we defined expressions for both net tax revenue and net exports in Chapter 6, we assumed those items away when we derived the model solution and the multipliers. Now it is time to incorporate those expressions into the model.

To recap, the net tax function has an intercept, $\bar{T}$, and a slope, t, and is written as: $T = \bar{T} + tY$. Clearly, the slope is positive since tax revenues rise with income. With regard to net exports, we continue to assume that exports are exogenous and equal to $\bar{X}$, but imports increase with income according to mY. Accordingly, the net export function is $X - IM = \bar{X} - mY$.

We develop the model in small steps, beginning with the new consumption function. Consumption is assumed to be a linear function of disposable income, YD, which is income minus net taxes, T. Net taxes (or taxes net of government transfers) are a function of gross income. Thus, the three equations for the consumption function are:

$C = A + mpc\,YD$ Consumption as a function of disposable income
$YD = Y - T$ Definition of disposable income
$T = \bar{T} + tY$ Expression for net taxes

These equations fit together like Russian dolls. We can substitute the third equation into the second, and then the second into the first to get:

$$C = A + mpc\ (Y - \bar{T} - tY)$$

Grouping the Y terms gives us the new consumption function, an equation we will dignify by calling it equation (7.1):

$$C = A - mpc\,\bar{T} + mpc(1-t)Y \tag{7.1}$$

Next, we derive the expression for AE, continuing to assume that investment and government spending are exogenous. The three equations involved are:

$$AE = C + \bar{I} + \bar{G} + X - IM$$

$$C = A - mpc\bar{T} + mpc\ (1-t)Y$$

$$X - IM = \bar{X} - mY$$

Substituting the expressions for consumption and net exports into AE yields:

$$AE = [A - mpc\bar{T} + mpc\ (1-t)\ Y] + \bar{I} + \bar{G} + [\bar{X} - mY]$$

Grouping the autonomous expenditure terms in one bracket, and the "Y" terms in another yields the AE function, equation (7.2):

$$AE = \underbrace{\left[A - mpc\bar{T} + \bar{I} + \bar{G} + \bar{X}\right]}_{\text{Intercept of the AE function}} + \underbrace{\left[mpc(1-t) - m\right]}_{\text{Slope of the AE function}}Y \qquad (7.2)$$

In the simplified model of Chapter 6, the slope of the AE function was simply *mpc* because taxes and imports were assumed away. The modified slope expression in equation (7.2) can be read as the *marginal propensity to consume, out of gross income, on domestic goods*. Since this name is somewhat cumbersome, we will refer to it more simply as the *marginal propensity to spend* and denote it with the symbol *z*.

$$z = mpc\ (1 - t) - m \qquad (7.3)$$

To illustrate, suppose the marginal propensity to consume *out of disposable income, mpc,* is 0.7, but 20 percent of gross income is taken in net taxes. In this case, the marginal propensity to consume *out of gross income* is 0.7 × (1 − 0.2), which equals 0.56. Since we are interested in the marginal propensity to spend on domestic goods, we need to subtract the consumption of imported goods. If the marginal propensity to import is 0.15, then the marginal propensity to spend, *z*, will be 0.56 − 0.15 = 0.41.

As we will see, the smaller is the value of *z*, the smaller the autonomous spending multipliers. To solve the model we need to use the equilibrium condition, which is:

$$Y = AE \text{ in equilibrium} \qquad (7.4)$$

Substituting the expression for AE into the equilibrium condition, we get:

$$Y = [A - mpc\bar{T} + \bar{I} + \bar{G} + \bar{X}] + zY$$

Bringing the Y terms over to the left-hand side, we have:

$$Y(1-z) = [A - mpc\bar{T} + \bar{I} + \bar{G} + \bar{X}]$$

Finally, dividing both sides by (1 – z), the solution for the equilibrium value of Y is:

$$Y = \left[A - mpc\ \bar{T} + \bar{I} + \bar{G} + \bar{X} \right] / \left(1 - z\right) \qquad (7.5)$$

All but one element in the numerator of equation (7.5) has an implied coefficient of unity. That is true for A, $\bar{I}$, $\bar{G}$, and $\bar{X}$. But the coefficient in front of $\bar{T}$ is different. Besides being negative, it is equal to the *mpc*, which is less than one. Consider a change in $\bar{T}$ *holding all other elements constant*. Clearly, the change in $\bar{T}$ will affect "Y," but since we are assuming that all other elements are constant, the change in Y must be purely because of the change in $\bar{T}$. That is,

$$\Delta Y = -mpc\ \Delta \bar{T} / \left(1 - z\right)$$

Or, expressing this as the effect on output *per dollar* change in $\bar{T}$, we can write,

$$\frac{\Delta Y}{\Delta \bar{T}} = \frac{-mpc}{\left(1 - z\right)} \qquad (7.6)$$

All the other multipliers are identical with each other and are stated below:

$$\frac{\Delta Y}{\Delta \bar{G}} = \frac{\Delta Y}{\Delta \bar{I}} = \frac{\Delta Y}{\Delta \bar{X}} = \frac{\Delta Y}{\Delta A} = \frac{1}{\left(1 - z\right)} \qquad (7.7)$$

So, it is still true that each dollar of autonomous spending—whether it be from government spending, investment spending, net exports, or autonomous consumption—has the same impact on output. But a change in net taxes has a smaller effect (in absolute terms) than these other multipliers since the numerator of the net tax multiplier (7.6) is *mpc*, which is a fraction, rather than unity. Intuitively, the reason why the tax multiplier is (absolutely) smaller than the autonomous spending multiplier is that a change in taxes operates in an indirect fashion. First, it affects disposable income; then the change in disposable income affects consumption *via the marginal propensity to consume*, the effect of which is then multiplied in the usual way. So, the tax multiplier is the *mpc* multiplied by the autonomous spending multiplier.

The fact that the tax multiplier is smaller than the government spending multiplier implies that a balanced increase in government spending and taxation has a positive effect on output. This means there is no need for the government budget to go into deficit in order to stimulate the economy. This is worth emphasizing given possible concerns about government deficits and debt. A balanced increase in spending and taxation will stimulate the economy, though the multiplier effect will be much smaller than from a spending increase alone. We can show this using the multipliers we have already developed.

Suppose both $\bar{G}$ and $\bar{T}$ increase. The effect on Y will be the sum of the effects. Thus, from equation (7.5) we can write:

$$\Delta Y = \Delta \bar{G} \frac{1}{(1-z)} - \Delta \bar{T} \frac{mpc}{(1-z)}$$

Further suppose that the change in the government budget is balanced, such that $\Delta \bar{G} = \Delta \bar{T}$. In this case, we can call the balanced change in spending ΔB, where $\Delta B = \Delta \bar{G} = \Delta \bar{T}$. Substituting into equation (7.6) we get:

$$\Delta Y = \Delta B \frac{1}{1-z} - \Delta B \frac{mpc}{1-z}$$

Or, expressing the change in output per dollar change in the balanced budget we get:

$$\frac{\Delta Y}{\Delta B} = \frac{1-mpc}{(1-z)} \tag{7.8}$$

Since both *mpc* and *z* are positive fractions, we know that $\Delta Y/\Delta B$ is positive. Using the same illustrative numbers as before, if $z = 0.41$, then the autonomous spending multiplier (which is the inverse of $1 - z$) is about 1.7, and the balanced budget multiplier will be about 0.5 (equal to 0.3×1.7).

1.3 Automatic stabilizers

Many people imagine fiscal policy as always being the product of deliberate decisions. Such fiscal policy is called "discretionary" fiscal policy. For example, if the economy goes into recession and the government responds with a new budget that expands spending and cuts tax rates, the government has engaged in discretionary fiscal policy.

But in most countries, government transfer spending—on things like employment insurance and social assistance—automatically increases during a recession as more people become unemployed. Furthermore, income tax revenues automatically fall when GDP declines because taxable incomes falls. These provisions are known as automatic stabilizers and macroeconomists are generally careful to distinguish these changes from discretionary fiscal policy.

How automatic stabilizers work is illustrated in Figure 7.2. As usual, the symbol "G" denotes government spending on final goods and services, and the symbol "T" denotes net taxes (taxes minus transfers). Since tax revenues go up as output increases, and transfers go down, the slope of the net tax function is shown as quite steep. But since "G" does not include government transfer payments, we have shown the "G" line as unaffected by output.

Figure 7.2 assumes a special situation in which the government budget would be balanced if the economy operated at full employment output, Y^f. In this case, if the economy were to operate below full employment, at Y_1 say, the government would automatically run a budget deficit, and the lower the output level, the larger is the deficit. Since a government deficit is what is needed to help offset the recession, the dependence of net taxes on output creates an automatic stabilizer.

Similarly, if the economy were to operate above full employment, at Y_2 say, there would be an inflationary gap, and the government will automatically run a budget surplus. Since a government surplus helps offset the inflationary gap, automatic stabilizers work in both directions.

What all this implies is that the government budget balance may change considerably over the course of the business cycle even without any explicit decisions by the government to change taxes or spending. It also complicates efforts to analyze both the stance of the government budget and the sustainability of government spending. Therefore, analysts undertaking these tasks use the cyclically adjusted budget, which is explained next.

1.4 The cyclically adjusted budget

The cyclically adjusted budget is the budget balance that would obtain if the economy were at full employment. In Figure 7.2, the cyclically adjusted budget balance is zero.

Suppose the economy is in recession at Y_1 and unemployment is high. There may be popular pressure for the government to take action, to increase spending, and expand the economy. The government may claim that it is already actively fighting the recession—just look at the deficit! But this claim is false and can be refuted by calculating the cyclically adjusted budget. In this case, it would

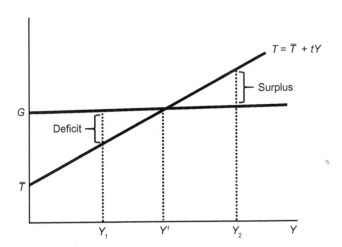

Figure 7.2 Automatic stabilizers

show that the government has done nothing *actively* to fight the recession. It has simply allowed the automatic stabilizers to kick in.

Alternatively, the deficit at Y_1 might worry fiscal conservatives, and they may start lobbying for a cut in government spending. But knowing that the cyclically adjusted budget is balanced demonstrates that there is no crisis of government profligacy or overspending. The fundamental point here is that the government should not be forced to run a balanced budget every year, since it would undermine the role of taxes and transfers as automatic stabilizers.

1.5 Factors that reduce the size of the income-expenditure multiplier

In Chapter 6, we defined the "simple multiplier" as $1/(1-mpc)$. In Section 1.2 of this chapter, we have shown that taxes and imports reduce the size of the income-expenditure multiplier. There are several other reasons to believe that the multiplier will be smaller still. The first revolves around the (implicit) assumption of constant interest rates. The second takes aim at the way we have specified the consumption function.

Allowing variable interest rates Removing the assumption that interest rates are constant opens up several feedback effects that may reduce the income-expenditure multiplier. The basic point is that any output increase, not supported by an increase in the money supply, is likely to increase interest rates, which would decrease investment spending.

Why is an increase in output likely to increase interest rates? The full explanation must wait until Chapter 9. But the simple explanation is that the economy is an engine that requires the grease of money to allow it to run. Money is required to facilitate transactions: the more transactions, the more money is required. As output increases, transactions increase, and the demand for money increases. Individuals therefore try to rebalance their portfolios of financial assets, selling bonds in an effort to obtain more cash. The increased sale of bonds drives down bond prices, which drives up interest rates. (Remember bond prices and interest rates are inversely related.)

In a closed economy, the increased interest rates will decrease investment spending, which reduces the size of the income-expenditure multiplier.

In an open economy, the increased interest rates will attract inflows of foreign financial capital, putting pressure on the exchange rate to appreciate. What happens next depends on whether the exchange rate is fixed or flexible.

- In a flexible exchange rate regime, the exchange rate appreciates, leading to a decrease in exports (since they are now more expensive in foreign currency terms). To the extent to which the inflow of foreign money mitigates the increase in interest rates, it is exports that are crowded out rather than investment.

- In a fixed exchange rate regime, the central bank must prevent the exchange rate from appreciating by buying up the increased inflows of foreign financial capital using domestic currency. And since there is only one place that domestic currency can be spent—in the domestic economy—this leads to an increase in the supply of domestic currency, which helps to stimulate the economy. This is the one case where allowing interest rates to vary may not reduce the size of the income-expenditure multiplier.

In summary, allowing variable interest rates makes fiscal policy less effective when the economy has a floating exchange rate, but may have no effect on the multiplier when the economy has a fixed exchange rate.[5]

The nature of the consumption function and Ricardian equivalence Higher values of *mpc* imply a bigger multiplier; lower values a smaller multiplier. But how small can the *mpc* be? An extreme possibility is the *mpc* could be zero if households base their consumption decisions on their *wealth* and ignore fluctuations in their *current income*.

Most modern theories of consumption put more emphasis on the importance of wealth. For example, the Lifecycle Theory of Consumption proposed by Ando and Modigliani (1963) suggests that people's consumption is determined by their needs at different ages, with their stream of lifetime consumption limited by their *expected* lifetime income. Similarly, Milton Friedman (1957) hypothesized that current consumption is determined by "permanent income"—by which he meant *expected* long-term average income—and that people will want to smooth out consumption over time.

You should notice that these modern theories of consumption put much more importance on expectations. This has several implications. For example, tax increases reduce consumption from the moment they are expected (or announced), not from when they are implemented. More interestingly, if households perceive that an increase in government spending implies future tax increases, households will decrease their consumption. To understand this, we need to delve into a basic accounting truth about bonds.

It is intuitive that the value of a perpetuity (a bond that is never redeemed) equals the discounted stream of interest payments it pays. It follows that if a government were to sell such a bond and then set aside money from the proceeds to cover the future interest payments, it would have to set aside the entire proceeds! The key point is that bond issue does not generate any extra net revenue. It merely redistributes revenues over time. Bonds represent *deferred* taxes.

Therefore, government spending financed by borrowing (issuing bonds) is really financed by future taxes. If this is understood by households, they will adjust down their expected lifetime disposable income, and hence decrease their consumption now. In the extreme case, the decrease in consumption completely offsets the increase in government spending. This possibility is known as *Ricardian equivalence*.

The Ricardian equivalence result requires households to understand fairly sophisticated logic. But even without Ricardian equivalence, both the lifecycle theory and the permanent income theory suggest that a *temporary change in current income* will have only a very small effect on current consumption. There are two reasons for this. First, a temporary change in income will have only a small effect on permanent (or expected lifetime) income. Second, whatever effect it does have will be spread equally over all future periods, making the effect on any one period minimal. This means that a temporary income tax cut, or temporary increase in government spending, would have only a small multiplier effect via consumption.[6]

1.6 Supply-side effects of taxes

More government spending requires more government revenue, and this requires higher taxes. No matter what form the taxes take, they always have adverse supply-side effects. This can offset the demand-side effect of the income-expenditure multiplier.

Income taxes In the labor market, shown in Figure 7.3, the income tax has no effect on the demand for labor, since this depends only on labor productivity and labor cost (which is the real wage rate). But workers look at the after-tax wage when deciding how much to work. Therefore, an income tax shifts the labor supply curve leftward to LS + tax. The vertical distance between the LS curve and the "LS + tax" curve measures the amount of income tax. With the reduced supply of labor, the before-tax wage rises to $25 an hour but the after-tax wage falls to $15 an hour. The gap created between the before-tax and after-tax wage is called the tax wedge. The net result is a reduction in the quantity of labor employed *at full employment*, from L_1^* to L_2^*, which in turn reduces potential GDP. A tax *cut* would have the opposite effect: it would increase the supply of labor, increase equilibrium employment, and increase potential GDP.

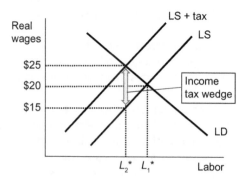

Figure 7.3 The supply-side effects of income taxes

Taxes on consumption Taxes on consumption expenditure add to the tax wedge. By raising the price for consumption goods, they are equivalent to a cut in the real wage rate. This weakens the incentive to supply labor in the same way as income taxes do. If the income tax rate is 30 percent and the consumption tax rate is 10 percent, a dollar earned buys only 60 cents worth of goods and services. Therefore, the total tax wedge is 40 percent.

Empirical estimates The 2004 Nobel Memorial Prize winner in economics, Edward Prescott, has written several papers suggesting that the supply-side effect of taxes is extremely significant. For example, in 2002 he estimated the tax wedges for a number of countries, including the United States and France. He found (for the year 2000) that the total tax wedge (consumption taxes plus income taxes) was 82 percent in France, but only 45 percent in the United States, and that this difference explains why potential GDP in France is 30 percent below that of the United States (per working-age person). This underlines the importance of adverse supply-side effects of taxes.

Macroeconomic impact of tax cuts We use the AD–AS model to illustrate why some economists believe that tax cuts are a superior way to stimulate the economy than increasing government spending. In Figure 7.4, the movement from A to B represents the aggregate demand effects of a tax cut. However, if tax cuts also have significant supply-side effects, then aggregate supply will also shift left, and output will move to point C. Because of this, the tax multiplier stated in equation (7.6) would underestimate the effect of tax cuts on output.

Tax revenues and the Laffer curve Developed by Arthur Laffer, one of President Reagan's economic advisors in the 1980s, the Laffer curve illustrates a theoretical relationship between rates of taxation and government revenue. Clearly, there will be no government revenue at a zero tax rate. As the tax rate increases from zero, revenue will initially increase. But at a 100 percent tax rate, tax revenue must again be zero, since no-one will have any incentive to work. Therefore, there must come a point, labeled T^* in Figure 7.5, at which tax revenues begin to decline.

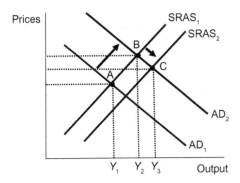

Figure 7.4 The macroeconomic effects of tax cuts

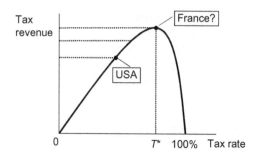

Figure 7.5 A Laffer curve

For supply-siders, the curve illustrates two opposing forces in operation. On the one hand, a higher tax rate brings in more revenue *per dollar earned*, but on the other, it reduces the number of dollars earned. Initially, the first effect dominates, but eventually, the second effect takes over. Parkin (2018: 335) remarks, "Most people think that the United States is on the upward sloping part of the Laffer curve. But France might be close to the maximum point or perhaps even beyond it."

The supply-side debate In the early 1980s, Laffer (and other supply-siders) convinced President Ronald Reagan of the virtues of cutting taxes. They not only argued that tax cuts would increase employment and output, but that it would also increase tax revenues. This latter claim requires that the United States be on the *downward sloping portion* of the Laffer curve—a highly unlikely situation given that tax rates in the United States are among the lowest in the industrialized world. In fact, the result of the Reagan tax cuts was a reduction in tax revenues and a ballooning deficit. This tarnished the reputation of supply-side economics. The standard view of mainstream economists today is to recognize that tax cuts can provide a fiscal stimulus and to emphasize that they provide supply-side incentives, but to admit that they will reduce government revenues.

1.7 Timing problems when using discretionary fiscal policy

Many economists caution that fiscal policy is too slow an instrument to stabilize the economy.

Given the many lags involved with fiscal policy, the time that fiscal policy is needed is rarely the time it has its effect. It is even possible fiscal policy might end up destabilizing the economy.

For example, suppose the economy is hit by a negative demand shock and the economy enters a recession. First, there is a *recognition lag*. The government has to realize that the recessionary gap exists. The data must be collected and analyzed, and recessions are often recognized only months after they have begun. Second, there is a *planning lag*. The government has to develop a spending plan, which can itself take months, particularly if politicians take time debating how the money should be spent and passing legislation. Third, there is *the implementation lag*: it takes time to spend money. By the time all this happens, the need for stimulus may have disappeared. Indeed, the economy may be entering a boom, and the stimulus will be precisely the wrong medicine.

1.8 Long-run issues: deficits and debt

Budget deficits need to be financed. There are only two ways to do this: the government can print money, or it can borrow money. Only in exceptional circumstances do governments print money to pay for their deficits since this can lead to hyperinflation, a topic we consider in a later chapter. Normally, governments finance their deficits by borrowing money, and they do this by issuing bonds. In Chapter 6, we discussed the crowding out problem: in long-run equilibrium, government borrowing absorbs loanable funds that would otherwise go to fund investment. But there is also a debt problem.

The outstanding stock of government bonds represents the government's debt. The usual measure of a government's capacity to carry debt is the debt-to-GDP ratio. As the debt-to-GDP ratio grows, so do the interest payments on the debt. If those interest payments start to absorb an ever-larger proportion of government revenue, the debt burden may become unsustainable.

In a typical scenario of unsustainable government debt, the debt-to-GDP ratio reaches a point where lenders (those who purchase the government's bonds) become worried the government will default on its payments. This higher risk means that lenders will only continue to purchase the debt if it carries a higher interest rate. So, the government must increase the interest rate on its bonds, which forces up interest rates throughout the economy. This not only chokes off economic growth but also increases the amount the government must pay to finance its debt, making matters worse.

Clearly, this is a vicious circle that could push the country into default, or push it to seek assistance from other countries or international institutions. If it takes the latter route, it may be obliged to implement "structural adjustment policies" to reassure international lenders that the government will be able to generate budget surpluses to get its debt under control. It may be forced to decrease government spending and increase taxes to generate a budget surplus, and this may plunge the economy into a deep recession. A recent example is provided by Greece.

Just before the Greek sovereign debt crisis began, in early 2009, Greek interest rates were comparable to German rates. But in October 2009, after its budget deficit was announced at 12.5 percent of GDP, and its debt-to-GDP ratio hit 125 percent, a crisis of confidence erupted. A mere six months later, in late April 2010, interest rates on Greek bonds were 10 percentage points higher than comparable German bonds. In early May 2010, the Greek government announced a bailout package of $143 billion financed by the European Union (EU) and the International Monetary Fund (IMF), and at the same time announced austerity measures.[7]

But these were just the beginning. Between 2010 and 2016, the government enacted eleven more rounds of austerity and was forced to seek three more bailout loans. The consequences for the Greek economy have been devastating, plunging it into a depression as deep as, but longer-lived than, the United States experienced during the Great Depression. Between 2009 and 2013, real GDP per capita in Greece fell by 22 percent, while the unemployment rate increased from 9.6 percent to 27.5 percent. Perhaps the worst aspect of the story is that the fall in GDP was so severe that the debt-to-GDP ratio actually increased from 127 percent in 2009 to 179 percent by 2017.

Clearly, the consequences can be disastrous if the debt-to-GDP ratio gets too high. While this is easy to acknowledge as a general point, it is difficult to know the level beyond which adverse consequences occur. Recently, however, an influential paper by Reinhart and Rogoff (2010) found empirically that a debt-to-GDP ratio over 90 percent is the tipping point. Beyond this level, long-term growth prospects are severely impaired.

But even a lower level of debt, which is *theoretically* sustainable, is still dangerous because it decreases a government's maneuvering room. There is always the possibility that a worldwide recession might occur just as a government is struggling to keep its debt level manageable. If so, the deficit automatically gets worse. The government might succumb to the temptation to restrict fiscal policy, which would worsen the recession. Or, if it does not, the debt levels might grow to unsustainable levels.

1.9 Concluding thoughts: fiscal policy versus monetary policy

The problems associated with fiscal policy (outlined above) help explain why monetary policy is nowadays the preferred stabilization tool.

We have seen that expansionary fiscal policy typically involves running government budget deficits, which adds to the stock of government debt. If the growth of government debt is greater than the growth of GDP, as is likely during a recession, the debt-to-GDP ratio will rise. In contrast, expansionary monetary policy involves cutting interest rates, which reduces the deficit by reducing the debt service burden. Further, if it succeeds in increasing GDP, it also reduces the debt-to-GDP ratio. So, from a debt point of view, monetary policy is preferable.

Monetary policy is also superior from a timing perspective. While both monetary and fiscal policy require the same recognition lag, the planning and implementation lags are shorter with monetary policy. Monetary policy is not subject to the same political wrangling as fiscal policy. Nor does it require implementing specific projects that require planning and environmental approvals, which can sometimes take years to acquire.

There are also other issues. Fiscal policy expansions usually increase interest rates, which may crowd out investment (or exports), whereas monetary expansions decrease interest rates, which "crowds in" investment and will help growth.

All the above, coupled with concerns about the size of the fiscal multiplier, helps explain the current mainstream preference for monetary policy over fiscal policy as the main stabilization tool. Fiscal policy should be assigned the job of keeping the government debt sustainable, not stabilizing the economy. Monetary policy should be assigned the job of stabilizing the economy.

2 THE ANTI-TEXT

Macroeconomic issues are inherently complex, which means that definitively proving anything in the field is inherently difficult.

Kenneth Rogoff (2019)

2.1 Introduction: the lack of a consensus

Normally, mainstream textbooks are so similar they could be clones of one another. But on this topic—fiscal policy—there is a wide diversity of treatment. For example, some textbooks did not mention the supply-side effects of taxes—though most did mention the topic, and some even left the reader with the impression that it contained a profound truth. Others did not mention Ricardian equivalence—though most did, and a few discussed it at length. Some downplayed worries about accumulating government debt, while a few gave the impression it imposed a serious limit on how much debt-financed spending all governments could undertake.

Strangely, they all agreed on one thing, however: not to pass judgment on the usefulness of fiscal policy. Instead, after biasing the discussion one way or another, they all limited themselves to outlining the "issues up for debate."[8] These diverse treatments reflect a lack of consensus in mainstream economics about the usefulness of fiscal policy. The tactic to refrain from reaching a conclusion, but merely to outline the "issues up for debate," seems designed to paper over this division. But the divisions could not be papered over in the aftermath of the Great Financial Meltdown. Pitch battles broke out over the size of the government expenditure multiplier, in particular, whether it was greater than zero.

One would have thought that such a basic question could have been answered by appealing to the empirical evidence. And one would expect to find that empirical evidence quoted in the textbooks. But no such luck. Instead, we find that all the textbooks, without exception, confine themselves to presenting *illustrative numbers*: "reasonable parameter values" are inserted into the multiplier formulas, and the formula is solved to generate the size of the multiplier. But there is no actual empirical evidence for real economies.

To understand why, we need to backtrack to the Great Financial Meltdown and delve into the stimulus debate of 2009.

2.2 The problem of evidence: the stimulus debate of 2009

By early 2009, central banks had flooded the banking system with liquidity, and interest rates were practically zero. That meant central banks were out of conventional ammunition. With the recession continuing to deepen, most industrialized countries engaged in fiscal stimulus. In the United States, President Obama proposed a fiscal stimulus of some $800 billion. This proposal ignited a fierce debate between New Keynesian and New Classical economists.

While New Keynesians worried that $800 billion might be too small—Paul Krugman suggested an amount twice as big—New Classical economists argued that fiscal policy had been debunked, and that neither a balanced budget expansion nor debt-financed government spending would have any effect. For example, Robert Lucas, the winner of the 1995 Nobel Memorial Prize in economics and Professor Emeritus at the University of Chicago, said,

> If the government builds a bridge ... by taking tax money away from somebody else, and using that to pay the bridge builders, then it is just a wash. ... [If] you apply a multiplier to the bridge builders, then you've got to apply the same multiplier with a minus sign to the people you taxed to build the bridge. And then taxing them later isn't going to help, we know that. (Lucas 2009a)

In the quote above, Lucas begins by asserting that the balanced budget multiplier—increased government spending financed by increased taxes—is zero. His last sentence asserts that postponing the tax increase by bond-financed fiscal policy is equally useless.

John Cochrane, senior fellow of the Hoover Institution at Stanford University, focused on bond-financed government spending when he said,[9]

> If money is not going to be printed, it has to come from somewhere. If the government borrows a dollar from you, that is a dollar that you do not spend, or that you do not lend to a company to spend on new investment. Every dollar of increased government spending must correspond to one less dollar of private spending. This is just accounting, and does not need a complex argument about crowding out. (Cochrane 2009)

At the outset, it seems that Lucas and Cochrane have just forgotten their basic economic theory. As we have seen in Section 1.2 of this chapter, taxes have their effect on spending via consumption, whereas government spending has a direct effect on AE. As long as *mpc* is less than one, the balanced budget multiplier will be positive, as equation (7.8) shows. Can it be possible that they made such a basic error?

To understand their thinking, we need to remember that New Classical economists prefer models that embody Ricardian equivalence. These models not only incorporate all accounting identities and budget constraints but also assume rational expectations and perfect access to capital markets. This means households will consider the expected future burden of taxes needed to pay for government spending. Since households attempt to smooth their consumption over time, any increase in government spending would be completely offset by a fall in consumption, regardless of whether it was paid for with higher taxes or more borrowing.

New Keynesians responded with real-world empirical evidence showing the effectiveness of fiscal policy. In a position paper, Christina Romer and Jared Bernstein (2009) gathered multipliers from private forecasting firms, government models, the Federal Reserve, and the broader literature. The multipliers were detailed. They distinguished between direct and indirect fiscal measures, allowed for the openness of the economy and possible effects on interest rates. For the case where the central bank (the Federal Reserve) held its key policy interest rate constant (the federal funds rate), they found that, after eight quarters, the government spending multiplier converged to around 1.6 and the tax multiplier to about 1.

But these numbers were dismissed by the New Classical economists as meaningless, or even pulled from thin air for political purposes.[10] We must remember that modern macro responded to the Lucas critique in the 1970s by putting overriding emphasis on logical consistency over what seems to be empirical success. The force of the Lucas critique meant that gathering empirical evidence from myriad diverse models as Romer and Bernstein had done—none of which was necessarily from an internally consistent model of the sort that New Classical economists favor—could not convince them.

The textbooks, wanting to appeal to both New Keynesian and New Classical professors, do not definitively take sides on the problematic relationship between macroeconomics and empirical evidence. This is the most likely reason why they fail to provide any real-world empirical evidence on the size of the fiscal multipliers.

> Question for your professor: In normal circumstances, what would be the multiplier effect of an increase in government spending? Why doesn't the textbook cite any empirical evidence on this issue?

2.3 The problem of evidence: Ricardian equivalence

How likely is Ricardian equivalence? In 1820, David Ricardo first noted the possibility of what has come to be known as Ricardian equivalence. But ironically, he did not think the proposition had any empirical relevance. Nor should we. Ask yourself, do you study the government's deficit and debt situation to determine your future taxes, and then use that estimate to determine your consumption? Do you know anyone who does? Ricardo himself believed that we are too myopic—or short-sighted—to do so.

But even if we were fully knowledgeable of the economy, and far sighted, and rational (in the way that neoclassical economics defines it), there are still lots of reasons why Ricardian equivalence has no empirical relevance.

First, Ricardian equivalence requires perfect capital markets. Section 2.6 of Chapter 5 discussed many reasons why capital markets are not perfect but are instead characterized by imperfect and asymmetric information. And if households are unable to borrow when their income is low—that is, if they are *liquidity constrained*—then putting more money in their hands *now* (by tax reductions, for example) will affect their consumption behavior *now*. They will not simply save it to pay future taxes.

Second, the "government" has a longer life than does the average person. Economists talk about the government being "infinitely long-lived." Clearly, ordinary mortals are not. It is reasonable, therefore, for people to think that by the time the government is forced to raise taxes to pay for its debt, they will be long gone. To avoid this difference in time horizon, New Classical economists must invoke infinitely long-lived households, filled with people who care as much about their descendants (who may not even exist) as they do about themselves.

Third, there is the question as to whether the government debt *ever* needs to be paid off—a question to which we will return.[11]

Given the fact that the conditions required for Ricardian equivalence are so extraordinarily unrealistic, why do the textbooks not dismiss the possibility? Again, it is because the textbooks want to appeal to both New Keynesian and New Classical professors, and therefore avoid taking a stand on even the most basic issue. They are papering over the cracks in the edifice of mainstream economics.

> Question for your professor: The conditions required for Ricardian equivalence are so unrealistic, I am wondering why textbooks even bother mentioning it. What relevance does it have?

2.4 The problem of evidence: the austerity debate of 2010

Whereas the stimulus debate of 2009 was about whether the government spending multiplier was zero, the austerity debate of 2010 was about whether the government spending multiplier could be *negative*. Again, the debate was *within* mainstream economics.

In early 2009, governments around the world implemented fiscal stimulus packages. By 2010, the worst was seemingly avoided. The postcrisis recession had bottomed out, and a recovery was under way in most countries. But output and employment were still far below normal. It was at this point that many countries reversed their fiscal policy stance and implemented austerity! This had exactly the effect that one would predict: the recovery in those countries was delayed; both the depth and duration of the recession was needlessly increased. Why was it done?

Perhaps the most important reason was the descent of Greece into a full-blown debt crisis in October 2009. No country wanted to be the next Greece—even though, as Figure 7.6 shows, no country was even close to being that.[12] The Greek crisis fed into the political nexus: neoliberals looking for any opportunity to shrink the public sector; politicians seeking ways to win elections; and electorates who resonate with analogies to family finances and "living within one's means." However, it is doubtful the turn to austerity would have happened without two hugely influential pieces of empirical economic research by mainstream Keynesian economists located primarily at Harvard University.

The first piece of research, by Alberto Alesina and Silvia Ardagna (2010), identified all large fiscal policy changes in advanced countries between 1970 and 2007, and found evidence that spending cuts were often associated with economic expansions rather than recessions! They suggested this was because—*when debt levels are high*—spending cuts create "confidence," the positive effects of which outweigh the direct negative effects of reduced spending. In effect, they proposed an "expansionary austerity doctrine"— which is to say, a negative government spending multiplier.

The second piece of research, by Carmen Reinhart and Kenneth Rogoff (2010), claimed to have found an answer to the long-standing question: what level of government debt is too high? Using a dataset that consisted of 3,700 annual observations of 44 countries spanning 200 years, they concluded that a debt-to-GDP ratio over 90 percent severely impaired long-term growth prospects. As Figure 7.6 shows, even though no country was close to being another Greece, many European countries were either beyond, or approaching, the treacherous 90 percent ratio.

Both pieces of research played their part in the turn to austerity that occurred all across the Western world.[13] The example of Greece, and the Reinhart–Rogoff results, helped spread fear about too high a level of debt; the Alesina–Ardagna results soothed that fear with the crazy notion that fiscal austerity would stimulate the economy.

Both results were widely reported in the media, quoted by right-wing politicians, and endorsed by both the European Central Bank and the Bank for International Settlements. For example, on June 24, 2010, Jean-Claude Trichet, then president of the European Central Bank, said, "As regards

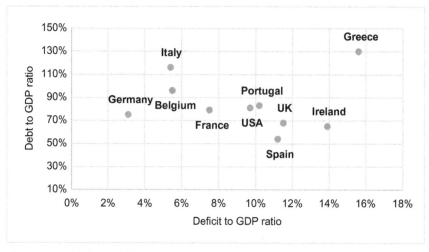

Figure 7.6 Deficits and debt ratios to GDP, 2009

the economy, the idea that austerity measures could trigger stagnation is incorrect. I firmly believe that in the current circumstances, confidence-inspiring policies will foster and not hamper economic recovery, because confidence is the key factor today."[14]

But it did not take long before both papers were thoroughly discredited. It turned out that both papers were riddled with computational errors.

The Alesina–Ardagna paper A review by the IMF in October 2010 found the methods used to identify periods of sharp austerity produced many misidentifications.[15] Correcting these mistakes reversed the results: *contractionary policy in fact led to contractions.* However, this 2010 IMF analysis itself substantially underestimated the size of the contraction that would occur if austerity took place when (1) there was an economic slump, and (2) interest rates were up against the zero lower bound. (Of course, these were the exact conditions that prevailed in 2010.) In October 2012, the IMF's chief economist, Olivier Blanchard, apologized on behalf of the IMF and admitted that the earlier analysis had substantially understated the damage of austerity in the context of a weak economy: the true effect was nearly three times larger than they expected.[16]

Canada illustrates how the contractionary effect of austerity can be avoided if it occurs at the right time. In the 1990s, Canada massively reduced government spending, but this was offset by interest rate cuts of 10 percentage points between 1990 and 1998. This led to a 35 percent devaluation of the Canadian dollar, which caused an export boom. The Canadian economy had healthy growth during the 1990s because monetary stimulus and the export boom more than offset fiscal austerity.

The Reinhart–Rogoff paper Many computational errors were discovered after they shared their data and spreadsheets with Thomas Herndon (see

Herndon et al. (2013)), a graduate student at the University of Massachusetts, Amherst. First, Reinhart-Rogoff omitted relevant data for five countries by accident. Second, they weighted each "episode" of high debt the same, whether it occurred during one year of bad growth or seventeen years of good growth.[17] Finally, their dataset failed to include the experience of several nations—Canada, New Zealand, and Australia—that emerged from the Second World War with high debt but nonetheless posted solid growth. Correcting these errors caused the 90 percent debt cliff to vanish.

According to Krugman (2015), the "austerian" ideology that dominated elite discourse in 2010 had collapsed by 2013. He says, "It is rare, in the history of economic thought, for debates to get resolved this decisively." If only this were true. Unfortunately, it is not—because of four reasons.

First, even though the IMF no longer supports austerity, many other international financial institutions—such as the Bank for International Settlements—continue to do so.[18] Second, the original researchers continue to defend their results. Most notably, Reinhart (2013) defends a slightly modified Reinhart-Rogoff debt cliff result, while Alesina has a 2019 book—described by Rogoff (2019) as a "towering scholarly achievement"—defending the expansionary austerity view.[19] Third, even though many European nations abandoned austerity in 2013, Ortiz and Cummins (2019) document how austerity measures are still central to the "prevailing policy playbook" and have become the "new normal" around the world.

Fourth, expansionary austerity will always be an empirical possibility that can never be definitively defeated. If it has not yet occurred, it is always possible that one day it might. Its possibility stems from the mainstream belief that too much government debt can lead to a crisis, which would necessarily weaken "confidence" and investment. It is this belief that needs to be softened or deconstructed, in order to undermine the austerity argument. As we will see, the case against ongoing government deficits is actually quite weak. Mainstream textbooks are exaggerating the problem.

> Question for your professor: When government debt is in some sense too high, is it possible the government spending multiplier could be negative? Do you know of any situation where "expansionary austerity" has occurred?

2.5 The effects of austerity on output and debt

Just as in the Great Depression, fiscal consolidation in the middle of a downturn worsened the crisis. By 2014, most European countries—Ireland, Italy, the Netherlands, Portugal, and Spain—had abandoned austerity. Only two European countries continued the bleeding: Greece because it was forced to continue, and the UK because it chose to continue. In the case of the UK, fear about deficits and debt was used as a political weapon by the Conservatives against Labour, and was endorsed by business interests and the popular press. Business generally likes it when their "confidence" is the primary issue.

What about the value of the fiscal multiplier? The October 2010 analysis by the IMF recognized that the government spending multiplier was positive—not negative as the expansionary austerity doctrine claimed—but estimated its value at around 0.5. In October 2012 when Blanchard issued his apology, the IMF suggested that fiscal multipliers might even be as high as 1.7—a number very close to the 1.6 value suggested by Romer and Bernstein in 2009. Multipliers this high imply that austerity was not only the wrong policy in terms of stabilizing output but also the wrong policy in terms of stabilizing debt!

For example, a multiplier of 1.7 means that a $1 decrease in government spending will decrease output by $1.70. If the overall marginal tax rate were 0.5 (say), then tax revenues would fall by 85 cents (equal to 0.5 × 1.7) for every dollar reduction in government spending. In other words, we would sacrifice a lot in terms of output, and in terms of government provided services, but get only a tiny improvement in the deficit—in our example, only 15 cents for every dollar cut from spending. What is worse is that since the deficit is only slightly reduced, the rate of growth of debt will be only slightly reduced, while the growth rate of output will be much harder hit, by the full multiplier of 1.7. This combination practically guarantees that the debt-to-GDP ratio will actually increase, not decrease, as a result of austerity.

Indeed, this is precisely what happened to those countries following austerity policies. The debt-to-GDP ratio increased between 2010 and 2013 for Ireland, Spain, Italy, Portugal, and the Netherlands. As soon as austerity was abandoned in 2014, those same countries enjoyed falling debt-to-GDP ratios. In the UK, the debt-to-GDP ratio gradually increased from 70 percent in 2010 to 85 percent in 2016, as the UK stuck blindly to its austerity policies.

> Question for your professor: Is it possible that cutting government spending could increase a country's debt-to-GDP ratio?

2.6 The necessity for government deficits in a "real balance sheet" recession

Financial crashes happen periodically. Japan suffered one in 1990, after an asset price bubble that developed throughout the 1980s finally burst. As expected, the Japanese economy went into a serious recession. What was unexpected was the length of stagnation that followed. It lasted throughout the 1990s, and even further into the new millennium. Richard Koo was studying the reasons why the Japanese economy was failing to bounce back when the Great Recession hit in 2008, and he concluded that the two events were fundamentally similar. His name for this type of recession is a "balance sheet recession," and he argues that: (1) monetary policy cannot fix it, and (2) the government *must* run large budget deficits for an extended period afterward.

Koo's (2008) main insight is microeconomic. When a debt-financed bubble bursts, asset prices collapse while liabilities remain, leaving millions of private sector balance sheets "underwater"—meaning the value of assets is less than the value of debt. A firm in this position is technically bankrupt. We expect this to happen when a firm makes repeated losses over time. But after a financial crash, even profitable firms—that are cash flow positive—can find themselves technically bankrupt.

In order to regain their financial health and credit ratings, households and firms are forced to repair their balance sheets by increasing savings and paying down debt. This act of deleveraging reduces aggregate demand. But this cannot be repaired using monetary policy. Even zero interest rates will not reverse this process. The process only ends when the balance sheets are repaired.

In Japan's case, the corporate sector shifted from being a substantial borrower to repaying debt at the rate of more than 6 percent of GDP a year. On top of that, the household sector was also saving more than 4 percent of GDP a year, all with interest rates at zero. In this situation, monetary policy cannot work, no matter how much liquidity the central bank tries to inject, because there are no willing borrowers.

To understand why the government must run fiscal deficits, it is helpful to use the "sectoral financial balances" framework pioneered by Wynne Godley.[20] The essential idea is that since income has to equal expenditure for the economy as a whole, the difference between income and expenditure for each sector must sum to zero. Thus, a rise in the surplus of one sector must be matched by an offsetting change in the others.

The analysis is based on accounting identities. When discussing the sources of national savings in Chapter 5, we derived identity (5.11), which we repeat below:

$$I \equiv S_{\text{Private}} + (T - G) + (IM - X)$$

Rearranging we obtain:

$$(G - T) + (I - S_{\text{Private}}) = (IM - X) \tag{7.9}$$

The left-hand side of (7.9) denotes the financial balances of the government sector $(G - T)$, plus the private sector $(I - S_{\text{Private}})$. The identity tells us the sum of these balances must equal the balance of trade. Koo's (2011) idea is to look at the world as a whole in balance sheet recession. In the context of the whole world, we can simplify equation (7.9) since the sum of world imports must equal the sum of world exports. This allows us to drop the term $(IM - X)$ and write:

$$(G - T) = (S_{\text{Private}} - I) \tag{7.10}$$

From equation (7.10), it is now apparent that since private savings are greater than investment, the right-hand side is positive. This means the left-hand side must also be positive, showing that governments—on a world scale—must run deficits. The only thing the government can do is the opposite of the private sector—it has to borrow and spend. As Koo (2011, p. 33) explains,

> That is what we did in Japan. We gave it a fiscal stimulus and the economy improved. Then we said, "Oh, the budget deficit is too large" so we cut it and the economy weakened again because the private sector is still deleveraging. So, we did it again—gave it more stimulus, and when the economy improved we cut it again, and it fell again. So, Japan had a zig-zag for a full 15 years.

The only remedy for a balance sheet recession is large and sustained government deficits. The government sector must run financial sector deficits to allow the private sector to run financial sector surpluses, which are necessary to allow the private sector to repair their balance sheets.

Question for your professor: After a financial crash, many firms and households will likely be in a negative net asset situation, and will therefore be trying to save. If the nongovernment sector is saving, then the government sector must be dissaving, or running a deficit. Do you agree?

2.7 Does the national debt ever need to be paid off?

Mainstream textbooks warn that if governments incur too much debt, lenders will demand higher interest rates to compensate for increased risk. Higher interest rates increase debt service costs and choke off economic growth. Both effects make matters worse, and a vicious spiral can set in. But what level of debt is too high?

Reinhart and Rogoff (2010) claimed to have discovered the magic number was 90 percent. However, that was thoroughly debunked. We now know that we do not know the magic number. Is it possible that something so elusive may not even exist?

In Olivier Blanchard's (2019) presidential address to members of the American Economic Association, he goes a long way to saying just that. Public debt may not matter because it never has to be paid off—it can always be rolled over without increasing taxes later. As Blanchard (2019: 1197) says, "Put bluntly, public debt may have no fiscal cost." The only requirement is that the rate of interest must be lower than the rate of growth of output. One of the important contributions of Blanchard's (2019) presidential address was to show that this is the normal situation in the real world.

Blanchard shows that for the United States, in the seven decades between 1950 and 2019, the nominal interest rate was lower than the nominal output growth rate in six of them. And the same is true for a large number of countries, over long periods of time.[21] Blanchard explains that this implies that the government's intertemporal budget constraint—which believers in Ricardian equivalence put so much emphasis on—is not binding. Governments can issue debt with no tax consequences. The debt-to-GDP ratio will decline without ever needing to raise taxes or pay back debt.

For example, Figure 7.7 plots the debt-to-GDP ratio for the UK, from 1900 to 2018. Looking at the figure it seems hard to believe that anyone could ever think that the UK would fall off a debt cliff if debt exceeded 90 percent of GDP. After the Second World War, government debt was 230 percent of GDP, and yet the UK enjoyed rapid postwar growth with no debt crisis. Indeed, that rapid growth is the reason the debt ratio fell. It was not brought down by running budget surpluses and paying back debt.

Figure 7.7 UK debt-to-GDP ratio, 1900–2018

How does the debt-to-GDP ratio fall if we never pay back any debt? The necessary and sufficient condition is $g > d$, where g is the rate of growth of GDP and d is the rate of growth of government debt. Digging deeper, the growth rate of debt is determined by the rate of interest paid on the debt, r, plus the rate at which new debt is added. The appendix to this chapter shows that the growth rate of debt, d, equals "$r + \theta/D$" where "D" denotes total government debt, and θ is the primary budget deficit—meaning the deficit that exists when we ignore debt service costs (the interest payments on the government debt). Thus, if inequality (7.11) holds, the debt-to-GDP ratio falls over time.

$$g > r + \theta/D \qquad\qquad (7.11)$$

To understand better what equation (7.11) means, let's use the UK as an example. Blanchard explains that "currently"—that is, in 2019—the excess of g over r is about 2.3 percentage points in the UK. If the UK's primary budget deficit were eliminated (meaning θ is zero), the debt-to-GDP ratio would fall by 2.3 percent a year without any debt needing to be repaid. Alternatively, the UK could run a primary budget deficit of less than 2.3 percent of outstanding debt, while still allowing the debt-to-GDP ratio to fall over time.

Does this mean that a high debt-to-GDP ratio does not matter at all? Can we run big deficits for "X" number of years, and have a steadily climbing debt ratio, safe in the knowledge that as soon as we decide to control the deficits, the debt will melt away on its own? While this is a tricky question, the answer is essentially "yes." We know there is no debt cliff because the debt itself never has to be "paid back." It will melt away once we stop adding to it.

It might seem that a larger debt implies larger debt service payments, which will make it harder to stop adding to the debt. But a close look at inequality (7.11) tells us this is not the case. The last term, θ/D, is the *primary* budget deficit—meaning the deficit that exists when we ignore debt service costs. So, as long as the government can pay for its programs, *ignoring* interest payments on the debt, the debt-to-GDP ratio will fall.

The only worry from a stability of debt perspective is the possibility that inequality (7.11) may not always hold. If growth slows down, or interest rates rise, the government's intertemporal budget constraint could reassert itself. Until that time, public debt may have no fiscal cost.

Question for your professor: Olivier Blanchard has stated, "put bluntly, public debt may have no fiscal cost." If this is true, why do textbooks continue to emphasize that the fiscal cost of higher public debt is higher taxation later?

2.8 The MMT view on debt and deficits

MMT stands for "modern monetary theory." It is a relatively new set of ideas forming (arguably) a coherent school of thought, with roots going back to Keynes and the post-Keynesians. It is delightfully fresh and controversial. It has been developed over the last 20 years by Randall Wray, Bill Mitchell, and Stephanie Kelton, with significant input from ex-investment banker Warren Mosler. Besides Keynes, it builds on the ideas of Hyman Minsky, Wynne Godley, and Abba Lerner.

MMT has been gaining traction and popularity partly because of the rise of blogging—all its adherents are prolific bloggers—and partly because it has been endorsed by left-wing politicians in the United States like Bernie Sanders and Alexandria Ocasio-Cortez. But perhaps the most important reason for its rise in popularity is its radically new ideas that—from this author's perspective—seem essentially correct.

At the outset, it needs to be emphasized that the MMT conclusions apply only to monetarily sovereign governments (meaning they have their own currency and central bank), a floating exchange rate, and no significant foreign currency debt. According to MMT theorists, such governments face no financial constraints on their spending. Such a government cannot run out of money since it can pay all its bills by issuing currency.

This really is the starting point for MMT: a monetarily sovereign government could pay all its bills by issuing currency. Taking this to its logical conclusion, such a government never needs to borrow money, nor to levy taxes! Unlike households and firms, a monetarily sovereign government does not face a *financing* constraint. But the lack of a financing constraint does not mean the lack of *any* constraint. For currency-issuing governments, the macroeconomic constraint on fiscal policy is resource availability, not revenue. Alternatively phrased, *the only limit on government spending is inflation.*[22]

As Keynes taught, the aim of the government should be to balance the economy, not to balance its budget. A balanced economy is one that achieves full employment without inflation. Like mainstream economists, MMT theorists believe inflation is caused by excessive total spending—by aggregate demand outstripping aggregate supply. Since taxes are not necessary to pay for government spending, *taxes should be used to target and limit inflation.* Taxes can be adjusted to keep total spending—government and private—at a level that will not be inflationary. Inflation is something that MMT takes seriously.

MMT proponents insist that the budget deficit and public debt debate reflect a misunderstanding as to what constitutes an economic cost. The real cost of any program is the extra real resources that the program requires for implementation. Following the advice of mainstream economists, politicians are currently obsessed with something that does not matter—balancing their budget over whatever arbitrary period—and are ignoring many things that do matter—such as renewing infrastructure, transitioning to a green economy, and eliminating unemployment. In general, when there is persistent and high unemployment, there is an abundance of real resources available. So, in some sense, when the economy is weak the opportunity cost of many government programs is zero.

A question like "Can the government afford this?" is really asking whether there are sufficient real resources to underpin the program. The nominal outlay is just an accounting entry; it does not necessarily reflect the real resource cost. Similarly, a statement that a nation is "living beyond its means" makes no sense when there is a significant output gap and large-scale hidden unemployment.[23]

Clearly, MMT theorists are not afraid of deficits, nor of the idea that government deficits should be taken as the normal situation. They apply the lessons of Godley's "sectoral financial balances" framework to argue that government budget deficits allow the nongovernmental sector to run financial surpluses, to save and accumulate assets. Conversely, government budget surpluses force the nongovernment sector into deficit and the accumulation of ever-increasing levels of indebtedness to maintain its expenditure. *It is ongoing government surpluses that are unsustainable for the private sector—not ongoing government deficits.*

At this point, we have explained three core statements at the heart of MMT. (1) Monetarily sovereign governments face no purely financial budget constraints. (2) All governments face real and ecological limits to what can be produced and consumed. And (3) the government's financial deficit is everybody else's financial surplus.[24]

Endogenous money and "crowding out" Another idea at the heart of MMT is the notion that the money supply is endogenous: banks create money in accordance with market demands for money. This leads to the seemingly topsy-turvy conclusion that taxation and bond sales are not even capable of financing government spending, since collection of this revenue implies their destruction (see Stephanie Bell-Kelton 1998). Indeed, the idea that taxation involves the destruction of money is one of the novel insights of MMT. Essentially, you pay your taxes by writing a check (or an electronic deduction) from your bank account, paid to the government. When that check clears, the central bank deducts that money from your bank's account at the central bank, and credits it to the Treasury's account at the central bank. Essentially, that money has been taken out of circulation or destroyed.

The idea that money is endogenous is one reason why MMT theorist reject crowding out. Since banks create money in accordance with market demands for money, there is no trade-off between loaning to governments and loaning to businesses. Hence, there is no tendency for interest rates to rise when governments borrow too much. Certainly, if deficits are "financed" by issuing currency, it is clear that the money supply expands with the deficit. Again, it must be stressed that this makes sense when the economy has real resources sitting idle.

Debt stability MMT theorists recognize that governments may choose to issue bonds. One reason is that government bonds play a useful role in the financial system by providing a highly secure asset. Abba Lerner (1943) gave a different reason for the government to issue bonds: to increase interest rates. If the public has too much cash, and attempts to lend it out, interest rates might be driven down to very low levels. This might cause "too much" investment spending in the sense that it generates inflation. When the government issues bonds, it absorbs some of the public's money and drives up interest rates. For Lerner, the government could either issue bonds or redeem them for currency, to achieve the rate of interest that results in the most desirable level of investment.

On the other hand, some MMT theorists suggest that interest rates should be held very close to zero, so as to avoid large government interest payments on the debt that go to the wealthier sections of society, and that may be regressive in its effect on income distribution.[25] According to MMT, the government (or central bank) can set any interest rate it wants.

In any event, even if the government borrows money by issuing bonds to pay for its deficit, and even if interest rates are positive, a debt crisis is inconceivable. Lerner (1943: 42–3) argues as follows. No matter how much interest has to be paid on the debt, it can be paid by borrowing still more. If the public becomes reluctant to keep on lending, the government can pay by issuing currency, which the public can either hoard or spend. If the public hoards the money, the only effect is the public holds currency instead of government bonds and the government is saved the trouble of making interest payments. If the public spends the money, this increases total spending, reducing the government's need to spend to maintain full employment. And if the rate of spending becomes too great, *then* is the time to tax to prevent inflation.

Lerner's explanation ignores the response of foreign lenders. Suppose they perceive an increased risk of default as the debt grows larger. They might sell domestic government bonds and repatriate their money, causing the exchange rate to depreciate. This would stimulate aggregate demand via an increase in net exports. Worries about solvency end up helping economies in a time of weak growth and low inflation, rather than leading to a vicious death spiral.

Monetary versus fiscal policy The mainstream consensus is to assign fiscal policy the job of keeping the government debt sustainable, not stabilizing the economy. Monetary policy is assigned the job of stabilizing the economy, by manipulating interest rates. Of course, once interest rates hit the zero lower bound, then the government must use fiscal policy to boost aggregate demand. But normally, it is the job of the central bank.

MMT sees very different roles for monetary and fiscal policy. Many MMT theorists think that the interest rate set by the central bank should always be zero, while fiscal policy should make all the adjustments (see Mitchell 2009). Certainly, since 2008, monetary policy has been extremely weak.[26]

Critics of MMT argue that trying to use fiscal policy to stabilize the economy would fail because of timing problems. And they say politicians cannot be relied upon to impose pain on the public through higher taxes or lower spending to squelch rising inflation. The MMT response is that they also oppose fine-tuning and instead want to use automatic stabilizers to keep the economy on track. One aspect of this is their Job Guarantee Program—discussed in Chapter 10—which would ensure that spending would automatically fall as the economy recovered. Furthermore, they assert that progressive income taxes work well, and can be made to work even better. Wray (2019) says of the US economy, "every time the economy grew rapidly by 5%, tax revenue exploded and was growing 16% per year. So, our tax system automatically does this."

Concluding thoughts MMT is challenging mainstream orthodoxy on a fundamental level. In response, some in the mainstream, like Larry Summers, have ridiculed MMT as being a "recipe for disaster." One contentious issue is whether their theories apply to all economies at all times.

For example, Summers (2019) suggests that if MMT theories were applied in emerging economies they would experience hyperinflation. He also cites the UK and Italian experience of balance of payments difficulties during the 1970s as further evidence. But these criticisms are really missing the point. MMT theorists have made it clear that their theories do not have blanket application to all economies at all times; their models only apply to monetary sovereign governments, with their own currency, a flexible exchange rate, and no significant foreign currency debt. Significantly, the UK and Italy did not have flexible exchange rates during the 1970s.

What about other debt crises? The European debt crises that affected Portugal, Italy, Ireland, Spain, and especially Greece occurred to countries that were not monetarily sovereign. Their adoption of the Euro was the origin of their problems. They had no nationally controlled central bank that could back up their debts and/or pay their obligations by issuing currency. Other debt crises, to countries that are monetarily sovereign such as Argentina (2002), occurred because they issued debt denominated in US dollars. This is always a bad idea. It means that a depreciating exchange rate increases the value of the foreign denominated debt.

Certainly, MMT is controversial. We will return to the MMT school of thought again when we discuss unemployment and inflation.

Question for your professor: Could a government that has its own currency, a floating exchange rate, and no significant foreign currency debt ever experience a public debt crisis?

2.9 Timing issues

Mainstream textbooks say that the implementation of fiscal policy involves long time lags, longer than those required for monetary policy, and is therefore too slow an instrument to stabilize the economy. Let us deconstruct this claim.

First, both fiscal and monetary policy involve the same recognition lag. With regard to the second and third lags—the planning and implementation lags—we need to consider how interest rate changes affect the economy. Most textbooks assume that investment is the interest-sensitive component of spending. If so, why would investment spending have shorter planning and implementation lags than government spending? All spending is planned. Why should corporate planning and implementation lags be shorter than those of the government?

Perhaps textbook authors have in mind a political situation such as the United States where different branches of government are controlled by different parties, leading to long periods of wrangling. But the political situation of the United States, over the most recent period, is a poor basis for generalizations about fiscal policy in all economies.

Parliamentary systems can respond quite quickly. Even though national budgets are traditionally only once a year—usually in March—governments can respond earlier than that. For example, when the Canadian economy began to slow mid-2000, the government brought forth a mini-budget in October 2000. Similarly, following the downturn that became undeniable by November 2008, a stimulative budget was announced in late January. Indeed, in 2009 an extremely wide range of economies responded in timely fashion to the call by the IMF and the G20 for expansionary fiscal policy to counter the unfolding global recession.

Further, austerity has created a backlog of suitable projects ready to be implemented. And currently there is the overriding need for government investment in a Green New Deal to wean economies off fossil fuels.

There seems very little substance to the view that monetary policy necessarily involves shorter time lags than fiscal policy. Mainstream textbooks fail to look critically at the usual claim concerning the relative lags of fiscal and monetary policy.

Question for your professor: Why do textbooks presume that the planning and implementation lags of the nongovernment sector are shorter than the planning and implementation lags of the government sector? Isn't all spending planned?

2.10 Supply-side effects of taxes

The notion that high tax rates have significant adverse supply-side effects is an example of what John Quiggin (2010) calls a "zombie idea": no matter how much evidence kills it, it keeps returning because it serves the interest of the rich and powerful.

The textbooks tell us that tax cuts would increase the supply of labor, increase equilibrium employment, and increase potential GDP. These claims are usually supported by a diagram depicting an aggregate labor market with an upward sloping labor supply curve, which is shifted to the left by the imposition of income taxes (see Figure 7.3). But are we sure the aggregate labor supply curve is upward sloping? If it were vertical, there would no adverse supply-side effects of higher taxes. If it were backward bending, an increase in taxes would elicit more labor supply—a situation consistent with people trying to achieve a given after-tax income. The diagram proves nothing. Standard economic theory does not predict the response of labor supply to income taxation; a tax increase may lead a rational person to work less, more, or the same.[27]

It seems we need to know the slope or, more accurately, the elasticity of aggregate labor supply. But analysts agree the elasticity of aggregate labor supply is not a unique structural parameter. For example, Attanasio et al. (2018) say,

> The most important conclusion from our analysis is that the macro elasticity [of labour supply] is not a structural parameter; it is simply the result of highly nonlinear aggregation, which depends on demographic structure as well as the distribution of wealth and the particular point in the business cycle. This implies, for instance, that to understand the consequences of income tax changes, we need to be explicit about whose tax is changing.

This is the key point: we need to be explicit about whose tax is changing. In suggesting that tax cuts have beneficial supply-side effects, the mainstream texts are obscuring this question, and seem to be supporting blanket tax cuts—even for the rich. But Attanasio et al. (2018) conclude that the beneficial supply-side effects of lower taxes occur much lower down the income distribution. For example, if taxes are lowered on women who are working few hours, or are working for low wages, the responses to changes in take-home wages are substantial.

Of course, conservative economists argue there are beneficial supply-side effects when taxes are cut for the rich. But the argument is not that their labor supply increases. Rather it is that they will invest more, employ more people, and create more jobs. Peter Diamond, Nobel Memorial Prize in economics winner in 2010, disagrees. He points out that the top 1 percent have wealth and an ability to borrow. If they want to start a new business, they are not going to be limited by having to pay a higher tax on their earnings. If the objective of a tax cut is to create jobs, it may be better to lower taxes on those who are further down the income ladder (the middle class). Those are the people having trouble starting businesses. Since Diamond disputes the premise that the wealthy need low taxes to create jobs, he sees little harm in rising the highest tax rate.[28]

Conservatives will respond with strong a priori beliefs that high taxes discourage an economic activity. We tax cigarettes to discourage smoking. If we tax work effort, we discourage work effort. But while that may be true in a "ceteris paribus" sense, in the real world "all other things" are not constant. People may prefer to live and work in a high-tax jurisdiction— where there is low inequality, low crime, and state-provided health care— than in a low-tax jurisdiction where there is high inequality, high crime, and high cost of private health insurance.

But what about Prescott's (2002) empirical results that the lower total tax wedge in the United States compared to France explains why potential GDP (per working-age person) is higher in the United States than in France. Of course, we need to be highly skeptical of such claims. Labor supply is affected by many factors such as the availability of jobs, the mix of skills required versus the skills available, the demographic mix of the population, and even the availability of affordable day care. Further, comparing across national economies runs into problems of different cultural preferences for work versus leisure. For all these reasons, Prescott's results are not convincing.

What we need are "natural experiments" where culturally similar, and economically similar, jurisdictions have different tax rates. So, it is noteworthy that when the state of Kansas slashed its tax rates in 2012, its labor force participation rate continued to lag behind its higher-tax neighbor, Nebraska.[29] Another problem for Prescott's worldview is that the labor force participation rate in Canada is higher than in the United States, despite significantly higher tax rates.[30]

Looking at a broad sweep of history, most Western countries had some of the highest tax rates in their history in the 1950s, yet enjoyed rapid growth. Sweden and Denmark have enjoyed faster long-term growth than the UK or the United States, despite much higher tax rates. It seems low tax rates are neither necessary nor sufficient for faster growth. Rather, low tax rates contribute to high inequality, and high inequality is bad for growth (as we have documented in Chapter 4).

But the facts of the matter do not stop conservative think tanks—and some mainstream textbooks—from trotting out the same old pap.

Questions for your professor
#1: When we talk about the supply-side effects of
    taxes, shouldn't we be more specific about whose
    tax rates are changing?

#2: If higher taxes have the terrible effects that
    the textbook shows, then why have Sweden and
    Denmark enjoyed faster long-term growth than
    the UK or the United States, despite much
    higher tax rates?

2.11 Conclusion

Economics textbooks like to present the subject as an objective science, characterized by a wide consensus about established theory and an agreed understanding of core empirical relationships. This chapter is where the mask falls off, revealing deep divisions within the mainstream camp. What can be a more basic relationship than the consumption function? Yet there is no consensus between New Keynesians and New Classical economists about the role of Ricardian equivalence in determining households' consumption spending. What can be a more central magnitude than income-expenditure multipliers? But we have seen that—at a time when the world economy desperately needed fiscal stimulus—the profession was in complete disarray over its likely impact.

In 2009, New Classical economists claimed the government expenditure multiplier was zero. In 2010, some Keynesian economists claimed that—when government debt got too high—the government expenditure multiplier could be negative!

While the textbooks keep up the pretense of there being a wide consensus, they fail to answer definitively the key questions raised in these debates. They do not take a position on the empirical importance of Ricardian equivalence. They do not provide empirical evidence on the size of fiscal multipliers in real-world economies. Instead, after biasing the discussion one way or another, they all limit themselves to "outlining the issues up for debate." The textbooks paper over these schisms and try to appeal to both Keynesian and New Classical professors. In so doing, they are trading off a more honest treatment of the state of the subject, with an attempt to sell more textbooks.

Some on the mainstream, such as Paul Krugman, like to portray those who supported (and continue to support) the notion of "expansionary austerity" as members of a "cult" who are "deluded." On the other side of the debate, Rogoff (2019) talks about the "anti-austerity thought police" and predicts that Alesina and his coauthors "will be tarred and feathered for daring to suggest that ... fiscal retrenchment can sometimes be expansionary."

The anti-text agrees with Krugman about the tremendous harm that austerity has done—not only by worsening the depth and duration of the Great Recession but also by worsening debt-to-GDP ratios! But what Krugman is failing to recognize is the link between the expansionary austerity doctrine and the mainstream belief that too much government debt can lead to a crisis. Since it is impossible to definitively defeat an empirical possibility, the only way to defeat the expansionary austerity doctrine is by abandoning the mainstream dogma about the dangers of high levels of government debt. Much of the rest of the anti-text gives reasons for doing just that.

First, we explore Richard Koo's theory of balance sheet recessions. This makes it clear that—particularly after a financial crash—the government sector must run large and persistent deficits to allow the nongovernment sector time to repair their balance sheets. It is here that we introduce Wynne Godley's "sectoral financial balances" framework, and we learn that government sector deficits equal nongovernment sector surpluses, and vice versa.

Second, we explain Olivier Blanchard's (2019) analysis that hinges on the inequality $g > r$. Blanchard has two main points. First, as long as the inequality holds, public debt may have no fiscal cost. Second, the normal state of the world is where the inequality holds. This means there can be no debt cliff because the debt itself never has to be "paid back." It will melt away once we stop adding to it.

Third, we explore the views of MMT that are applicable only to monetarily sovereign countries, with a flexible exchange rate. The message is loud and clear: fear of deficits comes from a profound misunderstanding of the nature of money; panic over government debt is a misguided and atavistic remnant of the gold standard.

The two remaining issues are time lags and supply-side effects of taxes. The anti-text argues there is very little substance to the view that monetary policy necessarily involves shorter time lags than fiscal policy. Mainstream textbooks have failed to look critically at the usual claim concerning the relative lags of fiscal and monetary policy.

With regard to the supply-side effects of taxes, the textbooks that chose to cover this material do a dismal job of it. Just like conservative think tanks, the textbooks trot out the same zombie ideas.

3 APPENDIX: DEBT DYNAMICS

The stock of government debt increases when the government runs budget deficits. The "primary budget deficit" (which we will denote as theta, θ) is the deficit that exists when we ignore debt service costs (the interest payments on the national debt). Denoting total government debt in nominal terms as D, and the nominal interest rate as i, then nominal debt service costs are iD. The increase in total nominal debt, ΔD, can then be written as:

$$\Delta D = \theta + iD \tag{A1}$$

Dividing through by "*D*," we can write the increase in nominal debt in proportionate terms as:

$$\Delta D/D = \theta/D + i \tag{A2}$$

With regard to the debt-to-GDP ratio, since *D* represents nominal debt, we need nominal GDP in the denominator. Using our usual symbols—*P* to denote the average price level, and *Y* to denote real GDP—we have *PY* equals nominal GDP. Denoting the debt-to-GDP ratio as λ , we write:

$$\text{Debt-to-GDP ratio} = \lambda = D/PY \tag{A3}$$

The rate of change of a ratio is the growth rate of the numerator (the term on the top) minus the growth rate of the denominator (the term on the bottom). The denominator is a compound term, the growth rate of which is the sum of the growth rates of each item. Thus, we have:

$$\Delta\lambda/\lambda = \Delta D/D - [\Delta P/P + \Delta Y/Y] \tag{A4}$$

Denoting the growth rate of prices ($\Delta P/P$) as π, and the growth rate of real output ($\Delta Y/Y$) as *g*, and eliminating $\Delta D/D$ using equation (A2), we have:

$$\Delta\lambda/\lambda = \theta/D + i - [\pi + g] \tag{A5}$$

Defining the real rate of interest, *r*, as ($i - \pi$), we can write,

$$\Delta\lambda/\lambda = \theta/D + r - g \tag{A6}$$

Finally, we can write the condition for $\Delta\lambda/\lambda$ to be negative:

If $g > r + \theta/D$ then $\Delta\lambda/\lambda < o$ (A7) = equation (7.11) in the text.

Chapter 8

MONEY AND BANKING: CRONY CAPITALISM AND THE CORRUPTION IT BREEDS

> Credit is the pavement along which production travels, and the bankers if they knew their duty, would provide the transport facilities to just the extent that is required in order that the productive powers of the community can be employed at their full capacity.
>
> John Maynard Keynes[1]

I THE STANDARD TEXT

The focus of this chapter is money and banking. We probe the nature of money and the inherent riskiness of banking. We will show that while banks cannot print money, *they do routinely create it.* The key questions are how to preserve stability of the banking system and the instruments used by central banks to control the money supply.

1.1 What is money?

In everyday speech, if someone has a lot of "money" we understand that person to be "wealthy." But in economics, money and wealth are not the same thing. To understand better what money is, consider its functions. The key function of money is that it serves as a *medium of exchange*: it is generally accepted as representing finality of payment once it changes hands.

The medium of exchange function requires money to be a *store of value:* it must hold its value over time. If it lost its value too quickly, it could lose its acceptability as payment. In addition, money needs to be a viable *unit of account,* such that we can express prices in terms of money, and in this way calculate relative values. While the three functions—medium of exchange, store of value, and unit of account—are mutually interdependent, the key function is its acceptability as a medium of exchange. Focusing on this key function, we can define money as any asset that can *easily* be used to purchase goods and services. Since "easily" is a relative term, there is an element of arbitrariness to the definition of money.

The narrowest definition of money is the most liquid. It only includes currency in circulation (cash held by the public) and checking accounts with banks. This is usually referred to as "M1." As we move to broader definitions, we include "near-money" assets that are less, and less, liquid. These assets may not be *directly* usable as a medium of exchange but can be quickly converted. For example, including savings accounts yields a measure of the money supply called M2; and further adding "term deposits" (which are fixed term but can be converted at a cost) yields a measure called M3. Further, since deposits at "near banks" (such as trust companies, mortgage and loan companies, money market mutual funds, and credit unions) can easily be transferred into commercial bank deposits, perhaps they too should be included. Doing so yields a measure called M3+.

Historically, many things have been used as money. *Commodity money* refers to the use of objects that have intrinsic value. Examples include precious metals such as gold and silver, or coins with precious metal content. A classic example of commodity money is cigarettes, which were used in the Second World War prisoner-of-war camps. When red-cross packages arrived, and cigarettes were plentiful, the value of a cigarette in terms of other items (such as blankets) was low; but as cigarettes were smoked, they became scarcer, and their value rose. Prices denominated in cigarettes rose and fell depending on the relative scarcity of cigarettes, illustrating how changes in the quantity of money can cause inflation and deflation.

Moving on from commodity money, the next level of abstraction is money that has no intrinsic value but is convertible into something that does. This is known as *commodity-backed money*. For example, from 1944 to 1971, US dollars were convertible into gold at the official exchange rate of $35 per ounce.

Nowadays, money is everywhere *fiat money*, meaning that it has no intrinsic value, nor is it officially convertible into anything else that does. Its value derives entirely from its official status as a means of payment.

Credit cards are not part of the money supply. They simply allow individuals to access credit. The story is different for debit cards. While they are not in themselves money, they allow people easy access to their bank accounts, which are part of the money supply.

So, having defined money, and determined that *bank accounts* are a crucial part of the modern money supply, we move on to consider banking in more detail.

1.2 Banking

A bank is a financial intermediary where money can be deposited for safekeeping and can be withdrawn on demand. Typically, banks then lend this money to borrowers, charging a higher rate of interest than they pay on deposits. In effect, banks borrow short term (from their depositors) and lend long term.

This is known as *maturity transformation*. Households with excess cash may not want to lend long term, while borrowers may need the security of long-term funds. Banks bridge this mismatch, increasing the funds channeled from savers to borrowers, and earn a profit in the process.

Banks can operate in this way because on any given day, withdrawals are small and steady. Banks require only a small cash reserve to meet withdrawals. So, banks keep a small amount of cash on hand as reserves and lend out the rest. The occasional large outflows can be met by borrowing temporarily from another bank, or the central bank.

Banks get financial resources not only from accepting deposits but also, like other companies, from issuing equity and debt. The equity that it issues to its owners is called bank capital. All of these are liabilities that the bank owes to (respectively) its depositors, creditors, and shareholders.

Table 8.1 shows a commercial bank's simplified balance sheet, known as a T-account, showing assets (on the left) and liabilities (on the right). We see the bank's total liabilities are $37 million, of which deposits are $30 million, debt is $6 million, and bank capital (or owners' equity) is $1 million.

Banks use their financial resources to generate profit for their owners. It not only makes loans and holds reserves but also buys financial securities such as stocks and bonds. We see these on the left of Table 8.1. By the rules of accounting, total assets on the left of the balance sheet must always equal total liabilities on the right. This occurs because the value of the owners' equity is a residual. It equals total assets minus the value of its other liabilities (deposits and debt).

On the left of Table 8.1, we see the bank has lent out $26 million, bought securities worth $8 million, and has cash reserves of $3 million. We note in passing that reserves do not need to be held by banks as cash in their vaults. Banks could deposit some of their cash reserves at the central bank; these deposits are regarded as equivalent to cash reserves in their vaults. (Bank reserves are not considered part of currency in circulation.)

From the data in Table 8.1 we can calculate two important ratios. First, the *reserve ratio* is the ratio of reserves to deposits, or $3 million divided by $30 million, making a reserve ratio of 0.1, or 10 percent. The second is the *leverage ratio*. From Section 2.3 of Chapter 5, we learnt that the leverage ratio is the ratio of assets to capital. The bank depicted in Table 8.1 has $1 million of capital, implying the leverage ratio is 37. This is heavily levered. Remember that leverage multiplies both gains and losses. A 1 percent increase in the value of the bank's assets

Table 8.1 A bank's T-account (in millions)

Assets		Liabilities	
Reserves	$3	Deposits	$30
Loans	$26	Debt	$6
Securities	$8	Capital (or owner's equity)	$1
TOTAL	$37		$37

will produce a 37 percent increase in the bank's equity. On the other hand, a 2.7 percent decrease in the value of assets would wipe out the value of equity $(-2.7 \times 37 \approx -100 \text{ percent})$, and anything larger implies negative equity.

Bank Runs—Illiquidity versus Insolvency If the value of equity should ever become negative, the bank would be technically *insolvent*. This could trigger a "bank run" where depositors attempt to withdraw their money as quickly as possible before bankruptcy occurs. *But a key point is that even solvent, well-run banks with positive equity are vulnerable to a bank run.* No bank can pay back all the money deposited with them at a moment's notice: there simply is not enough cash on hand. Even worse, the loans that banks extend—a key asset of the bank—are *illiquid*. So, if a *solvent* bank is forced into a distress sale of its assets to raise cash quickly, it may have to sell at such low prices that it becomes *insolvent*!

  Further, there is always a risk of contagion: if a run occurs at one bank, jittery depositors may doubt other banks, and even sound banks may be driven to failure. Such a *systemic crisis of confidence* could bring down the whole structure of financial institutions. Confidence is crucial for the smooth running of financial intermediaries because their maturity transformation function means they never have enough cash on hand to meet unusually large withdrawals of deposits.

1.3 Government oversight of banks

There is a three-pronged solution for bank runs. First, central banks are committed to lending to solvent banks that are short of liquidity—they stand ready to be "lender of last resort." Second, bank deposits in most countries are protected by deposit insurance. Usually, a national agency collects a small tax on bank deposits—where the tax is like an insurance premium—and guarantees depositors against loss, up to some maximum amount, if their bank fails.[2] By protecting depositors against bank failure, deposit insurance seeks to reassure depositors and reduce the likelihood of bank runs. Third, banks are subject to regulation and oversight. Sometimes this oversight is done by the country's central bank, sometimes by a separate regulatory body.[3] There are two main forms of regulation: capital requirements and reserve requirements.

  The capital requirement is a minimum amount of capital a financial institution must hold, relative to a measure of its assets. There is a global voluntary agreement, called the Basel III Accord, that stipulates banks must maintain a minimum of 7 percent "Tier 1" capital to asset ratio. Tier 1 capital is the core capital of a bank, which includes equity capital and disclosed reserves. To illustrate, in Table 8.1, the bank's equity was $1 million, and its cash reserves were $3 million, while its total assets were $37 million. This implies a Tier 1 capital ratio of approximately 11 percent $(4 \div 37 = 0.108)$.[4]

  As a final safeguard against bank runs, most central banks impose *minimum required reserve ratios*. For example, in the United States, the minimum reserve ratio for checkable bank deposits is 10 percent. In contrast, five countries have abolished reserve requirements: Australia, Canada, New Zealand, Sweden, and the UK. The argument is that banks know best the level of reserves they need, and in any event, the central bank always stands ready to loan cash to banks that may become short of reserves.

1.4 How banks create money

Without banks, the money supply would equal currency in circulation—the notes and coins issued by the government. Banks affect the money supply in two ways: first, they take some currency out of circulation and keep it as reserves in their vaults; second, banks offer deposits, which are counted as part of the money supply. In fact, this section will show that through the process of lending and creating deposits, *banks create money*! In what follows, we will make two crucial assumptions: first, banks desire to maintain a 10 percent reserve ratio; second, the general public has all the cash it needs—anyone receiving more cash will simply deposit it in a bank. At the end of this section, we consider the effect of relaxing these assumptions.

To begin, suppose Tony decides not to keep his life savings in a biscuit tin under his bed. Instead, he decides to deposit the grand sum of $1,000 in an account with First Canadian Bank. Table 8.2 shows the effect on First Canadian Bank's T-account.

So far, there has been no effect on the money supply. Currency in circulation fell by $1,000, but checkable bank deposits rose by the same amount. Since banks desire to maintain a 10 percent reserve ratio, First Canadian Bank only needs to hold $100 in reserves. It can increase its profits by lending out the other $900. Suppose it lends the money to Brian, who wishes to buy a new billiard table. The effect on First Canadian Bank's T-account is shown in Table 8.3.

First Canadian has now maximized its lending given its desired 10 percent reserve ratio. It is therefore maximizing its profits and is in equilibrium. But the banking system is not.

After Brian buys his new billiard table from Canadian Billiard Inc., the company deposits the $900 into its account at Second Canadian Bank, which will keep

Table 8.2 Effect of $1,000 deposit at First Canadian Bank

Assets		Liabilities	
Reserves	+ $1,000	Deposits	+ $1,000

Table 8.3 Effect after First Canadian loans $900 to Brian

Assets		Liabilities	
Reserves	+ $100	Deposits	+ $1,000
Loans	+$900	Debt	No change
Securities	No change	Capital (Equity)	No change

10 percent of the new bank deposit as reserves ($90), and lend out the rest. Suppose it lends the remaining $810 to Rose who uses the money to buy a new saddle from Albion Saddlemakers. They deposit the money in (say) the Third Canadian Bank, which duly holds 10 percent as reserves ($81) and lends out the rest ($729).

Clearly, the total increase in bank deposits is an infinite progression. So far, we have the initial deposit of $1000 by Tony, plus the $900 deposited by Canadian Billiard Inc., plus $810 deposited by Albion Saddlemakers, plus $729 that is just about to be spent and redeposited. Denoting the total increase in bank deposits as T, we can write:

$$T = \$1,000 + \$900 + \$810 + \$729 + \cdots$$

Or equivalently, $T = \$1,000\{1 + 0.9 + 0.81 + 0.729 + \cdots\}$

Considering the numbers in the curly brackets, can you guess what number would appear next? To get the next number in the series, we would multiply the previous number by 0.9. This is one minus the desired reserve ratio of 0.1. Denoting the *desired reserve ratio* by "*rr*," we can write:

$$T = \$1,000 \{1 + (1 - rr) + (1 - rr)^2 + (1 - rr)^3 + \cdots\}$$

The expression in the curly brackets is a geometric progression where each subsequent number is getting smaller. We could *derive* the solution to this, but instead we will just *state* the general mathematical solution for such progressions. It is $a/(1 - g)$, where "*a*" is the first term in the series, and "*g*" is the common ratio. Using this, we get:

$$T = \$1,000 \times \frac{1}{1 - (1 - rr)} = \$1,000 \times \frac{1}{rr}$$

Thus, to calculate the total increase in bank deposits from the initial $1,000 deposit, we must multiply that initial deposit by the inverse of the reserve ratio. This reserve ratio can be the *required* or the *desired* reserve ratio. In our example, *rr* is 0.1, its inverse is 10, and the total increase in bank deposits is $10,000. In summary, the reserve ratio is a key magnitude. The inverse of the reserve ratio is the deposit multiplier.

$$\text{The Deposit Multiplier} = \frac{1}{rr}$$

Before moving on, we should note that the effect on the money supply is $9,000, not $10,000. While the total change in bank deposits is $10,000, there is now $1,000 less currency in the hands of the public.

$$\text{The Change in the Money Supply} = \frac{\$1,000}{rr} - \$1,000$$

Tony no longer has $1,000 in his biscuit tin under his bed. That money is now dispersed throughout the banking system and is being held as reserves to support an extra $10,000 of deposits.

Relaxing the initial assumptions The money multiplier process and the deposit multiplier formula depend on our two initial assumptions: banks maintain a specific reserve ratio (required or desired), and the public already has all the cash it needs. But if banks do not foresee profitable and secure opportunities to make loans, they may prefer to hold "excess reserves," and the money deposited will not be lent out. This is most likely to occur when business conditions are depressed, such as in a recession. In times like that, the propensity of banks to hold excess reserves can turn the deposit-creation process into one of deposit destruction. We also assumed that the public has all the cash it needs. However, if the public wants to hold extra cash, perhaps because of an increase in uncertainty, the money spent will not be redeposited in the banks. Either way, the money multiplier process will be short-circuited.

An important example of money multiplier working in reverse occurred in the United States during the Great Depression. After a wave of bank runs and bank closings in the early 1930s, households withdrew deposits from banks, preferring cash. Meanwhile, to protect themselves from bank runs, bankers increased their reserve ratios. As a result, between 1929 and 1933 the money supply fell by 28 percent.[5] In an influential book published in 1963, Milton Friedman and Anna Schwartz argued that the fall in the money supply was the main cause of the Great Depression, and the US Federal Reserve could and should have prevented it.[6]

1.5 Central banks

All central banks are owned by their respective governments, but beginning in the 1980s, many central banks won a degree of autonomy from their governments. This was granted because it was recognized that political interference with monetary policy can be harmful. In particular, governments are sometimes tempted to fund their spending by printing money, which could lead to inflation. Central bank autonomy separates the power to spend (which the government has) from the power to print money (which the central bank has).

The central bank oversees and regulates the country's banking system and implements monetary policy. In some ways central banks are just like ordinary banks: they accept deposits and give loans; they have assets and liabilities; and they make a profit (which is remitted to the government). But unlike commercial banks, central banks do not have the objective of maximizing their profits: their objective is to maximize the national interest, however that may be defined.

Central banks have two clients: the government and commercial banks. The functions of central banks are related to the clients they serve. So, we can say central banks serve two main functions: they act as the government's bank and they act as the "bankers' bank" (the bank for commercial banks).

We will illustrate the functions of a typical central bank using the balance sheet of the Bank of Canada as an example. Table 8.4 shows the Bank of Canada's assets and liabilities as of December 31, 2017. Its four key functions are illustrated.

The central bank acts as the government's bank Line 1 of Table 8.4 shows how the central bank acts as banker for the government: on the liability side, it accepts deposits from the government; on the asset side, we see that it makes loans to the government by buying government bonds. Indeed, Canadian government bonds represented over 90 percent of the Bank's total assets on December 31, 2017.

The central bank issues currency As the government's bank, a key role of the central bank is to issue currency. It is the central bank's responsibility to prevent counterfeiting, and to ensure that the supply of bank notes meets public demand. In line 2, on the liability side of Table 8.4 we see there was nearly $86 billion worth of bank notes in circulation, which amounted to over 75 percent of the Bank's total liabilities.

The central bank conducts monetary policy As the government's bank, the central bank conducts monetary policy. This may involve controlling interest rates, the quantity of money, the exchange rate, or some combination. Since the central bank may occasionally intervene in foreign exchange markets to moderate fluctuations in the value of the Canadian dollar, it needs to hold foreign currency. We see these holdings on the asset side of line 3.

The central bank acts as the bankers' bank On the asset side of line 4, reflecting the central bank's "lender of the last resort" function, we see "advances to commercial banks." No loans were actually outstanding on that date. On the liability side of line 4, the central bank accepts deposits from commercial banks. Rather than holding large cash reserves in their own vaults, it is safer for commercial banks to deposit some cash with the central bank. This permits

Table 8.4 The Bank of Canada's assets and liabilities, December 31, 2017

Line	assets ($ millions)		Liabilities and equity ($ millions)	
1	Government of Canada bonds	$100,457.4	Government deposits	$21,454.2
2	Other short-term loans	9,478.5	Banknotes in circulation	85,855.9
3	Foreign currency assets	14.6	Other liabilities	2,326.1
4	Advances to commercial banks	---	Deposits of commercial banks	968.5
5	Other assets	1149.8	Equity	495.6
	Total assets	**$111,100.3**	**Total liabilities**	**$111,100.3**

the central bank to settle payments between commercial banks at the flick of a keystroke—merely by debiting one account and crediting another.

1.6 Monetary policy tools

Having studied the banking system and the functions of the central bank, we move on to consider how the central bank manages monetary policy. In general, central banks have three main tools at their disposal: reserve requirements, the central bank's policy interest rate, and open-market operations. We consider each in turn.

Reserve requirements Changing the required reserve ratio is a potentially potent tool of monetary policy. Increasing the required reserve ratio forces banks to reduce their lending and hold more reserves, and this reduces the money supply. However, in practice central banks rarely use this tool because it would cause immediate liquidity problems for banks (unless they happen to be holding sufficient excess reserves). One exception is the central bank of China, which regularly changes required reserve ratios to control the money supply. Of course, this tool is not available in countries that have abolished required reserve ratios.

The central bank's policy interest rate In the normal course of doing business, some banks may become short of cash, while others may have excess. To cope with this possibility, most well-developed financial systems have an institutional arrangement—a market—where banks can easily borrow and lend short-term funds among themselves. Often, as in Canada, it is called the "overnight" market (since funds are loaned overnight); in the United States it is called the "federal funds" market (since it is the Federal Reserve that requires banks to have sufficient funds). The interest rate is set by supply and demand, and gets its name from the market. Thus, in Canada it is called the "overnight rate" and in the United States it is called the "federal funds rate." In both cases, the central bank influences the supply of funds to bring this interest rate in line with its target. *Thus, the overnight market rate is the central bank's policy interest rate target.*

Banks that are unable to get sufficient reserves from the overnight market can borrow directly from the central bank itself, though at a penalty interest rate. This interest rate is usually called the *bank rate* (though in the United States it is called the *discount rate*), and is set above the overnight market rate in order to discourage banks from turning to the central bank. How much the bank rate exceeds the overnight rate depends on the central bank. In Canada, it is always one-quarter of a percentage point higher.

Banks that have excess reserves, and do not wish to lend to other banks in the overnight market, can deposit those reserves with the central bank and earn interest on their deposits. In Canada, this interest rate is called the "deposit rate" and is set at one-half of 1 percentage point (or "50 basis points") below the bank rate. (In the United States, it is called "IOER," denoting the "interest rate

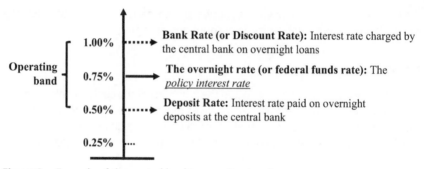

Figure 8.1 Example of the central bank's operating band

on excess reserves.") The gap between the rate at which the central bank lends to commercial banks (the top of the band) and the rate paid by the central bank on commercial bank deposits (the bottom of the band) is known as the central bank's *operating band*. Figure 8.1 illustrates this operating band when the policy interest rate is 0.75 percent.

The overnight rate must be within the operating band. No bank would borrow from another bank at a rate higher than it would be charged by the central bank; similarly, no bank would lend to another bank at a rate lower than it could receive from the central bank. In practice, the central bank intervenes in the overnight market such that the overnight rate is directly in the center of the operating band, and equal to the central bank's policy target rate. In Canada, the UK, and the United States, the central bank announces its policy target rate at regular intervals throughout the year, usually every six weeks. Central banks then use "open-market operations" to achieve the target rate, a method discussed both in the next section and also in Chapter 9.

Changes in the bank rate affect the money supply because it affects the cost to commercial banks of finding themselves short of reserves. Thus, commercial banks are more willing to extend loans when the bank rate is reduced, and less willing to extend loans when the bank rate is increased.

Furthermore, changes in the bank rate affect other interest rates in the economy. Because of substitutability between different assets, the different interest rates tend to rise and fall together, from short-term lines of credit to longer-term interest rates that are more relevant for determining consumption and investment spending. However, as discussed in the next chapter, announcing changes to the bank rate is not enough to induce interest rates to change. The central bank must take additional actions—open-market operations—to ensure that interest rates in the economy move in the desired direction.

Open-market operations This is the principal tool of monetary policy. Central banks can increase the *monetary base*, defined as currency in circulation plus bank reserves, by buying government bonds from banks and paying for them with cash. For example, suppose the central bank bought $100 million of government bonds from First Canadian Bank.

Table 8.5 An open-market purchase of $100 million

Central Bank	Assets		Liabilities	
	Government bonds	+ $100m	Banknotes in Circulation	+ $100m
First Canadian Bank	Assets		Liabilities	
	Government bonds Reserves	– $100m + $100m	No change	

Table 8.5 shows that both the assets and liabilities of the central bank increase by $100 million. Simultaneously, the assets of First Canadian Bank are modified: $100 million worth of government bonds are replaced with cash. Now First Canadian Bank has excess reserves and would normally respond by increasing its loans. This starts the multiple expansion of deposits that increases the money supply.

From whom the central bank buys the bonds is unimportant. If the Bank of Canada bought the bonds from a private individual instead of a bank, the individual would deposit the money with a commercial bank, and the money multiplier process is again set in motion.

Open-market operations and the foreign exchange market It is crucial to understand that it doesn't matter what asset the central bank buys and sells when it conducts open-market operations. Instead of buying bonds, the central bank could just as easily buy $1 million worth of office furniture using freshly printed dollar bills. In this case, on the asset side of its balance sheet, other assets (office furniture) would increase by $1 million; and on the liabilities side of its balance sheet, "banknotes in circulation" would increase by $1 million. When this cash is deposited with a commercial bank, a multiple expansion of the money supply is again set in motion.

Of course, central banks do not often buy (or sell) office furniture. However, there is one other asset (besides bonds) that it does frequently buy and sell, and that is foreign currency. Suppose, for example, that the country's exchange rate is appreciating relative to its trading partners, and this is adversely affecting the country's exports. If the central bank wants to limit this appreciation, it will enter the foreign exchange market and sell domestic currency, thus reducing its price. In return it will receive foreign currency. In effect, it has bought foreign currency using Canadian dollars. On the asset side of its balance sheet "foreign currency assets" increase, and on the liability side "banknotes in circulation" increase.

Since the only place one can spend domestic currency is in the domestic economy, sooner or later that money will be spent and deposited into the commercial banking system, leading to a multiple expansion of the money supply. In effect, the central bank has made an open-market purchase of foreign exchange.

The bottom line is this: it doesn't matter what asset the central bank buys—bonds, furniture, or foreign exchange. All of them lead to a multiple expansion of the money supply.

Similarly, if the central bank wants to support the value of the country's exchange rate, it will buy domestic currency on the foreign exchange market using its foreign currency reserves. On the asset side of the central bank's balance sheet "foreign currency assets" decrease, and on the liability side "bank notes in circulation" decrease. In effect, the central bank has made an open-market sale (of foreign currency) that will lead to a multiple contraction of the money supply. Again, it does not matter what asset the central bank sells: bonds, furniture, or foreign exchange. All of them lead to a multiple contraction of the money supply.

The key point to all of this is that attempts by the central bank to influence the value of the exchange rate necessarily affect the supply of money. Therefore, a "fixed" or "pegged" exchange rate is inconsistent with independent monetary policy since it requires the central bank to continually intervene to offset those market forces that would otherwise change the exchange rate. Effectively, the central bank loses control over both the timing and magnitude of its open-market operations (those that involve buying and selling foreign currency).

An independent monetary policy is only possible when the central bank adopts a "floating" (or "flexible") exchange rate regime and allows market forces to determine the exchange rate with no intervention of any sort on its part.

1.7 Interest rate targets versus money supply targets

As will be explained more fully in the next chapter, every central bank has a choice—it can choose to target the money supply (and let interest rates adjust) or it can target interest rates (and let the money supply adjust to changes in desired money holdings). But which policy is better? There are several reasons why central banks have now adopted a policy of targeting interest rates.

The first reason is that the money supply cannot be controlled very precisely. Although central banks have substantial power to influence the money supply (primarily through open-market operations) changes in household and banking preferences can also change the supply of money. For example, if households choose to hold more cash there will be less for the commercial banks to hold as reserves. Or, if commercial banks feel that the economic environment is too risky, they may increase their reserve ratio. In both cases, the money supply will decrease.

Another reason why the money supply cannot be controlled very precisely is that it is not clear what it is. As we have seen, there are many measures of the money supply, from M1 to M3, as well as M1+ to M3+. These measures differ not just in magnitude but also in their annual growth rates. At any given time, some measures of the money supply may be increasing, while others may be decreasing.

On the other hand, while the central bank cannot control the money supply very precisely, it can control its key policy interest rate almost perfectly. As we mentioned, the central bank announces a target for the overnight rate, and conducts open-market operations so as to keep the overnight rate within a narrow band of that target. However, in practice central banks can hit the target with precision.

There is one further advantage of an interest rate target over a money supply target: changes in interest rates are more meaningful to firms and households than changes in the money supply. For example, if we hear that mortgage lending rates at commercial banks have decreased by 1 percentage point, we can readily understand what this means for our plans to buy a new house. In contrast, if we hear that the money supply has just increased by $5 billion, it is not clear what this means.

These reasons explain why, since the late 1980s, most central banks conduct monetary policy by targeting interest rates rather than the money supply. An interest rate target has two big advantages over a money supply target: it is more easily achieved, and it is more easily understood.

1.8 The financial crisis of 2007–8

It is clear that the maturity transformation function of banks—lending long but borrowing short with a promise to pay back on demand—makes them extremely vulnerable to crises of confidence and "bank runs." But prior to 2007, there had not been a major crisis in advanced economies since the 1930s. It was thought that government oversight of banks—as well as capital requirements, required reserve ratios, deposit insurance, and the central bank's lender of the last resort function—was sufficient to create a safe and reliable financial sector.

Yet, beginning in the late 1990s, excessive lending created the biggest house price bubble in US history. While it lasted, this spectacular boom, mirrored in other countries, helped drive the entire world economy and its stock markets. When the inevitable bust occurred in 2007, many banks incurred losses big enough that they were technically insolvent. The uncertainty caused widespread panic and a freezing of financial flows. There were many actual, as well as near, bankruptcies of financial institutions beginning in 2007 and extending well into 2009.

The feedback loops between credit markets, real estate markets, stock markets, and real economic activity generated the Great Recession—the biggest world recession since the Great Depression. So, what went wrong? How did it occur? The following discussion is organized around four factors: deregulation, financial innovation, monetary policy mistakes, and irrational exuberance.

Deregulation The deregulation was essentially fourfold. First, both the interest rates that could be charged on mortgages and the terms and conditions of mortgages were deregulated in the early 1980s, setting the scene for the entry of predatory mortgage brokers. Second, the Glass–Steagall Act was repealed in 1999, which had prevented the consolidation of commercial and investment banks. Ostensibly, this was to allow banks to enjoy economies of scale, but it exposed commercial banks to the increased risk associated with investment banking. Third, one year later, "over-the-counter" derivatives were deregulated, which meant that there was no oversight of the trillion-dollar growth in credit default swaps, the vehicle that (supposedly) insured mortgage-backed securities. Fourth, the same bill (the Commodity Futures Modernization Act, 2000) slashed the budget of the Securities and Exchange Commission, weakening the oversight body at a time when the material needing oversight was growing enormously.[7]

Financial innovation Unlike deregulation, which can be clearly articulated with specific actions on specific dates, the evolution of financial innovation was more organic and subtle. However, two elements stand out. First, mortgage-backed securities became more complex and opaque, which hid the increased risk they came to embody as a result of subprime lending.[8] Second, shadow banks—insurance companies, pension funds, investment banks, mutual funds, and hedge funds—were deeply involved, and they were not protected by the same suite of tools provided to commercial banks.[9] (See Section 2.4 of Chapter 5 for more details of both the deregulation and the financial innovation that occurred in the United States.)

Monetary policy mistakes Besides deregulation and financial innovation, the financial crisis also had its origin in monetary policy mistakes. There were two specific mistakes, and one general mistake.

The first specific mistake was the policy of very low interest rates implemented after the 2001 recession. To promote a faster recovery, the Federal Reserve pushed its policy interest rate down to 1 percent in June 2003 and held it there for an entire year. This pushed up the demand for houses and fed the house price boom. Since the return on safe government bonds was so low, it also encouraged investors to seek higher returns both by purchasing riskier securities and by increasing leverage.

The second specific mistake was the US government decision to allow Lehman Brothers—the fourth largest investment bank in the United States—to go bankrupt on September 15, 2008. It was the largest bankruptcy in US history and precipitated worldwide financial panic: stock prices plummeted and credit markets froze. Making Lehman Brothers "reap what it sowed" was intended to serve as a warning to financial institutions that they could not count on always being bailed out. But three days later, after witnessing the consequences of the Lehman bankruptcy, the government did bail out AIG, then the world's largest insurance company. These two very different solutions in "too big to fail" institutions left government policy in a state of confusion.

So much for the two specific mistakes. The general mistake was that monetary policy was excessively focused on inflation control and paid insufficient attention to the health of the financial system, including factors that could increase systemic risk. Nowadays, there is more talk about the importance of "macro prudential policy" that focuses on whether financial imbalances are developing that could pose systemic risks to the financial sector.

Irrational exuberance The last element is, of course, human nature. As we know, human beings are prone to irrational exuberance; we forget about the last bust and believe "this time is different." As people came to believe that house prices would rise forever, mortgage lending standards dropped, and leverage ratios increased. Ability to pay the mortgage seemed unimportant if the house could be resold at a profit in a matter of months. Irrational exuberance is the element emphasized in classic books on the boom and bust cycle—books like John Kenneth Galbraith's *A Short History of Financial Euphoria* (1990), or Charles Kindleberger's *Manias, Panics, and Crashes: A History of Financial Crises* (1978).

1.9 What actions were taken

The situation was saved (to paraphrase Star Trek's tagline) by central banks boldly lending where no central bank had lent before—and on a scale never seen before. In the United States, the Federal Reserve went beyond its mandate of lender of the last resort to commercial banks, and became lender of the last resort to many shadow banks including the investment banks Goldman Sachs and Morgan Stanley, and the insurance giant, AIG. These institutions pledged their assets on hand as collateral. Besides lending funds to financial institutions, the Federal Reserve also extended loans directly to nonfinancial companies by buying their "commercial paper"—unsecured, short-term debt issued by corporations, typically to finance payrolls.

Further, in October 2008, the "Troubled Asset Relief Program" (or TARP) was approved, whereby the US government would buy $700 billion of mortgage-backed securities that nobody wanted, and were clogging up the financial system. At least, that was the plan. Instead, the money was used to recapitalize the banks directly—they were supplied with cash in return for shares. The effect was to partly nationalize the financial system.

Recent data show that the US Federal Reserve lent no less than $3.3 trillion to prop up the world's economy, including to the Bank of England. The amount of money "lent, spent, or committed" was an incredible $7.7 trillion according to the influential financial firm Bloomberg, which points out that even that number might be an underestimate.[10]

By 2010, the worst was over. Almost all of the Federal Reserve loans had been repaid, and the bank shares bought under the TARP had been sold for a profit of $12 billion for the US taxpayer. The combination of extreme actions by the Federal Reserve and other central banks, coupled with expansionary fiscal policy, brought the economy out of its slump and restored economic growth. But it was a very close call.

1.10 Financial reform in the United States

The Wall Street Reform and Consumer Protection Act of 2010—generally known as "Dodd–Frank Act"—attempted to address the many weaknesses exposed by the financial crisis. Its aim was essentially fourfold: first, to improve transparency in the financial system; second, stop banks from taking excessive risks; third, end "too big to fail" (and the necessity for bailouts); and fourth, extend protection to consumers against abusive financial practices. How were these aims achieved?

The Act increased transparency by requiring that derivatives—such as credit default swaps—be traded on centralized exchanges where they could more easily be monitored. Excessive risk was limited by a provision known as the "Volcker Rule," which restricts the ways banks can invest, limiting speculative trading and eliminating proprietary trading.

"Too big to fail" was addressed by empowering the Federal Reserve to supervise financial institutions that are deemed to be systemically important, and subjecting these large institutions to a tougher regulatory regime. In addition, regulators were authorized to seize any big, tottering financial firm and wind it down in an orderly fashion. This was to be handled by a new agency, the Financial Stability Oversight Council.

Finally, to protect borrowers from being exploited through seemingly attractive financial deals they do not understand, the Consumer Financial Protection Bureau (CFPB) was created.

One of the main weaknesses exposed by the financial crisis was lack of regulation of shadow banks. The Dodd–Frank Act repaired this by the transparency required in the derivatives market and also by the "too big to fail" legislation, which applied to all financial institutions.

The Dodd–Frank Act is complex, itself 848 pages long, with many of those pages directing dozens of regulatory agencies to revise or create even more regulations. Critics have argued that its complexity makes it too burdensome on financial businesses, especially small ones that lack the resources to meet all the new regulatory requirements. Some of its provisions have already been rolled back. In 2018, the rules on all but the largest banks were relaxed, auto dealers were exempted from the CFPB, and the budgets of the regulatory agencies were restricted.

Virtually everyone agrees that prior to the meltdown, the financial system operated with far too much leverage. In part, excessive leverage can be traced to lax regulation and inadequate laws—which Dodd–Frank tries to fix. But a great deal of it reflected poor business (and household) judgments.

1.11 Conclusion

In summary, money is whatever is accepted as a means of payment. To be accepted, it must be a viable store of value and a unit of account. Bank deposits constitute the biggest component of the money supply. Since there are various types of bank deposits with varying liquidity, there is an arbitrary element to the quantitative measure of the money supply.

Because withdrawals are steady and normally predictable, banks only need to hold a fraction of their deposits as reserves, and can lend out the rest. The banking system as a whole can create (or destroy) money through this lending process. The maturity transformation function of banks—borrowing short but lending long—coupled with the nature of fractional reserve banking makes banking inherently risky. Not even solvent banks with positive net equity value can withstand a bank run.

There are several lines of defense that mitigate the risks of a bank run: deposit insurance, required reserve ratios, required capital ratios, central bank willingness to be the lender of last resort to banks, and regulatory oversight.

The central bank can control the money supply through open-market operations, provided the exchange rate is allowed to float. In practice, central banks nowadays prefer to target interest rates rather than the money supply.

The worldwide financial crisis was partly caused by the development of a shadow banking sector outside the regulation and oversight of the central bank. It was also caused by policy mistakes and irrational exuberance. Financial reform in the form of the Dodd–Frank Act of 2010 has crucially brought more transparency and regulation to the shadow banking sector. While time will tell how well the reforms work, we must acknowledge that no legislation can change human nature nor its occasional tendency toward irrational exuberance.

2 THE ANTI-TEXT

The global "Occupy Movement" began with a call to occupy New York's Wall Street financial district on September 17, 2011. It was born from frustration with extreme inequality, political corruption, and corporate influence of government. Nowhere was this corruption and influence more evident than the events surrounding the global financial meltdown. Criminal activity had been systemic in driving the subprime bubble, and bankers had earned huge rewards in the process. Even while the banks were being bailed out, the bankers continued to give themselves huge bonuses. No Wall Street CEOs were sent to jail. And this contrasts with the last big financial scandal in the United States—the Savings and Loan (S&L) Crisis of the 1980s—a scandal that was only one-seventieth as big, where hundreds of Wall Street executives went to prison.

In the anti-text, we discuss various strands of explanation. One strand is the free market ideology that takes at face value the "contribution" of the financial sector to GDP. This view assumes that competition drives earnings, and financial traders and bank executives earn what they are worth. We assess this view, using both economic theory and the evidence of endemic criminal behavior in banking. We enquire into the bailouts: was all the money paid back? Was there an alternative solution? And finally, we address the question of the solution: is it more regulation, better regulation, or something else entirely?

Before embarking on our intellectual journey, we begin by reconsidering the key questions of how to define money, and whether the quantity of money matters. The answers turn out to be relevant to Modern Monetary Theory (MMT).

2.1 What is money?

In defining money by focusing on its functions, all mainstream textbooks ignore the most critical element of money: the government. The textbooks explain that modern fiat money is not backed up by anything. And while it is true that fiat money cannot be exchanged for anything at a bank other than itself, it is not true that it is not backed up by anything. On the contrary, all modern money is backed up by the *power of the state*. This point is emphasized by MMT.

With a couple of exceptions (such as the Euro) every country has its own currency. This is not a coincidence. It is bound up with sovereign power, political independence, and fiscal authority. Money is always the state's IOU. In buying real resources, and paying in its IOU, the state "spends its currency into existence." People accept the state's IOU because they need it to pay the government what they owe in taxes, fees, and fines. That is because all governments demand payment in its own IOU, its own currency. MMT theorists say, as a shorthand, that "taxes drive money."

Bitcoin and other cryptocurrencies This perspective helps shed light on the question of whether a cryptocurrency (such as Bitcoin) could pose a serious challenge to national currencies. Whatever supposed advantages Bitcoin might possess in terms of speed of settlement, smaller transaction fees, and "decentralized ledger," it has the massive flaw that governments will not accept it.[11] No government would be willing to give up its power to buy resources by issuing its own IOUs—by "printing money." Therefore, we can be confident no cryptocurrency will ever become the usually accepted means of payment.[12]

But what if households suddenly tire of banks, tire of their scandals, or for some other reason decide that a cryptocurrency is their preferred means of payment? If so, central banks will unveil their own digital currencies, denominated in the government's IOU (pounds for the UK, dollars for the United States), one that is superior to a privately provided cryptocurrency. Such digital currencies, called "CBDCs" (central bank digital currencies) are ready to be unveiled if the public mood should shift away from conventional bank money. What would a CBDC look like? It would amount to a digital "coin"—like a bitcoin. But instead of being paper money in a wallet, it would be a digital wallet, carrying money (the government's IOU) that would be a direct claim against the central bank.

Final question: why can we be confident the central bank's digital currency will be superior to a cryptocurrency like Bitcoin? Would it have a superior "blockchain technology"?[13] The answer here is that a CBDC would not need blockchain technology. Blockchain is really just a glorified spreadsheet that registers transactions and trades on public decentralized peer-to-peer ledgers. It is the accuracy of this ledger that gives people confidence in the cryptocurrency. But because we already trust the central bank's currency, we don't need a distributed ledger to believe we have just received final payment. This gives the central bank's digital currency a crucial advantage not only in terms of trust but also in terms of the real resources (electricity) required to create it.

2.2 Why does the quantity of money matter?

Mainstream textbooks reassure the reader that central banks can control the supply of money, despite two difficulties: first, banks may not lend out their excess reserves; and second, the public may change the amount of cash it desires to hold. Nearly all of them omit the most important difficulty: the central bank's commitment to being "lender of the last resort." If commercial banks need more reserves, they can sell government treasury bills to the central bank. As "lender of the last resort" the central bank cannot refuse to buy. This means that *commercial banks might themselves be the ones initiating open-market operations!* And this makes the quantity of money endogenous. Central banks cannot control the supply of money while maintaining their role as lender of the last resort. But why should this matter?

The textbooks are not clear on why the quantity of money matters. There seems to be a residual element of belief in the quantity theory of money—an old theory coming out of the Chicago School—which asserts a link between the quantity of money and nominal GDP, and in the long run (when output is at full employment) a link between the rate of money growth and inflation. Indeed, the very commonly included discussion of prisoner-of-war camps during the Second World War, and the fluctuation of prices (denominated in cigarettes) as the quantity of cigarettes changed, is precisely a quantity theory of money explanation. But this is not consistent with the AD–AS model presented in mainstream textbooks.

What matters in the AD–AS model is the rate of interest, the cost of borrowing money. This is an important determinant of consumption and investment spending, which we know are important for determining AD. Normally, knowing the rate of interest is sufficient, we don't need to know the quantity of money. And central banks can accurately target interest rates despite the endogeneity of the money supply. So, the central bank's inability to control the supply of money does not matter.[14]

From the government's perspective, there is only one monetary aggregate that matters: the monetary base. This is the total amount of currency in existence in the economy whether held by the public, commercial banks, or the central bank. This is the government's IOU, and an increase in the monetary base means the government has purchased resources by "printing money." As emphasized by MMT, spending by monetarily sovereign governments is not constrained by hard financial limits. Moreover, an increase in government IOUs will have no necessary consequences in terms of inflation. Even mainstream textbooks argue that inflation will only be generated by excess AD.

The clear link between the monetary base and the government's ability to spend is revealed once we tear down the veil between the government and the central bank. In technical language, this tearing down the veil is called "consolidating their accounts." [15]

> Question for your professor: Does the quantity of money really matter? Does its rate of growth matter? Would different definitions of money have different rates of growth? How would we know which one mattered?

2.3 Banking irregularities: the incompetent, the immoral, and the illegal

After reading the mainstream textbooks, you would be forgiven for thinking that the financial meltdown was the result of honest mistakes; for thinking the core problem was irrational exuberance and too much leverage—spiced up by financial innovation, deregulation, and the development of shadow banking—producing an outcome no-one could have foreseen. But such a view is a complete whitewash of what went on. The subprime bubble and the financial crash could not have happened without systemic criminal behavior at the highest executive levels.

William Black (2010) talks of criminal behavior in banking as epidemics. He was a senior financial regulator and litigation director, and played a central role in the effort to stop the S&L frauds that occurred in the 1980s. He successfully prosecuted hundreds of their senior executives. But there was no similar effort to prosecute senior executives for their criminal behavior in the years following 2008. Only the *banks* were prosecuted—not the *people* responsible. As a result, criminal behavior has been, and is still, rampant in the financial sector.

Here is an exercise. Go to your favorite internet search engine, and type in "bank scandals." Where to start? The fifteen most recent? The ten biggest?

As John Lanchester (2013) put it, there is so much lurid wrongdoing in the world of finance, the accusations can become a cacophony which drown out—or somehow normalize—specific instances of wrongdoing.

Given the avalanche of examples, the hard part is finding an organizing principle to present them. For brevity and succinctness, we proceed as follows. First, we forget any scandal that occurred before the meltdown, since the point is to show that no lessons were learnt from the meltdown. Second, we divide the scandals into three types depending on which feature is most dominant: incompetency, immorality, or criminality.

The incompetent We begin with the incompetent, and two fiascos that illustrate that—contrary to the claims made by mainstream textbooks—the financial system does not necessarily reduce risk. Indeed, even complex financial derivatives created to control risks can instead become vehicles used by traders to gamble big time.

Both fiascos occurred in London at big international banks. The "UBS rogue trader scandal" occurred in 2011 when Kweku Adoboli lost around $2 billion betting on "forward-settling ETF positions." Because he hid his losses (by entering false information into UBS's computers), he was sentenced to 7 years in prison for fraud. The "London Whale" fiasco occurred in 2012, when a trader at JPMorgan Chase lost $6.2 billion betting on an index of credit default swaps. The trader, Bruno Iksil, was fired. In both cases, the banks were fined for having inadequate internal controls and oversight.[16]

Traders are not necessarily pointy-headed nerds with IQs over 150. Instead, they are just people gambling with other people's money. As we will discuss in more detail below, the incentives built into banker's pay mean that traders have a one-sided incentive to make the biggest bets possible. It is a market failure that requires government regulation to fix.

The immoral We focus here on bank bonuses—paid while the banks were being bailed out by taxpayers.[17] In a 2009 report by New York Attorney General Andrew Cuomo, it was calculated that in 2008 nine US banks received $175 billion in taxpayer funds and paid out—wait for it—$32.6 billion in bonuses![18]

One of the most egregious cases was a shadow bank. It was the insurance giant AIG, the firm that was at the center of the credit default swaps disaster. AIG is notable for posting a loss of $61.7 billion in the fourth quarter of 2008, the largest ever for any corporation, and receiving a bailout of $85 billion on September 16, 2008—a bailout that would eventually grow to roughly $180 billion. Despite the losses and the bailout, AIG paid out $165 million in bonuses to the executives in its financial services division. Bonuses for the entire company were close to $1.2 billion!

Similarly, Merrill Lynch paid its employees $4 billion in bonuses in December 2008, days before it was saved from bankruptcy by being taken over by the Bank of America.

As Cuomo's 2009 report stated, "When the banks did well, their employees were paid well. When the banks did poorly, their employees were paid well. When the banks did very poorly, they were bailed out by taxpayers and their employees were still paid well." And yet, bonuses are justified as a reward for good performance.

Incidentally, as a sidebar to this discussion, you may remember from Chapter 6 that many countries cut government spending in 2010 as they embraced austerity. This led to an interesting contrast in fortunes between the bankers, who caused the mess, continuing to receive mega bonuses, and retired teachers, nurses, and firefighters—folks who had worked hard all their lives—having their pensions cut. These frustrations helped fuel the Occupy Movement.

The final category of "banking irregularity" concerns their criminal behavior. This category is so big it needs its own section heading.

2.4 Criminal wrongdoing

We begin by taking an aggregate look at all the fines imposed on banks for criminal wrongdoing by US regulators between 2008 and 2017. This breaks down into two parts. First, we have the criminal activity directly related to the subprime crisis. This amounts to $150 billion paid between 2008 and 2017, about 60 percent of which was to settle charges that banks deliberately misled buyers of mortgage-backed securities—that is, they knowingly sold toxic assets while pretending they were low-risk securities. The remainder was for a variety of criminal conduct ranging from the faulty underwriting of mortgages, improper foreclosure practices (the infamous "Robo-signing" scandal), and discriminatory lending. Second, we have criminal activity unrelated to the subprime crisis—the more recent activity. This includes laundering drug money, terrorist financing, rigging benchmark interest rates, and violating US sanctions law. Including the fines for this activity brings the total to a staggering $242 billion.[19]

The Bank of America leads the ignominious tally with $76 billion in fines to cover the institution's own mortgage sales as well as the conduct of subprime mortgage lender Countrywide and broker Merrill Lynch—two companies it had acquired which were at the epicenter of fraudulent practices. JPMorgan Chase, the owner of Bear Stearns and Washington Mutual, has been fined the second largest amount of nearly $44 billion. Several other big banks have been fined over $10 billion.[20] The eleven banks listed in Figure 8.2 make up 93 percent of the total fines imposed.[21] Fines of this magnitude are not imposed for honest mistakes. They are imposed for criminal behavior.

So, did anyone go to jail? You bet they did! US prosecutors convicted 324 individuals of crimes linked to the crisis: mortgage lenders, loan officers, and real estate brokers. They even convicted a few CEOs and executive vice presidents of tiny regional banks and subsidiary banks.[22] But no senior

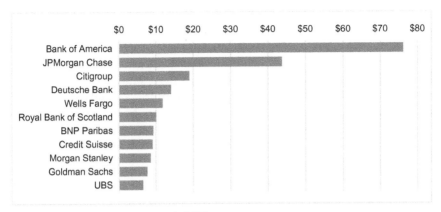

Figure 8.2 Bank fines 2008–17, in billions

executives from the big banks listed in Figure 8.2 went to jail.[23] And only one Wall Street CEO was prosecuted and that was Angilo Mozilo, the CEO of Countrywide Financial—the mortgage originator that issued more toxic mortgages than any other; the company that would give anyone a loan as long as they could "fog a mirror." He got away with a fine.[24]

We address the question of *why* no big fish have gone to jail in the next section. But for now, let us content ourselves with asking why it matters. After all, the companies were hit with big fines. Isn't that punishment enough? The answer here is a resounding "no." In the classic paper, Akerlof and Romer (1994) explain how banks can be looted by their executives. William Black put it in simpler language in the title of his 2005 book, *The Best Way to Rob a Bank Is to Own One*. Think of it this way: we don't fine banks for being robbed! We catch the criminals. Furthermore, who suffers when a bank is hit with a huge fine? Not the white-collar criminals; it is the shareholders. And if white-collar crimes of that magnitude are left unpunished, then criminal activity will flourish. And flourish it has.

In Appendix 1 at the end of this chapter, I present a list of the major big bank scandals that have come to light since the subprime meltdown. It shows that banks have knowingly laundered money for drug cartels, terrorists, and Russian mobsters. They have been complicit in Ponzi schemes. They have forged documents on a mass scale and illegally foreclosed mortgages. They have sold insurance products they knew provided no coverage. They have systematically cheated their own clients. They have manipulated the key international benchmark interest rate, underpinning $350 trillion of derivatives. They have manipulated gold prices, other precious metals prices, and exchange rates. They have rigged auctions and ripped off municipalities. There is no criminal organization with whom the banks won't do business, provided there is sufficient profit. There is no price they won't illegally manipulate. There is no auction they won't try to rig. There is no-one the banks won't rip off. If you think this is an exaggeration, go read Appendix 1 now.

As Robert Prasch (2012) succinctly put it (when talking about the big banks), "fraud was not an aberration at these firms, it was their core business strategy." The consequences have been fines that look huge—but, in reality, are just a few weeks of profit—and some small fish—traders mostly—have gone to jail. Big bank CEOs have not been prosecuted, and have rarely even lost their bonuses! The consequences have been borne by the owners of the banks—the shareholders—which in one ironic instance meant that the burden of a fine fell on the government that imposed it.[25]

Question for your professor: The economist Robert Prasch said that fraud was not an aberration at the big banks but their core business strategy. Do you think it is any different now?

2.5 Why did no big bank CEOs go to jail?

In his 2016 book on corporate crime, Sam Buell—a Duke law professor—argues that it is almost impossible to punish CEOs of corporations that do even the most nefarious actions because of the difficulty proving criminal responsibility. He talks of corporations being "big, fancy responsibility-diffusion mechanisms."

But if it is "almost impossible" to prosecute CEOs, then the prosecutions in the 2015 Volkswagen case should not have occurred. When it was discovered that VW had employed a "cheat device" to make it appear that its diesel vehicles passed emissions standards in the EU, the United States, and elsewhere, the company was fined and *the people responsible* have been held accountable. In 2017, Oliver Schmidt, the executive in charge of Volkswagen's US environmental and engineering office, was sentenced to seven years in prison and fined $400,000 for his role in the conspiracy to defraud. In 2019, the ex-CEO Martin Winterkorn and four other executives were charged in Germany with knowing about the conspiracy as early as 2014 but failing to inform regulators or consumers. They face up to ten years in prison.[26]

Big bank CEOs were all implicated by hard evidence—whistleblower evidence, email evidence, and testimony given under oath. The whistleblower stories of people like Alayne Fleischmann (who was a JPMorgan Chase banker), or Carolyn Wind, or Everett Stern (who were whistleblowers at HSBC), or Michael Winston (who was a whistleblower at Countryside Financial, and who cofounded "Bank Whistleblowers United") all reveal that the very top bosses knew exactly what was going on, and reacted vindictively to the person worrying or complaining about it.[27] Furthermore, hundreds of Wall Street executives went to prison during the fraud-fueled bank crisis known as the S&L Scandal of the 1980s.[28] So, what changed with regard to the financial sector?

Many economists argue that what changed was the financial system becoming ever more concentrated, ever more dominated by a few large firms. It happened in part because of the repeal of the Glass–Steagall Act in 1999, which allowed investment banks and commercial banks to merge.[29] And it happened in part because of the 2007 financial crisis and the subsequent Great Recession, when weak banks were either bought up by stronger banks or went bankrupt.[30] Fewer banks, and larger banks, that are more interconnected increase the systemic risk to the whole system of prosecuting any one bank. It is argued that banks are *"too big to jail."*

This argument was articulated in a famous memo written by Eric Holder in June 1999, when he was Deputy Attorney General under President Bill Clinton.[31] The memo was sent to "all component heads and US attorneys" and asserts that the "collateral consequences" from prosecutions—including corporate instability or collapse—should be considered when deciding whether to prosecute a big financial institution. It explains why, when Holder became US Attorney General from 2009 to 2015, the Justice Department's approach was to collect incriminating evidence, threaten public disclosure of criminal behavior, and then extract a huge financial settlement in exchange for keeping the evidence sealed.

The "too big to jail" sentiment was echoed by Holder's "enforcement chief," Lanny Breuer, in December 2012.[32] In a press conference, Breuer announced that HSBC bank would be fined $1.9 billion for nearly a decade of knowingly laundering drug money for Mexican drug cartels—among other high crimes and misdemeanors. He explained that he chose not to criminally prosecute the bank, nor jail any of its officers, because "HSBC would almost certainly have lost its banking license in the United States. The future of the institution would have been under threat and the entire banking system would have been destabilized."[33]

But this argument strains credulity. Individuals perpetrating crimes need to get arrested, fined, and/or imprisoned. The bank does not need to lose its banking license. If there is no risk to the bank, there is no systemic risk. It's all baloney.

If the "too big to jail" argument is not plausible, what explanations remain? What remains is that the banking industry has effectively captured governments in Western democracies. This has certainly operated through primitive lobbying and campaign contributions—the banking-and-securities industry has become one of the top contributors to political campaigns in the United States. But more importantly it has amassed a "cultural capital"—a belief system or ideological view—that it is the golden goose, the most important source of wealth generation in the economy.[34]

One channel of influence is, of course, the flow of individuals between the banking sector and the government. Appendix 2 lists some of the more important names of Wall Street bankers who have moved into key government positions in the past four US administrations. Note that the treasury secretary is the principal economic advisor to the president, playing a critical role in policymaking. That position has been held by an ex-banker nearly 70 percent of the time. If we were to highlight any name in Appendix 2, it would have to be Robert Rubin. He was cochairman of Goldman Sachs before becoming Bill Clinton's treasury secretary. It was Rubin who recommended against regulating derivatives, and steered through the 1999 repeal of Glass–Steagall—both key elements paving the way for the subprime bubble.

Appendix 2 is striking. But we must realize that it underestimates the influence of Wall Street on government policy for at least four reasons. First, it ignores individuals who go to Wall Street *after* leaving government, possibly as a reward for services rendered. Second, it ignores people who were not bankers per se but were employed by bankers or represented bankers— people, in fact, like Eric Holder and Lanny Breuer who were lawyers before entering public service, and represented the interests of bankers.[35] Third, it ignores the personal connections from overlapping social circles. And fourth, it focuses on only the very upper echelons of power, whereas the personal connections were multiplied many times over at the lower levels of government. Even so, it is apparent from Appendix 2 that it is irrelevant whether the administration is Democrat or Republican, Wall Street bankers are inside the government, holding key policymaking positions. It is what William Black calls "the modern face of crony capitalism." When talking about why no big bank CEOs went to jail, Black says, "It's all about power. And it is not just economic power—it's political power. It is the great threat, not just to our economy, but also to our democracy. I could have never imagined that in my lifetime an administration would actually say that there were entities too big to prosecute."[36]

But what about the belief that the financial sector is the golden goose, the most important source of wealth generation in the economy? Is it true?

Question for your professor: There was criminal wrongdoing by big banks during the subprime meltdown. Many CEOs were implicated by hard evidence—whistleblower evidence, email evidence, and testimony given under oath. Why did none of the CEOs go to jail?

2.6 The economic contribution of the financial sector

We see the importance of the financial sector by the increased depth and duration of recessions following a financial crisis. A financial crisis brings the economy to its knees. But what about the positive contribution finance makes in normal times?

The value-added of a sector is often used as an indication of its relative importance to the overall economy. For the United States, the value-added of the financial sector is currently about 8 percent of total GDP, and in the UK, it is slightly higher at about 10 percent of GDP. But what is more telling is that in both countries this share has increased almost *fourfold* since the Second World War.

The elevated position of the financial sector is even more obvious when we look at corporate profits. Figure 8.3 shows the share of US financial corporate profits as a percent of total corporate profits.[37] In the first couple of decades following the Second World War, this share was around 16 percent. After 1980, at the beginning of the period of financial deregulation, it began a very rapid increase. Recently, it has been averaging over 40 percent, and before the subprime meltdown it was as high as 53 percent. That is staggering. Superficially at least, this seems to support the view that the financial sector *is* the most important source of wealth generation in the economy. But does this stand up to scrutiny?

Because of the difficulty in measuring the value of the huge number of products and services the banking sector produces, statisticians use the income method described in Chapter 2: they measure the value of output in the banking sector by the incomes generated within it. *Yet, there are many reasons why the value of those incomes—wages and profits—may exceed*

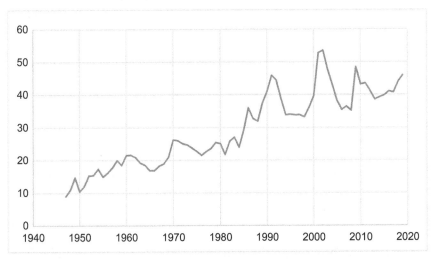

Figure 8.3 US financial corporate profits as a share of total corporate profits

the value of its output. For example, if we take the last section seriously, and accept that the core business strategy of banks was (and still is?) fraud, then we could see the financial sector as a parasite eating its host. Common thieves may make high incomes, but they do not add to output.

It is even difficult to accurately measure the economic contribution of honest banks, for three big reasons. First, banks receive income for both bearing risk and managing risk, but bearing risk is not a productive economic activity. Second, the risks taken by banks have actually been borne by society, not the banks themselves. Third, banks may provide services that have negative spillovers.

As Haldane and Madouros (2011) explain, bearing risk is not by itself a productive activity. For example, someone who buys a corporate bond is bearing risk but not contributing to economic activity. While the bond transaction reallocates risk, it does not change its nature or size. For that reason, statisticians do not count bond purchases as contributing to GDP. On the other hand, the management of risk *is* a productive economic activity. When banks use resources to assess the creditworthiness of borrowers and monitor them, or to assess their own vulnerability to liquidity shocks, they *are* performing productive economic activities.

Unfortunately, statisticians do not distinguish between *risk-bearing* and *risk management* when measuring economic activity. Revenues that banks earn as compensation for risk-bearing—the spread between loan and deposit rates—are counted like any other revenue. So a bank balance sheet expansion—like the one that occurred before the financial crisis—counts as increased output of the banking sector. This is a particularly egregious error when the risk itself is mispriced and mismanaged! According to Colangelo and Inklaar (2010) this effect could lead to an overestimate of the financial sector's output by between 25 percent and 40 percent.

The second reason why the national accounts overstate the value-added of the financial sector is that the risk taken by banks is passed on to society, through government bailouts. This lowers the risks associated with investing in banks, which means lower funding costs and fatter bank profits. Haldane (2011) has sought to estimate the implicit subsidies to banking arising from its too big to fail status. For the largest twenty-five or so global banks, the *average annual* subsidy between 2007 and 2010 was hundreds of billions of dollars—in other words, the annual subsidy is the same order of magnitude as the profits they make.

The third reason the national accounts overstate the value-added of the financial sector comes from negative spillovers that exist even in normal times. As Wouter den Haan (2011) explains, the financial sector may provide services that are useful to a client but not to society as a whole. For example, a financial institution may help to structure a firm's financing in such a way that the firm pays less taxes. Similarly, as Samuelson (1957) noted, getting information milliseconds before others may make banks a lot of money on their trading desks but would create zero social value.

For all of the above reasons, even in normal times, the measured value-added of the financial sector will overstate its actual contribution to GDP, and the profits generated in this sector will exaggerate its economic importance. All of this suggests that incomes generated in the banking sector exceed its output. In effect, the banking sector is transferring value-added from other sectors, and from the economy as a whole via the taxpayer. Thanassoulis (2009) uses these facts to build a case to regulate bankers' pay.

Indirect evidence that much of the activity in the banking sector is not socially useful is provided by Chari and Kehoe (2009). They use US firm-level data and find that 84 percent of firms use internally generated funds to finance their investment. This seriously erodes the view perpetuated in mainstream textbooks that the key role of the banking sector is channeling savings into investment. If the huge banking sector is doing very little of that key role, what is it doing? And how efficiently does it do it?

Direct evidence that the banking sector is actually inefficient is provided by Philippon (2011). He abandons the methodology used in the national accounts—which assumes that incomes generated must equal the value of output created—and instead measures the output of the financial sector directly. He constructs a weighted average of all the financial assets created by the financial sector for the real economy and computes the liquidity benefits of deposits and money market funds. Then he puts all the pieces together to obtain a series for output for the finance industry. Dividing this by the cost (the sum of the profits and wages paid) he finds that the financial sector is less efficient than it was in 1910. He titles his paper "Where is Wal-Mart when you need it?" The point being that we actually want a small financial sector—one that is efficient and of low cost. Indeed, in the 1960s outstanding economic growth was achieved with a much smaller financial sector.

Finally, direct empirical evidence on the link between economic growth and the size of the financial sector was provided in a highly cited paper by Arcand, Berkes, and Panizza (2015). They used many different datasets and empirical approaches to check the robustness of their results. But they consistently found that at high levels of financial depth, more finance is associated with less growth—a result consistent with the view that there can be "too much" finance.

All this leads to the question of how best to reform the financial sector? And will the new regulations introduced as a result of the subprime meltdown actually work?

Question for your professor: How can we measure the output of banks? If criminal wrongdoing by big banks is as prevalent as it seems, would this bias our measure?

2.7 Evaluating the renewed regulation

Will the new rules prevent another financial collapse? No they won't. Both the US-specific Dodd–Frank Act of 2010 and the international Basel III Accord of 2009 are overly complex, poorly designed, and do not go to the heart of the problem.

But what is the heart of the problem? What is the root cause of financial instability? There are so many contenders! Is it that bank executives are paid in ways that encourage excessive risk-taking? Is it that banks are allowed to take trading positions that are so large they could endanger their own financial well-being if the investment turns out badly? Is it that banks are simply too big—too big to fail? Arguably, all of those issues are just symptoms of the real problem, which is ... *too much leverage.*

Recall that *leverage is the ratio of assets to equity capital.* There are basically two ways for a corporation to raise money to buy assets: it can raise equity capital by selling shares or it can borrow and incur debt. The more debt it incurs, the less equity capital it needs to raise, and the greater that equity is levered.

Most nonfinancial corporations rely on equity capital because it is safer. If things go wrong, they can reduce their dividend payments; but they cannot alter the interest obligations associated with their debt. The average equity financing level for nonfinancial corporations in the United States is around 60 percent.[38] Technology companies such as Google often have as much as 95 percent of their assets funded by shareholder equity.

On the other hand, financial corporations usually have very little shareholder equity. For example, in 2013, the eight largest American banks together derived less than 5 percent of their funding from shareholders. This means that financial corporations are incredibly highly levered: shareholder equity of 4 percent, for example, implies a leverage ratio of 25. This is great when asset values increase but disastrous when asset values decrease. Clearly, a decrease in asset values greater than 4 percent wipes out all shareholder value and makes the corporation insolvent (with its debts worth more than its assets). Financial corporations operate this way because they want all the upside, while shoving the downside risk onto the taxpayer through bailouts. Excessive leverage is the most important source of the systemic risk associated with the banking sector.

This suggests a very simple solution to the problem of redesigning banking regulation. Instead of creating vastly complicated rules about what banks *do with their money*—what kinds of assets they hold, dividing these assets into "Tier 1" and "Tier 2" capital depending on their perceived safety, and so on—regulators should worry more about where that *money comes from.* This perspective has been cogently argued by Anat Admati and Martin Hellwig in their 2013 book, *The Bankers' New Clothes: What's Wrong with Banking and What to Do About It.* They argue that banks should be made to move much closer to the average equity financing level of nonfinancial companies.

Needless to say, bankers have resisted this. Martin Wolf (2013, p. 28) writes,

> The UK's Independent Commission on Banking, of which I was a member, made a modest proposal: the proportion of the balance sheet of UK retail banks that has to be funded by equity, instead of debt, should be raised to 4 per cent. This would be just a percentage point above the figure suggested by the Basel Committee on Banking Supervision. The government rejected this, because of lobbying by the banks.

Martin Wolf is saying that the banking sector in the UK successfully lobbied against a miniscule increase in their equity capital, from 3 percent to 4 percent. Whereas, what Admati and Hellwig want is "another digit" of equity capital—an increase from 3 percent to 30 percent. They note there is nothing magic about 30 percent equity funding; it could be 20 percent or 40 percent. Their point is to move to that order of magnitude; not from 3 to 4, or 4 to 5.

Of course, when banks lobby governments against such a move, they argue that the proposed changes would not only be bad for them but also bad for the economy! For example, the US trade association representing big banks argued that more equity capital ties up money that could otherwise be lent out, leading to less investment and less economic growth.[39] Admati has stated that a big motivation for her work was finding such errors repeated in finance textbooks.[40]

The claim that *more equity capital leads to less lending* is wrong on a practical as well as a theoretical level. In practice it is wrong because a large fraction of the money banks borrow is not used to make loans. It is used to trade complex derivatives—like the 2012 London Whale fiasco, where one trader at JPMorgan Chase placed a bet that lost more than $6 billion.

More importantly, it is wrong on a theoretical level because equity capital, like debt, is just a kind of *funding*. As in the simplified balance sheet shown in Table 8.1, equity capital and debt both appear on the liability side of the bank balance sheet. They both do the same work: they both support loans. They are interchangeable. If this rebuttal is still not clear, consider one way in which banks could increase their equity capital: they could temporarily suspend their dividend payments. With the billions not distributed as dividends, they could build up their cash reserves *and* acquire assets—in particular, they could make more loans to businesses and households. It is clear, in this case, that increasing equity capital actually implies more lending, not less lending.

A second important argument made by banks (against increasing their equity capital) is that it would increase their costs of doing business, resulting in higher interest rates. But while it is true that equity requires a higher return than debt (because it is more risky), it is not clear that requiring banks to have more equity would increase their financing costs. As Admati and Hellwig explain, this is because the riskiness of banks decreases when banks use more equity capital. The net effect on bank interest rate markups would likely be very small. Indeed, David Miles (2013) correlates bank equity capital to interest rate spreads in both the United States and the UK over the last 140 years. He finds that between 1880 and 1960 equity-capital ratios were, on average, about twice as high as the level of recent decades, but spreads between reference rates of interest and the rates charged on bank loans were no higher.

These two arguments against increasing bank equity capital (and hence reducing bank leverage ratios) are just scratching the surface of the erroneous arguments, flawed claims, and spin put out by the banking lobby. Admati and Hellwig (2013) group them into the categories: "much has been done already," "it's very complicated," "there will be unintended adverse consequences," and "we must maintain a level playing field." They rebut them all.

Are there any other solutions that might work? If one of the severe problems is that banks are too big to fail, what about breaking them up into smaller bits? This has had high-profile proponents, most notably the US Senator, Bernie Sanders, and has been endorsed by people like Neel Kashkari, the president of the US Federal Reserve Bank of Minneapolis.

If the banks were deemed too big to fail in 2007–8, we know they are much bigger now. If we focus on the twenty-eight largest global banks, the average bank in this group had assets equal to $1.8 trillion as of 2013. To get an idea of the size of that number, Admati (2018) supposes we had $1,000 bills. If we stack them up to make $1 trillion, the stack would be 68 miles high. Focusing again on the largest global banks, the average bank had derivatives that would reach over 2000 miles into the sky in 2013. Certainly, these measures are alarming. "Let fail" defies credibility. So, should we break them up?

It is not clear that this is the correct solution. Canada sailed through the global financial crisis of 2008–9 more easily than almost any other country, and its financial system is dominated by just five large banks. Furthermore, the United States experienced widespread bank runs in the 1930s, when its financial system still comprised thousands of small banks.

On the other hand, there is a way of making banks smaller that would solve the problem: split the two main functions of banks—deposit-taking and credit-creation—into separate institutions. This radical approach has a long and distinguished academic lineage. The idea was hatched in the 1930s at the University of Chicago by Irving Fisher and Henry Simons, and as a result has come to be known as "The Chicago Plan." More recent luminaries such as Nobel Prize winners Milton Friedman and James Tobin have both advocated it. Benes and Kumhof (2012)—two researchers at the IMF—confirm the proposal is eminently workable.[41]

The Chicago Plan proposes that "banks" would be institutions that accept deposits that are backed one-for-one with reserves at the central bank. Their primary job is to clear payments, and they would compete to offer the most convenient services without putting anyone's savings at risk. They would make money by paying a lower interest rate than they receive from their reserves at the central bank, or by charging fees, or both. This business model is simple and straightforward, eliminating the need for deposit insurance and regulation.

Credit-creation would be handled by lending companies funded by people who consciously choose to put their savings at risk. The new credit vehicles could take a variety of forms. Some might resemble bond mutual funds. Others could operate more like venture capital funds, complete with long lockup periods. From the perspective of borrowers, things might not look that different. Large corporations already borrow mainly by issuing bonds, so the change for them would be relatively inconsequential. Smaller firms and retail borrowers could obtain financing from institutions that look like local banks, but instead of relying on deposits, these outlets would actually be subsidiaries of lending companies funded by equity investors.[42]

Of the two ways of reforming banking that would work, Admati's plan of increasing bank equity is the simpler, more obvious approach. In commenting on her failure to have any impact on policy, Admati (2018) focuses on the lobbying power of banks coupled with the need of politicians for campaign contributions. Of course, the ideological view that the financial sector is the "golden goose" of the economy is hard to smash. And in the UK, a class-based explanation would have much merit too, whereby big banks are stuffed full of private school, then Oxbridge-educated, members of the ruling class.

Question for your professor: Given the lobbying power of banks and the need of politicians for campaign contributions, do you have any hope for meaningful bank reforms?

2.8 A brief assessment of the bailouts

First, consider the often-asked question, "was all the bailout money paid back?" The conventional answer, endorsed by all the mainstream textbooks that address the question, is that it was. But in reality, the question is practically unanswerable. As the inimitable Matt Taibbi (2019) puts it, "trying to compute [the size of] the bailout is a fool's errand, because it was so all-encompassing."

The US bailout included trillions of dollars in short-term loans from the Federal Reserve at below-market interest rates. It included then paying above-market interest rates, on the same money, that the banks held as excess reserves at the Federal Reserve.[43] It included a ban in 2008 on short selling of nearly 800 financial stocks. It included the granting of commercial bank status to Goldman Sachs and Morgan Stanley (two investment banks), so they could have lifesaving access to borrowing at the Federal Reserve's discount window. It included buying toxic assets at inflated prices. It included tax breaks. Researchers who have tried to compute the value of all that have reached figures in the trillions. Ivry, Keoun, and Kuntz (2011) make it $7.7 trillion. Felkerson (2011) makes it $29 trillion. We will never be really sure. But we can most certainly be sure that flaccid claims about all the money being paid back are staggeringly inaccurate.

Finally, was there any alternative but to give this massive bailout? It is understandable that none was perceived at the time. The financial sector was going down in flames and pulling the real economy down with it. Every second counted. Personally, I think it was extremely fortunate that Ben Bernanke was head of the Federal Reserve from 2006 to 2014, and was in charge during the meltdown. Prior to joining the Federal Reserve, he had devoted much of his academic career to studying the causes of the Great Depression. There was no-one better qualified to be in charge of monetary policy during the financial meltdown.

But now, years later, we have the luxury of calm assessment. Could we have let the market work its magic and put the Wall Street banks out of business?

As Dean Baker (2019) points out, the US government has a long history of keeping a bank operating through a bankruptcy. The Federal Deposit Insurance Corporation (FDIC) takes over the running of a bank when it becomes insolvent, and depositors (for the most part) don't notice anything different. The government could also have taken over the commercial paper market, where corporations borrow money to meet payroll obligations.

Furthermore, a widespread stock market meltdown could have been avoided by direct intervention in the stock market in a manner suggested by Roger Farmer (2010). He proposes that the central bank should define a stock market index—ideally one that includes every publicly traded stock, weighted by market capitalization. The central bank should then buy shares in all publicly traded companies in proportion to their weights in the index.

In brief, there is nothing to stop central banks from targeting stock price indices in addition to targeting domestic interest rates.

Of course, there may have been glitches. Having so many banks implode would have put a huge burden on the FDIC. Nevertheless, in Baker's opinion "having these glitches imply a Second Great Depression (ten years of double digit unemployment) involves some very serious hand waiving."

So, perhaps the trillion-dollar bailouts were not necessary. Perhaps more countries could have gone the Icelandic route of letting their big global banks go bankrupt and then sending the CEOs to jail for the corrupt practices that led to the bankruptcies. Subsequently, Iceland resisted world pressure to nationalize their banks' debt, something that Ireland did not do. In the Irish case, the bank debt crisis was transformed into a sovereign debt crisis.

2.9 Conclusion

This chapter's anti-text begins with two fundamental points. First, mainstream texts miss the most important element when defining money: the power of the state. Second, mainstream texts are unclear as to why the quantity of money matters. They display vestiges of a quantity theory of money perspective, inconsistent with the AD–AS model. In fact, printing money to pay for government spending will only generate inflation if it generates excess demand at full employment.

The bulk of this chapter's anti-text (Sections 2.3, 2.4, 2.5, and the appendix) is devoted to providing a record of systemic criminal behavior throughout the banking sector—especially in the United States but also globally—and then evaluating why no big bank CEOs have been held criminally responsible. Two reasons stand out. First, rampant cronyism between the government and the banking sector; and second, an incorrect belief that banking is the source of great wealth creation.

Section 2.6 argues that the incomes generated in the financial sector are greater than its output. The financial sector is also too big and inefficient. National accounting methods of measuring value-added fail to distinguish between risk-taking activity and risk-management activity. It also fails to account for the government subsidy given through the implicit commitment to bail out big banks. As Haldane and Madouros (2011) remark, "If risk-making were a value-adding activity, Russian roulette players would contribute to global welfare. And if government subsidies were the route to improved well-being, today's growth problems could be solved at a stroke." With regard to the financial sector being too big, Tobin (1984) puts it like this, "we are throwing more and more of our resources, including the cream of our youth, into financial activities remote from the production of goods and services, into activities that generate high private rewards disproportionate to their social productivity."

Current reforms are not close to being sufficient. The key problem is too much leverage. One way to reduce leverage is to regulate minimum equity-capital requirements for financial firms that are similar in magnitude to what is normal for nonfinancial firms. This is Admati and Hellwig's solution. In making banks safer, and reducing leverage, the return on bank equity would fall. Bankers who have been feasting on profits from excessive risk-taking will see their pay fall too. This might also help to slow the 30-year trend toward greater income inequality. Given the financial sector's resistance to even tiny increases in their equity capital, we should not hold our breath for meaningful reform.

The more radical approach to make the financial system safer is the Chicago Plan. This involves separating deposit-taking from credit-creation by having these functions performed by entirely different institutions.

While neither Admati's solution, nor the Chicago Plan, have any chance of being implemented in the near term, it is important to keep the blueprints ready for the next crisis. Another massive crisis is bound to occur sooner or later. To turn the neoliberal slogan on its head, "we shouldn't let a good crisis go to waste." Public outrage is necessary to force governments to implement the radical reform required.

Finally, the claim that "all the money lent to banks was paid back" is staggeringly inaccurate. Moreover, with the benefit of hindsight, there were other ways of avoiding a second Great Depression besides throwing trillions of dollars at the banking system.

APPENDIX I: MAJOR BANK SCANDALS REVEALED SINCE THE SUBPRIME MELTDOWN

Dating the scandals is a problem. Should we date them by when the scandalous action took place? But usually we do not really know. Likely the prosecution will have evidence for just a portion of the time the scam was in place. Should we date them by when the scandal was settled in court? But this may occur years after the scandal was discovered. Should we date them by when the scandal was first revealed? Whenever possible, I try to present some idea of all three dates, to provide a timeline.

2009: assisting illegal tax evasion. UBS paid $780 million in fines for helping American clients illegally evade taxes using concealed offshore accounts.

2009: complicit to Bernie Madoff's Ponzi scheme. On March 12, 2009, Madoff pleaded guilty to operating the largest private Ponzi scheme in history. He defrauded investors of around $65 billion. According to both Madoff himself and internal memos, the big banks were passively complicit in the fraud, allowing it to continue (and make money from Madoff's funds) instead of reporting their (well-founded) suspicions to the SEC as they were duty bound to do.[44]

2009–2012: foreclosure-gate. In their haste to issue as many mortgages as possible with as little verification as possible, originators of subprime mortgages had either not created the necessary legal documents or had not filed them with the proper authorities. Since these documents were needed to evict people who had defaulted on their mortgage payments, the big banks (Bank of America, JP Morgan, Wells Fargo, Ally Financial, and Citigroup) set up "factories" of temporary workers—or robo-signers—who would robotically sign reams of documents without any knowledge of the facts being attested to. This mass production of forged legal documents led to a widespread epidemic of improper foreclosures, including people evicted from their homes when their mortgage payments were not in arrears!

Early 1990s–2011: the payment protection insurance (PPI) scandal. This involved British banks aggressively selling credit insurance that would not benefit the client. It was sold to all borrowers, whether they were taking out a mortgage, car loan, or personal loan, and was supposed to guarantee loan payments if the borrower should fall ill, become injured, or unemployed. Borrowers were often told their loan application would be denied if they refused it. Often it was sold to people who would not be eligible to claim it, such as the self-employed, and it was structured to limit the chances of a payout to someone who was genuinely ill. Often it was added on to the cost of a loan without the client's knowledge. Finally, PPI was horrendously expensive, with premiums often adding 20 percent to the cost of a loan, and in the worst cases over 50 percent. Salespeople chased their commissions, bosses chased higher profits, and the banks' own retail clients were systematically cheated.[45]

2012: unfair billing. The CFPB announced that JPMorgan Chase agreed to pay refunds totaling $309 million to more than 2 million customers after the Office of Comptroller "found that Chase engaged in unfair billing practices for certain credit card 'add-on products' by charging consumers for credit monitoring services that they did not receive."

2002–2012: money laundering for drug lords and mobsters. In early December 2012, HSBC was fined $1.9 billion—or about five weeks' profits—as a punishment for nearly a decade of knowingly laundering hundreds of millions of dollars for Mexico's Sinaloa drug cartel, Al Qaeda, Hezbollah, and Russian mobsters; for helping Iran, the Sudan, and North Korea evade sanctions; and for helping hundreds of common tax cheats hide their cash. Matt Taibbi (2013) commented that while people may have "outrage fatigue" about Wall Street, aiding and abetting murderers and terrorists went way beyond expectations.

Internal memos show how the bank group actively found ways around international controls. Astonishingly, it ignored reams of official warnings about its behavior. And when its compliance chief, Carolyn Wind, raised concerns at a Board meeting in 2007, she was fired. HSBC was eventually busted when another compliance officer, Everett Stern, became a whistleblower and turned over a ton of evidence to the FBI and the CIA. Not a single HSBC official was punished with jail time or a personal fine.

2002–2019: money laundering and sanctions violations. Another British bank, Standard Chartered, was busted in 2012 for concealing illegal transactions with Iran, Sudan, Libya, and Burma for over a decade. According to New York's Department of Financial Services the bank falsified records and withheld information from regulators in "evident zeal to make hundreds of millions of dollars at almost any cost."[46] In 2012, it was granted a deferred-prosecution agreement, which meant it would not be charged as long as it cleaned up its act, and was fined $327 million. But it didn't. It was fined an additional $300 million for continued violations in 2014, and another $427 million in 2019 for continued violations. At that point, the bank was granted an amended deferred-prosecution agreement, again dependent on cleaning up its act. So, the bank has been fined over $1 billion, and given one last chance, and then another last chance, and still no criminal charges.[47]

Early 1990s–2012: LIBOR interest rate manipulation. Libor—an acronym for the London Inter-bank Offered Rate—is a key international benchmark interest rate. Besides underpinning about $350 trillion in derivatives trading, Libor also influences the interest rates charged on government and corporate debt, as well as car, student, and home loans, including over half of US flexible-rate mortgages. It was calculated—before the scandal— by the British Bankers' Association (BBA) polling a representative panel of global banks about the interest rate at which they could borrow unsecured funds from other banks.[48] The highest and lowest 25 percent of responses were discarded, and the remaining rates averaged. Calculated for five different currencies, the rate for each currency was set by panels of between eleven and eighteen banks.[49]

Beginning in 2012, an international investigation revealed a widespread plot by multiple banks—notably Barclays, Deutsche Bank, UBS, Rabobank, and RBS (Royal Bank of Scotland)—to manipulate the Libor interest rates for profit. Traders would make bets based on movements in Libor, then influence the rate itself by communicating with Libor rate "submitters" (those who respond to the BBA poll) at multiple banks.

Prosecutions from regulatory bodies have led to bank fines totaling over $9 billion. Civil suits are still being settled, but could easily cost the banks upward of $35 billion.[50] Thirteen people were charged by the UK Serious Fraud Office, of whom eight were acquitted, and five sent to prison. No bank executives were charged, only traders, brokers, and rate-submitters— despite evidence that the fraud extended right up to the CEO level.[51]

One irony is that as a result of the financial crisis bailouts, RBS was government owned. Therefore, the only people hurt by its fines were taxpayers!

2012: bid rigging. In 2012, US federal prosecutors released details from a ten-year investigation into bid rigging involving most of the major American finance institutions, including JP Morgan Chase, Bank of America, UBS, Lehman Brothers, Bear Sterns, Wachovia, and GE Capital. Municipalities routinely issue bonds to raise money for infrastructure—such as water, schools, hospitals, and libraries—but the money is not spent all at once. Rather than have idle money in the town's bank account, local officials seek to invest it in a GIC (guaranteed investment contract). They hire a financial firm to set up a public auction and invite banks to compete for the town's business. The competitive bidding process should guarantee that the municipality gets the highest possible interest rate. But the bidding process was rigged.

The prosecution focused on the period between 1999 and 2004, and showed that bank representatives colluded to rig bids on the money raised from about $3.7 trillion worth of municipal bonds. The bankers gave kickbacks to the organizers of the auction, who in turn gave kickbacks to politicians to ensure they were given future auctions to organize.

Matt Taibbi (2012) commented that the crimes "were virtually indistinguishable from the kind of thuggery practiced for decades by the Mafia, which has long made manipulation of public bids for things like garbage collection and construction contracts a cornerstone of its business."[52]

2015: the Forex scandal (Foreign exchange market manipulation). Many of the same banks involved in the Libor manipulation colluded to manipulate global currency markets. In May 2015, five banks—Citigroup, JP Morgan Chase, Barclays, Royal Bank of Scotland, and UBS—pleaded guilty to criminal charges of manipulating foreign exchange markets for over a decade, agreeing to pay over $5 billion to the US Justice Department and other regulators. No individuals were charged.[53]

2014—Investigation still ongoing: manipulation of gold and other precious metal prices. After the Libor and Forex scandals, regulatory bodies began to investigate whether precious metals markets—such as gold, silver, platinum, and palladium—have also been manipulated. The main discovery was a form of manipulation called "spoofing," where hundreds or even thousands of orders are placed but are cancelled before they can be executed. The goal is to induce other market participants to trade at prices or quantities they otherwise would not have traded, thus influencing the price of the commodity and benefiting a preexisting trading position. By 2019, US Federal prosecutors lodged spoofing cases against fifteen traders in the big banks.[54] Several traders have claimed they were taught how to spoof by senior traders and that supervisors knew of their actions.[55] Deutsche Bank, UBS, HSBC, and JPMorgan Chase have paid fines and face civil suits.

2016: wells Fargo account fraud scandal. In September 2016, various US regulatory bodies fined Wells Fargo for creating millions of savings and checking accounts—with associated credit cards—without their clients' consent. As a result, millions of Wells Fargo customers had credit card, checking, and other accounts without even knowing about them. The episode led to the firing of more than five thousand bank employees, and then-CEO John Stumpf ended up giving up substantial portions of his pay and leaving the company in October 2016.

2017: unnecessary car insurance for vehicle loans. Wells Fargo has found itself at the center of numerous troubling incidents over the past few years. Following internal reviews conducted as a result of the fake-account scandal, the bank found in 2017 that hundreds of thousands of auto-loan customers were forced to pay for comprehensive and collision insurance coverage for their vehicles—even if they already had their own coverage. That extra cost led to many people defaulting on their car loans and having their vehicles repossessed, further damaging Wells Fargo's already tarnished reputation. As a result of both the account fraud and the insurance fraud, Wells Fargo faces civil and criminal suits estimated $2.7 billion by the end of 2018.[56]

Ongoing: the UK as the money-laundering capital of the world. Lest the reader feels that this appendix has been overly focused on US banking scandals, let us finish by noting that several writers identify the UK as the money-laundering capital of the world, a role that is likely to increase after Brexit. Several factors contribute to this. First, when setting up shell companies, there are no identity checks in the UK! Anyone can register their company using fictitious names and addresses. This was instrumental to the world's biggest known money-laundering scheme, the Danske Bank scandal of 2017–18, where several hundred billions of dollars were laundered mainly from Russia.[57]

An additional favorable factor is that banks in the City of London are exempt from the UK's freedom of information laws, creating an extra ring of secrecy. The final element is the use of British territories—the British Virgin Islands, Bermuda, and the Cayman Islands—as places to process and hide vast sums. These places are effectively satellites of the City of London. But because they are overseas, the City can benefit from "nefarious activities ... while allowing the British government to maintain distance when scandals arise."

APPENDIX 2: THE WALL STREET–WASHINGTON REVOLVING DOOR (GS DENOTES GOLDMAN SACHS)

Name	Wall Street Position	Government Position
The Clinton Administration (1993–2001)		
Robert Rubin*	Cochairman GS, 1990–2 Chairman of Citigroup, 1999–2009	Treasury Secretary, 1995–9
Kenneth Brody	Partner GS, 1971–93	Head of US Export–Import Bank, 1993 Chair of Presidential Committee on US-Pacific Trade and Investment Committee, 1996
The George W. Bush Administration (2001–2009)		
Stephen Friedman	Cochairman of GS	White House chief economic advisor
Joshua B. Bolten	Executive director for Legal and Government Affairs, GS London, 1994–9	White House Chief of Staff, 2006–9
Robert K. Steel	Vice chairman of GS	Under secretary of the Treasury
Henry Paulson	CEO of GS	Treasury secretary, 2006–9
Neel T. Kashkari	Investment banker for GS	President of Federal Reserve Bank of Minneapolis
The Obama Administration (2009–2017)		
William C. Dudley	Partner of GS	President of Federal Reserve Bank of New York
Gary Gensler	Partner of GS	Chairman of the Commodity Futures Trading Commission
Jacob Lew	COO of Citigroup, 2006–8	Treasury secretary, 2013–17
The Trump Administration (2017–20)		
Steven Mnuchin	GS Partner, 1994–2002 CEO of his own hedge fund, 2002–9	Treasury secretary, 2017–20
Gary D. Cohn	Partner GS, 1994 President and COO of GS, 2006–17	Director of the National Economic Council, 2017–18 Chief economic advisor, 2017–18
James Donovan	Managing director of GS, 1993–current	Member of President's Intelligence Advisory Board, 2017–current
Dina Powell	Partner GS, 2015–17 Partner GS, 2018–current	Deputy national security advisor, 2017–18

Chapter 9

MONETARY POLICY: THE FIXATION ON INFLATION

In theory, theory and practice are the same. In practice, they are not.[1]

I THE STANDARD TEXT

In the last chapter we studied the banking system and learnt how central banks can affect the money supply through open-market operations. The focus of this chapter is monetary policy. We will look at how the money supply affects interest rates, and how interest rates affect the economy as a whole.

1.1 The liquidity preference model

Households and businesses must make a choice about how to hold their financial wealth, and they face a trade-off concerning liquidity and return. Money has the lowest return—practically zero—but is also the most liquid. This is why the demand for money is called the "liquidity preference function": it reflects firms' and households' preferences to hold their wealth in its most liquid form. The *liquidity preference model* explains how the interest rate is determined in the short run by the demand and supply of money.

We begin by focusing on the demand for money. We will draw it with the interest rate on the vertical axis, and the quantity of money on the horizontal. We need to determine its slope and the most important shift factors.

With regard to the slope, the demand for money will be negatively sloped like most other demand curves. Clearly there is no return from holding cash, and the interest rate on bank chequing deposits is negligible—especially after deducting the many different banking fees. And while the return on savings deposits is very slightly better, it is just a fraction of the rate on short-term Treasury Bills. Therefore, other things being equal, a higher interest rate increases the opportunity cost of holding money, causing the quantity demanded to fall. But are we talking here of the real or the nominal interest rate?

Table 9.1 The real versus the nominal cost of holding money

	Nominal return	**Real return**
Bonds	i	$i - \pi$
Money	0	$-\pi$
Opportunity cost	$i - 0 = i$	$(i - \pi) - (-\pi) = i$

Once we incorporate inflation into the model, we need to clarify that it is the nominal rate of interest that is the opportunity cost of holding money, not the real rate of interest. The alternative to holding *financial* wealth in the form of money is holding it in bonds. As shown in Table 9.1, whether we think in real or in nominal terms, the opportunity cost of holding money is still the nominal interest rate. Thinking in nominal terms we must subtract the nominal return from holding money (which is zero) from the nominal return form holding bonds, which yields the nominal interest rate (i). Thinking in real terms we must subtract the real return from holding money (which is "$-$") from the real return form holding bonds (which is $i - \pi$), which again yields the nominal interest rate (i).

What about the shift factors? There are two important shift factors in the short run: prices and real income. An increase in the aggregate price level means consumers must spend more money to buy a given basket of goods. This shifts the demand curve for money to the right, increasing the quantity of money demanded at any given interest rate. Indeed, other things being equal, the quantity of money demanded will increase in proportion to the price level. So, a 50 percent increase in the price level will lead to a 50 percent increase in the quantity of money demanded.

The other shift factor is real income. As real income increases so does spending. Hence more money is required to facilitate purchases, shifting the demand for money to the right at any given interest rate.

In brief, we may write the demand for money, MD, as the function below, where the sign above the variable indicates its effect on the quantity of money demanded:

$$MD = H\left(\overset{-}{i}, \overset{+}{Y}, \overset{+}{P}\right)$$

Changes in banking technology have no place in the demand for money equation because they are a slower, long-run phenomenon. However, it is worth noting that as banking technology has improved, the demand for money has fallen. For example, the invention of ATM machines in the 1970s made it easier to get cash whenever and wherever it was needed, and therefore reduced the amount people needed to carry with them. Similarly, the internet has widened the acceptability of credit cards and reduced the need for cash.

So much for the demand for money. To determine the equilibrium level of interest rates, we need to confront the demand for money with the supply. In Chapter 8, we noted that the supply of money is determined by the interaction of the central bank, the private sector, and commercial banks. Importantly, even though there is a good deal of endogeneity, the central bank can affect the money supply through its open-market operations. We shall draw the supply of money as a vertical line because it is not affected by changes in interest rates.

Figure 9.1 shows the demand and supply of money intersecting at an interest rate of i_e. How will the market arrive at this equilibrium? Suppose the interest rate is too high at i_H. At this interest rate, the demand for money, M_H, is less than the supply of money, $\bar{M}$, meaning there is an excess supply of money. Therefore, households and businesses try to hold less money by buying other financial assets such as bonds. This drives the price of those assets up, and the interest rate down. Recall from Chapter 5 that as bond prices increase, the interest rate on bonds decreases. Substitutability between assets ensures that the interest rate on all similar short-term assets will also decrease. As the interest rate falls, the quantity of money demanded rises until equilibrium is reached.

Similarly, if the interest rate is below equilibrium at i_L, there is an excess demand for money and households and businesses sell other financial assets such as bonds in an attempt to get more money. This causes the price of bonds to fall, and interest rates to increase. This continues until the quantity of money demanded equals the supply, $\bar{M}$.

Figure 9.1 can also be used to illustrate how the central bank achieves its interest rate target. Suppose initially the money supply is M_H and the equilibrium interest rate is i_H. If the central bank wants to lower interest rates to i_e it simply engages in open-market purchases of bonds until the money supply is increased to $\bar{M}$.

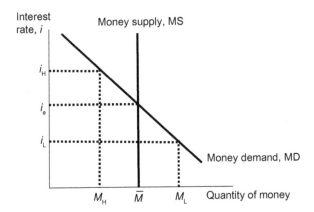

Figure 9.1 Equilibrium in the money market

In the last chapter, we explained that most central banks target the overnight interest rate—the rate at which banks lend to one another overnight. This interest rate is usually in the middle of a band. (You might want to refer to Table 8.5 in Chapter 8.) The top of the band is the interest rate at which the central bank will lend to commercial banks. (It would be foolish to borrow at a higher rate than that available from the central bank.) And the bottom of the band is the interest rate paid on reserves deposited by commercial banks with the central bank. (It would be foolish to lend to another commercial bank at a rate lower than can be obtained from the central bank.) So, clearly, the rate at which banks will lend to each other overnight is bounded by interest rates set by the central bank. What we did not explain in the last chapter was how the central bank established the precise value of the overnight rate—how it makes this rate hit its target. Now we know it is done by open-market operations that change the money supply and the availability of bank reserves.

1.2 Longer-term interest rates

When the central bank changes its policy interest rate, short-term interest rates will move in parallel fashion. On the other hand, longer-term interest rates—like the rate on five-year mortgages—do not move in lockstep with the overnight rate as do short-term rates. This is because longer-term interest rates are influenced not just by the current short-term interest rate but expected future short-term interest rates. This link is known as *the expectations hypothesis of the term structure of interest rates.*

Take a simple example. Imagine you need a two-year loan, and your options are to take a two-year loan, or take a one-year loan this year and another next year. Which one is better depends on the rates currently prevailing, and crucially on the *expected* one-year rate next year. In equilibrium, there should be no difference between the two methods of financing. And this suggests that long-term interest rates are determined by current and expected future short-term interest rates.

To make things concrete, suppose you could get a two-year loan at 5 percent a year. And the current one-year rate is 3 percent. This suggests that we can solve for the one-year rate that is expected next year (denoted as "x") using the equilibrium condition:

$$(1 + 0.05)(1 + 0.05) = (1 + 0.03)(1 + x) \tag{9.1}$$

Solving for "x" yields a value slightly over 7 percent. The point here is that to drive down long-term mortgage rates, the central bank might have to cut short-term interest rates several times *to reduce expectations of future short-term rates.* Normally, repeated cuts in short-term interest rates will significantly reduce long-term rates. Alternatively, the central bank could announce that it intends to keep short-term rates low in the future. (This is referred to as giving *forward guidance.*) Once long-term interest rates fall, there will be an expansionary effect on housing starts, corporate investment, and other big-ticket items, and then through multiplier effects on the whole economy. The details of how this works are described as the monetary transmission mechanism.

1.3 The monetary transmission mechanism

Interest rates affect aggregate demand (AD) through two channels: direct and indirect. The direct channel is through consumer and investment spending. However, in countries where foreign trade is a significant part of the economy, the equally important indirect channel is through net exports via the exchange rate. Consider the case where the central bank pursues an expansionary monetary policy designed to shift AD to the right, depicted in Figure 9.2.

Expansionary monetary policy begins with the central bank announcing a reduction in its policy interest rate target, and expanding the money supply through open-market purchases of Treasury Bills so as to achieve its target. The direct effect of lower interest rates is to stimulate both consumer and investment spending. The indirect effect is that a lower interest rate will cause an outflow of financial capital, causing the exchange rate to depreciate, which will stimulate net exports. The indirect effect on net exports *reinforces* the direct effect on consumption and investment spending. This makes monetary policy particularly effective, especially in a world where financial capital is extremely mobile.[2]

An important fact about our increasingly globalized world is that financial capital is very mobile across international borders. Bonds from similarly advanced free market economies are close substitutes for one another. So, a fall in (say) Canadian interest rates makes Canadian bonds less attractive compared to foreign bonds. Consequently, investors will react by selling some of their Canadian bonds and buying more of the higher-return foreign bonds. To

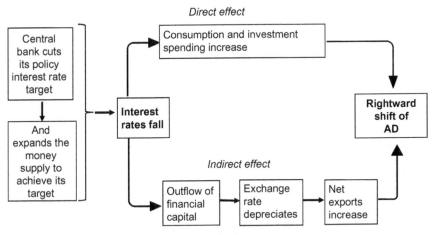

Figure 9.2 The monetary transmission mechanism

do that, they will convert Canadian dollars into foreign currency, and this will put downward pressure on the Canadian exchange rate. As the Canadian dollar depreciates, Canadian goods and services become cheaper relative to those of other countries. Consequently, Canadian imports will fall, and Canadian exports will rise. The greater the mobility of financial capital internationally, the stronger is the effect on the exchange rate, and the stronger is the indirect effect.

With *contractionary monetary policy* designed to shift the AD curve to the left, the same transmission mechanism works in reverse. In this case, the central bank announces an increase in its policy interest rate target and contracts the money supply to achieve it. The direct effect of higher interest rates is a decrease in both consumer and investment spending. The indirect effect is that domestic bonds are more attractive relative to foreign bonds, so investors (both domestic and foreign) sell some foreign bonds and convert the resulting foreign currency into domestic currency to buy domestic bonds. The purchase of domestic currency puts upward pressure on the domestic exchange rate. As the exchange rate appreciates, domestically produced goods become more expensive relative to foreign goods, causing both exports to decrease and imports to increase. The fall in net exports reinforces the contractionary effects on AD from decreased consumer and investment spending.

1.4 Monetary policy and stabilization policy

Monetary policy and fiscal policy are both tools that the government can use, and both have their limitations. In Chapter 7, we discussed the problem of long lags involved with discretionary fiscal policy. It takes time to gather statistics about the economy, time to recognize that action is necessary, and time to plan the response. Any discretionary fiscal response may involve a political fight, with right-wing parties wanting tax cuts, and left-wing parties wanting increased government spending. The response time will be especially long if the government wants to spend on infrastructure projects since these will need planning and environmental assessments that could take years. Because of these time lags, the effect of the fiscal stimulus may arrive when the economy no longer needs it.

While monetary policy has the same information gathering lag, and the same recognition lag, the response lag is much shorter. Many central banks routinely update markets about their interest rate intentions every six weeks. Those occasions are designed to announce policy interest rate changes. Furthermore, a central bank can change its policy interest rate any time it wants. So, on the question of time lags, monetary policy is superior to discretionary fiscal policy. However, monetary policy has one major weakness: central banks might run out of room to lower interest rates. We will discuss this in Section 1.6 momentarily. Assuming that interest rates are not bumping up against the "zero lower bound," monetary policy is the main tool for macroeconomic stabilization, because it has shorter lags than fiscal policy.

Stabilization means keeping output as close as possible to full employment and ensuring price stability. But can one policy lever achieve two goals?

Conceivably it can because inflation depends in part on how the economy is performing relative to its potential. All else being equal, an economy operating above potential creates inflationary pressures, and an economy running below potential pushes inflation down. So keeping inflation equal to its target rate may involve holding output at its potential full employment level.

In 1993 Stanford economist John Taylor suggested that central banks should follow a simple rule that included both a full employment goal and a low inflation goal. In general terms, the so-called "*Taylor Rule*" is stated below:

$$i - \pi = \rho + \alpha\left(\pi - \pi^*\right) + \beta\left(Y - Y^f\right) \tag{9.1}$$

In equation (9.1), we have the usual symbols for inflation ($\neq$), output (Y), and full employment output (Y^f). The new symbols are π^*, which is the target rate of inflation, and rho (ρ), which denotes the "natural rate of interest"—the real interest rate that prevails when the economy is in long-run equilibrium. We can see that when inflation equals its target ($\pi = \pi^*$), and output equals full employment output ($Y = Y^f$), the only term left on the right-hand side is ρ. The term on the left-hand side ($i - \pi$) is the real rate of interest. So, this confirms that when the economy is in long-run equilibrium (since $\pi = \pi^*$ and $Y = Y^f$), the real rate of interest equals its long-run equilibrium value.

To see this equation as an interest rate adjustment rule, we should move the π term from the left-hand side to the right-hand side. This yields equation (9.2):

$$i = \pi + \rho + \alpha\left(\pi - \pi^*\right) + \beta\left(Y - Y^f\right) \tag{9.2}$$

Inflation (π) appears twice on the right-hand side of equation (9.2). This means, ceteris paribus, a 1 percent increase in inflation should be met by increasing nominal interest rates by more than 1 percent. This is necessary since spending responds to the real interest rate ($i - \pi$), and to remove an inflationary gap the real rate must be increased.

Taylor suggested specific policy parameters that were "straightforward" and "captured the spirit of recent research." His suggestion involved setting both ρ and π^* to 2 percent and setting both α and β to 0.5. What is both interesting and surprising is that Taylor was able to show that actual monetary policy in the United States between 1987 and 1992 appeared to be following that rule. Similar findings have been made by subsequent researchers for periods prior to the Federal Reserve's formal embrace of inflation targeting in 2012.

1.5 Inflation targeting

First adopted by New Zealand in 1990, the practice spread to other advanced economies in the 1990s, and to emerging markets in the 2000s. By far the most common target is 2 percent, sometimes with a permissible range of fluctuation from 1 percent to 3 percent , and sometimes without.[3]

There are three differences between inflation targeting and the Taylor rule. First, inflation targeting is "forward looking" whereas the Taylor rule is "backward looking." This means that when central banks use inflation targeting, they adjust interest rates based on forecasted future inflation, not past inflation. Second, inflation targeting is much clearer and transparent than a Taylor rule. Public knowledge of the objective that guides monetary policy reduces uncertainty and helps provide an anchor to inflationary expectations. Third, commitment to an inflation target makes it easier to assess the central bank's performance, and this makes it more accountable.

The adoption of inflation targeting can be interpreted as setting the "β" coefficient on the output gap term in equation (9.2) to zero. This could be seen as excessive focus on achieving low inflation, and ignoring the goal of full employment. In 1991, when Canada formally adopted inflation targeting, many economists became so concerned about this that they raised a clarion call to reform the Bank of Canada (BOC). They wanted to make it more responsive to the democratic wishes of the electorate. Was this warranted?

Figure 9.3 considers two cases: in Panel A, a negative AD shock; and in Panel B, a negative AS shock. In both cases we begin in long-run equilibrium at E_1 initially. This means the short-run aggregate supply ($SRAS_1$) curve and the AD_1 curve initially intersect at potential output (Y^f).

In Panel A on the left, a negative AD shock causes both output and prices to fall— or in the context of ongoing inflation, it causes inflation to decrease. If the central bank is committed to keeping inflation near the midpoint of the target band, it will lower interest rates to shift the AD curve to the right as quickly as possible, keeping the economy as close as possible to potential output in the process.[4] Clearly, inflation targeting stabilizes output when the economy is buffeted by shocks to the AD curve. But what happens if there are shocks to aggregate supply (AS)?

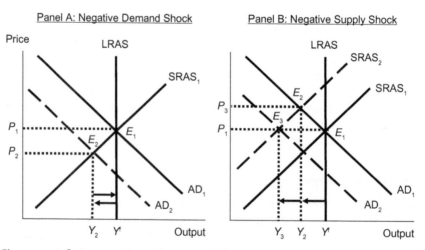

Figure 9.3 Inflation targeting and output stability

In Panel B on the right, a negative AS shock pushes AS up and to the left, from $SRAS_1$ to $SRAS_2$. This causes output to fall to Y_2 and prices to increase to P_3. In the context of ongoing inflation, this means that inflation has increased above its target. Inflation targeting implies that the central bank will react by raising interest rates to reduce AD to AD_2. This brings inflation back to the midpoint of its target band, but at the expense of output, which is pushed even lower, from Y_2 to Y_3.

Negative supply shocks—like an increase in world oil prices—simultaneously increase prices and decrease output. We can either offset the effect on output by increasing AD, which worsens the effect on prices; or we can offset the effect on prices by decreasing AD, which worsens the effect on output. There's no easy fix. With inflation targeting, however, the response will always be to stabilize prices, which means always worsening the effect on output.

While this is a serious problem, there is a solution. The solution is for the central bank to target an inflation measure that has the effect of supply shocks removed! Such a measure of inflation is called "core inflation" and it is obtained by removing from the consumer price index the effect of changes in energy prices and other supply-determined prices. For example, the BOC's measure of core inflation removes eight of the most volatile elements from the consumer price index including certain types of fruit and vegetables (whose prices are determined in world markets), and energy prices. Core inflation is much less volatile than inflation measured using the consumer price index.

It is noteworthy that most of the period of the Great Moderation—the period from 1985 to 2007—came after the adoption of inflation targeting. It would appear that inflation targeting did *not* destabilize output—quite the reverse actually.

1.6 The zero lower bound and quantitative easing

It used to be believed that interest rates could not go below zero. Why hold an asset yielding a negative return when there is always the option of holding cash, which offers a zero return? But it turns out that slightly negative interest rates are possible because handling large quantities of cash is costly—it requires vaults, armored cars, and security guards. Nevertheless, holding cash becomes more attractive the more negative rates become. And this suggests that there is a lower bound to interest rates, though it might be slightly less than zero. Slightly negative interest rates have been observed in Switzerland (since 2014), Denmark, Japan, and the eurozone (since 2016).

As we noted in Chapter 7, by early 2009 policy interest rates around the world were perilously close to the lower bound. With practically no room for further interest rate reductions, conventional monetary policy could do no more. But with the Great Recession continuing to deepen, central banks turned to unconventional measures and in particular to quantitative easing (QE).

Conventional monetary policy operates via central banks, making open-market purchases of short-term assets—like 3-month Treasury Bills—thus influencing short-term interest rates. QE involves open-market purchases of medium- and long-term assets. There are several ways this could influence aggregate spending. First, by pumping more liquidity into the economy it could increase bank lending, and hence increase spending. Second, it puts downward pressure on longer-term interest rates, which might increase spending. Third, by increasing the prices of a vast array of financial assets it creates a positive wealth effect, again possibly increasing spending. Fourth, if risky assets are bought by the central bank, QE could lower the interest rate differential between safe and risky assets—an aspect known as "credit easing."

The US Federal Reserve implemented several waves of QE: in 2008, 2010, 2012, and more recently as a result of the Covid-19 pandemic, in 2020. The first of these included the purchase of mortgage-backed securities. As Blinder (2010) notes, it was squarely aimed at compressing the interest rate differential between safe and risky assets.

QE has been criticized by right-wing economists who worry that since it is pumping money into the economy, it will dramatically increase inflation. Left-wing economists have criticized it for being an ineffective substitute for fiscal policy.

Empirical studies on the effect of QE on output have produced a range of results from negligible at one end to a significantly positive though small effect at the other (see MacLean 2015). It seems that QE had only a small positive effect on output at best. Predictions of high inflation have failed completely—at least thus far.

1.7 Monetary neutrality: output and prices in the long run

Assuming no zero lower bound constraint, what would happen if there was a monetary expansion when the economy was already at long-run equilibrium? This is illustrated in Figure 9.4. The process begins with the money supply increasing from $\bar{M}_1$ to $\bar{M}_2$ in Panel A, causing equilibrium interest rates to fall to i_2. In the short run the monetary transmission mechanism causes AD to increase from AD_1 to AD_2 in Panel B, and output to increase to Y_2. The economy is in short-run equilibrium in Panel B at E_2, where there is now an inflationary gap, equal to $Y_2 - Y^f$. Over time the economy's self-correcting mechanism kicks in.

While wages are sticky and slow to change, they will eventually be bid up. As nominal wages increase, the SRAS curve shifts up and to the left. As this occurs, the short-run equilibrium moves up and along AD_2 and prices increase as output falls. The process stops only when the SRAS curve arrives at $SRAS_2$ and the economy finds itself in a new long-run equilibrium at point E_3. In Panel A, the increase in prices has shifted the money demand function up to MD_2, which has restored interest rates to exactly the same level they were at initially. The long-run effect of an increase in the money supply, then, is that the aggregate price level has increased from P_1 to P_3, but aggregate output is back at potential output, Y^f, and interest rates are unchanged at i_1. In the long run, a monetary expansion raises the aggregate price level but has no real effects on the economy.

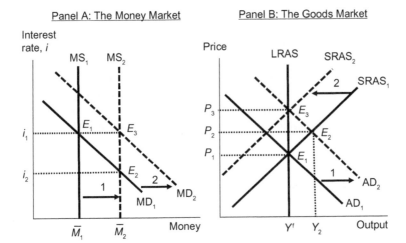

Figure 9.4 Long-run monetary neutrality

So far, so good. But now a key question: in the long run, how much does the price level change in response to the change in the money supply? The answer is that the price level changes in direct proportion to the change in the money supply. For example, if the money supply rises 5 percent, the aggregate price level rises 5 percent in the long run.

How do we know this? Fundamentally, it is because the demand for money increases proportionally to the price level. An increase in the aggregate price level means consumers must spend more money to buy a given basket of goods. So, a 5 percent increase in the price level leads to a 5 percent increase in the quantity of money demanded. This means that at the new equilibrium E_3 in Panel A, the amount of real money balances, M/P, is the same as it was at the original equilibrium, E_1.

If you still have any doubt about the long-run proportional relationship between the money supply and the price level, consider the following thought experiment. Suppose *all* prices in the economy double—output prices, input prices, and asset prices all double. Wages and salaries will have doubled since they are an input price. And while incomes will have doubled, no-one is any better off since all prices have doubled. Now suppose the money supply doubles at the same time. What difference does this "doubling experiment" make to the economy in real terms? The answer is none. All real variables in the economy—including real income, real asset values, and the real value of the money supply—are all unchanged. So there is no reason for anyone to behave any differently.

This analysis demonstrates the concept known as *monetary neutrality*, in which changes in the money supply have no real effects on the economy—no effects on real GDP or its components. The only effect of an increase in the money supply is to raise the price level by an equal percentage. Importantly, in the long run the rate of change of prices—or inflation—is equal to the rate of growth of the money supply.

Now we can understand why some economists worried that QE would lead to inflation—because in the long run increases in the money supply are predicted to lead to proportionate increases in prices. And a massive increase in the money supply implies a massive increase in prices at some point. But that prediction only applies when the economy is in the long-run equilibrium. QE was undertaken during the Great Recession. That is not at all the same thing.

2 THE ANTI-TEXT

The textbooks do a good job describing the monetary transmission mechanism and the determination of interest rates. And some texts do a reasonable job explaining that while the money supply is essentially endogenous, this does not prevent central banks from determining short-term interest rates through open-market operations.

Where they fail is in downplaying the limitations of monetary policy, both conventional and unconventional. They also fail to critically consider alternatives to inflation targeting, nor—if inflation targeting were retained—what the optimal inflation target should be. Most importantly, they fail to consider the impact of inflation targeting on employment and the distribution of income. Finally, long-run monetary neutrality is a cornerstone of the mainstream model but has surprisingly weak foundations.

2.1 The limits of conventional monetary policy

The mainstream textbooks emphasize that conventional monetary policy is unable to stimulate the economy once the zero (or slightly negative!) lower bound has been reached. But they fail to note that this failure can occur at *any* interest rate. It does not depend on a lower bound being reached. It simply requires that a recession be sufficiently severe.

In a deep recession, firms will have idle (or underutilized) capital equipment and laid off workers. Lower interest rates are unlikely to convince firms to build new capacity when they already have too much. Furthermore, in a deep recession, prospects for future sales will be dim. Again, lower interest rates are unlikely to convince firms to build new capacity to make products that won't sell. Finally, in a deep recession, banks may be unwilling to extend loans to customers given the higher prevalence of bankruptcies and general uncertainty. Open-market purchases by the central bank may succeed in lowering interest rates and increasing the banking system's excess reserves, but banks cannot be forced to increase their lending.

For these reasons, expansionary monetary policy may not help the economy recover from a deep recession, *even when interest rates are not at their lower bound*. Spending may simply be unresponsive to reductions in the cost of borrowing. On the other hand, when the economy is booming and firms are seeking loans to build investment capacity, an increase in the cost of borrowing—if it is sufficiently large—will affect their thinking. Since there is no upper limit on how high interest rates can go, it is reasonable to suppose that contractionary monetary policy can be effective in a boom.

For these reasons, monetary policy has been compared to "pushing on a string." The metaphor captures the idea that monetary policy can pull the economy back from being overheated, but cannot push it out of a deep recession.

There is another, quite different reason why expansionary monetary policy might be ineffective—the economy might be in a "balance sheet recession." This is likely after a financial crash when households and firms are focused on paying down debt. Since debt is fixed in nominal terms, but the value of assets is not, the bursting of a debt-financed bubble and the collapse of asset prices cause private sector balance sheets to be "underwater." This means that the value of their assets will be less than the value of their debt. In order to regain their financial health and credit ratings, households and firms are forced to repair their balance sheets by increasing savings and paying down debt. This act of deleveraging reduces AD. *But this cannot be repaired using monetary policy.* Even zero interest rates will not reverse this process. The process only ends once debt has been paid down and "balance sheets" have been repaired.

The theory of "balance sheet" recessions was developed by Richard Koo (2008). He points out that the situation is a perfect Paradox of Thrift, where everyone wants to save, and no-one wants to invest. We have already discussed Koo's ideas in Chapter 7 when dealing with fiscal policy. The point we made in that chapter was that only public sector deficits can prevent a multiple contraction of output in a "balance sheet" recession. But it also forms a nice segue into the next section, since it helps to explain why QE has been mostly unhelpful.

2.2 The limits of QE

We begin by showing that QE had no effect on bank lending in the United States when it was implemented after the financial meltdown. Figure 9.5 plots three key monetary variables: the monetary base (currency in circulation plus bank reserves), the money supply (measured as M2), and excess reserves of commercial banks.[5] The period begins in 2008 and extends out four years. We see that QE produced a dramatic threefold increase in the monetary base (the dashed line and left-hand axis), but this had almost no effect on the money supply (the solid line and right-hand

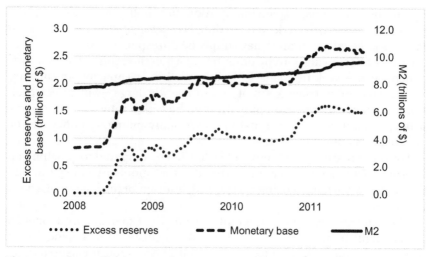

Figure 9.5 The ineffectiveness of QE

axis).[6] So, where did all the money go? It went into the excess reserves of commercial banks. Figure 9.5 clearly shows bank reserves moved in lock step with the monetary base. Why was QE so ineffective at increasing bank lending and the money supply? The economy was in a balance sheet recession. Firms and households did not want to borrow. The extra cash sat in bank vaults.

An interesting fact about this period is that banks were rewarded by the Federal Reserve for keeping their money idle. As Figure 9.6 shows, the Deposit Rate—which is the interest paid by the Federal Reserve on commercial bank deposits—was above the Federal Funds rate—which is the going market rate at which commercial banks lend to each other.[7] In effect, the Federal Reserve was paying above-market interest rates on commercial bank reserves. These excess interest payments were a clear, though well-hidden, subsidy to the commercial banks. Over the period 2009–16, the excess interest payments amounted to a cool $1.8 trillion. Why so big? As Figure 9.5 shows, while the interest rate differential itself was quite small—it was 0.18 percentage points at its largest—the quantity of the excess reserves on which it was paid was huge.[8]

In contrast to what happened in the United States, many countries adopted negative base interest rates (as noted in Section 1.6). This means that commercial banks actually had to pay to keep excess reserves at the central bank, which encourages them to lend. Yet, as Koo (2011) shows, QE in those countries was also ineffective in increasing bank lending since the private sector was focused on repairing their "balance sheets."

What about the other avenues through which QE might have an impact? In the text section, we mentioned that it could push down long-term interest

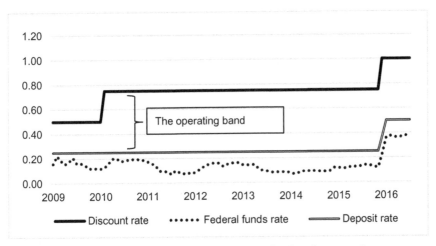

Figure 9.6 The US federal funds rate and the operating band, 2009–16

rates, create a positive wealth effect, and reduce the interest differential between safe and risky assets. Has any of this benefited employment?

With regard to the effect of QE on employment, empirical results range from zero effect at one end to a small positive effect at the other. In other words, despite massive QE, the employment effects were either small or nonexistent. With regard to the effect of QE on income and wealth inequality, results are also inconclusive. One would suppose that since QE pushes up asset prices, and since lower income households do not own many assets, QE would widen inequality. Certainly, some empirical studies suggest this is the case.[9] But on the other hand, the effect of pushing down longer-term interest rates reduces the income from interest earning assets. And to the extent it mildly stimulates employment this benefits mainly lower income households. Both of these are offsetting effects. A recent survey by Colciago et al. (2019) summarizes the results by saying, "With various forces driving inequality in opposite directions, the total distributional effect is small or insignificant."

There is one big exception to this rather negative view on QE—when QE is used to buy newly issued government debt. In this case, QE becomes money-financed fiscal policy, a policy that post-Keynesians and MMTs would endorse. For example, as a result of the Covid pandemic, and the increased support spending it necessitated, the Federal government deficit in Canada ballooned from a projected deficit of about $20 billion in 2020 to an estimated deficit (at the time of writing) of around $343 billion. At the same time, the BOC announced a program of buying $5 billion government of Canada bonds every week, providing money financing of $260 billion—about 75 percent of the deficit. These central bank purchases of newly issued government debt become assets of the central bank and do not increase the net debt of the public sector, though the measured debt-to-GDP ratio of the government would increase. It is amusing to hear mainstream economists publicly pronouncing that soon the government will be bankrupt, or that a burden is being created for future generations. It is the same old debt hysteria.

Question for your professor: Given that the express purpose of QE is to increase all financial asset prices, wouldn't this benefit primarily the rich?

2.3 The limits of other monetary policy options

Forward guidance This is a method of trying to lower long-term interest rates. According to the expectations hypothesis of the term structure of interest rates, long-term rates are a weighted average of expected future short-term rates. So, if the central bank can convince markets that it will keep short-term interest rates low for the foreseeable future, long-term rates should fall. QE attempts to do the same thing by buying longer-term securities. Many central banks have adopted forward guidance along with QE, with either small or nonexistent results.

Negative interest rates As mentioned, some central banks have already adopted slightly negative interest rates. However, some economists propose making whatever institutional changes are necessary to permit seriously negative interest rates! The point here is that interest rate reductions have become the main weapon against recessions, and those reductions have averaged about 9 percentage points over the last four recessions.[10] But with interest rates close to zero since 2009, there is not sufficient room for the required reductions. A possible solution is to look seriously at deeply negative interest rates—rates as low as –6 percent, or even lower.

One proponent of this approach is Kenneth Rogoff.[11] Rogoff recognizes that imposing negative interest rates on regular household deposits at banks would be undesirable. Such deposits should therefore be exempt. However, large bank deposits held by firms would not be exempt. He suggests that to avoid a flight to cash, cash should simply be abolished—we should go completely digital. He suggests this would mostly inconvenience criminal elements.[12]

The big worry about such radical proposals is that whoever is subjected to deeply negative interest rates would shift away from government fiat currency and into cryptocurrencies. Perhaps because of these concerns, no central bank is currently considering implementing the changes necessary to set interest rates into deeply negative territory.

Rogoff's position is understandable given his ideological perspective. He has a phobia about public debt, and prefers free market solutions over government-directed spending. You will remember that in 2010 Rogoff and Reinhart published a hugely influential paper claiming that debt-to-GDP ratios over 90 percent severely impaired long-term growth prospects. While the results were quickly debunked, their paper contributed to the absurd adoption of austerity policies between 2010 and 2014. So, given his hostility to fiscal policy solutions, the ineffectiveness of unconventional monetary policy, and the necessity to do something, his support for negative interest rates is at least consistent with his other views.

Increasing the inflation target The mainstream textbooks do not explain why so many central banks have decided on an inflation target of 2 percent. Basic optimization theory suggests that we should be equating the marginal cost of one more percentage point of inflation against the marginal benefit. But the mainstream texts make no mention of even the possibility of a cost–benefit analysis. Practically all textbooks discuss the costs of inflation, but none discuss the benefits, leaving readers to think there are no benefits.

The costs and benefits of inflation depend on whether it is accurately anticipated. By definition, inflation *is* accurately anticipated in the long run. Unanticipated inflation is a short-run phenomenon.

In the short run of the mainstream model, an increase in inflation gives output and employment a temporary boost—a boost that disappears as expected inflation catches up. So, there is a temporary output gain from an increase in inflation, but we are left with a permanently higher inflation rate.[13]

A permanently higher inflation rate (one that is anticipated) generates two kinds of costs: *menu costs* and *shoe leather* costs. Menu costs comprise all the costs of changing prices more frequently. (The name comes from the idea that restaurants will need to print new menus more often.) Shoe leather costs comprise all the costs of economizing on money holdings as a result of higher nominal interest rates. (The metaphor is that people will wear out their shoes making more frequent trips to the bank.)

Mainstream thinking runs as follows. If there are no benefits of inflation, then we should minimize the costs. This seems to suggest that zero inflation would be optimal. But Milton Friedman (1969) pointed out that to eliminate *all* costs, the inflation rate should be negative! The idea is that money balances are useful but costless to produce, implying the socially optimal price is zero. Since the nominal interest rate is the opportunity cost of holding money, it should be set to zero. This implies (from Fisher's equation, repeated as equation (9.1)) the optimal inflation rate equals minus "*r.*"

$$i = r + \pi \qquad\qquad (9.1)$$

It is important to note that Friedman did not worry about lower bound problems and monetary policy running out of room to maneuver. He believed the appropriate instrument of monetary policy was the quantity of money, not the interest rate.

While Friedman's suggestion of negative inflation never gained traction in the profession, the idea of zero inflation did. The 1980s saw a slew of research seeming to demonstrate that zero inflation would have a small but significantly positive impact on productivity growth. John Crow (the governor of the BOC from 1987 to 1994) was a believer, and under his watch the BOC unilaterally began a quest for "price stability." During the early 1990s interest rates were kept high despite there being both a huge recessionary gap and core inflation well *below* the 2-percentage-point band. This unannounced experiment with price stability ended in 1994 when John Crow's term expired. Nowadays, the flow of papers purporting to demonstrate a positive relationship between productivity growth and price stability has decreased to a mere trickle—though they still continue.

Mainstream macroeconomists now recognize that more inflation does have one important benefit: it helps to ameliorate lower bound problems. As a result, many economists—such as Olivier Blanchard (2010) and Krugman (2013)—have called for an increase in the target inflation rate from 2 percent to 4 percent. However, central banks feel it is too dangerous to disturb the status quo. It is said that after two decades of targeting 2 percent inflation, and being quite successful at hitting this target, expectations of inflation are now anchored at 2 percent. Increasing the inflation target might reignite an inflationary spiral.

There are two other benefits from a higher rate of inflation. All economists recognize that inflation erodes the real value of nominal debt. Mainstream economists rarely count this as a benefit and prefer to call it an "unintended redistribution effect." Post-Keynesians argue that this can be extremely helpful in a recession, especially in a balance sheet recession.

The last benefit from a higher inflation is extremely controversial. Post-Keynesians and other heterodox economists argue that *full employment output* is positively related to inflation—at least up to a point. This will be explained and discussed more fully in the next chapter.

Question for your professor: Both Olivier Blanchard and Paul Krugman have called for an increase in the target inflation rate from 2 percent to 4 percent. Do you think this is a good idea?

2.4 The fundamental problem of inflation targeting

The fact that targeting inflation also stabilizes output is—in the words of Blanchard and Jordi (2007)—something of a "divine coincidence." As long as the economy is subject to demand shocks, monetary authorities can hit two targets using one instrument. While the divine coincidence does not exist in the face of supply-side shocks, their impact on inflation can be removed by targeting "core" inflation.

This divine coincidence can be illustrated using Figure 9.7 that shows a short-run Phillips curve trade-off. While this construct will be extensively discussed in the next chapter, it is useful to introduce it here because it illustrates the relationship between inflation and output. The mainstream view is that the trade-off between inflation and output exists only for given expectations of inflation, which means it only exists in the short run.

In Figure 9.7, expectations of inflation are assumed to be 2 percent, denoted by the "star." When actual inflation is 2 percent, expectations are correct, and the economy is at full employment, Y^f. If expected inflation were to increase to 4 percent, the entire short-run Phillips curve trade-off would shift up by 2 percentage points such that the star would lie on the dotted Y^f line at 4 percent inflation. In the long run, when we assume that expectations are correct, there is no trade-off. Or equivalently stated, the long-run Phillips curve is vertical situated at Y^f.

The divine coincidence exists because of the nature of the short-run trade-off. If output is below full employment output, then inflation is below target, and both "problems" can be solved by expansionary monetary policy. Alternatively, if output is above Y^f, then inflation is above target. This time,

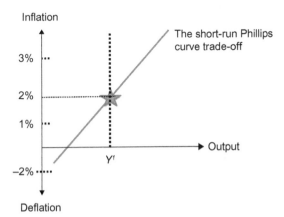

Figure 9.7 The Phillips curve trade-off and the divine coincidence

contractionary monetary policy solves both issues. At least, this is how the "divine coincidence" is supposed to work.

However, the short-run Phillips curve has broken down over the last two decades. As we will see in the next chapter, it has always been somewhat of a "will-o'-the-wisp"—the definition of which (by the way) is an "atmospheric ghost light seen by travelers at night, especially over bogs or swamps." So, the short-run Phillips curve has appeared and disappeared. We know it is not stable. It shifts systematically not only with expected inflation but also with a host of other factors. Many argue it does not exist at all. And certainly, if it ever did exist, it seems not to yield the "divine coincidence" anymore.

We will keep this discussion short since it will be taken up in the next chapter. Consider, however, Figure 9.8 that shows a kinked short-run Phillips curve, with the kink located at Y^f. In fact, a kinked trade-off makes more sense than a linear one since wages and prices go up much more easily than they go down. Figure 9.8 depicts a situation where the kink is exaggerated to the point where inflation no longer falls in response to a recessionary output gap.

Why has this occurred? Frankly, it is at present still unclear. It may be because of the anchoring of expectations at 2 percent, so prices continue to increase at 2 percent even though output is below Y^f. It may be because of changes in the nature of work described in Chapter 2. It may be because of the increasingly globalized nature of world trade. Whatever the reason, the fact is undeniable. Since the global financial crisis of 2008, we have witnessed some very wide fluctuations in output but relatively small changes in the inflation rate.

In this situation, if monetary authorities continue to believe in the "divine coincidence" and continue targeting inflation, they will take no action when output falls below Y^f. This has led many economists to call for the abandonment of inflation targeting.

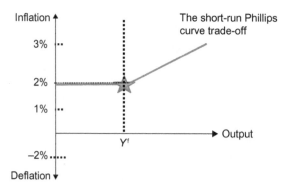

Figure 9.8 The Phillips curve trade-off may be broken

> Question for your professor: Have SR Phillips
> curves become flatter? Could they become horizontal
> at output levels below Y^f? If so, what are the
> implications for unemployment from just targeting
> inflation?

2.5 The need for a dual mandate

Central banks continuously review their performance and occasionally will undertake a full-scale review that includes a request for public feedback. The BOC undertook such a process in 2020. The BOC's review questionnaire discussed four alternatives to inflation targeting: price level targeting, average inflation targeting, nominal GDP targeting, and a dual mandate. The first two are minor deviations to the current inflation targeting regime. Let us consider the options in more detail to better understand why a dual mandate is best.

Under *price level targeting* the central bank could choose to target 2 percent growth in the price level. This seems the same as targeting 2 percent inflation. Indeed, if inflation proceeded at exactly 2 percent, it would be the same. The difference concerns what happens if inflation is temporarily higher or lower than 2 percent. Under the current system, such temporary deviations are *ignored*. This means that the price level is permanently affected by temporary deviations. Under price level targeting, past deviations of inflation from its target would not be ignored. Price level targeting implies that periods where inflation is above target would be followed by periods where it is below target, so as to get the price level back onto its 2 percent growth line.

It is thought that this could be helpful in the context of recovery from a recession. Presumably, inflation would have been below target during the downturn. Just getting inflation back on target would require less monetary stimulus than getting the price level back onto its 2 percent growth trajectory, and this could be advantageous to the recovery. Of course, the downside is that a boom, which would involve higher inflation than the target, would be stamped out more firmly to get the price level back down to its 2 percent trajectory. In other words, monetary policy would be turned up a notch or two—more aggressive in general. Unfortunately, implicit in this suggestion is that the "divine coincidence" continues to hold. It does nothing to solve the problem depicted in Figure 9.8 where inflation—and implicitly the price level trajectory—is detached from changes in output, when output is below Y^f.

Average inflation targeting This is a minor variant where the central bank would target a 2 percent target "on average." This would give more flexibility to monetary policy. It might want to achieve a 2 percent price level trajectory, or it might not. Either way, it doesn't solve the problem depicted in Figure 9.8.

Nominal GDP targeting This is a creative option. Essentially, the central bank would target the growth rate of nominal spending. Prior to the Great Recession, a growth rate of 5 percent was being discussed in the blogosphere.[14] The idea here is that real GDP was growing at around 3 percent, and the inflation target was 2 percent, implying a 5 (=3+2) percent growth of nominal GDP. This *does* address the problem depicted in Figure 9.8. If real GDP growth were to fall, but inflation was unaffected, nominal GDP growth would fall, and the monetary authorities would receive a signal to give the economy a monetary stimulus.

However, there are several drawbacks with nominal GDP targeting. Whereas inflation targeting is easily understood, the split of nominal GDP between the price level and real GDP is confusing. Would the public understand what is being targeted? Maybe not. Would this provide an anchor to expected inflation? Probably not. These difficulties would be compounded by the lags in getting real GDP data—it takes at least one-quarter to get provisional estimates—and by their frequent and large ex post revisions. The big drawback, however, is we do not know with any certainty the growth of potential real GDP, and hence we do not know the optimal growth of nominal GDP. And each change in the growth rate of potential GDP implies the necessity to change the target level of nominal GDP.

A dual mandate This is the best option—something for which post-Keynesians and heterodox economists in Canada have been actively lobbying.[15] Isn't it time that full employment became a priority again, as it was prior to the emergence of monetarism in the 1970s? A dual mandate would specify that maximizing employment along with keeping inflation low and stable are the joint goals of the central bank.

Post-Keynesians do not believe in coincidences—divine or otherwise. They argue it is not a coincidence that the era of inflation targeting has seen countries experience continued high levels of unemployment, growing inequality, and slower growth.[16] They point out that while moderate inflation may be inconvenient for some (particularly the wealthy), the costs of excessive unemployment are extremely damaging to society as a whole—loss of production, loss of employee skills, more stress, mental illness and family breakdowns, and worsening gender and racial inequalities.

Defenders of the status quo might contend that in targeting inflation, central banks try to estimate the output gap, and therefore there is, indirectly, a full employment target.[17] (Essentially, this is the divine coincidence argument.) But under the status quo, what happens when there is a range of unemployment rates consistent with roughly constant inflation, as depicted in Figure 9.8? Central bankers are instructed to be averse only to the risk of inflation. If they achieve their inflation target, they have fulfilled their mandate—even if unemployment is at the top end of the stable inflation-unemployment range. Indeed, given that the whole exercise of inflation targeting is replete with uncertainty—uncertainty of theory, forecasting methodology, and future events—there is an incentive to minimize the chances of excess inflation and *aim* for the top end of the stable range.[18]

As Osberg (2020: 124) explains, "When monetary policy is motivated solely by inflation avoidance, policy makers do not assign themselves the harder task of navigating the risks of unnecessarily high unemployment and possible inflation surges. However, the rest of society bears the large social and economic costs of their incentive structure."

Is the superiority of a dual mandate supported by any empirical or theoretical evidence? One empirical approach would be to compare the economic performances of countries that operate under a dual mandate with those that simply target inflation. In fact, the United States has had a dual mandate for decades. Yes, it embraced inflation targeting in 2012. But its formal mandate was established by the Humphrey–Hawkins Act of 1978, which specifies the goals of achieving "stable prices" and "maximum employment." And following its first public review, in August 2020 the Federal Reserve reasserted its dual mandate of price stability and maximum employment, modifying, however, its 2 percent inflation target into an average inflation target.

Given their geographical proximity and close economic connections, a natural comparison is the United States and Canada. Fortin (2020) notes that over the past 25 years the average unemployment rate has been 0.75 percentage points lower in the United States than in Canada.[19] Meanwhile, CPI inflation excluding food and energy has averaged 2.1 percent in the United States, but has been below target at 1.6 percent in Canada.

The theoretical approach involves building a macroeconomic model and seeing how it performs when the central bank follows different decision rules, and the economy is subject to a variety of shocks. We would need to specify some sort of "loss function" that would weigh the economic "bad" of inflation against the economic "bad" of unemployment. Many central banks have done such work. Indeed, this is the "bread and butter" of macro theorists. But because the results will depend crucially on how the loss function and the model are specified, and given all that we know about the state of macroeconomics these days, one would not expect an easy consensus. Having said that, it is worth noting that economists at the IMF, Debortoli et al. (2017) gave a resounding "Yes" to the question as to whether a dual mandate was desirable.

It is encouraging to note that the Reserve Bank of New Zealand—which was the first central bank in the world to adopt inflation targeting—abandoned it in favor of a dual mandate in early 2018. Besides targeting inflation at 2 percent, the central bank's new mandate adds that it will "contribute to supporting maximum sustainable employment within the economy."[20]

Finally, Bill Mitchell, one of the leading proponents of MMT, puts the problem of inflation targeting in terms of its implication that fiscal policy must be passive. He says (2009), "The real costs of inflation targeting lie in the ideology that accompanies it such that fiscal policy has to be passive (that is, the pursuit of surpluses given the logic adhered to). The failure of economies to eliminate persistently high rates of labour underutilisation despite having achieved low inflation is directly a consequence of this fiscal passivity."

2.6 The need for a green mandate!

We have emphasized the challenges posed by the climate emergency in Chapter 3. In brief, we need zero net emissions by 2050, and about a half-trillion tons of negative emissions between 2050 and 2100. Given that efforts thus far have not stopped *continuing increases* in global emissions, the scale of the task is truly gargantuan. It is astonishing that macroeconomic textbooks continue to ignore this reality.

A carbon price alone is not sufficient. We need to "wage war" on climate change, and the Second World War was not won with a "Hitler tax." Like all war efforts, this one requires the government to coordinate and to help fund the effort. This may seem like a task for fiscal policy alone, but increasingly central banks are realizing that there is a big role for monetary policy—for various reasons.

One reason is that climate change, as a source of financial risk, falls squarely within central bank mandates. The insurance industry, for example, is exposed to increasingly uncertain liability risks that could bring insolvency. Furthermore, as the world weans itself off fossil fuels, trillions of dollars of assets will become "stranded"—effectively worthless.[21] This leaves financial markets vulnerable to a meltdown similar to that of the subprime meltdown of 2008. Recognizing this reality, in 2017 many central banks formed the Network for Greening the Financial System (NGFS). Currently, the NGFS comprises seventy-four central banks and regulators, including China and Russia, but excluding (as of 2020) India and the United States.

There are a range of measures that central banks could take. For example, they could move to "green quantitative easing." Currently, when central banks buy corporate debt as part of QE, they abide by a "market neutrality" principle, and buy bonds strictly in proportion to outstanding totals. As a result, polluting oil, energy, and mining firms benefit from lower borrowing costs. Adopting green QE would exclude such firms, and could focus on buying the debt of renewable energy companies.

Central banks could also put pressure on commercial banks by imposing higher capital ratios on banks that lend to polluting corporations. More generally, they could set standards for green lending that their regulated banks will have to apply.

Currently, such measures are merely being discussed. Giving the central bank a green mandate would provide an incentive to central bankers to green the financial sector and help power the green revolution.

```
Question for your professor: Many economists
suggest expanding the central bank's mandate beyond
targeting inflation. Do you think a dual mandate
that includes full employment is a good idea?
What about a green mandate where the central bank
encourages commercial banks to hold assets in the
"green economy"?
```

2.7 Long-run monetary neutrality: the quantity theory rides again!

Mainstream texts assert that there is monetary neutrality in the long run. This means that the price level changes in direct proportion to the change in the money supply. For example, if the money supply rises 5 percent, the aggregate price level rises 5 percent in the long run. It implies that monetary policy has no real effect in the long run. Clearly, this is the quantity theory of money making its reappearance.

How strange this is! In the previous chapter on "money and banking" the mainstream texts are generally very good at explaining how the definition of money is a "gray area." The usual definition of money is "any asset that can *easily* be used to purchase goods and services." Since "easily" is a relative term, there is an element of arbitrariness to the definition of money. That is why there are so many definitions of money. We have M1, M2, and M3—all related to measures of money held in the commercial banking system. When we start to include near bank financial intermediaries, then we add "+" signs to these definitions, or even double "+" signs, giving us nine widely used measures of the money supply.

What makes this sudden conversion to monetarism even stranger is that when discussing why most central banks now target interest rates and not the money supply, the texts are explicit that given the plethora of definitions of the money supply, it would not be clear which one is the appropriate target.

So, long-run monetary neutrality tells us that the price level changes in direct proportion to the change in the money supply. We might ask: which one? It matters. While some definitions of money might be increasing rapidly, others might be falling. This problem of deciding on the definitive measure of money is not easily solved. In the 1970s monetarism was tried by many central banks. They tried to control inflation by controlling the quantity of money. The experiment failed for precisely this reason.

Besides this problem, there is an even deeper issue concerning the possibility of *hysteresis*—where the path toward equilibrium determines the nature of the equilibrium itself. What is at issue is whether potential output might be influenced by the short-run fluctuations of actual output.

Potential output is determined by the economy's resources—both capital and labor—and by its technological know-how. Increases in the labor force, and increases in both physical and human capital, as well as technological innovation, all shift potential output to the right. It follows, therefore, that the loss of human capital will decrease potential output. One argument for hysteresis is that deep recessions, which cause long periods of unemployment, destroy human capital. But there are other avenues through which hysteresis can occur, especially involving innovation. We will consider this argument in more detail in the next chapter.

2.8 Conclusion

There are strong reasons to believe that monetary policy is like pushing on a piece of string.

It can pull the economy back in a boom, but cannot push it out of a recession—particularly a deep recession. In a balance sheet recession many businesses will be technically bankrupt and are focused on paying down debt. They will not borrow (and spend) even with zero interest rates.

QE is an interesting attempt to ameliorate the situation. However, the private sector's spending has not been sensitive to changes in interest rates, neither long nor short. To the extent to which it had a wealth effect, it has benefited the wealthy contributing to increased inequality. But this increased wealth has not translated into more spending. The most useful aspect of QE is the implicit financing of fiscal policy. QE has moved us a step closer to a MMT world.

An interesting "sidebar" to the QE story is the way it was implemented in the United States. The Federal Reserve paid above-market interest rates on commercial banks' excess reserves. This was an implicit subsidy to the banking sector amounting to many trillions of dollars over a period of years.

Finally, inflation targeting is no longer blessed by the "divine coincidence." Most of the other possible targets—price level targeting, average inflation targeting—are no better. Nominal GDP targeting is an interesting alternative but has several critical flaws. This seems to be the moment when central banks should formally adopt a dual mandate and add the full employment goal to the central bank's mandate. Making full employment a priority again is long overdue.

Chapter 10

INFLATION AND UNEMPLOYMENT: THE POLITICAL ECONOMY OF UNEMPLOYMENT

I THE STANDARD TEXT

In this chapter, we examine inflation and its relationship to output and unemployment. We investigate the causes of an accelerating inflation rate and the costs of disinflation. In the process, we explain the forces determining the full employment level of unemployment and possible policies to reduce unemployment.

1.1 The Phillips curve

In 1958, a New Zealand economist named A. W. Phillips published a paper that showed a negative relationship between the unemployment rate and inflation.[1] Phillips concluded that inflation and unemployment were linked in a way that economists had not previously appreciated. While Phillips used UK data from 1861 to 1957, a flurry of subsequent research showed that the relationship could be generalized to other economies and other time periods. It was believed that a fundamental relationship had been discovered—a stable trade-off between inflation and unemployment. For a short while it seemed that policymakers could choose where on that trade-off they wanted the economy to be.

However, it soon became clear that a key shift variable was expected inflation, and in the long run when expectations are (by definition) correct, the Phillips curve would be vertical and there would be no trade-off.

We have already introduced Phillips curves in Figure 9.8 of Chapter 9, but we have not yet provided an explanation or derivation. This is our next job.

1.2 Lipsey's (1960) micro-underpinnings to the Phillips curve

In 1960, Richard Lipsey provided a theoretical explanation for the traditional Phillips curve relationship between inflation and unemployment: both its shape and its one-for-one shift with expected inflation. Using Lipsey's approach, we begin by deriving the relationship between inflation and output. This is the version best adapted to inclusion in macro models. Later, in Section 1.6, we provide the link to the traditional curve—the relationship between output and the unemployment rate.

Lipsey's analysis is centered in the labor market, and he postulates a normal price adjustment mechanism—that the real price of labor will respond to excess demand or supply of labor. Letting "N" denote employment, and "N^f" full employment, we can specify excess demand for labor as $(N - N^f)$, and write:

$$\text{The rate of change of}\left(\frac{W}{P}\right) = \beta\left(N - N^f\right), \qquad \text{where } \beta > 0$$

This says that real wages will increase if there is an excess demand for labor $(N > N^f)$, and decrease if there is an excess supply $(N < N^f)$. Furthermore, the greater the excess demand (or supply), the faster real wages will change.

Next, Lipsey recognizes the importance of labor market contracts, which implies that the prices that will prevail during the length of the contract need to be expected. Thus, it is the wage divided by the expected price level that adjusts.

$$\text{The rate of change of}\left(\frac{W}{P^e}\right) = \beta\left(N - N^f\right)$$

Next, note that the rate of change of a ratio is the difference between the rate of change of the numerator and the rate of change of the denominator. Writing the rate of change of wages as $\dot{w}$ and the rate of change of expected prices (which is the same thing as the expected rate of inflation) as π^e, we can write the real wage adjustment equation as:

$$\dot{w} - \pi^e = \beta\left(N - N^f\right) \tag{10.1}$$

Since employment and output are positively related through the production function, we can replace the $\left(N - N^f\right)$ term with a term measuring the output gap, $\left(Y - Y^f\right)$. When we make this substitution, we replace the β term with a new term ϕ to reflect the link between labor and output through the production function. Moving expected inflation to the right-hand side, we get:

$$\dot{w} = \pi^e + \phi\left(Y - Y^f\right)$$

The final stage is to link wage inflation to price inflation. Assuming labor is the only variable factor of production, and assuming no productivity growth, price inflation would be the same as wage inflation, allowing us to write the inflation–output Phillips curve as in equation (10.2).

$$\pi = \pi^e + \phi\left(Y - Y^f\right) \tag{10.2}$$

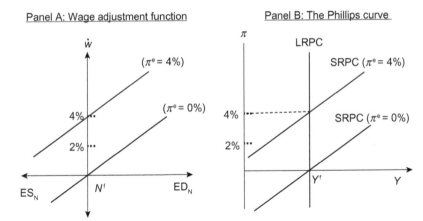

Figure 10.1 Lipsey's derivation of the Phillips curve

Figure 10.1 illustrates the expected real wage adjustment line (equation 10.1) in Panel A alongside the Phillips curve (equation 10.2) in Panel B.

In Panel A, excess demand and excess supply of labor (ED_N and ES_N respectively) are measured on the horizontal axis. The intersection of the vertical and horizontal axes indicates full employment. Employment increases as we move toward the right. When expected inflation is zero, excess demand for labor $(N > N^f)$ generates wage inflation $(\dot{w} > 0)$, while excess supply $(N < N^f)$ generates wage deflation $(\dot{w} < 0)$. An increase in expected inflation shifts up the wage adjustment line one-for-one.

In Panel B of Figure 10.1, we utilized the production function to replace employment with output and we changed the measure of inflation to "price inflation" (π) on the vertical axis. The main difference between the panels is the placement of the vertical axis. In Panel B, the vertical axis is shown in its more familiar location on the extreme left of the diagram. What was the vertical axis in Panel A becomes the position of the long-run Phillips curve (LRPC) in Panel B. In the long run, expected inflation must equal actual inflation, and whenever this occurs, output is at its full employment level. Hence, the LRPC is a vertical line located at Y^f.

1.3 The Phillips curve as a dynamic aggregate supply curve

Lipsey (1960) was the first to provide a theoretical explanation for the Phillips curve. There have been many explanations since then, using many different approaches. However, the key point to note is that there is a close relationship between aggregate supply and the Phillips curve. Indeed, the inflation–output Phillips curve is often referred to as a "dynamic aggregate supply curve." We can see this correspondence visually in Figure 10.2, which depicts a Phillips curve in Panel A, alongside an aggregate supply curve in Panel B.

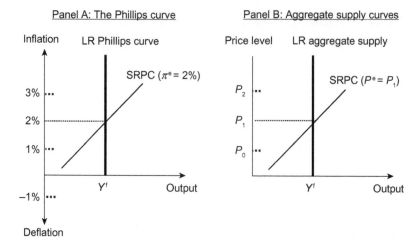

Figure 10.2 Phillips curves versus aggregate supply curves

Notice that we have made one slight modification to the "old-fashioned" aggregate supply curve: instead of making the position of the short-run aggregate supply (SRAS) curve dependent on the given level of wages, we make it dependent on expected prices. (In Figure 10.2, the expected price level is P_1.) This formulation is more modern since it recognizes that the supply of output depends on the relationship between actual prices and expected prices. (If you prefer, think of the key determinant of wages as expected prices.)

For those who are mathematically inclined, we can easily derive the Phillips curve from an equation for the aggregate supply curve. We write the equation for the aggregate supply curve as:

$$Y = Y^f + S\left(P - P^e\right)$$

Since S is positive, $Y > Y^f$ when $P > P^e$, which is the SRAS curve, and $Y = Y^f$ when $P = P^e$, which is the long-run aggregate supply (LRAS) curve. So, this one equation describes the aggregate supply nexus. Next, rearrange the equation putting the price level on the left-hand side.

$$P = P^e + (1/S)\left(Y - Y^f\right)$$

Now subtract last period's price level P_{-1} from both sides, and write $(1/S)$ as ϕ.

$$(P - P_{-1}) = \left(P^e - P_{-1}\right) + \phi\left(Y - Y^f\right)$$

If "P" denoted the log of prices, then $\left(P-P_{-1}\right)$ would be inflation, π, and $\left(P^e-P_{-1}\right)$ would be expected inflation, π^e. Making these substitutions, we get equation (10.2) from the previous section.

$$\pi = \pi^e + \phi\left(Y - Y^f\right)$$ (10.2) (again)

So, the Phillips curve is simply a dynamic aggregate supply curve, *and there are many different approaches to deriving the aggregate supply curve*. In particular, there is a major difference between the New Classical and New Keynesian approaches.

New Classical economists favor market clearing models and explain short-run fluctuations either through real shocks or through expectational errors.[2] Keynesian economists—both old and new—favor nonmarket clearing models where wages (or prices) are sticky. It can be shown that the SRAS curve derived from the New Classical market clearing model is steeper than that from the New Keynesian wage (or price) stickiness model, which means that the New Classical short-run Phillips curve (SRPC) will be steeper than the Keynesian SRPC. Given empirical uncertainty about the slope of the Phillips curve in reality, these theoretical differences inform different policy positions about the costs of disinflation. The steeper the SRPC, the smaller is the output cost of disinflation.

Another important difference concerns the interpretation of cyclical unemployment. Keynesians are committed to the view that unemployment caused by a recession is involuntary and has high social costs. In contrast, there is no involuntary unemployment in a market clearing story. Yes, fewer people work in a recession, but that is their choice. They have chosen more leisure and less work since the expected real wage has fallen. Keynesians ridicule the New Classical story as saying that "recessions are just vacations" and really bad recessions are mass vacations. New Classicals argue that the distinction between voluntary and involuntary unemployment is not clear. After all, people do not voluntarily make expectational errors.

1.4 What determines the long-run inflation rate?

Long-run equilibrium is consistent with any inflation rate as long as inflation is correctly anticipated. So, what determines the long-run inflation rate?

While the determination of inflation can be quite complex in general, the specific determination of the inflation rate in long-run equilibrium is very straightforward. The key point is that in long-run equilibrium all real variables must be constant. In order for the real money supply, M/P, to be constant, the rate of growth of the money supply must be equal to the rate of inflation. Thus, it can be correctly said: *in the long run, inflation is a monetary phenomenon*. The long-run equilibrium rate of inflation is determined solely by the rate of growth of the money supply.

1.5 Accelerating inflation

Suppose policymakers set themselves the objective of increasing output beyond full employment output, Y^f, and keeping it there. Perhaps an election is approaching, and a booming economy gives the incumbent government a big advantage. Or perhaps policymakers are committed to achieving full employment and they mistakenly believe that full employment output is higher than it really is. The precise policy mix used to achieve the objective—whether fiscal or monetary or both—does not matter. The point of the exercise is to investigate the consequences to the economy *if* the government succeeds in its objective.

We begin with the economy at point A in Figure 10.3, with both expected and actual inflation equal to 2 percent. Now the government pursues expansionary policies and output expands to Y_1. As the economy moves up the SRPC from point A to point B, inflation increases to 4 percent. The economy will enjoy the boom, but there is inherent tension: actual inflation is greater than expected, and eventually, people will adjust their expectations upward.

While opinions differ on how quickly this adjustment will occur—New Classicals prefer the assumption of *rational expectations* and quick adjustment, while Keynesians generally argue that slower adjustment is more realistic—the adjustment must occur eventually. Once people come to expect 4 percent inflation, the SRPC shifts up and the economy moves to point C. Output is still greater than Y^f and inflation has increased to 6 percent, which is greater than the now 4 percent expected. Once again, expected inflation will eventually catch up, shifting up the SRPC and moving the economy to point D. The process continues in this way with inflation ever accelerating, which is why this result is known as the *accelerationist hypothesis*.

We should note that if policymakers attempt (and succeed) in holding output *below* full employment, the process works in reverse with ever-accelerating *deflation*.

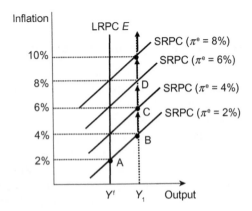

Figure 10.3 Accelerating inflation

This result is bad news for policy activism. What makes it even worse is the realization that policymakers do not know the value of Y^f with any accuracy. So, given the uncertainty of knowing Y^f, and the destructive consequences of aiming for the wrong level, the message is to abandon the attempt to achieve a full employment goal. The silver lining is that the economy is stable, and so it will tend toward full employment on its own.

The accelerationist hypothesis suggests a limited role for policy. In normal circumstances, monetary policy should restrict itself to targeting inflation, and fiscal policy should focus on balancing the government's budget over the business cycle. Active stabilization policy is best reserved for those rare situations when a recession is deep and (expected to be) prolonged.

Note that the unemployment that exists at full employment, Y^f, is the natural rate of unemployment (NRU), u^*. Now we see why u^* is sometimes referred to as the nonaccelerating inflation rate of unemployment, or NAIRU: whenever the unemployment rate is less than u^*, inflation will tend to accelerate.

The fact that inflationary expectations can influence actual inflation implies that managing expectations is critical. Once high inflation becomes expected, it will persist, even when output is at Y^f. That is why inflation targeting is thought to be such an important tool: it anchors expectations.

1.6 The standard Phillips curve in inflation-unemployment space

The success of stabilization policy is usually judged by how well the economy has avoided the twin evils of unemployment and inflation. That means replacing the output gap on the right-hand side of equation (10.2) with the unemployment rate gap. For convenience, equation (10.2) is repeated below.

$$\pi = \pi^e + \phi\left(Y - Y^f\right) \tag{10.2}$$

The two gaps are negatively related via Okun's law:

$$\left(Y - Y^f\right) = -v\left(u - u^*\right) \qquad \text{Okun's law}$$

Okun's law is not a result derived from theory but is an empirical observation first made by the American economist Arthur Okun in the 1970s. The value of "v" may vary between countries and may change over time. It is clear that the two gaps will be negatively related: as output increases, so employment increases, and unemployment will decrease. What may not be clear is why the value of "v" is greater than one, and is often closer to three. That is to say, a 1 percentage point reduction in the unemployment rate may require a 3 percentage point increase in output. One reason for this "slippage" is that the participation rate may increase as employment increases (and more jobs become available). In addition, both hours of work and productivity increase as output increases.

Using Okun's law, we can replace the output gap in equation (10.2) with the unemployment gap, yielding a typical Phillips curve, where $\lambda = v\phi$.

$$\pi = \pi^e - \lambda(u - u^*) \tag{10.3}$$

Besides incorporating Okun's law, we need to make another change to explain historical observations of inflation and unemployment: we must abandon the simplification that labor is the only variable factor of production. In particular, we must include imported intermediate inputs into the production process. Increases in the cost of raw materials, whose prices are determined in world markets, are the source of supply-side shocks. For example, if the world price of oil were to increase, this would push up the prices of domestically produced goods.

Denoting the rate of change of prices of imported intermediate inputs as $\dot{z}$, we can write our new inflation–unemployment Phillips curve as in equation (10.4).

$$\pi = \pi^e - \lambda\left(u - u^*\right) + \gamma\dot{z} \tag{10.4}$$

Using words, equation (10.4) says:

Inflation = Expected inflation + Demand-pull inflation + Cost-push inflation

While equation (10.4) makes us much better equipped to explain historical observations, a new unknown has entered the analysis: the NRU, $u*$. In Chapter 3, we mentioned that the word *natural* does not mean that it is determined by *nature*. The NRU is determined by institutions and policies. Before we can attempt to explain historical observations of inflation and unemployment, we need to consider the determinants of $u*$. We turn to that task next.

I.7 The determinants of the NRU

The NRU, $u*$, has two components: frictional and structural. Frictional unemployment occurs *when there are enough jobs for everyone*, but the process of matching workers to jobs takes time. Structural unemployment occurs when there are structural barriers that prevent wages from falling to their equilibrium level, causing *a surplus of job seekers*. There is also the possibility that the components of $u*$ (both frictional and structural) could be dependent on their past history, a possibility known as hysteresis.

Frictional unemployment The essence of frictional unemployment hinges on two facts. First, the economy is constantly churning—people enter the workforce and others leave; new jobs are created, and existing jobs destroyed. Second, workers (and jobs) are heterogeneous—no two workers (or jobs) are alike. Since workers have different preferences and abilities, and jobs have different attributes and requirements, it makes sense for both workers and firms to spend time searching for the best match. This implies that there will always be some frictional unemployment, even at full employment.

Obviously, the amount of job search will be positively influenced by the generosity of government benefits while unemployed. (These are often called unemployment insurance benefits.) But while higher benefits mean higher frictional unemployment, this is not necessarily a net cost to the economy. It permits a better matching of worker skills with job requirements, which improves efficiency.

Less obvious is the influence of demography. Younger workers tend to have higher quit rates (and hence more frequent incidence of job search) than older workers. People usually try several jobs before settling into one for a longer period of time. Therefore, the higher the proportion of young people in the labor force, the greater the number of people searching for jobs, even at full employment.

The extent to which the economy "churns" can be influenced by things like free trade agreements or technological change. Both of those can create jobs requiring new skills, and eliminate jobs requiring old skills. Matching worker to job can be particularly difficult if workers need to retrain or relocate. This can produce quite lengthy spells of unemployment.

We should note that some economists label longer spells of unemployment due to mismatch as "structural unemployment." This is logical since the mismatch occurs between the structure of the labor force—in terms of skills or geographic locations—and the structure of the available jobs. The problem with this definition is that there is no clear dividing line between search with everyday heterogeneity and search with mismatch. How often would a worker leave one job, only to take another using exactly the same skills as before, or in exactly the same location as before? And how big a difference must there be to warrant the associated job search being called "structural" instead of "frictional"?

We (and other economists) reserve the term "structural unemployment" for when there is *a persistent surplus of job seekers*, over and above the available vacancies, due to real wage rigidity.[3] Frictional unemployment, whether with mismatch or without, refers to a situation where the number of vacancies equals the number of job searchers.

Structural unemployment This is caused by structural impediments preventing wages from falling to the point where the quantity of labor supplied is equal to the quantity demanded.

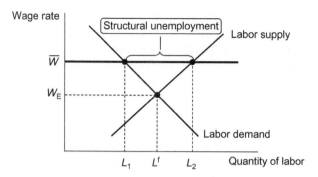

Figure 10.4 The effect of a binding minimum wage

Consider a typical labor market shown in Figure 10.4. Even at the equilibrium wage, W_E, there will still be some frictional unemployment. That's because there will always be some workers engaged in job search even when the number of jobs available is equal to the number of workers seeking jobs. But there wouldn't be any structural unemployment at W_E. However, if the wage rate were stuck at $\overline{W}$, structural unemployment would equal the difference between L_2 and L_1. This can occur for two main reasons: employers might choose to pay higher wages in order to get employees to work harder, or there might be institutional barriers to lowering wages.

When it is hard to monitor worker effort, firms might choose to pay above equilibrium wages, or *efficiency wages*, as an incentive for better performance. Suppose workers who are caught shirking will be fired. Workers might not care about this risk, and choose to shirk if a similar job at similar pay could easily be found. But if the firm paid a wage above market equilibrium, being caught shirking now implies a lower wage in an alternative job. Hence worker effort improves. If all firms pay efficiency wages, the penalty for being caught shirking is a period of structural unemployment.[4]

There are three institutional factors that cause structural unemployment: unions, minimum wages, and job protection regulations.

Unions give workers greater bargaining power. Collective bargaining usually results in higher wages than the market would have otherwise provided. The effect is the same as a minimum wage: labor unions push the real wage that workers receive above the equilibrium real wage, leading to structural unemployment.

A minimum wage is a government-mandated floor on the price of labor. While the minimum wage is always stipulated in nominal (or dollar) terms, there is a tendency for it to be increased to reflect increases in the cost of living. To the extent to which this occurs, the minimum wage is actually a *real wage floor*. For many types of labor, the minimum wage is irrelevant; the market equilibrium wage is well above this price floor. But for some types of labor, the minimum wage may be binding. In Figure 10.4, if the minimum wage were equal to $\overline{W}$ it would cause structural unemployment equal to $L_2 - L_1$.

Job protection regulations make it hard to fire workers. This has the effect of reducing worker effort. Because workers are less productive, employers want to hire fewer of them. This can exacerbate structural unemployment if there are other factors making it hard for wages to fall. It can also increase frictional unemployment by encouraging employers to search longer to find a good match. This makes workers less willing to leave jobs, creating a less flexible labor market. In France and Italy, employers need to have a government-approved reason to fire a worker. The resulting increase in structural unemployment in these economies has been dubbed "Eurosclerosis."

Hysteresis This term is applicable to any system where the equilibrium is path dependent. Hysteresis implies that periods of high unemployment might increase the NRU, u^*. Some avenues suggest an effect on frictional unemployment, while others suggest an effect on structural unemployment. For example, long durations of unemployment might erode workers' skills making it harder for them to find work, hence increasing frictional unemployment.

Another mechanism involves unions and collective bargaining. Suppose unions want to negotiate the best deal for their currently employed members. The size of this group of "insiders" might shrink if there is a negative demand shock. The newly unemployed union members become "outsiders" whose unemployment exerts no downward pressure on wages. Hence their unemployment becomes "locked in" and structural unemployment increases. Since European countries are heavily unionized, many commentators have emphasized this insider–outsider hypothesis as a cause of "Eurosclerosis"— persistently high unemployment rates in the EU.

1.8 Explaining historical observations of inflation and unemployment

Now that we understand the determinants of u^*, we can use the Phillips curve (as expressed in equation 10.4) to explain historical observations of inflation and unemployment. The theory can be applied to any well-developed market economy. For example, consider Canadian data from 1962 to 2009, a period ending at the start of the Great Recession.[5] Figure 10.5 shows a scatterplot of annual observations of the CPI inflation rate and the unemployment rate for all adults aged fifteen to sixty-five. Many observations are labeled by year, so that we can trace the historical movement of the economy through inflation–unemployment rate space. The initial impression of Figure 10.5 might be that the movements of the economy look like a tangled ball of thread. But in fact they are amenable to explanation.

The first thing to notice in Figure 10.5 is the presence of clockwise loops. Generally, in the upward phase of a loop, excess demand moves the economy up and along the SRPC, and the economy moves in a northwest direction as inflation increases and unemployment falls. When expected inflation catches up, the SRPC shifts up and to the right, moving the economy in a northeast

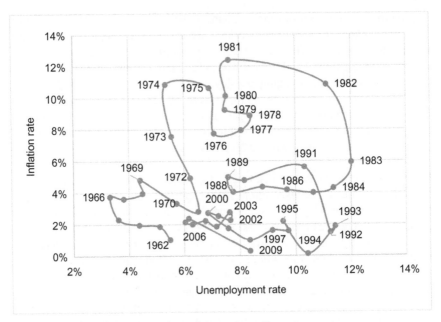

Figure 10.5 Canada's economic performance, 1962–2009

direction. For example, this explains the movement from 1962 to 1969, and *to some extent* the movement from 1971 to 1975. (The proviso is explained in the paragraph after next.)

Generally, in the downward phase of a loop, the central bank acts to increase interest rates, pushing the economy into a recession, increasing unemployment and decreasing inflation as the economy moves down the SRPC in a southeast direction. Eventually expected inflation also falls, shifting the SRPC down. (This is depicted in Figure 10.6.) As the central bank relaxes monetary policy in the recovery phase, the economy moves in a southwest direction. For example, this explains the movement of the economy from 1974 to 1976, from 1981 to 1988, and from 1991 to 1994.

A key component in explaining the origin of double digit inflation, and the movements from 1973 to 1981, is massive supply-side shocks occurring in 1973 and 1979, producing big upward shifts in the SRPC. In 1973 the Organization of the Petroleum Exporting Countries (OPEC) choked back their supply of oil to engineer a *fourfold* increase in world oil prices. In 1979, before the world economy had fully digested that first shock, there was *another* 150 percent increase in world oil prices. These supply shocks led to *stagflation* on a massive scale: both double digit inflation *and* double digit unemployment rates.

1.9 The costs of disinflation

Once inflation has become embedded in expectations, reducing it may require a sacrifice of lost output and higher unemployment. The size of the sacrifice

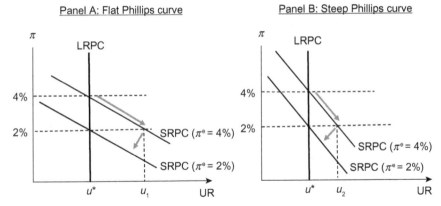

Figure 10.6 Disinflation and the depth of the recession

depends on the slope of the Phillips curve and the speed with which expected inflation adjusts.

As illustrated in Figure 10.6, for every percentage point reduction in inflation, the increase in unemployment is greater if the Phillips curve is relatively flat (as in Panel A). Suppose we begin in long-run equilibrium, with both actual and expected inflation equal to 4 percent, and the money growth rate also equal to 4 percent. If the money growth rate is reduced to 2 percent, interest rates increase, spending falls, and the economy travels down the initial SRPC ($\pi^e = 4\%$) to u_1 in Panel A. In comparison, unemployment only increases to u_2 if the Phillips curve is relatively steep, as in Panel B. The economy will be stuck in recession until expected inflation falls to 2 percent and the SRPC shifts down.[6] Thus, the slope of the Phillips curve determines the depth of the recession, while its duration is determined by the speed with which expectations adjust.

The "sacrifice ratio" is a measure of the cost of disinflation. It is the percentage of a year's real GDP that must be forgone to reduce inflation by 1 percentage point. For example, the 1990–2 disinflation in Canada reduced inflation by roughly 4 percentage points. Suppose the total output loss over this period was $80 billion, and further suppose potential GDP at the time was equal to $400 billion. Using these numbers, 20 percentage points ($= 80 \div 400$) of potential output was lost, implying a sacrifice ratio of 5 percentage points of GDP ($20 \div 4 = 5$) for each percentage point reduction of inflation.

While typical estimates of the sacrifice ratio range between 2 and 4, it is not a given parameter but depends on many specific factors. Some New Classical economists go so far as to suggest that a zero sacrifice ratio might be possible if the central bank announces in advance of wages bargains being set that its inflation target is being reduced, and it has a reputation for credibility.

Keynesian economists agree that credible policy announcements by the central bank can be helpful in resetting inflationary expectations. But they do not agree that painless disinflation is possible. They point out that wage contracts overlap, new wage bargains are continuously occurring, and that relative wages are an important component in setting wages. Therefore, it is not possible to announce a policy change "in advance of wage bargains being set."

To conclude, we consider two extreme cases: deflation and hyperinflation.

1.10 The danger of deflation

While disinflation means reducing inflation to a lower positive rate, deflation means negative "inflation." Disinflation is a classic example of short-term pain (the sacrifice ratio) for long-term gain (lower inflation). Deflation has no long-term gain. In fact, deflation can become a dangerous whirlpool from which it is very hard to escape.

The problem with *unanticipated* deflation is that it increases the real value of debt, crushing debtors and decreasing their spending.[7] This causes aggregate demand to fall, potentially leading to even more deflation, creating a vicious circle. While stuck in the deflationary trap, unemployment remains high.

The problem with *anticipated* deflation is the zero lower bound problem. According to the loanable funds theory, both the supply and demand for loanable funds shift up one-for-one with expected inflation. So, expected deflation shifts both lines down, which reduces the equilibrium nominal rate of interest. Other things being equal, this keeps the real rate of interest unchanged. (The real rate of interest equals the nominal rate minus expected inflation.) However, once the zero lower bound is reached, nominal interest rates cannot fall. At this point, an increase in expected deflation increases the real rate of interest, decreasing aggregate demand, leading to even more deflation. Once again, there is a vicious circle, but this time occurring in the context where conventional monetary policy is no longer effective.[8]

1.11 Hyperinflation: cause and cure

In a hyperinflation, price increases are so rapid that money no longer functions as a store of value, and the viability of the money supply is undermined. People will either refuse to accept it, or it becomes a "hot potato," passed from hand to hand as quickly as possible to minimize the loss of purchasing power suffered by those holding it. Savings are destroyed, with implications for the viability of the political system. The German hyperinflation in the 1920s, followed by the Great Depression in the 1930s, set the stage for the rise of fascism and the Second World War.

The conventional marker for hyperinflation is anything over 50 percent a month, but there are many examples where it has been much higher.[9] In postwar Hungary, the *daily* inflation rate was over 200 percent. In Zimbabwe in 2008, the daily inflation rate was nearly 100 percent. In 2019, the daily inflation rate in Venezuela rose to over 1,000 percent. How does a country get itself into such a mess?

As we already know, the long-run equilibrium rate of inflation is determined by the rate of growth of the money supply. So, hyperinflation is caused by hyperfast growth of the money supply. But why does this occur? The short answer is because the government is desperately short of money, is unable to borrow more, and is unwilling or unable to cut spending or raise taxes. So, it resorts to the printing press. But this sets up its own vicious circle. The more money it prints, the faster is the rate of inflation, and the less money people want to hold, which further increases the rate of inflation.

We can analyze the process more clearly by recognizing that inflation is a tax on those holding money. If inflation is 5 percent, then a year from now $1 will buy goods and services worth only 95 cents today. This is equivalent to a tax rate of 5 percent on the value of all money held by the public. The tax revenue in nominal terms is $(\Delta P / P) \times M$.

Dividing by the price level gives us an expression for the inflation tax revenue in real terms:

$$\text{The real inflation tax} = \left(\frac{\Delta P}{P}\right)\left(\frac{M}{P}\right)$$

The nominal revenue generated by the government's right to print money is known as "seigniorage," which is equal to the money supply it issues, or ΔM. In real terms, this seigniorage is ΔM divided by the price level, P, or $\Delta M / P$.

$$\text{Real seigniorage} = \frac{\Delta M}{P} = \left(\frac{\Delta M}{M}\right)\left(\frac{M}{P}\right)$$

In the equation above, we have multiplied and divided the right-hand side by M, leaving the result unchanged. The reason for doing this is because we want the rate of growth of the money supply on the right-hand side. Since this equals the rate of inflation, we can replace $\Delta M / M$ with $\Delta P / P$ to get the same expression as that for the real inflation tax.

$$\text{Real seigniorage} = \text{The real inflation tax} = \frac{\Delta P}{P}\frac{M}{P}$$

The above equation should come as no surprise. It simply says that the revenue raised in seigniorage equals the tax burden imposed.

The total revenue raised by any tax is always the tax *rate* multiplied by the tax *base*. In the case of the inflation tax, the tax rate is the rate of inflation, $\Delta P / P$, and the tax base is the real value of money that people hold, M / P. This is the key to understanding why hyperinflation can get out of control. People try to avoid paying the inflation tax by reducing their real money holdings. *This reduces the tax base and shrinks government revenues.* To restore its revenues, the government increases the rate of growth of the money supply, which increases the rate of inflation. This further reduces real money holdings, further reducing the tax base, causing the government to further accelerate the rate of growth of the money supply.

Once the vicious circle of hyperinflation has been ignited, dramatic policy remedies are required. Simply raising interest rates is insufficient. Hyperinflation has an expectations component. The vicious circle of increases in expected inflation leading to actual increases in inflation must be snapped. The crisis of confidence must be solved. Often central banks abandon the deflated currency and introduce a new one. But such measures do not go to the heart of the problem. Hyperinflation is a monetary phenomenon with an underlying fiscal cause. The budgetary problems of the government must be addressed. Either government spending must be cut or new sources of tax revenue must be found. These elements are inevitably found in any "structural adjustment program" advocated by the IMF or World Bank. Unfortunately, these policies are rarely popular.

1.12 Conclusion

When the Phillips curve is expressed as a relationship between inflation and output, it may be viewed as a dynamic aggregate supply curve. There are many possible ways of framing its micro-underpinnings. This version of the Phillips curve is easily transformed into the traditional relationship between inflation and unemployment using Okun's law to replace the output gap with the unemployment rate gap. When augmented with a term representing aggregate supply shocks, we can use this version of the Phillips curve to explain movements in inflation/unemployment space.

The accelerationist hypothesis demonstrates the danger of attempting to target full employment. If the government can succeed in hitting its target, then that target had better be exactly equal to full employment output. If it misses, there are serious adverse consequences in terms of accelerating inflation or deflation. Given the uncertainty surrounding the exact level of full employment output, the message is to abandon any attempt to target output.

The proper coordination of fiscal and monetary policy is of central importance to understanding hyperinflation. Hyperinflation is a monetary phenomenon with an underlying fiscal cause.

2 THE ANTI-TEXT

A natural rate that hops around from one triennium to another under the influence of unspecified forces, including past unemployment rates, is not "natural" at all. "Epiphenomenal" would be a better adjective; look it up.

Robert Solow (1987: S33)

2.1 The possibility of a nonvertical LRPC

We begin with a modest critique of the mainstream view: the possibility that the LRPC may be nonvertical. If true, there would exist a long-run trade-off between inflation and unemployment—a higher fully anticipated inflation rate would be associated with a lower natural unemployment rate, *at least up to a point.* For example, if the LRPC has a "tail" at low levels of inflation, as illustrated in Figure 10.7, then the trade-off disappears when inflation is higher than 3 percent. But an inflation rate lower than that leads to a permanently higher unemployment rate.

Clearly, this is an argument against aiming for an inflation rate that is too low, and is an argument with real empirical relevance given the low inflation targets most central banks have adopted. But it is a weak critique of the mainstream because it does not change anything fundamental. The system is still stable—it will return to a "natural rate" of unemployment eventually, though that rate may be dependent on the choice of the inflation target. Nor is the economy path dependent.

So, why should the LRPC have a tail? One often cited reason is the so-called "Tobin effect" named after James Tobin's 1972 presidential address to the American Economic Association.[10] In this paper Tobin notes the empirical fact that workers resist wage cuts. More importantly, workers are willing to accept cuts in their real wages brought about by price increases (with constant wages) but resist cuts in their real wages brought about by wage decreases (with constant prices). To a neoclassical economist this smacks of "money illusion"—a failure to understand what is happening in real terms because of a fixation on money values. But resisting wage cuts is rational when workers are concerned with relative wages, and relative wages are a real magnitude. Since there is no central economy-wide mechanism to alter all money wages together, the desire to preserve relative wages translates into resisting wage cuts.

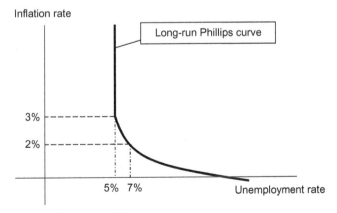

Figure 10.7 Nonunique natural rate

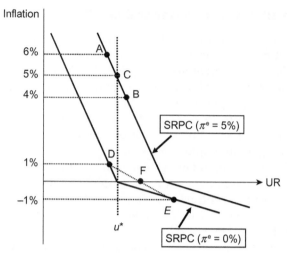

Figure 10.8 Implications of a Tobin effect

The Tobin effect creates a kink in the SRPC at zero inflation, as shown in Figure 10.8. When expected and actual inflation are zero, the kink occurs at u^*. But when expected inflation increases, the kink does not move upward as the Phillips curve shifts up, but rather remains situated at zero inflation. This means the kink no longer occurs at u^* but at a higher unemployment rate. Adding dispersion creates the tail in the LRPC. In his 1972 paper, Tobin talks about spatial dispersion (across different labor markets), but temporal dispersion (over time) gives precisely the same result.[11]

Consider first the situation where average inflation is high enough that the kink is not relevant. For example, suppose the economy has average inflation of 5 percent, and expected inflation is anchored at 5 percent. Now we add temporal shocks that push the economy back and forth between points A and B (Figure 10.8). The average outcome is point C, which corresponds to the natural unemployment rate, u^*. On the other hand, if average inflation is low enough, such that the economy is bouncing back and forth around the kink, average unemployment will be greater than u^*.

For example, suppose average (equals expected) inflation is zero but fluctuates between plus and minus 1 percent. The economy moves between points D and E. Half-way along the line that connects these points gives us the average unemployment outcome at point F. The kink produces an average unemployment rate greater than the natural rate.

With temporal dispersion, the tail appears in an average outcome sense. With spatial (geographic) dispersion, the tail appears in an aggregate sense. The size of the tail depends on the slopes of the Phillips curves around the kink and the amount of dispersion.[12] The possibility of a tail in the LRPC is a strong argument for targeting an inflation rate far enough away from zero.

> Question for your professor: If workers resist wage cuts, could this cause the SR Phillips curve to have a kink at the zero inflation? If so, could volatility in inflation around its average level cause the LR Phillips curve to have a tail?

2.2 The possibility of not enough jobs

As should be clear by now, mainstream economics is not particularly concerned about jobs. Unemployment is either "natural" or a cyclical short-run problem that will resolve itself. Sure, growing GDP is an objective, but GDP can grow without significant job growth. This contrasts dramatically with everyday concerns about jobs. We worry as the inexorable march of technology eliminates wave after wave of jobs. Political parties make jobs the centerpiece of election platforms, and their success is judged on whether they have created enough jobs. Jurisdictions compete using grants, subsidies, and tax holidays to attract firms and jobs. And when a new facility is announced it makes headline news.

None of this makes any sense according to mainstream theory. There is no need to fret. *The forces of demand and supply establish full employment on their own.* Trust in the force, Luke! Indeed, trusting in the force is practically a religious belief among mainstream economists. Leijonhufvud calls demand and supply the econ tribe's most powerful totem. It is simple enough—just "two carved sticks joined together in the middle." In glorious satire he describes the tribe's most sacred ceremony where the elder holds the totem above his head, and leads the grads of the village on an epic tortuous trek over forbidding terrain. And just when all seems hopeless, at long last the totem begins to vibrate, then oscillate, until finally quivering, the elder pronounces, "Behold, the Truth and Power of the Macro."[13]

It is astonishing the hold it has over the profession's collective imagination. We already know (from the Cambridge Capital Controversies discussed in Chapter 5) that the aggregate demand for labor could have upward sloping regions. And even if it were monotonically declining, *we cannot rule out* that there simply aren't enough jobs. For example, the situation could be as shown in Figure 10.9, with a surplus of labor even at a zero wage. What would determine the wage and employment in this scenario? Good questions! Wages might be determined by institutional factors, or by the minimum subsistence level. Alternatively, we could redraw Figure 10.9 with the two lines intersecting at a positive wage, but the positive "equilibrium wage" could be below the subsistence wage—which is just another way of saying there aren't enough jobs that pay well enough

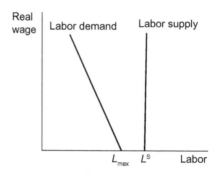

Figure 10.9 The possibility of not enough jobs

to live. If so, given the wealth the rich developed nations enjoy, isn't this an argument for a Job Guarantee (JG) program? (This is discussed more fully later in this chapter.)

2.3 The possibility of fragile equilibria

Once we abandon belief in the crude totem, more interesting possibilities become apparent. For example, Blanchard and Summers (1988) call for "theories of fragile equilibria" where both the demand and supply curves have backward bending sections and multiple intersection points. In these models, outcomes are very sensitive to shocks and may be history (or path) dependent.

To avoid overly complicating matters, we allow labor demand to be monotonically declining but incorporate two backward bending sections in labor supply. Besides simplicity, the advantage of this approach is that the backward bending labor supply curve is well accepted in mainstream neoclassical economics. The disadvantage is that it gives the impression of a negative relation between real wages and employment—coming from the monotonically declining labor demand curve. If we allowed for backward bending sections of labor demand, this would not be the case.

Consider Panel A of Figure 10.10, and in particular the section of the labor supply curve above W_s. As wages rise there are two offsetting effects on the quantity of labor supplied: a substitution effect and an income effect. As the reward to working (and the cost of not working) increases, so people substitute work for leisure. The substitution effect suggests people work more as wages increase. On the other hand, higher wages mean higher incomes, which increases people's demand for normal goods. Since leisure is a normal good, people "buy" more leisure by working less. Initially, this substitution effect dominates, leading to an upward sloping supply curve between W_s and W_L. However, when wages get high enough the income effect dominates (because people can afford to buy more leisure), leading

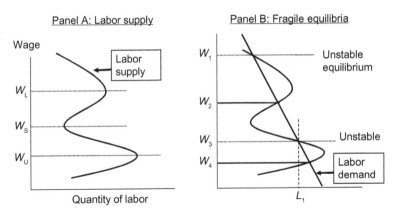

Figure 10.10 Fragile equilibria in the labor market

to a backward bending section above W_L. A labor supply curve with one backward bending section is actually fairly standard, and is often found in mainstream textbooks.

Prasch (2008) supplements this standard story by considering what happens when wages fall toward (and even go below) subsistence levels. When wages go below the level necessary to maintain minimum living standards with normal working hours, households increase their labor supply to abnormal levels. They might hold two jobs or work fourteen-hour shifts. So, below the subsistence wage, W_s, labor supply increases as wages fall, accounting for the bend in the labor supply curve at W_s.

As wages continue to fall, they will eventually reach the point where the total hours of work required are simply unsustainable. Below the unsustainable wage, W_U, hours worked fall precipitously. As Prasch explains, "the primary workers and his or her family will be forced by exhaustion, disease, despair, and disrepair to abandon their effort to maintain a standard of living consistent with effective membership in the labour force and consequently civil society. They become homeless, petty thieves, or beggars, with strong prospects for a relatively short and miserable life" (2008: 88). This explains the third bend occurring at W_U.

When we confront this labor supply function with a standard downward sloping labor demand function, we get four possible equilibrium points, as shown in Panel B of Figure 10.8. Of these, both W_1 and W_3 are unstable. (At a wage slightly below either of these levels, supply exceeds demand, causing wages to continue to fall; similarly, at a wage slightly above either of these wage levels, demand exceeds supply, causing wages to continue to increase.) This leaves two stable equilibria—one of which offers wages quite a bit higher than the subsistence level, W_2; while the other is a poverty trap where wages are substantially below subsistence, W_4.

Prasch uses this construction to show the potential usefulness of minimum wage laws and maximum hour provisions. Either a minimum wage set above W_3 or maximum hours restriction set below L_1 would preclude the poverty trap equilibrium. Interestingly, in this model the legislation pushes the economy to a desirable equilibrium at W_2, but once at this equilibrium neither restriction appears "binding." That is to say, the equilibrium wage would be above the legal minimum wage and the offered hours would be less than the legal maximum, so the legal restrictions would appear to be redundant. He notes that this is "a nice illustration of how market forces can interact with legislation to bring about results that are not immediately evident or expected" (p. 93).

This forms a nice segue into the determinants of the natural rate.

Question for your professor: Do you think the fiction of an aggregate labor market is best described as perfectly competitive? Do we have confidence that both the demand and supply of labor are monotonic functions of the real wage?

2.4 The NRU assumes an irrelevant and inappropriate market structure

According to the textbooks, the NRU is composed of frictional and structural components, where both may possibly be influenced by hysteresis. However, this textbook discussion is based around the assumption that the labor market is perfectly competitive. To quote Galbraith (1997: 95), it is based on a "failed metaphor, unsuitable for use as a foundation for theory."[14] What remains of this theoretical treatment if we dare to jettison this piece of totem worship? We begin by considering the textbook treatment of structural unemployment.

The structural component What keeps real wages from falling to their equilibrium level? Mainstream economics emphasizes efficiency wages and "institutional factors." Unfortunately, while there is some evidence that some firms pay efficiency wages in some industries, there is literally no empirical evidence that efficiency wages increase *aggregate* unemployment.[15]

That leaves institutional factors, which are a "grab bag" of mainstream bogey men: minimum wages, unions, and job protection legislation. Let us take them in turn.

The evidence on whether minimum wages adversely affect employment is dealt with extensively in the *Microeconomics Anti-Textbook* (2021). To be brief, while most mainstream microeconomics textbooks continue to claim that minimum wages decrease employment, and some continue to quote a long outdated estimate dating back to 1982 (!), the evidence is so mixed that there is no longer a consensus in the profession on the issue of minimum wages. It remains a highly contentious issue.[16] Why should it be so?

Testing whether the minimum wage adversely affects employment is equivalent to testing the applicability of the competitive model to the real world—the usefulness of the totem itself. This is the key point. If the market is not perfectly competitive, increases in the minimum wage may actually increase employment. In noncompetitive markets, the minimum wage works to limit the market power of employers.

In the context of labor markets, firms are not simply wage-takers: they have some short-run (or dynamic) market power to set wages lower than other firms without losing all their workers. This power may derive from the time and resources necessary for a worker to find a new job, or because taking another job might entail moving home or increased costs of commuting. Either way, moderate minimum wage increases may offset the market power of employers without causing job losses—indeed, they may even cause job gains. The same is true of unions.[17]

The bottom line is that the structural component of the natural rate is predicated upon a market structure that is not relevant or appropriate. In the real world, firms have power to set their own prices and power to set their own wages. They have both monopoly and monopsony power. In this world, workers aren't fully compensated for unpleasant or dangerous work, workers have to work more hours than they want, and employers can set the wage structure to discriminate among workers. In this real world, unions play a socially useful role. They provide "countervailing power." By offsetting the market power of firms, unions and job protection legislation may improve economic efficiency. The *presumption* that unions cause "structural" unemployment is bogus.

That is not to say that in *some* circumstances unions might dominate the bargaining process and succeed in forcing wages up so much that employment falls. Lye and McDonald (2006) argue that this occurred during the 1970s in Australia, when over 50 percent of the workforce was unionized. At that time, wage bargaining was highly centralized and unions competed over relative wages, with each new bargain leapfrogging the last.

But in general, when unions operate in specific labor markets they will have no overall quantity effects in the labor market.[18] Instead, as unions make wage gains, employment decreases in the unionized sector and increases in the nonunionized sector. Certainly, unionized workers will earn a wage premium over nonunionized workers. But the only way this wage premium can generate unemployment is through so-called "wait" unemployment. Supposedly, workers remain unemployed while "waiting" for a job in the union sector. This is as ridiculous as assuming that the only way workers can search for a job is by being unemployed—an assumption that is universally made in job search theory, and one that is patently false.

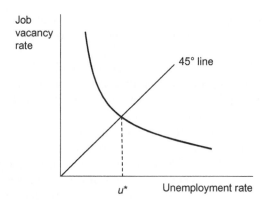

Figure 10.11 The Beveridge curve

The frictional component Frictional unemployment is caused by the time it takes to match worker with job vacancy. The relationship between the vacancy rate and the unemployment rate is known as the Beveridge curve, depicted in Figure 10.11. There we see that the vacancy rate moves with the business cycle: when the unemployment rate is low, the job vacancy rate is high, and when the unemployment rate is high, the job vacancy rate is low. If the matching process improves, the entire Beveridge curve will shift toward the origin. If the degree of mismatch gets worse, the curve will shift out. The frictional unemployment component of the natural rate occurs where the curve cuts a 45-degree line. Or, since we believe the structural arguments are bunkum, it yields an estimate of the full employment level of unemployment, which we denote as u^f. Using data on vacancy rates suggests u^f is between 2 and 3 percentage points, at least for the United States and Canada.[19]

McDonald (2007) provides an interesting alternative approach to estimating the full employment level of unemployment. He argues that the disappearance of long-term unemployment could be regarded as a necessary but not sufficient condition for full employment. To be classified as unemployed, a person has to be searching for a job. Searching for a job for more than a year after one's previous job does not sound like full employment. Therefore, he statistically relates (using "regression analysis") the long-term unemployment rate and the aggregate unemployment rate. It turns out that the two rates are very closely related, and he is able to predict that the long-term unemployment rate would be zero if the aggregate unemployment rate were around 3 percent.[20]

Hysteresis All mainstream macro textbooks mention some reasons why the economy is characterized by path dependency. But the reasons discussed are always restricted to the labor market. Those workers just keep on losing their skills after a period of unemployment. Or, in the insider/outsider story it's those terrible unions again. Furthermore, hysteresis is always just a *possibility* that *may* occur. Once the possibility of hysteresis is noted, it is promptly forgotten. The strategy, common in the mainstream textbooks, is to "note but ignore."

But we should not ignore hysteresis. It is a phenomenon that is completely corrosive of the mainstream model. As Mankiw and Scarth (2020: 468) acknowledge in their intermediate macro textbook, "it not only affects the costs of disinflation it affects our entire discussion of economic fluctuations in the past four chapters." The mainstream analysis of economic fluctuations is based on the natural rate hypothesis, which permits the study of short-run fluctuations independent of long-run growth. If there is hysteresis, all of this collapses. Along with it goes the doctrine of the long-run neutrality of money. A monetary disturbance that has real effects in the short run can *not* be presumed to have no real effects in the long run.

It is time to turn to the empirical evidence.

Question for your professor: How important is hysteresis? Given how likely it seems, how much of our previous analysis about stabilization policy would we have to modify?

2.5 Evidence on the NRU: problems predicting inflation and deflation

Let's begin with the question of estimating the NRU. To do so, we need to estimate a Phillips curve. This entails deciding on a specific functional form, and which shift variables to incorporate. The shift variables will necessarily include expected inflation, and may include union density, unemployment insurance benefits, and measures of supply-side shocks. Once the shift variables are decided upon, we need to determine how to measure them. Using Canadian data, Setterfield, Gordon, and Osberg (1992) explored these issues and showed that seemingly innocuous decisions led to very big differences in the estimates of the NRU. The difference between the lowest estimated NRU and the highest was as big as $5\frac{1}{2}$ percentage points. Moreover, the resulting estimating equations were all statistically satisfactory and economically reasonable. There was no good basis for deciding between very different estimates. They suggest that the effort to estimate the NRU as like searching for a will-o'-the-wisp.

Staiger, Stock, and Watson (1997) came to similar conclusions using US data. While arguing that an NRU was present in the data, they concede that it could not be pinned down with any precision. Moreover, knowledge of the NRU did not much matter from the perspective of forecasting

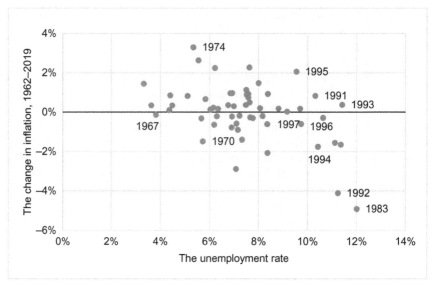

Figure 10.12 The change in inflation, Canada, 1962–2019

inflation (which is essentially the same point). Further, there were much better indicators than the unemployment rate (or the gap between the unemployment rate and the NRU) for forecasting inflation.

To sum up, if the NRU exists, we do not know its value with any certainty. It could be practically anything. *We can actually see this in the data ourselves.* The basic point of the accelerationist hypothesis—which requires a long-run vertical Phillips curve—is that when the unemployment rate is less than the NRU, inflation should increase; when unemployment is greater than the NRU, inflation should decrease; and when unemployment equals the natural rate, the change in inflation should be zero. Figure 10.12 plots the *change* in the inflation rate on the vertical axis, against the unemployment rate on the horizontal, for Canada.

There does appear to be an overall negative slope to the scatter of points in Figure 10.12. As expected, really big recessions bring down the rate of inflation, as occurred in 1983 and 1992. But if zero change in inflation occurs at the NRU, then the NRU apparently fluctuated from less than 4 percent in 1967 to over 10 percent in 1996. Furthermore, we can find pairs of years with nearly identical unemployment rates that have very different changes in their inflation rates. Compare 1992 and 1993, for example. In both cases the unemployment rate was just over 11 percent. But in 1992 inflation fell by over 4 percentage points, while in 1993 inflation increased slightly. Since these were adjacent years, one could hardly claim that the NRU had changed significantly.

Fortin (2003b) generalizes this point by calculating the deflation that should have occurred during the 1990s using consensus estimates of the

NRU and the slope of the SRPC. He determines that inflation should have declined by 9.7 percentage points from 1992 to 2000.[21] But in fact the annual level of inflation in the year 2000 (1.5 percent) was unchanged from its 1992 value. Given this *missing deflation puzzle* he argues in favor of a nonvertical LRPC, similar to that shown in Figure 10.7.[22]

2.6 Evidence on the NRU: wild gyrations of the NRU

An alternative line of enquiry is suggested by Farmer (2013). He points out a simple way of jointly testing the natural rate and rational expectations hypothesis.

According to the rational expectations hypothesis there should be no systematic error between actual and expected inflation. This implies they must differ only by a random disturbance term. Over a decade, the probability that average expected inflation will differ from average actual inflation should be extremely small.

Further, according to the natural rate hypothesis (NRH), unemployment will differ from its natural rate only when expected inflation differs from actual inflation. Therefore, a ten-year average of actual unemployment rates will yield the natural rate. If NRU were constant, a plot of decade averages of inflation against unemployment should reveal a vertical line at the NRU. While Farmer presents ten-year averages for the United States, Figure 10.13 shows the results for Canada (from 1962 to 2019). The two diagrams are qualitatively very similar. In neither one is there a tendency for the points to lie on or around a vertical line.

Farmer argues that those who believe the NRU is time varying need to provide us, in advance, with a theory of how the NRU varies over time. Without such a theory, the NRH has no predictive content. As he puts it (2013: 6), "A theory like this, which cannot be falsified by any set of observations, is closer to religion than science."

Robert Gordon—a supporter of the NRH—mused about what it would take to reject the NRH (and therefore a vertical LRPC). He answers (1997: 28), "wild gyrations of the estimated NRU over a range too wide to be explained by microeconomic changes in market structure and institutions." The data in Figure 10.13 fit that description. Sure, there were changes in market structure; there always are. But the changes in these variables cannot explain the gyrations we see in Figure 10.13.[23]

Question for your professor: If workers resist wage cuts, could this cause the SR Phillips curve to have a kink at zero inflation? If so, could volatility in inflation around its average level cause the LR Phillips curve to have a tail?

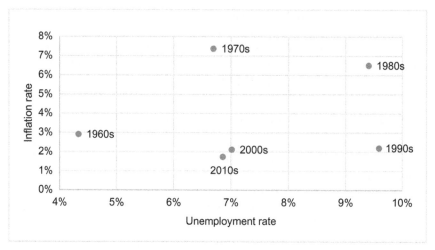

Figure 10.13 Average inflation and UR by decade

2.7 Alternatives to the neoclassical consensus #1: a post-Keynesian view

It is important to realize the NRU hypothesis follows directly from the neoclassical conclusion that unemployment is caused by wage stickiness. Since wages will adjust given enough time, unemployment will eventually return to its full employment level. This result is the very embodiment of the neoclassical synthesis: "Keynesian" in the short run and classical in the long run.

In the anti-text of Chapter 6 we presented a critique of this view. We argued that when debt effects dominate, the aggregate demand curve will be upward sloping. This yields a result very much in keeping with Keynes's own views: falling wages will make the situation worse, not better. (This is shown in Figure 6.11.) However, it is high time that we broke free of the neoclassical straitjacket, and presented an alternative model that provides a more realistic view of how capitalist economies work. Here we present a post-Keynesian model based on the work of Michal Kalecki.

As explained in Joan Robinson's (1976) article entitled "Michal Kalecki: A Neglected Prophet," both Keynes and Kalecki were searching to explain the breakdown of the market economy in the Great Depression, and both independently discovered the theory of employment. They had the same diagnosis and the same remedy: increased government spending financed by borrowing.

But there were important differences between their theories. In particular, Keynes accepted that labor markets could be treated as reasonably competitive. This is perhaps the single most important reason why the "Keynesian revolution" misfired. It made his system, where real wages are above their equilibrium level whenever there is unemployment,

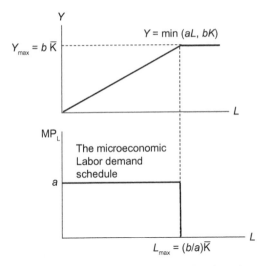

Figure 10.14 The Leontief fixed-proportions production function

hard to differentiate from a system where there is unemployment *because* real wages are above their equilibrium level.

In contrast, Kalecki assumed markets are oligopolistic (dominated by a few firms), and firms set their prices by adding a gross profit margin to prime labor costs. He linked output to employment in the short run via a Leontief fixed-coefficients production function, illustrated in Figure 10.14. The marginal product of labor (MP_L) is constant until all the capital stock is fully utilized. Beyond this point, the marginal product of labor falls to zero. Interestingly, this type of production function has the property that the capital stock might be too small to provide employment for the whole workforce, a possibility discussed earlier in this chapter, in Section 2.2.

Kalecki was critical of Keynes's treatment of investment (his "Marginal Efficiency of Investment" schedule) and instead emphasized that investment expenditures are determined by decisions taken in previous periods.[24] Because of this time lag, investment is treated as exogenous in the current period.

To express Kalecki's key ideas, consider a simple model of a "pure" capitalist economy that excludes foreign trade and government activity. Real output, Y, is then the sum of consumption expenditure, C, and investment expenditures, I.

$$Y = C + I$$

Looking at real GDP from the income side, income can be classified as employment income, wL, and property income, J.

$$Y = wL + J$$

where "w" is the average real wage rate, L is total employment, and J is the flow of profit (including interest and rent). In Kalecki's model, the distribution of income between wages and profits is important because wage recipients spend all their income and only profit recipients save. (If we recall the distribution of wealth discussed in Chapter 4, this assumption approximates reality.) The consumption function of profit recipients (or "capitalists") has an intercept, A, and a component that varies with their profits, αJ. This implies that savings, S, are simply:

$$S = -A + (1 - \alpha)J$$

In equilibrium, we have the usual savings equals investment condition. This allows us to write:

$$-A + (1 - \alpha)J = I$$

Since both "A" and "I" are exogenous in the short run, the above equation solves for profits, J.

$$J = \frac{I + A}{(1 - \alpha)}$$

This tells us that gross profits come from the spending of capitalists on investment, I, and their spending on consumption out of profits, A. The more each capitalist spends, the greater the profits they all receive. This conception highlights a vicious circle: if investment is low, profits are low, leading to a weak inducement to invest.

We can complete the model by writing down the aggregate consumption function. This is the sum of workers' consumption, C_w, and capitalists' consumption, C_c. Since workers spend all that they earn, the aggregate consumption function is:

$$C = C_w + C_c = wL + [A + \alpha J]$$

Substituting this into the expenditure definition of real GDP we get:

$$Y = wL + A + \alpha J + I$$

Eliminating Y using the production function, $Y = aL$, and rearranging slightly, we get:

$$aL = wL + (I + A) + \alpha J$$

Finally, eliminating J using its solution equation, we have:

$$(a - w)L = (I + A) + \frac{\alpha(I + A)}{(1 - \alpha)}$$

The solution for employment, L, follows easily once we group the $(I+A)$ terms and put them over a common denominator. This yields:

$$L = \frac{(I+A)}{(1-\alpha)(a-w)}$$

Since α is the marginal propensity to consume of capitalists, we know it is a fraction. Further, "a" is the average (and marginal) product of labor before we reach L_{max}. This has to be greater than the real wage, "w," otherwise firms would not even be covering their labor costs. So, we know that both $(1-\alpha)$ and $(a-w)$ are positive.

The key issue is the relationship between employment, L, and real wages, w. As w increases, $(a-w)$ decreases, and L increases. Thus, the *macroeconomic* labor demand curve is upward sloping in real wage/employment space.[25] The reason for this is simple enough. Workers spend all their income, so an increase in real wages will increase consumption and hence the demand for labor.

If we assume a vertical labor supply function, we can draw the macroeconomic labor market relation as shown in Figure 10.15.[26] Any increase in investment, I, or autonomous consumption, A, will shift the macroeconomic labor demand curve to the right. But at a given real wage associated with an excess supply of labor, such as w_o, there is no self-correcting mechanism to bring the economy back to full employment. *If wages were flexible downward, and falling wages succeeded in reducing real wages, the effect would be to make matters worse.* Only an increase in discretionary spending, and/or an *increase* in real wages, can bring the economy back to full employment.

Now we have developed the model in real terms, we next focus on the relationship between inflation and unemployment.

Post-Keynesians see inflation as the result of a struggle over income shares. We can illustrate this process by adding a price setting equation, and a wage equation linked to real wage claims of workers. For example, assuming firms set prices by adding a markup to their prime costs, and defining the markup as "u," and the nominal wage as "W," we may write:

$$P_t = \frac{(1+u)}{a} W_t$$

where W/a equals $(WL)/Y$ (from the production function) and is prime labor costs per unit. If both the markup, "u," and the average product, "a," are exogenous, the price markup equation yields a solution for real wages as $a/(1+u)$. Pitchford (1978) calls this "the real wage offer" of firms.

Now suppose there is the usual asymmetric information requirements, whereby firms know their own product price, but no-one knows the aggregate general price level. When we aggregate over price setting equations we obtain the price markup equation as written above. But in forming their real wage claims, workers must form expectations of the general price level. Denoting the real wage claim of workers as "B" we may write:

$$W_t = B P^e_t$$

Finally, supposing a simple regressive price expectation formation, whereby $P^e_t = P_{t-1}$, we can write:

$$W_t = B P_{t-1}$$

Substituting the wage equation into the price markup equation we get:

$$P_t = \frac{(1+u)B}{a} P_{t-1}$$

Dividing both sides by P_{t-1} and then subtracting one from both sides yields,

$$\frac{P_t}{P_{t-1}} - 1 = \frac{(1+u)B}{a} - 1$$

Putting the price terms over a common denominator, we realize that the term on the left is the inflation rate, allowing us to write:

$$\pi_t = \frac{(1+u)B}{a} - 1$$

Inflation is the ratio of the real wage claim by workers, "B," divided by the real wage offer of firms, $a/(1+u)$. If income claims are excessive this ratio exceeds unity. The more excessive are income claims, the higher is the inflation rate generated.

It will be noted that in the current formulation, real wages are determined by the real wage offer of firms. This could be modified by having firms base their prices on last period's unit labor costs, perhaps because of the necessity to post prices in advance of sales (through advertising). In general, it is possible to construct models where neither the "real wage offer" of firms, nor the "real wage claim" of workers, is always achieved. The result may depend upon which group has more accurate expectations, or the precise time lags involved, or it may depend on the state of the labor market that influences the bargaining process.[27]

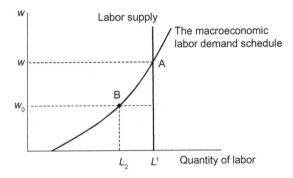

Figure 10.15 Macroeconomic labor market relation

In summary, this post-Keynesian model denies many key mainstream notions. It shows that capital accumulation does not depend upon household savings, but rather the investment process itself generates the necessary savings. It shows that factors of production do not receive a "reward equal to their contribution" (meaning incomes are determined by marginal products): capitalists' income depends on their spending, and labor's marginal product is greater than its real wage. There is no automatic tendency to restore equilibrium. There is no NRU in a post-Keynesian model; the economy could get stuck at any unemployment rate. Flexibility of wages does not help. Indeed, falling wages would make the situation worse if they succeeded in reducing real wages. And finally, inflation results from the struggle of people to maintain their income shares. Any unemployment rate can coincide with any inflation rate, even in equilibrium.

Can the post-Keynesian model explain the observed data? Can it explain both the data that A. W. Phillips himself observed, and the breakdown of that relationship in the 1970s and beyond?

First, note that in a purely mechanical sense the post-Keynesian model contains the following prediction: all other things being equal, if the complex interactions between wage and price inflation lead to an increase in real wages, unemployment will decrease as inflation rises, giving the appearance of a conventional Phillips curve. Conversely, if those interactions lead to a decrease in real wages, unemployment will increase, giving the appearance of an upward shift of the Phillips curve as the economy moves northeast in inflation–unemployment space. However, this mechanical explanation misses the heart of the post-Keynesian view of inflation: the struggle over income shares.

So, a better rendering of the post-Keynesian explanation for the data would emphasize the social contract emerging after the Second World War, based on full employment. Excess demands would have emerged in certain markets, leading to gentle inflation. Rapid growth led to increasing real wages. These were ideal conditions to observe a Phillips "trade-off": rising inflation coinciding with a falling unemployment rate.

All this changed with the oil price shocks of the 1970s. These massive price increases represented a transfer of real income from the oil importing countries (the developed Western economies) to the oil exporting countries. This ignited a struggle over income shares, resulting in inflation and a wage-price spiral. This struggle was decisively won by the property owning class with the elections of Margaret Thatcher in the UK, Ronald Reagan in the United States, and the dawning of the neoliberal era. This was the end of full employment. Essentially, large-scale unemployment was used to intimidate the working class.

Question for your professor: Could inflation be caused by a struggle over income shares?

2.8 Alternatives to the neoclassical consensus #2: Roger Farmer's view

The idea that any unemployment rate can coincide with any inflation rate—even in equilibrium—comes not only from the Kaleckian post-Keynesian models but also from the ultra-modern real business cycle models developed by Roger Farmer. This short section presents a brief overview of his work.[28]

Farmer is an "old-style Keynesian" insofar as he believes that unemployment is not due to wage stickiness but from insufficient spending. Like Keynes, he emphasizes the importance of investor confidence. (Keynes referred to "long-term expectations" of investors as being like their "animal spirits.") However, he is a "New Keynesian" insofar as he accepts both the necessity for expectations to be formed rationally and the necessity for macro models to have sound microeconomic underpinnings. In addition, he believes that the traditional Keynesian consumption function, which bases consumption on income, is wrong. Instead, he accepts the modern theories of consumption based upon wealth.

Farmer identifies the key problem in mainstream real business cycle models as their treatment of labor markets. Yes, they are constantly churning, but no, they are not auction markets. In the face of both worker and job heterogeneity, and lack of information, firms face a problem in filling their vacancies.

Ideally, in a fully specified model, this problem would be solved by "job-matching firms" selling "producing firms" a "worker-job match." The "job-matching firms" would buy from a worker the right to find that person a job, and would buy from the firm the right to fill a particular vacancy. Those would be its input costs. Then they would sell to the "producing firms" their output—a worker-job match. However, this solution faces a moral hazard problem: workers may refuse the match and continue to sell the right to be matched. This creates an incomplete factor market problem. This is the fundamental reason why factor markets do not clear and leads to an indeterminacy.

Farmer regards the Beveridge curve, shown in Figure 10.9, as defining the technology required to produce a new job. The curve shows the combinations of vacancies and unemployed workers capable of producing a certain number of job matches. But there is no equation to get us to the optimal point on the curve. There is a missing equation.

Farmer closes his model by adding another equation—a "belief function," fundamentally similar to Keynes's "state of long-term expectations." Employment is determined by the demand for workers, which is determined by capitalists' beliefs about the demand for their goods. And crucially, whatever they believe turns out to be self-fulfilling. While this diagnosis is very reminiscent of Keynes's own, Farmer's solution is rather different.

Since Farmer does not accept the traditional Keynesian consumption function, he believes the fiscal multiplier is small. Furthermore, Farmer has traditional mainstream concerns about public debt overhang that can come from debt-financed government spending. As a result, he suggests using monetary policy to boost asset prices, affecting consumption through increased household wealth. This suggestion is similar to the quantitative easing (QE) policies implemented after the Great Financial Crash. But he wants to expand the program, and have the central bank use it as an ongoing tool to stabilize the economy.

Farmer suggests that monetary policy should attempt to stabilize confidence directly, by putting a floor and a ceiling on the value of the stock market. This could be done by first defining an index containing a weighted average of all publicly traded companies (where the weights would be periodically updated). Private investment companies would be encouraged to create mutual funds based on the overall index—in other words, "index funds." They would sell shares of the index fund to the public, and use the funds to buy shares in the private companies according to the weights in the index. Control over the overall value of the stock market could be achieved by the central bank buying and selling blocks of shares in the index funds.

Question for your professor: What do you think of Roger Farmer's suggestion of having the central bank stabilize the stock market by trading an index fund reflecting the entire market?

2.9 Alternatives to the neoclassical consensus #3: Richard Lipsey's new view

While Lipsey provided micro-underpinnings for the mainstream expectations-augmented Phillips curve in 1960, in his recent work he regards this "unique equilibrium fixation" as a key error introduced into macroeconomics. In recent years, Lipsey has frequently published articles in the *Journal of Evolutionary Economics* (yes, there is one!)[29] and made substantive contributions to understanding the importance of endogenous technical change and the pervasiveness of uncertainty. This work helps us to better understand the sources of hysteresis.

Uncertainty is where the full range of possible outcomes cannot be identified, and we cannot attach probabilities to the outcomes that can be identified. The key implication is that two identical individuals—with the same endowments, tastes, and information—faced with the same choice between two courses of action may make different choices.

Hysteresis and path dependency follow immediately, since even if economic agents could return to the same initial conditions, "there is no guarantee that they would retrace their steps exactly, since the outcome of successive actions subject to uncertainty may be different at each point in time" (Lipsey and Carlaw 2012: 740).

Furthermore, what is discovered and/or innovated today influences what can be discovered and/or innovated tomorrow. What is potentially profitable to search for today depends on current capabilities, which depends on what was searched for in the past. This introduces path dependency and inertia in technological choices.

For all of these reasons, Lipsey suggests we must reject the idea of a unique NRU, a unique long-run equilibrium position, or a unique equilibrium growth path.

In its place, evolutionary economists do not have single agreed-upon alternative model. Given the reality they emphasize, it is not possible to have one. But on one important aspect, the unemployment-inflation relationship, Lipsey does have a preferred framework, one that he calls the NAIBU, or nonaccelerating inflationary band of unemployment.

Lipsey embraces many of the elements of a post-Keynesian view: noncompetitive firms, prices marked up over unit prime costs, and horizontal short-run cost curves up to capacity output. Firms respond to short-term fluctuations in demand by varying output, holding their prices constant. In the labor market, wages do not continually equilibrate labor demands and supplies. Rather, wages are sticky—often both up and down. This implies that the economy can vary over a wide range of output and unemployment (the NAIBU) without triggering either wage or price inflation or deflation that would push it back toward some unique full employment equilibrium. In Figure 10.16, this range is between U_H and U_L.

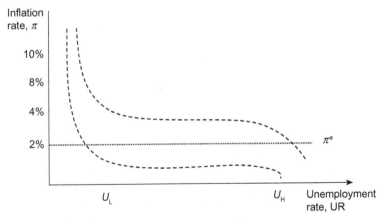

Figure 10.16 The band of nonaccelerating inflation (NAIBU)

The midpoint of the band is situated at the expected rate of inflation. If expected inflation increases, so the whole band shifts up. It is clear that between U_H and U_L, any unemployment rate can coincide with any inflation rate, even in equilibrium. Within this range, the inflation rate will vary around expected inflation, depending on things like changes in productivity, or changes in the price of oil and food. But inflation will not vary systematically with variations in unemployment.

The U_H boundary is set by the existence of both jobs and expenditures that are recession-proof. The latter includes consumption expenditures financed from past savings, newly acquired debt, or the social safety net.

The U_L boundary is set by the maximum output of firms. As the economy moves toward this boundary, excess demands begin to set in at different times and by different amounts in different labor markets.

Beyond the upper and lower boundaries, Lipsey invokes conventional forces to return the economy to the NAIBU, just like a conventional Phillips curve. For example, in major recessions falling wages and prices will depress interest rates and stimulate investment. And in major booms, rising prices will eventually increase interest rates and reduce aggregate demand unless the inflation is validated by the central bank.

2.10 Achieving genuinely full employment

The anti-text has suggested that the full employment level of unemployment might be as low as 3 percent. This would be equivalent to Lipsey's U_L in Figure 10.16. The acid test of whether this is true is to get the economy to that point and see whether excessive inflation is generated. Economics is, after all, an empirical science.

What should we do if inflation starts to accelerate at a higher level of unemployment? What if the mainstream is right that the full employment level of unemployment is closer to 6 percent? And on top of that, there is all that hidden unemployment! To address this problem, many economists have recommended a Job Guarantee (JG) program—an option never even mentioned in mainstream textbooks.[30]

A JG Program While a JG program goes under many different names (such as Employer of Last Resort (ELR) policy, or a Public Sector Employment Program (PEP)) the idea is that the government should stand ready to provide a job with a basic wage and benefits to anyone wanting to work.

Besides curing involuntary unemployment and much poverty, the JG program would help to stabilize the economy: government spending on the program would automatically increase in a recession. And of course, having a JG program would help alleviate fears of job loss (whether transitional or permanent) due to automation, globalization, or the shift to a green economy.

In addition, much needed public work could be accomplished. Various plans have been published outlining the types of jobs that could be included.[31] These include the repair of infrastructure, energy-efficient upgrades to buildings, ecological restoration, community development projects, school services (preschool, after-school, and teachers' aids), and elder care.

Before we get too fixated on whether the unemployed have the skills required for such jobs, and the administrative difficulties involved in running a JG, we should note that it's been done before, at least in the United States.

During the Great Depression, as part of his New Deal, President Roosevelt created two job programs—the Works Progress Administration and the Civilian Conservation Corps (aimed at young unemployed men)— which between 1935 and 1943 employed between them around 9.5 million Americans. These programs provided almost every type of work imaginable, from infrastructure construction to pest extermination. More than 600,000 miles of new roads were constructed, along with 100,000 bridges and viaducts, and 35,000 buildings. Other work included the prevention of forest fires, floods, and soil erosion and the construction or repair of paths and fire lanes in the national parks and national forests.[32]

Proponents of a JG program argue that it is an inherently "green idea" because it addresses the neglect and destruction of both natural and human capital.

What about the cost of such a program? Here we need to distinguish between the financial cost and the real resource cost. As the Modern Monetary Theorists (MMTs) point out, if the only alternative to working in a JG program is remaining unemployed, then the real resource cost is nil—there are only benefits from the restoration of human and natural capital. Yes, some resources will be pulled out of other uses. Some prices could be bid up. The huge increase in spending could be inflationary. To this, MMTs respond: the cure for inflation is increased taxes. Taxes might need to be increased, not to fund the program but to calm inflation. The limiting factor is not the government's deficit and debt but real resource availability.

With regard to pay, many studies propose starting out with pay at the minimum wage, but incorporate plans to increase the minimum wage to a "living wage." Setting the pay at the national minimum wage would set a floor for private sector wages, eliminating the need for minimum-wage legislation and its attendant compliance costs.

```
Question for your professor: Would a JG Program be
a good way to eliminate involuntary unemployment,
build and repair public infrastructure, and even
retrain people for different jobs?
```

2.11 Conclusion

The NRU hypothesis is just the dynamic version of the neoclassical conclusion that unemployment in Keynes's model depends upon the assumption of wage rigidity. If you reject the latter, you must reject the former.

The anti-text highlighted the empirical problems with the NRU hypothesis—it does a poor job explaining changes in inflation and a poor job explaining changes in the NRU itself. Estimated NRUs exhibit wild gyrations over a range too wide to be explained by microeconomic changes in market structure and institutions.

Furthermore, the theoretical basis for the NRU depends upon the assumption of perfectly competitive markets—a market structure that is both irrelevant and inappropriate. In noncompetitive market structures there is no presumption that minimum wages or unions decrease employment. Rather, they may offset the market power of firms and may even increase employment.

The anti-text presented three alternative views to the mainstream model, none of which contained a natural rate. Indeed, in all three, any unemployment rate could coincide with any inflation rate, even in equilibrium. Beyond this point, however, the models were very different. The Kaleckian post-Keynesian model was mostly presented in real terms, reflecting a very diminished role for money. This could be because the money supply is assumed endogenous, or because expenditures are assumed to be interest inelastic. The reason is not spelled because it is not necessary. Inflation is not seen as being caused by excess demand, or "too much money chasing too few goods," but by a struggle over income shares—or in this specific formulation, a struggle over real wages.

The second alternative view—Farmer's view—was radically different in construction, though it contained the essential post-Keynesian truth: unemployment is involuntary and caused by insufficient demand for goods, a situation not helped by falling wages. This model has explicit microfoundations and assumes rational expectations. Indeed, it was a modified real business cycle model.

The third alternative view—that of Lipsey—goes a long way back toward the conventional mainstream model, insofar as the usual monetary transmission mechanism is operating in the background. Instead of a unique NRU, Lipsey proposes a NAIBU—a band of possible unemployment rates consistent with stable inflation. However, more radically, Lipsey's views of technological change under uncertainty cause him to reject any model that contains unique equilibrium growth paths. History matters.

Why is any of this important? It is important because we need to clear away notions that the economy will return to full employment on its own, or that the unemployment we have observed in Western economies since the 1970s has been anything close to full employment. Full employment needs to be restored as a key goal of macroeconomic policy. It is a key element in the fight against increasing inequality. And fear of job loss in the fossil fuel industries is slowing down the much needed transition to a green economy.

Finally, a JG program has been proposed as a way of removing any involuntary unemployment remaining once the economy reaches the nonaccelerating inflation level of unemployment. This would provide an automatic stabilizer for the economy, and help restore both natural and human capital.

Part 4

CONCLUSION

Chapter 11

SUMMING UP

The aim of this short chapter is to gather together the key points raised about what is unsatisfactory with the standard macroeconomic textbook—and why it matters.

1 THE OVEREMPHASIS ON PERFECTLY COMPETITIVE MARKETS

In *The Microeconomics Anti-Textbook*, we argue that the ubiquitous use of demand and supply in mainstream microeconomic textbooks creates (or perhaps reflects) an ideological bias in favor of laissez-faire and against government intervention. The key to understanding this bias is knowing that supply curves only exist in perfectly competitive markets. Therefore, the demand and supply framework is shorthand for (and synonymous with) perfect competition. In this market structure, no market participant has any market power, and everyone has perfect (or near perfect) information. Unless there are specific externalities, such markets will be socially efficient. The textbooks use this as their starting point to analyze the effects of price ceilings (such as rent controls) or price floors (such as minimum wages). The obvious conclusions follow—both price ceilings and floors lead to inefficiencies. The rabbit that was put in the hat is now pulled out to great applause. No mention is made of the fact that noncompetitive market structures lead to different conclusions.

The overemphasis on perfectly competitive markets continues in macroeconomic textbooks. Whenever a market is depicted, it is always using demand and supply. This is particularly important in two markets: the financial (or loanable funds) market and the aggregate labor market.

The fact that the financial market is depicted as efficient, with all participants having perfect information, contributes to the view that the financial system is the source of great wealth creation, rather than a source of instability and a center of white-collar crime.

Criminal behavior runs rife in the financial sector because information is imperfect and asymmetrically distributed. This gives rise to a cluster of well-known problems associated with the distortion of incentives—the principal-agent problem, moral hazard, and adverse selection. As explained in Chapter 5, all of these played a role in the 2008 financial crisis. And as explained in Chapter 8, the subprime bubble and the financial crash could not have happened without systemic criminal behavior throughout the financial sector, behavior that extended to the highest executive levels.

Financial markets are the beating heart of the capitalist system, bridging the time between receipts and payments, financing debts, and facilitating investment. A financial crisis is an economic heart attack. Minsky's "financial instability hypothesis" (examined in Chapter 5) provides a theory that predicts both small cycles and full-scale crises as the financial sector breaks free of its regulatory constraints. What drives these cycles is excessive leverage. This multiplies gains and allows for huge bonuses when times are good. But it puts the entire system at risk when times are bad.

How does this relate to the pervasive use of demand and supply? It relates because the perfectly competitive goggles cannot see power. In a perfectly competitive market structure no economic actor has any power. This means that the textbooks are blind to power and the nexus between money and politics. And this gives them a completely naïve view of the possibilities of easy and successful financial reform.

As Admati convincingly argues, meaningful financial reform needs to address the fundamental problem of excessive leverage. What is required is about a tenfold increase in bank equity funding. This would take them from around 3 percent equity funding to around 30 percent, which would still be less than half the amount of equity funding of nonfinancial US corporations.

But given the huge political clout of the financial sector, there is almost zero likelihood of such reform occurring. In the UK, the banks lobbied the Independent Commission on Banking against any increase in equity funding. Eventually, the Commission recommended an increase of 1 percentage point in 2011. But even this miniscule increase was rejected by the government because of continued lobbying by banks.

When it comes to the labor market, the reflexive application of perfect competition allows mainstream textbooks to parade minimum wages and unions as villains responsible for increasing structural unemployment, thereby hurting those they are meant to help. It is a great storyline. But there is no presumption of truth in a realistic noncompetitive world. The costs of searching for a new job (and possibly having to retrain or move house) give employers *dynamic monopsony power.* In this context, minimum wages and unions can offset the market power of employers and increase both wages and employment.

Finally, there is a nuanced connection between the perfectly competitive conception of the aggregate labor market and the conclusion that the economy has a unique equilibrium at full employment. If we draw the demand and supply curves as is habitually done, we will have a monotonically declining labor demand curve intersecting a monotonically increasing labor supply curve in real wage-employment space, giving rise to a unique full employment equilibrium. But this conception is vastly oversimplified. On the one hand, the Cambridge Capital Controversies (discussed in Chapter 3) have shown that the demand for capital (and by implication the demand for labor) can have backward bending regions. On the other hand, as discussed in Chapter 10, the supply curve of labor can also have backward bending regions. Either one of those is sufficient to give us multiple possible equilibria.

2 HYSTERESIS AND MULTIPLE EQUILIBRIA

Backward bending labor supply and/or labor demand curves are not the only possible source of nonuniqueness. For example, Lipsey and Carlaw (2012) have emphasized endogenous technical change as another source. Farmer emphasizes the fact that the labor market is incomplete. Yes, labor markets are constantly churning, but no, they are not auction markets. In the face of both worker and job heterogeneity, and lack of information, firms face a problem filling their vacancies. This leads to an indeterminacy: there are many combinations of unemployment and vacancies, which are possible equilibria. Another source of multiple equilibria is the possibility of a nonvertical long-run Phillips curve due to "Tobin effects," as discussed in Chapter 10. All of these are examples of hysteresis.

Hysteresis means that the nature of long-run equilibrium is dependent on the path the economy takes moving toward it. This implies that there are all kinds of possible long-run equilibria and brings the emphasis back onto the short run. As Lipsey and Carlaw emphasize, the short run is where investment decisions are made by people groping into the fog of an uncertain future. In this context, what is a sound decision—let alone an optimal decision—can only be known after the event. Even if decision-makers could return to the same initial conditions, there is no guarantee the same decisions would be made. Innovation is an endogenous process, influenced by what has gone before. In contrast with the textbook treatment, history matters.

This means that the notion of a natural rate of unemployment (NRU) to which the economy automatically returns must be rejected. As many analysts have argued, a unique NRU is an idea "past its sell-by date." It is neither consistent with good theory nor consistent with the data.

3 THE MISFIRING OF THE KEYNESIAN REVOLUTION

Even if there were a unique full employment position for the economy, there is no guarantee that we would get there. As explained in Chapter 5, the stability mechanisms emphasized by textbooks are surprisingly weak.

In the textbook neoclassical model, the fundamental cause of cyclical unemployment is nominal wage stickiness. If nominal wages were perfectly flexible, both the short-run and long-run aggregate supply (AS) lines would be vertical, and aggregate demand (AD) would be irrelevant to the determination of output. Nominal wage stickiness makes the short-run

AS line upward sloping and allows AD to matter—but only in the short run. Over time, nominal wages will fall, allowing the short-run AS line to move down and to the right, bringing the economy back to full employment.

Such an economy is stable. The NRU and even the accelerationist hypothesis are the dynamic corollaries of attributing cyclical unemployment to wage stickiness. Why? Over time even sticky variables adjust. Therefore, the economy will tend toward its unique full employment point. This wage stickiness explanation for unemployment is not qualitatively different from the pre-Keynesian classical economists.

The key element in this conception is the downward sloping AD line. It is derived from the aggregate expenditure model, a model that embodies Keynes's own views about the importance of spending and its multiplier effects. This model assumes fixed prices. The key question is: what happens to aggregate expenditure when prices fall? The neoclassical model argues that aggregate expenditure *increases* when prices *fall* for three reasons—a wealth effect, an interest rate effect, and a net export effect. But none of these effects are at all convincing.

The wealth effect requires an asset with a fixed nominal value, so that it increases in real value as prices fall, causing an increase in spending. The required asset is money. But textbooks do not explain that only *outside* money (cash in circulation) is appropriate. *Inside* money—or money in bank accounts—is precisely offset by nominally denominated debts that also increase in real value as prices fall, redistributing wealth from debtors to creditors. Since creditors have a higher marginal propensity to save than debtors, this effect will shift the aggregate expenditure function down. Since inside money dwarfs outside money, it is highly unlikely that the wealth effect will work in the required direction.

Things are no better for the interest rate effect. Given that most central banks now set interest rates, the argument that a decrease in prices will automatically reduce interest rates is simply obsolete.

Finally, the net export effect requires that trading partners will not retaliate against countries attempting to capture more of their markets through deflation.

In sum, the downward sloping AD curve is a straw upon which rests all the weight of the stability requirements of the textbook neoclassical model. It simply can't support the weight. There are many possible reasons for the misfiring of the Keynesian revolution. But the idea that aggregate expenditure is automatically increased by deflation is the most obvious way to explain the problems at an introductory level.

4 THE EMPHASIS ON LONG-RUN EQUILIBRIUM

Given that much modern theory suggests the economy is not characterized by a unique long-run equilibrium, and given that we cannot rely on the stability properties of the model to get us to a unique long-run equilibrium should it exist, it is frustrating that mainstream textbooks now emphasize the properties of a unique long-run equilibrium in the early chapters. These chapters cover the financial system and growth (and sometimes include a discussion of the determinants of the NRU and even the long-run equilibrium inflation rate).

Of course, in long-run equilibrium there is no Paradox of Savings. Anything that increases savings must increase investment. Therefore, to stimulate growth, we can confidently recommend policies that increase savings. It is a strange place, this long-run equilibrium world, since it is a world we do not inhabit. What use is knowing its properties?

The emphasis in the early chapters of macro textbooks on long-run issues is analogous to the emphasis in the early chapters of micro textbooks on perfect competition. Both give an aura of efficiency to the free market economy. Remember, in the long run, we must be at full employment. For Keynes, putting emphasis on the long-run properties of an economic system was foolish. He quipped, "in the long run we are all dead!"

5 THE NEGLECT OF UNCERTAINTY

Uncertainty is different to risk. Risk is defined as a situation where we can assign probabilities to the likelihood of future events. Uncertainty is where we cannot. There is a big difference. The efficient market hypothesis relies on the über-rational traders to not make any mistakes. By buying low and selling high, they are supposed to bring asset prices back to their fundamental value and efficiently allocate the economy's savings to the best possible investment projects. But as explained in Chapter 5, the argument is flawed. What something is worth depends upon what other people expect other people are willing to pay, and this is fundamentally uncertain. This uncertainty and the fact that markets can stay irrational longer than the rational can stay solvent are why asset markets are prone to boom and bust.

Uncertainty was central to Keynes's theory. He used the term "animal spirits" to describe how people arrive at financial decisions. Uncertainty is central to why Lipsey and Carlaw believe that history matters: investors are "groping through a fog" when making their decisions.

But mainstream neoclassical economics prefers things to be mathematically concrete. Partly this is because of the limitations of falsifiability. Since empirical tests are rarely definitive, how can we decide which models are good? As discussed in Chapter 1, this has led to weight being placed on consistency with optimizing underpinnings (through an infinite time horizon) as a second criterion for model selection. To make these mathematical problems tractable the exercise is carried out for a representative agent in a situation where there is a range of known outcomes with a probability distribution attached to them. As argued in Chapter 1, focusing on a representative agent means the loss of the Fallacy of Composition. We now see a second consequence: mathematical tractability has obscured the importance of uncertainty.

6 THE ADDICTION TO GROWTH

It is not just neoclassical economics that is addicted to growth. It is a pervasive cultural phenomenon. Sporting clubs, cities, regions, and countries all want to grow bigger without question. Never is it asked, "what would be our optimal size?" Bigger comes with more congestion, more pollution, a larger ecological footprint, and weaker community ties. In the context of macroeconomics, only a tiny fraction of economists dares to consider degrowth.

Macroeconomic textbooks contain no critical thinking about the merits of growth. The "happiness literature" (discussed in Chapter 4) has shown that beyond a threshold, more "stuff" does not make us any better off. What matters is relative position, not absolute consumption.

This would be important at any time. But at this time—as we face an existential ecological crisis—it demands our attention. We simply cannot continue to consume more stuff no matter how "green" that stuff may be.

7 BLINDNESS TO OUR CHALLENGES

The challenges that we face—an existential ecological crisis, massive inequality, and poverty—are barely mentioned in macroeconomic textbooks. The climate crisis is exacerbating the inequality crisis, with its worst effects—drought and famine—falling first on the poorest nations. We are facing the consequences of our growth addiction and the belief that the only way to solve poverty is through growth. It follows that we must not wean ourselves from fossil fuels since doing so would slow down growth. And we must not interfere with the market, because the market knows best.

The challenges we face today require government action. As Mazzucato and Skidelsky (2020) put it, "It is time to embrace the state's unique and profound capacity for steering economic life in the interest of the common good."

This embrace requires breaking free of the prevailing economic orthodoxy that has vastly exaggerated the perils of government deficits and debt. Massive government investment is needed in clean energy and smart grids, and the extraction of CO_2 from the atmosphere. We need to extract about a half-trillion tons of CO_2 between 2050 and 2100. It is the largest industrial project human beings have ever undertaken.

We need a state that actively fights inequality and poverty. It is not rocket science. Billionaires are paying less taxes than the average household. We need higher taxes on the rich, higher minimum wages, and labor market policies that give workers a fair chance of unionizing. It requires policies that reign in the ability of CEOs to pay themselves three hundred times the average salary in the corporation. We also need genuinely full employment, a concept currently rendered unthinkable by the doctrine of the natural rate.

Unfortunately, the standard macroeconomic textbooks not only largely ignore these issues, but the views they advocate stand in the way of addressing them.

8 A FINAL COMMENT

The goal of this Anti-Textbook has been to provide macroeconomics students with the basic ideas with which they can begin to think critically about what they read in their textbooks. Without some guidance, students must think for themselves, not an easy matter to do alone. Indeed, many students may not realize that critical thinking is necessary given the textbooks' apparent stamp of professional approval.

The intention in writing this book has not been to discourage anyone from studying macroeconomics. After all, it deals with matters that are central to individuals' well-being and to the functioning and stability of the economic system in which they live. Yes, standard macroeconomics textbooks are seriously flawed, but understanding how and why this is the case opens the door to a new understanding of the subject and, even more importantly, to new possibilities for the future.

POSTSCRIPT: CLIMATE CHANGE, THE COVID PANDEMIC, AND GENUINELY FULL EMPLOYMENT

The Covid pandemic that began in January 2020 has continued to twist and turn. At the time of writing, December 2021, the world is facing an even more contagious mutation of the virus. What the future holds is totally uncertain. Up to this point, over 5 million people have died worldwide. Vast sections of the economy have closed, reopened, and closed again. Unemployment has shot up, GDP has tanked, and government deficits have spiked. An increase in poverty and household bankruptcies was avoided in most developed countries by relatively generous—though temporary—government assistance. Shortages of many goods have developed due to disruption in supply chains, causing many prices to increase.

At the same time, we are witnessing the terrible consequences of climate change. Much of western North America was stuck under a heat dome from late June to mid-July that broke records for how many records it broke. The heat wave sparked extensive wildfires, destruction of road and rail infrastructure, incinerating many small towns. Heat and drought across western North America, extending through to the Prairies, significantly reduced grain crops. Some months later, as winter approached, the Pacific Northwest broke all records for rainfall. Climatologists don't talk of clouds but of atmospheric rivers. Billions of dollars of damage was done by flooding and high winds. Dairy herds drowned in the fertile plains of the Fraser Valley. As a result, food prices rose by 7 percent in the last quarter. Climate change is driving up food prices.

Both climate change and the Covid pandemic are pushing prices up and have reignited the fear of inflation. Naturally, some conservative commentators are blaming government deficits and are suggesting the need for massive cuts in spending. Others are suggesting that central banks are now soft on inflation, and they should increase interest rates. Would such measures be beneficial? Reducing government spending would not repair infrastructure nor help restore supply chains. Cutting off assistance to households and allowing them to fall into poverty would not help the economy.

Essentially, we are faced with massive supply-side shocks that have historically been associated with an acceleration of inflation. Think of it in terms of income shares. The supply shock has reduced the economy's real income. If no group is willing to allow their real income to fall then cost-push inflation could generate an inflationary spiral. Inflation can be seen as a safety value that reconciles excessive real income claims with the available real GDP. It does so by essentially fooling some people into thinking their real income is higher than it is in reality, or by raising prices faster than some people can react. Yes, central banks can end the process by sufficiently large increases in interest rates. But that would further reduce output and increase unemployment.

It is true that in a situation of excessive income claims over a reduced total GDP, if the government cut its spending that would help alleviate the excessive income claims and mitigate the inflationary pressure. But given the need to rebuild infrastructure, and the need for the government to marshal massive resources to invest in greening the economy, that would be a disaster. We would be hamstrung as we plunge off the climate change cliff.

The fundamental solution to the inflation problem is a "social contract" that determines whose real incomes will fall. Essentially, this should be done by the government increasing taxes on the wealthy and assisting the poor. Government policies that enlist the help of the market, such as tax-based incomes policies (or TIPS), can also help break an inflation spiral by creating incentives to mitigate against wage and price increases.

Besides producing a supply-side shock, both climate change and the Covid pandemic have dramatically worsened inequality. White-collar workers can usually work from home in safety. Those that work directly producing goods (or the service and transportation sectors) either work and face the risk of getting sick, or stay home without income. To address the problem of heightened inequality, many have argued it is time for governments to implement a universal basic income (UBI) program.

At the same time, many heterodox economists talk of the need for genuinely full employment to alleviate the many social ills of unemployment, as well as poverty and inequality. To achieve this aim, modern monetary economists advocate a Job Guarantee (JG) program, as discussed in Chapter 10.

What are the relative merits of these programs, and is the cost–benefit calculus affected by the context of climate change and the Covid pandemic? After defining the meaning of UBI, this brief postscript contains a few thoughts on the issue.

I UNIVERSAL BASIC INCOME

UBI also has several different names such as Guaranteed Annual Income or Basic Income Guarantee. While everyone is eligible, it is taxed back in such a way that only those in poverty benefit. It guarantees a "basic" income close to the poverty line even if people choose to make no effort to help themselves. On the other hand, if recipients choose to work, they lose only cents of basic income for every dollar earned, with many plans suggesting a loss of 50 cents on the dollar. Clearly, the details can be refined.

Currently, in most rich nations, there is a patchwork of programs aimed at alleviating poverty, a patchwork that only got more complicated with the implementation of emergency Covid relief payments. Evelyn Forget (2021) calculated that in British Columbia, Canada, there are 194 uncoordinated programs offered by federal, provincial, and municipal authorities that offer support, in cash or in kind, to low-income people. Desperate people are forced to try to navigate through a complex bureaucracy, resulting in many not receiving benefits to which they are entitled. She explains, "This system is so ineffective that tent cities and food banks proliferate, and we treat the consequences of poverty in our emergency departments and jails." The simplicity of a UBI gives it a huge advantage over the current system.

Proponents of the JG approach, as well as most mainstream economists, worry that a UBI would have work disincentives. But basic income experiments have been carried out in various jurisdictions over the years—at least twenty-five by one count—and employment has never been adversely affected.[1] Indeed, the two-year experiment in Finland (that began in 2017) was branded a "flop" because the *increase* in employment among the recipients, though statistically significant, was smaller than was hoped for![2]

One of the earliest basic income experiments took place between 1974 and 1979 in Manitoba, Canada. Forget (2011) reports a reduction in hospitalization rates and contact with physicians for participants relative to controls, and reduced high school drop-outs. These results suggest significant health care savings associated with a UBI.

Another claim from right-wing critics is that money will be "blown" on alcohol or drugs. But in Stockton, California—a town with 23 percent of residents living in poverty—the randomly selected participants of a basic income experiment (that ran from 2019 to 2020) spent the extra $500 a month mostly on food, with merchandize, utilities, and car repairs accounting for 85 percent of the money.[3]

If there is one single result that stands out from all the experiments, it is a big increase in reported feeling of well-being (with less insecurity and less stress). When looking for economic gains from a UBI, the increase in people's reported well-being should not be ignored.

2 THE RELATIVE MERITS OF JG OR UBI IN THE CONTEXT OF COVID AND CLIMATE CHANGE

Clearly both programs have their merits. The big advantages of a JG approach are the public works that could be accomplished, the building of dykes, creating fire breaks in forests, and generally adapting to climate change. In addition, the JG program helps the maintenance of workers' skills and the possibility of incorporating on-the-job training. We know that involuntary unemployment is a source of many social ills.

The big advantage of a UBI is its simplicity. The government just sends out a check every month. It allows recipients to retrain, or engage in creative pursuits, or start their own business. And in the age of the pandemic, when much of the economy is shut down, UBI is the more robust program. Rather than scrambling to set up some kind of "emergency response benefits," as many governments did, a support system would already be in place.

Since both programs have their merits, why not have both? The UBI could effectively be "means tested" by having it as a taxable benefit. What is for certain is that conservative forces would oppose either of these measures. But such forces seem to be blind to the requirements of the current crises.

NOTES

Chapter 1

1 This is taken from Yoram Bauman's hilarious stand-up comedy routine called "Principles of economics, translated." It is available on YouTube, https://www.youtube.com/watch?v=VVp8UGjECt4 (accessed May 14, 2022).

2 This is taken from page 99 of Minsky's (1986) book entitled "Stabilizing an Unstable Economy," Yale University Press.

3 An earlier version of this chapter said, "Therefore, it is generally accepted that governments should attempt to reduce the severity of recessions, or stabilize the economy." A friendly reviewer questioned this, and noted that the textbook he used said that "business cycles are essentially optimal responses of the economy to fluctuations in total factor productivity, and nothing should be done about them." Astonishing!

4 This section contains more advanced material. It could be skipped without loss of continuity.

5 These conditions are known as the *Sonnenschein–Mantel–Debreu conditions*.

6 By June 1932, the Dow Jones industrial average was 791, whereas in August 1929 the index was as high as 5,523. See https://www.macrotrends.net/1319/dow-jones-100-year-historical-chart (accessed May 14, 2022).

7 The data are computed between 1929 and 1933. For the United States we use manufacturing wages. See https://fraser.stlouisfed.org/scribd/?item_id=20153&filepath=/files/docs/publications/employment/1960s/empl_081960.pdf&start_page=38 (accessed May 14, 2022). For Canada the data are found in http://www5.statcan.gc.ca/access_acces/archive.action?l=eng&loc=../pdf/5500095-eng.pdf, section E41, Earnings in Manufacturing industries, production, and other workers. Money wages in the UK fell surprisingly little between 1929 and 1933, only around 5 percent. The explanation is that the UK entered a mini-depression after the First World War, with money wages falling by over 20 percent between 1918 and 1922 and unemployment hovering just under 10 percent throughout the 1920s. So, the Great Depression had a smaller impact on wages in the UK since they were already in a mini-depression. See Hatton and Thomas (2010).

8 The insightful reader might be wondering where the leaked saving goes to, and whether that money can find its way back into the circular flow again. Obviously, if we stuffed the saved money under our mattresses, it would not find its way back. But usually people do not do that. They put the money in the bank, and maybe the bank lends the money out to someone wanting to borrow it. When the borrower spends it, the money will find its way back into the circular flow again. However, the important point is that there is nothing automatic about this. See the discussion in Section 2.6 "Digging Deeper into the Paradox of Thrift."

9   There have been: the development of the electric grid in the early twentieth century, the beginning of the automobile age, the atomic age, the computer age, and the information technology age.

10 In a complete description of the economy, there are three leakages (savings, taxes, and imports) and three injections (investment, government spending on final goods, and exports). Assuming there is no government eliminates a leakage (taxes) and an injection (government spending). Assuming there is no foreign trade eliminates a leakage (imports) and an injection (exports).

11 The paradox of thrift is an interesting application of the crude Keynesian model. However, normally, savings are a stable function of income, while investment is volatile.

12 In particular, in 1820 Thomas Malthus proposed a theory of gluts caused by redundant or idle savings. See, for example, the discussion in Pullen (2016).

13 He used the old-fashioned term "magneto" instead of "alternator." It eventually results in a dead battery. See Keynes, *Essays in Persuasion*, 1931.

14 The "Nobel Prize in Economics" is a commonly used term for "The Sveriges Riksbank Prize in Economic Sciences in Memory of Alfred Nobel." It was established in 1968 by the Bank of Sweden, which also funds it. It is not one of the original prizes established by Alfred Nobel.

15 In formalizing Keynes's ideas, the founders of the neoclassical synthesis forced Keynes's ideas back into a Classical framework. How did this happen and why? Partly it is because of the difficulty understanding exactly what Keynes was trying to say. The General Theory is a multilayered book. On a single page, Keynes moves from high theory to practical earth-bound considerations. It contains a rich appreciation for detail and many insightful asides and footnotes. As a result, it has been hard to pinpoint exactly what Keynes was trying to say. For example, we have said that Keynes did not attribute unemployment to wage rigidity and he thought that forcing wages down could worsen the problem of unemployment. But in analyzing unemployment in the General Theory, Keynes did sometimes assume wage rigidity: sometimes it was an empirical observation; sometimes it was a simplifying assumption; and sometimes it was a *policy recommendation*. Yet, the formalized versions of Keynes's theory, which became the neoclassical synthesis, do attribute unemployment to wage rigidity.

16 We say the short run is "pseudo-Keynesian" because it relies on wage or price stickiness for its existence, whereas Keynes did not think the problem of unemployment arose because of a failure of prices to adjust.

17 Besides Michal Kalecki, the post-Keynesian school was developed by Nicholas Kaldor, Paul Davidson, Piero Sraffa, Geoff Harcourt, and Charles Goodhart. An excellent and quite comprehensive introduction is provided by Marc Lavoie (2014).

18 The data were downloaded from https://fred.stlouisfed.org/series/ GDPC1 (accessed May 14, 2022). The series is real US GDP. The growth rate is calculated quarter to quarter and then annualized (multiplied by four).

19 Arguably, only six economists around the world predicted the crash: Nouriel Roubini, Ann Pettifor, Steve Keen, Dean Baker, Raghuram Rajan, and Peter Schiff. For further discussion, see https://www.intheblack.com/ articles/2015/07/07/6-economists-who-predicted-the-global-financ

ial-crisis-and-why-we-should-listen-to-them-from-now-on (accessed May 14, 2022).

20 Alberto F. Alesina and Silvio Ardagna (2010) argued for fiscal austerity on the grounds that it would be expansionary in a context where high government debt endangered private sector confidence. This was followed by an influential paper by Carmen M. Reinhart and Kenneth S. Rogoff (2010) who claimed to have found that a debt-to-GDP ratio over 90 percent severely impaired long-term growth prospects.

21 See https://krugman.blogs.nytimes.com/2009/01/27/a-dark-age-of-macroec onomics-wonkish/ (accessed May 14, 2022).

22 The schools of thought that reject neoclassical economics can be grouped under the umbrella term "heterodox" and includes Marxist, institutional, Austrian, ecological, and post-Keynesian (among others).

Chapter 2

1 This saying is often credited to American statistician W. Edwards Deming (1900–1993), but the line does not appear in his books.

2 According to recent Stats Canada data, women still do about twice as much housework as men—even when both have full-time paid jobs.

3 Data from the Bureau of Labor. The wage data were "average hourly earnings of production and nonsupervisory employees, total private. The price data was the CPI for all urban areas."

4 U6 includes (1) marginally attached workers who currently are neither working nor looking for work but indicate that they want and are available for a job and have looked for work sometime in the past 12 months, plus (2) involuntary part-time workers. Discouraged workers, a subset of the marginally attached, have given a job-market-related reason for not currently looking for work.

5 See https://tinyurl.com/y6te9fxw (accessed May 14, 2022).

6 See Cavallo and Rigobon (2016), page 152 for a description of government manipulation of inflation data between 2007 and 2015. Another account is provided in "Economic Data in Argentina: an Augean Stable," February 13, 2016, *The Economist*, https://www.economist.com/the-americas/2016/02/13/ an-augean-stable.

7 The survey was conducted by Edison Research in April 2017. The question was number 47 of the survey and asked: "How much do you trust the data about the economy that is reported by the federal government?" 18.3 percent did not trust it at all; 21.3 percent somewhat distrusted it; 43.8 percent somewhat trusted it; and 14.3 percent completely trusted it. Only 2.3 percent did not know.

8 John Williams made these remarks in an interview. See https://tinyurl.com/ yxljdrk5. Incidentally, Williams has a BA in economics, and an MBA from Dartmouth College, and calls himself "an economist."

9 This was said on September 28, 2015, in a press conference. See Jacobson (2015).

10 This has been clearly explained by Greenlees and McClelland (2008).

11 This is visually apparent when comparing the inflation series. John Williams admitted to doing no calculations in an interview with James Hamilton of Econbrowser. See https://azizonomics.com/2013/06/01/the-trouble-with-shadowstats/.

12 The data are available from their website: http://www.thebillionpricesproject. com/datasets/. The daily price index was averaged to produce a quarterly price index. The inflation rate is the quarter-to-quarter rate of change of the price index times four to "annualize" the result.

13 The Not-Working Rate can equivalently be written as:

$$\left\{ 1 - \frac{\text{Population}}{\text{Population}} \right\} + \frac{\text{Unemployed} + \text{Not in Labor Force}}{\text{Population}}.$$

This equals: $1 - \dfrac{\left\{ \text{Population} - \text{Unemployed} - \text{Not in Labor Force} \right\}}{\text{Population}}$

which can be simplified to:

$$1 - \frac{\text{Employed}}{\text{Population}}$$

14 Data obtained from the US Bureau of Labor Statistics. The employment–population ratio for prime-aged men is series LNS12300061Q.

15 Interestingly, data for the United States show no long-run increase in the incidence of involuntary part-time work. Data are from the OECD statistics and data directorate. http://www.oecd.org/sdd/.

16 An animated map of the United States, showing unemployment rates by county from 1990 to 2016, shows the important regional dimensions of the problem. https://www.youtube.com/watch?v=shqJR_oWdrI. It is remarkable how the propagation of unemployment resembles a living organism or virus.

17 An interesting metadata study of international results by Paul and Moser (2009) examines several variables of mental health, including mixed symptoms of distress, depression, anxiety, psychosomatic symptoms, subjective well-being, and self-esteem.

18 See Stuckler and Basu (2013).

19 See Lindo (2011); Bubonya, Cobb-Clark, and Wooden (2014).

20 See Reeves and Howard (2013).

21 Raphael and Winter-Ebmer (2001) examine the period from 1970 to 1997 and find that there are sizable effects of unemployment on the seven felony offenses recorded by the Department of Justice. Additionally, they find significant and sizable positive effects of unemployment on the rates of specific violent, as well as property, crimes. In a subsequent study, the authors find that nearly 40 percent (their most conservative estimate) of the decline in property crime rates during the 1990s is attributable to the concurrent decline in the unemployment rate.

22 See Fougére, Kramarz, and Pouget (2009).

23 See Darity (1999).

24 See Dan Bobkoff (2016), "What just happened to Apple, explained" Business Insider, August 30, https://www.businessinsider.com/what-just-happe ned-to-apple-explained-2016-8.

25 See Karen Weise, "Microsoft Pledges $500 Million for Affordable Housing in Seattle Area," *New York Times*, January 16, 2019, https://tinyurl.com/yd4xg5p2.

26 See Stefano Marcuzzi and Alession Terzi, "Are Multinationals Eclipsing Nation-States?" Project Syndicate, February 1, 2019, https://tinyurl.com/yxtmzwhb.

27 I would like to thank Brian MacLean of Laurentian University, Canada, for an exchange of ideas on this topic.

Chapter 3

1 See page 292 of the World Meteorological Conference on "The Changing Atmosphere: Implications for Global Security" that took place in Toronto Canada in 1988, WMO No. 710. The document can be found at: https://tinyurl.com/rx77epne (accessed May 14, 2022).

2 The "Rule of 70" is the appropriate approximation for continuous compounding. (More accurate, but less user friendly, is a "Rule of 69.3.") The "Rule of 72" is appropriate for variables that grow according to periodic compounding.

3 Malthus made this prediction in his pamphlet "An Essay on the Principle of Population."

4 He wrote "The Ultimate Resource," in 1981 (and updated it in 1996 as "The Ultimate Resource 2" [Princeton University Press]) and was constantly in the thick of controversy.

5 It is true that this massive gap in our understanding has received attention in the modern era. Unfortunately, models of "endogenous growth theory"— which make technical change endogenous—are merely based on ad hoc mechanistic assumptions. For example, one very common model distinguishes between labor used to make goods and services, and labor employed in "universities" to produce technical change. It is a fun exercise to play but reveals nothing about the process of technical change in the real world. On the other hand, the book by Philippe Aghion and Peter Howitt (1997) is one that better attempts to describe and understand real-world technological change.

6 Tobin originally proposed his "currency transaction tax" in 1972 in his Janeway Lectures at Princeton. He again proposed it in his Presidential Address to the Eastern Economic Association in 1978. See Tobin (1978).

7 A Tobin tax was backed by eleven EU members in 2013 but not implemented. In 2016, China drafted rules to impose a Tobin Tax, but has since kept the tax rate at zero (effectively not imposing it). Also in 2016, presidential candidate Hilary Clinton backed a version of the Tobin Tax.

8 In the nineteenth century, the average tariffs in the United States were nearly 45 percent. The beneficiaries were, first, the textile and iron industries and then steel. It was protectionism, rather than free trade, that made the United

States the world's fastest-growing economy in the nineteenth century and into the 1920s.

9   For example, Nokia got its early funding from public sources and the government agency kept an equity stake, which was sold when Nokia grew large enough. Similarly, Brazil has a public investment bank that takes an equity stake in companies in strategic areas such as biotech and renewables. As of 2015, this bank was making 20 percent return on equity. The government takes some of that money and redistributes it to health and education, and the investment bank gets to keep a part and reinvest.

10 There are around twenty countries that currently have negative or zero natural growth rates (excluding immigration). Among these are Japan, Spain, Portugal, and Italy for example. A useful reference website is: https://www.unfpa.org/data/world-population-dashboard.

11 The population density of Paris is 55,673 people per square mile. At that level of density, the current population of the world, which is around 7.7 billion, would require 138,308 square miles. Montana has a land size of 145,552 square miles, while Texas has a land area of 261,797 square miles. These facts were gleaned from the internet! The comparison is the idea of Tim de Chant, who has a website called Per Square Mile. https://tinyurl.com/jyw2kb6.

12 The estimate is provided from the Global Footprint Network. https://www.footprintnetwork.org/.

13 And what about the recycling scam where your recycled plastic is carefully bundled and shipped off and ends up on a beach halfway around the world? Most of the plastic has no value. It cannot compete against new plastic. See Ivan Watson et al. "China's recycling ban has sent America's plastic to Malaysia. Now they don't want it—so what next?" CNN.COM, April 27, 2019, https://tinyurl.com/y3b2yngp.

14 When we cut forests for timber, pulp, fuel, and other products and clear land for farms and communities, we also add GHGs to the air. This is because through photosynthesis, trees and plants absorb carbon dioxide when they grow and release it when they die or are disturbed.

15 Such a worldview has been attempted by Kate Raworth (2017) in her book *Doughnut Economics: Seven Ways to Think Like a 21st Century Economist.* Raworth begins by redrawing the circular flow diagram to embedding the economy into earth's natural systems.

16 This is the book by Krugman and Wells (2018). They have a section in the growth chapter on the cost of limiting carbon.

17 The data can be downloaded from: https://crudata.uea.ac.uk/cru/data/temperature/#datdow. For a discussion of the data see: https://crudata.uea.ac.uk/cru/data/temperature/CRUTEM4-gl.dat.

18 See Nuccitelli et al. (2012). This is explained for the layperson in the "skeptical science" website, https://tinyurl.com/y99oc8zf. Another useful reference is James Hansen's (2012) Ted talk, https://tinyurl.com/y3lftxv6.

19 The United Nations meeting in Rio de Janeiro agreed a climate change convention. The 1997 Kyoto Protocol established legally binding targets. The Paris Agreement of 2015 relies on voluntary targets that governments knew when they signed the deal are insufficient to keep the world below 2 degree Celsius warming let alone 1.5 degree Celsius.

20 Atmospheric concentrations can be found at: https://www.co2.earth/mont
    hly-co2.
21 See Hanson (2012).
22 See Homer-Dixon (2015).
23 Ecologists point out that one tried and true method is a massive increase
    in conservation and preservation of forests (and wetlands) and replanting
    of forests. Perhaps technologies can capture some emissions in the air. But
    massive regreening is essential.
24 Riahi et al. (2017). There is a very useful power point presentation on the
    "Global Carbon Project" website, http://www.globalcarbonproject.org/carbo
    nbudget/index.htm. They update this presentation every year, so the one
    I am referencing today (June 2019) may have changed when you reference
    it. Nevertheless, you should be able to skip to the section entitled "Emission
    scenarios." Look for the slide that shows the emissions necessary to meet the
    Paris targets. In the 2018 presentation, this was slide #50.
25 See https://tinyurl.com/yd7wqqoj and https://www.nytimes.com/interact
    ive/2017/08/23/climate/alaska-permafrost-thawing.html.
26 Three forms of carbon pricing are popularly discussed. There is the straight
    carbon tax (where the government may either use the extra revenue to
    incentivize greening the economy or to lower other taxes). There is the carbon
    tax and dividend (where the government gives the carbon revenue back to
    the people in a lump sum). And there is cap and trade (where the government
    issues licenses to emit carbon to producers who then buy and trade the
    licenses). There are advantages and disadvantages of each, though technically
    they can all produce an *efficient* reduction of carbon emissions.
27 See "Closing the Gap," Canada's Office of the Parliamentary Budget Officer,
    June 13, 2019.
28 President Macron is pledging to increase carbon taxes to C$130 a ton by
    2022. This is in line with the estimates of what is required to meet the Paris
    Agreement targets—at least according to the Report of the High-Level
    Commission on Carbon Prices (2017).
29 It seems passions were inflamed in France by the fact that the money raised
    was going to general revenues and used to reduce the national budget deficit,
    and by the fact that a recent budget hurt the poorest families. Nevertheless,
    it seems that carbon pricing or carbon taxes are a hard sell—especially in
    countries that have an oil sector (as in Canada) and where there are growing
    inequalities (practically everywhere).
30 The source is Chapter 2 "Mitigation Pathways Compatible with 1.5° C in the
    Context of Sustainable Development" page 152 of the IPCC Special Report
    called "Global Warming of 1.5° C." The authors state, "the price of carbon
    varies substantially across models and scenarios."
31 At least this was the claim made by the United States and the Harper
    government in Canada. But there is a good argument that this was just playing
    politics, and it all came down to "vested interest" in the end. In particular, the
    Kyoto Protocol was based on precedents set in the Vienna Convention and
    Montreal Protocol relating to ozone depletion where developing countries had
    a delayed timeline for reducing CFCs. In that case the "free rider effect" was
    not insurmountable.

32 See https://www.scientificamerican.com/article/exxon-knew-about-climate-change-almost-40-years-ago/.

33 The following is an incomplete list of the climate denial organizations and "think tanks" funded or established by Big Oil. These are: American Enterprise Institute; Americans for Prosperity; American Legislative Exchange Council (set up and funded by ExxonMobil; and the Koch brothers); Beacon Hill Institute at Suffolk University (in Boston); Cato Institute; Competitive Enterprise Institute; Heartland Institute; Heritage Foundation; Institute for Energy Research; and the Manhattan Institute for Policy Research. Why the need for so many? It is the echo chamber effect. If you hear something repeated enough, you start to believe it.

34 See Robert Brulle (2013) in the list of references.

35 The data are a result of several studies by the Climate Investigations Centre. It was reported by Bloomberg and the Calgary Herald. See https://tinyurl.com/yxt4zonn.

36 On June 18, 2019: on the same day that the Canadian Parliament declared a climate change emergency, the Canadian government approved a massive new pipeline—the Trans-Mountain Pipeline—that would permit an expansion of tar-sands oil extraction.

37 A good discussion of the history of Supreme Court decisions that led to the US campaign on finance laws becoming horrendously dysfunctional can be found at the website "citizens take action." See https://citizenstakeaction.org/supreme-court-decisions/.

38 A superb source for detailed examples of bias in British newspapers is Simon Wren-Lewis (2018).

Chapter 4

1 This is taken from Kate Raworth's (2017) book entitled *Doughnut Economics: Seven Ways to Think Like a 21st Century Economist*, Chelsea Green Publishing.

2 This is taken from Nelson Mandela's speech delivered at Trafalgar Square on February 3, 2005.

3 See, for example, Diener and Seligman (2004: 5): "there are only small increases in wellbeing" above some threshold. Clark, Frijters, and Shields (2008: 123) state, "greater economic prosperity at some point ceases to buy more happiness." And Frey and Stutzer (2002: 416) claim that "income provides happiness at low levels of development but once a threshold (around $10,000) is reached, the average income level in a country has little effect on average subjective wellbeing."

4 Kahneman (2010a) explains it is the "reflective self" that makes decisions. Insofar as economics is the study of how people makes choices, the "reflective self" and "life satisfaction" are clearly important. On the other hand, Layard (2010) explains how "experienced happiness" or "emotional wellbeing" is correlated with physical functioning (such as levels of cortisol) and measures of brain activity. From the point of view of "health" it seems that "experienced happiness" is most important.

5 See, for example, Stevenson and Wolfers (2008), and Sacks, Stevenson, and Wolfers (2012). The quote is from 2010. Wolfers also has a series of articles debunking the Easterlin Paradox on the *Freakonomics* website beginning in 2008 and going on through 2011. See, for example, https://tinyurl.com/y7q8h fug (accessed May 15, 2022).

6 Kahneman and Deaton controlled for health insurance, age, education, religion, sex, marital status, weekend, presence of children, caregiver, obese, divorced, health condition, headache, alone, and smoker.

7 Given the very narrow time dimension to the study, the lack of a satiation point for life evaluation is not surprising. Remember, the relative income hypothesis predicts that the rich will be happier than the poor at any point in time.

8 However, it may also be the case that income simply offers greater opportunities for happiness in wealthier regions. In other words, at very high levels, income may still be able to yield greater standards of living, which may not be the case in poorer regions.

9 Answers about happiness are also well correlated with measurements of bodily function, such as amounts of salivary cortisol, fibrinogen stress responses, blood pressure, heart rate, and (in some cases) immune system responses to a flu vaccination. With regard to brain activity, there is a correlation between "experienced happiness" and activity in the left dorsolateral prefrontal cortex. See Layard (2010).

10 It is not obvious that "happiness" should be the objective. There are attractive alternatives such as justice or virtue. For example, suppose 99.9 percent of the population were made ecstatically happy by the human sacrifice of a tiny minority, would we say that was OK? Turner (2010) recognizes problems such as this as nontrivial, but instead prefers to assert the negative hypothesis: we have no good reason for believing that additional growth in GDP per capita will necessarily, and limitlessly, deliver increased "happiness."

11 Surveys of the literature are provided in the IMF staff discussion notes by Ostry, Berg, and Tsangarides (2014) and Dabla-Norris et al. (2015).

12 Crucially, the dataset contains information on both market incomes (pretaxes and transfers) and disposable incomes (posttaxes and transfers). The dataset is the Penn World Tables version 7.1. They use data on 189 countries between 1950 and 2010. https://www.rug.nl/ggdc/productivity/pwt/.

13 See Persson and Tabellini (1994), Easterly (2007), and Berg, Ostry, and Zettelmeyer (2012).

14 They consider eleven different health and social problems: physical health, mental health, drug abuse, education, imprisonment, obesity, social mobility, trust and community life, violence, teenage pregnancies, and child well-being.

15 The measure of income inequality used throughout The Spirit Level is not the Gini coefficient but the 20:20 ratio: the size of the gap between the richest 20 percent and poorest 20 percent of the population. This reduces the effect of outliers at the top and bottom, and prevents the middle 60 percent statistically obscuring the worst effects of inequality.

16 The authors of *The Spirit Level* make their key slides freely available. The slides can be found here: https://www.equalitytrust.org.uk/resources/the-spirit-level.

17 Sanandaji et al. (2010) claimed they could not duplicate Wilkinson and Pickett's finding using OECD data on inequality. Wilkinson and Pickett responded that they used UN data on inequality since the OECD data were not intended

for cross-national comparisons. There has also been a book by Snowden (2010) (published by the right-wing think tank "the Democracy Institute") that attempts to ridicule the correlations in the Spirit Level by finding lots of amusing but spurious correlations. Any attempt at reducing inequality is branded as favoring "big government." It proposes trickle-down economics.

18 This figure appears toward the end of *The Spirit Level*. To produce our version of the figure, we went back to the original research published by Leon et al. in 1992 in the *British Medical Journal*. The data were drawn over the period 1985–6 for Sweden, and for 1983–5 for England and Wales.

19 The original source for the data shown in Figure 4.2 is Willms (1997).

20 The statistic "roughly 69 percent of US adults are overweight or obese" comes from Flegal et al. (2012).

21 The feeling that others can be trusted is inversely related to inequality. See https://ourworldindata.org/trust. If only 40 percent feel that others are trustworthy (as in the United States), this cannot be a problem of the bottom 20 percent alone. Similarly, variations in mental illness among the poor alone cannot account for why countries' prevalence rates for mental illness vary between 8 and 25 percent of the population (see *The Spirit Level*).

22 Source: http://www.oecd.org/social/income-distribution-database.htm. The data shown are Gini coefficients for disposable income, posttaxes, and transfers.

23 Globalization could not explain why inequality increased so dramatically in the United States between 1980 and 1990, despite trade as a percent of GDP hardly changing. It could not explain why globalization did not produce a shift toward more skill-intensive goods in the rich developed countries. It could not explain why inequality also increased in less developed countries. The technological change explanation was hampered by the fact that inequality increased even while productivity growth was flat—a fact that seems paradoxical.

24 The source for Figure 4.9 is the World Inequality Database, http://wid.world/data/.

25 Sources: Economic Policy Institute, Washington, DC. https://tinyurl.com/yak45qcm, Frydman and Saks (2008), and Dean Baker (2016, figure 6.1). The pay of CEOs includes stock options realized. Worker compensation is average annual compensation.

26 Baker (2016) chapter 6 summarizes a wealth of academic research supporting the argument that a large portion of CEO pay is rent, that is, not justified by performance.

27 Source: Statistica.com, https://tinyurl.com/yazgbnhg.

28 Source: Figure 4:12. Alvaredo, F., A. Atkinson, T. Piketty, and E. Saez (2013) "The Top 1 Percent in International and Historical Perspective." *Journal of Economic Perspectives*, vol. 27 (3): 3–30.
This figure combines both central and local government income taxes.

29 The data for 2015 come from the Oxfam Briefing Paper (2016), which itself relies on the "Global Wealth Databook" produced by the research branch of Credit Suisse. The prediction for 2030 comes from the British House of Common Library, as reported in *The Guardian*, https://www.theguardian.com/business/2018/apr/07/global-inequality-tipping-point-2030.

30 Source: US Bureau of Labor Statistics. Technically, the figure shows labor's share in the nonfarm business sector.

31 According to the OECD, labor's share declined in twenty-six out of thirty developed economies between 1990 and 2009. Source: International Labour Organization (2012) *Global Wage Report 2012/13*, Chapter 5.

32 Source: International Labour Organization (2015) *The Labour Share in G20 Economies*, Report for the G20 Employment Working Group, Turkey, February 26–27.

33 The advanced economies in this study are Australia, Austria, Belgium, Canada, Denmark, Finland, France, Germany, Ireland, Italy, Japan, the Netherlands, New Zealand, Norway, Portugal, Spain, Sweden, Switzerland, the UK, and the United States.

34 The result survives the inclusion of possible omitted variables that could both reduce unionization and increase inequality. These additional controls include changes in elected government, sectoral employment shifts such as the decline of industry and rise of services sectors, the strong expansion of employment in finance, and rising education levels.

35 In 1980, the top 1 percent captured around 10 percent of national income, while the poorest 50 percent took around 20 percent, in both blocs. By 2017, in Europe both groups has increased their share marginally: the top 1 percent captured 12 percent of income while the poorest 50 percent took 22 percent. But in the United States, the top 1 percent are now taking 20 percent, while the bottom 50 percent make do with only 10 percent.

36 All of Piketty's data and diagrams can be found at: http://piketty.pse.ens.fr/cap ital21c.

Chapter 5

1 This is taken from Stephen McBride's (2018) article entitled "Eight Things the Crisis Taught Us about Austerity." It appeared in the September edition of "The Monitor" published by the Canadian Centre for Policy Alternatives.

2 This raises perhaps an obvious question: why then are mutual fund managers paid fortunes? If markets are efficient, their marginal product is zero. But since their pay is very high, markets cannot be efficient.

3 On the other hand, if the government gave tax breaks specifically to households who increased their savings, this would change the incentive to save, and could increase total savings.

4 Output and income are held constant at the full employment level since this is long-run analysis where we are abstracting from the business cycle.

5 Assuming that world interest rates are not affected by domestic fiscal policy is, strictly speaking, only applicable to a "small open economy." Since the United States is "large," changes in its fiscal policy could affect world interest rates. An alternative argument is that Trump's tax cuts to corporations increased investment, while his tax cuts to the rich increased savings, and these effects may roughly cancel out.

6 The interest rate is the three-month prime rate on commercial paper. The inflation rate is derived from the CPI. All data obtained from the Federal Reserve of St. Louis. https://fred.stlouisfed.org/.

7 The 1980 deregulation was the Depository Institutions Deregulation and Monetary Control Act. The 1982 deregulation was the Alternative Mortgage Transaction Parity Act.

8 Note: "subprime" does not mean lending at an interest rate lower than prime. It means lending to high-risk borrowers.

9 Glass-Steagall was repealed by the Gramm-Leach-Bliley Bank Deregulation Bill (1999).

10 Three of the better known acronyms are SIVs (structured investment vehicles), CDOs (collateralized debt obligations), and ABCPs (asset-backed commercial paper).

11 This illustrates a crucial point: it is not sufficient to have regulations in place. The agency whose job it is to enforce the regulations needs a budget sufficient to do the job.

12 An interesting paper in this regard is by Gans and Shephard (1994) that explores the issue of rejected classic articles by leading economists. Apparently, George Akerlof's classic article on the market for "lemons" (dealing with the problems created if the product's quality is unobservable) was rejected three times by leading journals, twice on the basis that the result was trivial, once because it was too general.

13 For example, we weigh a dollar lost more heavily than a dollar won. And our decision is affected by the way the choice is framed: we are more likely to accept a medical procedure if it carries a 90 percent chance of survival, than if it carries a 10 percent chance of death.

14 Asset price movements are not always unpredictable. De Bondt and Thaler (1985) found that past "winners" over a period of years tend to underperform—and past "losers" outperformed—the market. Over shorter periods of six months to one year, stocks display momentum—the stocks that go up the fastest for the first six months of the year tend to keep going up. So, markets sometimes overreact and sometimes underreact (Mullainathan and Thaler 2004).

15 Of course, there is always an exception. Baumol and Blinder, in their 2020 *Principles of Microeconomics* textbook state on page 93, "The Great Recession of 2007–2009 is only one of many historical examples of recessions that have been triggered by stock market investors who irrationally followed the behavior of other investors (i.e., herd behavior)." No need to discuss the housing bubble, or the near criminal behavior of the financial sector. It was all the fault of irrational stock market investors!

16 The stories vary, but always seem convincing at the time. In the dot-com bubble the story was all about the new technology breaking the mold. Everything was going to be different. In real estate booms the story is usually about a fixed amount of land confronting a growing population and a growing economy that has always (and will always) propel prices higher. It's a myth, but people believe it during the boom.

17 Stock prices are much more variable than the discounted streams of profits investors are trying to predict. See, for example, Shiller (1981), Campbell and Shiller (1987), and Jung and Shiller (2005).

18 The reference is taken from Keynes's famous beauty contest analogy. He compared the difficulty of predicting asset prices to the difficulty of winning a newspaper competition asking contestants to pick (from a list of 100

female photographs) not the prettiest faces but the six faces that will be the most chosen by other entrants as the prettiest. Keynes says it is not a case of choosing the prettiest faces, "nor even those which average opinion genuinely thinks the prettiest. We have reached the third degree where we try to anticipate what average opinion expects average opinion to be. And there are some, I believe, who practice the fourth, fifth and higher degrees" (Keynes 1936: 156).

19 For example, when discussing the loanable funds equilibrium, Krugman and Wells (2018) state,

> The figure also shows that this match-up is efficient, in two senses. First, the right investments get made: the investment spending projects that are actually financed have higher payoffs (in terms of present value) than those that do not get financed. Second, the right people do the saving and lending: the savers who actually lend funds are willing to lend for lower interest rates than those who do not.

20 There is an extended discussion of the information requirements of perfect competition—of which the demand and supply framework is the shorthand version—in Hill and Myatt (2010: 55).

21 I would like to thank Brian MacLean for extended discussions on the topics in this section and the next. These sections encapsulate his ideas.

22 The Economist, "Saving by companies: the corporate savings glut," *Economist*, July 7, 2005, economist.com/node/4154491.

23 The Economist, "Dead money: cash has been piling up on companies' balance-sheets since before the crisis," *The Economist*, November 3, 2012, economist.com/node/21565621.

Chapter 6

1 This quote is taken from Axel Leijonhufvud (2009) "Stabilities and Instabilities in the macroeconomy," Vox CEPR Policy Portal, November 21, https://tinyurl.com/ya5j2u45.

2 This quote is taken from Roger Farmer's (2009) article entitled "Why Keynes Was Right and Wrong, and Why It Matters," originally published on May 27 on a webpage called The Economist's Forum, hosted by *The Financial Times*.

3 Data source: Cansim Tables 380-0017 and 36-10-0222-01.

4 This measure of the money supply is called "M2."

5 There is another model used to explain business cycles called the Real Business Cycle Model. Proponents of this model have a different explanation for recessions and booms and believe that they are "optimal" responses to technology shocks and therefore nothing should be done about them.

6 This is not news. It may have been news in 1968 when Leijonhufvud published his treatise "On Keynesian Economics and the Economics of Keynes," but it is not news now.

7 Currency outside banks is Cansim vector V37173, and in December 2018 this amounted to 88 billion, or about 4 percent of nominal GDP. At that time

bank deposits as measured by M2 was $1,667 billion, or about 75 percent of nominal GDP. (Nominal GDP is Vector, V41552796, in the Cansim database.)

8 Technically, currency is a liability of the central bank that issues it. At one time, during the Gold Standard era (that began in the nineteenth century) central banks pledged to convert their currency into gold. But this is no longer the case. Money is now purely "fiduciary," meaning its value is purely derived from its acceptance as a means of payment.

9 Negative nominal interest rates were observed in the years following the Great Financial Meltdown, but they were on specific bonds in high demand as a safe place to "park" money. They were very much the exception.

10 The likelihood of an upward sloping AD line, and its implications, has been discussed by Lavoie (2016).

Chapter 7

1 The quote is taken from a piece entitled "The Austerity Chronicles" that appeared on April 5, 2019, on the Project Syndicate website. Rogoff was endorsing the finding of Alesina et al. (2019). https://tinyurl.com/y2ja64fy (accessed May 15, 2022).

2 https://krugman.blogs.nytimes.com/2012/09/23/expectations-and-the-confidence-fairy/.

3 In Figure 7.1, we have added government transfer payments to "G" to obtain government expenditures, rather than subtracting transfers from taxation to get net taxes. This is a better way of showing the size of the government. For example, if a government had high tax rates but used all the money to pay for government transfers, both net taxes and "G" could be quite small, giving a misleading impression about the influence of the government on the economy.

4 Source: International Monetary Fund, *World Economic Outlook Database*.

5 If financial capital moves across international borders with perfect ease, the income-expenditure multiplier will be unaffected by removing the assumption of constant interest rates. The model where this result occurs is known as the Mundell–Fleming model.

6 On the other hand, a temporary sales tax cut will have a bigger effect on spending than a permanent sales tax cut because there is an incentive to make planned future purchases now to take advantage of the lower tax. Similarly, a temporary investment tax credit would have a bigger short-term impact than a permanent one.

7 Source: http://en.wikipedia.org/wiki/Greek_debt_crisis_timeline.

8 Only one book took a strong stand in defending the effectiveness of fiscal policy. Krugman and Wells (2018) list three arguments against the use of fiscal policy and then debunk each in turn. The only difficulties they cite are timing issues (lags). Long-run problems associated with rising debt are situated in the context of countries in the EU who no longer have separate currencies, or countries like Argentina that borrowed money denominated in US dollar terms.

9 We quote Lucas and Cochrane, but of course, there were many other voices besides them. An excellent source of quotes from other major figures in the

new classical school is Brad DeLong (2011). In that piece, we find quotes by Zingales, Levine, Cochrane, Lucas, Prescott, Fama, Boldrin, and Posner.

10 See Lucas (2009).

11 There are other issues as well. One key issue is whether government bonds constitute a component of net wealth. If they just represent deferred taxation, as the new classical economists believe, then they should not be regarded as a component of society's net wealth—at least from a theoretical point of view. Nevertheless, if people *perceive* government bonds as part of net wealth, then the issue of government bonds will have real effects on the economy.

12 In Figure 7.6, the data for the European countries were obtained from Eurostat. The data for the United States were obtained from the Federal Reserve Bank of St. Louis.

13 See Krugman (2013) and Blyth (2013).

14 See the article "ECB's Trichet: austerity plans don't risk stagnation" in Reuters, https://tinyurl.com/y2ybfmsm.

15 See Chapter 3 of the World Economic Outlook, October 2010. They note several glaring errors. For example, as part of its industrial policies the government of Finland holds equity stakes in companies it has subsidized (see Chapter 3, Section 2.3). In 2000 there was a stock market boom, which caused a surge in government revenue—but Alesina–Ardagna mistakenly identified this as a major austerity program. Further, there was a large fiscal contraction in Japan in 1997—the only modern large contraction to take place in the face of a liquidity trap. But Alesina and Ardagna don't pick up that contraction at all, instead identifying some spurious cases of austerity in other years. Nor do they pick up the huge Japanese stimulus policy in 1995.

16 See Blanchard (2012). He says on page 41: "The main finding, based on data for 28 economies, is that the multipliers used in generating growth forecasts have been systematically too low since the start of the Great Recession. Informal evidence suggests that the multipliers implicitly used to generate these forecasts are about 0.5. Actual multipliers may be higher, in the range of 0.9 to 1.7."

17 For example, one year for New Zealand—when it had a high debt ratio and the economy was in depression—was equal to (according to their weighting method) nineteen years where the UK had a high debt ratio and the economy grew reasonably well, at 2.5 percent.

18 For example, the 2013 Annual Report of the Bank for International Settlements has a full chapter supporting fiscal consolidation. They believe that "there is no compelling evidence" that fiscal multipliers are greater than zero, and blame the poor performance of economies undergoing fiscal austerity on "other factors" and continue to discuss the importance of credibility and confidence.

19 The new book is by Alesina, Favero, and Giavazzi (2019) published by Princeton University Press.

20 Wynne Godley popularized (if not pioneered) their use (at the UK Treasury during the 1960s) and enabled him, in 2000, to identify those imbalances in the US economy which would later cause the crash. See http://www.lrb.co.uk/v22/n13/wynne-godley/what-if-they-start-saving-again. They have been used by many others since then. For example, Martin Wolfe and Paul Krugman have used them in their blogs to point out the foolishness of cutting government

deficits when the private sector has moved into surplus to restore their net assets. Also see Godley (2007).

21 Details are provided in Blanchard (2019), footnote 4, p. 1201.

22 This catchphrase is often used by MMT theorists. See, for example, the piece by Fullwiler, Grey, and Tankus in a letter to the Financial Times, 2019, https://tinyurl.com/y4e638r7.

23 See Bill Mitchell (2013).

24 See Steven Hail (2017).

25 See Randall Wray (2019).

26 Since 2008, cutting interest rates has not done much. As of June 2019, there were $13 trillion of government bonds worldwide with negative interest rates, with no sign that it was stimulating demand sufficiently to hit the target rate of inflation. See https://tinyurl.com/y6berlj3.

27 See Manski (2012).

28 Peter Diamond made these remarks in an interview with Paul Solman on PBS News Hour entitled, "Taxes: How High Is Too High." See https://tinyurl.com/y6ew2r7d. Incidentally, In 2018–19, the highest income tax rate in the United States is 37 percent on incomes above $500,000. This is astonishingly low by international standards. Diamond would be comfortable with rates in the low 60s.

29 It was the usual story in Kansas. After taxes were slashed in 2012, the state's finances began to drown in red ink, but economic growth did not improve. Tired of waiting for the supply-side magic to materialize, the Kansas legislature voted in 2017 to roll back the tax cuts. See Noah Smith (2017) "Supply-Siders Still Push What Doesn't Work." Bloomberg, https://tinyurl.com/y3waxx8g.

30 See Noah Smith (2013) "A blow to the Prescott theory of Labor," Monday, December 16, https://tinyurl.com/yynlfzj4.

Chapter 8

1 The quote can be found in Keynes's collected works, volume VI, p. 197.

2 For example, in Canada all bank accounts are covered up to a maximum of $100,000 per account.

3 In Canada, the office responsible for supervising all financial institutions (not just banks) is the Office of the Superintendent of Financial Institutions, or OSFI.

4 Details of bank regulation get messy quickly. Besides "Tier 1" capital there is also "Tier 2" capital, which is used to absorb losses in the event of liquidation. The 7 percent cited in the text refers to "Common Equity Tier 1" (CET1) which is a ratio of Tier 1 capital to "risk-weighted" assets, and includes a mandatory "capital conservation buffer." In addition to this, Basel III introduced a "discretionary counter-cyclical buffer." This allows national regulators to require up to an additional 2.5 percent of capital during periods of high credit growth.

5 Source: US Census Bureau (1975) "Historical Statistics of the United States."

6 Friedman and Schwartz (1963) "A Monetary History of the United States, 1867–1960" Princeton University Press.
7 The Financial Crisis Inquiry Commission (FCIC) appointed by the US Senate to investigate the causes, said this (2011: xvii): "More than 30 years of deregulation and reliance on self-regulation by financial institutions ... had stripped away key safeguards, which could have helped avoid catastrophe."
8 Mortgages were gathered, cut into tranches, diced into bundles, and sold off as investment vehicles around the globe. Originally only federally insured mortgages were securitized, but after the terms and conditions of mortgages were deregulated, these bundles began to include noninsured mortgages and sub-prime mortgages, originating with agents working on commission who had no vested interest in the credit-worthiness of the borrower. Holders of these assets thought they were protected against default by taking out insurance known as credit default swaps.
9 Akerlof and Shiller (2009) argued the main problem was financial innovation, and in particular, the natural evolution of economic institutions to avoid existing regulations.
10 "Add up guarantees and lending limits, and the Fed had committed $7.77 trillion as of March 2009 to rescuing the financial system, more than half the value of everything produced in the U.S. that year" (Ivry, Keoun, and Kuntz 2011).
11 And this affects its role as a medium of exchange which puts its role as a trusted store of value into question, which further affects its role as an acceptable medium of exchange.
12 Nouriel Roubini (2018) points out that nearly all cryptocurrency transactions occur on centralized exchanges that are regularly hacked, that wealth in the crypto universe is even more concentrated than it is in North Korea, and that most crypto mining occurs in "bastions of democracy" such as Russia, Georgia, and China. The promise of "blockchain" was a ruse to separate retail investors from their hard-earned real money.
13 Blockchain is a transaction ledger that maintains identical copies across each member computer within a network. The fact that the ledger is distributed across each part of the network helps to facilitate the security of the blockchain. The basic advantages of blockchain technology are decentralization, immutability, security, and transparency, which allows for verification of data without having to be dependent upon third parties.
14 However, there is one exception: in a financial crash knowing the rate of interest does not tell us everything we need to know about the ease of borrowing money. In a crash, the central bank can reduce interest rates, but banks will not loan—perhaps because of elevated uncertainty, or perhaps because they are themselves insolvent—creating an excess demand for loanable funds.
15 The validity of this is disputed by some economists, even by some post-Keynesian economists. In particular, Thomas Palley (2015) argues that it is not justified.
16 Interestingly, Bruno Iksil's losses were not the most costly losses on record caused by a single rogue trader. That prize goes to Jerome Kerviel, a trader at Societe Generale, who in 2008 managed to lose $7.2 billion.

17 Clearly, this is just the tiniest tip of the iceberg. Whole books have been written on this subject. Wikipedia has a very informative page entitled "Goldman Sachs controversies," which is well worth exploring. Matt Taibbi has written extensively for Rolling Stone on bank scandals, and his essays are engrossing. He famously compared Goldman Sachs to "a great vampire squid wrapped around the face of humanity" (Taibbi 2010).

18 The report was entitled "The 'Heads I Win, Tails You Lose' Bank Bonus Culture."

19 See Goldstein (2018) and Bathke (2017).

20 To avoid another bankruptcy like Lehman Brothers, the Federal Reserve and the US Treasury engineered a number of takeovers of failing companies by bigger more solvent companies. Thus, the stated fines on Bank of America include fines they "inherited" on Countrywide and Merrill Lynch. The fines on Bear Stearns include fines on Washington Mutual, and the fines on Wells Fargo include fines on Wachovia.

21 If we also include fines imposed by European regulators the total rises to $321 billion. This is according to The Boston Consulting Group's 2017 publication "Global Risk 2017: Staying the Course in Banking." https://tinyurl.com/ybkxvrdq.

22 A great source of information on who was prosecuted, when it occurred, and the sentence they received can be found at the Office of the Special Inspector General for the Troubled Asset Relief Program. On their website they have a tab labeled "crimes and fines database." See https://www.sigtarp.gov/Pages/wd9er7g.aspx.

23 In some accounts it is said that "one senior Wall Street executive" went to jail. That person is Kareem Serageldin, a senior trader at Credit Suisse. He was given a 30-month sentence for inflating the value of mortgage bonds in his trading portfolio, allowing them to appear more valuable than they really were. However, Credit Suisse is hardly a Wall Street icon, and a senior trader is not a CEO.

24 In 2006, Countrywide financed nearly $500 billion in subprime mortgage loans. Mozilo was charged with fraud and insider trading. In 2010, he paid $67.5 million to settle with the SEC on insider trading charges. In 2016, the DOJ dropped charges of mortgage fraud. See the Marketplace piece, "You asked, we answered: Why didn't any Wall Street CEOs go to jail after the financial crisis?" https://tinyurl.com/y34c4vn4.

25 This occurred since the UK government was the majority shareholder in RBS (the Royal Bank of Scotland) after the bailouts needed because of the subprime crisis. See the Libor scandal in Appendix 1.

26 The case has not been heard at the time of writing. However, it is not looking good for Winterkorn. He received a memo in 2014 detailing the cheating, and approved €23m on a "useless" software update designed to continue to obscure the cheating. See https://tinyurl.com/y5jddltd.

27 See Appendix 1 for the discussion of the Libor scandal and the role played by Robert Diamond (CEO of RBS). See William Cohan (2015) for details about how a top JPMorgan Chase banker, Alayne Fleischmann, alerted her bosses that the bank was selling toxic assets. After sharing her concerns with her boss in a thirteen-page letter, Fleischmann was marginalized and then fired.

28 See Joshua Holland (2013).

29 Investment banks engage in riskier activities like stock picking and derivatives trading, while commercial banks focus on low-risk lending like home mortgages and small business loans. Glass–Steagall kept the two activities separate to protect the viability of commercial banks.

30 Wikipedia has a very useful list of banks acquired or bankrupted during the Great Recession. See https://tinyurl.com/hhzjbkf. In the United States the list includes Bear Sterns and Washington Mutual (both acquired by JPMorgan Chase), Countrywide Financial and Merrill Lynch (both acquired by Bank of America). Worldwide, the list is quite extensive, totaling eighty-six between 2007 and 2018.

31 See Cohan (2015) and Chittum (2014). As of June 2020, the memo could be downloaded from the US Department of Justice website, https://tinyurl.com/y7gdjdgb.

32 Breuer was the Assistant Attorney General for the Criminal Division of the Department of Justice.

33 Breuer articulated this view in more detail on the PBS TV show, "Frontline." See https://tinyurl.com/y7dpm4af.

34 The term "cultural capital" comes from Simon Johnson (2009).

35 Holder came from the white-shoe DC law firm Covington & Burling, which represented half of the top ten mortgage servicers. He brought along his Covington colleague Lanny Breuer as enforcement chief, and Breuer would play a key role in the lack of indictments of major executives. See Chittum (2014).

36 This was said in an interview with Joshua Holland (2013).

37 The data are from the Federal Reserve Bank of St. Louis and are computed from two data series. Total corporate profits before tax (without IVA and CCAdj) were series "A053RC1Q027SBEA." Nonfinancial corporate profits before tax (without IVA and CCAdj) were series "A464RC1Q027SBEA." I subtracted nonfinancial profits from total profits to obtain financial profits.

38 See Binyamin Appelbaum (2014) "When She Talks, Banks Shudder," *New York Times*, August 9, https://tinyurl.com/ycexq822.

39 See Binyamin Appelbaum (2014) and also Admati (2018).

40 See Admati (2018).

41 More recently, Boston University economist Larry Kotlikoff has argued for "limited purpose banking." It's basically the same idea.

42 See Matthew Klein (2013) for an interesting discussion.

43 Using data from the Federal Reserve Bank of St. Louis, it is possible to calculate the implicit subsidy given to "depository institutions" from interest payments on excess reserves that were higher than the federal reserve rate itself. Between 2009 and 2013, the excess interest payments amounted to $827 billion.

44 See the *Guardian* article by Dominic Rushe (2011), https://tinyurl.com/y9uuwdvf.

45 See Rupert Jones, "The end of a scandal: banks near a final release from their PPI liabilities." The Guardian, August 24, 2019, https://tinyurl.com/yxgp237g.

46 See Peter Schroeder (2012) "NY Regulator: British Bank Helped Iran Evade Sanctions, Hide Billions," *The Hill*, June 8, https://tinyurl.com/ya2mosgq.

47 See Elstein (2019) for more details.

48 In the aftermath of the scandal, Britain's primary financial regulator, the Financial Conduct Authority (FCA), shifted supervision of Libor from the British Bankers' Association to a new entity, the ICE Benchmark Administration (IBA), an independent UK subsidiary of the private US-based exchange operator Intercontinental Exchange, or ICE.

49 The five currencies were the US dollar, the Euro, the British pound, the Japanese yen, and the Swiss franc. See the explainer by James McBride (2016).

50 This estimate is contained in the article by McBride (2016). The source is an investment bank's (Keefe, Bruyette, and Woods) industry update, https://tinyurl.com/7zfvbno.

51 In 2008 the CEO of Barclays, Robert Diamond, instructed his subordinates by email to make a false Libor submission to make the bank seem healthier than it really was. This fact was told by a senior Barclays executive to a parliamentary hearing, and reported by Mark Scott in the *New York Times*. See Scott (2012).

52 Taibbi (2012) is an excellent reference for this story. Also useful is Stempel (2013), Walsh (2014), and Roberts (2015).

53 See Sebastian Chrispin (2015) "Forex Scandal: How to rig the market." May 20, BBC News, https://tinyurl.com/yb237ej8.

54 See Dan Mangan (2019).

55 See Son and Mangan (2018).

56 See "Attorney General Shapiro Announces $575 Million 50-State Settlement with Wells Fargo Bank for Opening Unauthorized Accounts and Charging Consumers for Unnecessary Auto Insurance, Mortgage Fees." Attorney General, Commonwealth of Pennsylvania, https://tinyurl.com/yboqze6t.

57 See Oliver Bullough (2019), George Monbiot (2020), and Tom Burgis (2020).

Chapter 9

1 Attribution of this quote is problematic. It has been attributed to baseball player and manager, Yogi Berra, to Albert Einstein, and to physicist Richard Feynman.

2 This conclusion is only true for floating exchange rates. Economists refer to two types of exchange rate regimes: fixed and floating. A floating exchange rate is one determined by market forces, in particular, the demand and supply for the currency. A fixed exchange rate is one where the central bank intervenes to ensure that currency markets clear at the preannounced exchange rate. Most countries adopted floating exchange rates in the late 1970s. Monetary policy is ineffective in a fixed exchange rate regime with perfect capital mobility. The necessity to keep the exchange rate at the preannounced level exactly offsets any central bank–induced changes in the money supply (and hence interest rates).

3 The actual target, or the center of the range, is 2 percent for the UK, the United States, Canada, Sweden, and New Zealand. Norway aims for 2.5 percent with a permissible range of 1.5–3.5 percent.

4 It is left to readers to convince themselves that inflation targeting also stabilizes output when there is a positive AD shock.

5   Source: Federal Reserve Bank of Saint Louis. The data are weekly and seasonally unadjusted.
6   The average annual rate of growth of the monetary base was 53 percent over the four-year period. In contrast, the average annual rate of growth of M2 was just 6.4 percent.
7   All data come from the Federal Reserve Bank of St. Louis.
8   Usually, the central bank's policy interest rate lies within the "operating band." Figure 9.6 shows a truly unusual situation where—in the United States—it lay below the lower bound.
9   For example, Georget (2019) suggests that QE increased wealth inequality in the United States by at least 25 percent.
10 That figure refers to Canadian data. See Fortin (2020). The US average interest rate reduction is slightly lower.
11 See Rogoff (2017) and Rogoff (2020). Another interesting piece is Altavilla et al. (2019).
12 As described in the appendix to Chapter 8, criminal elements are already able to launder their money through the banking system easily enough, so it is unclear whether they would be inconvenienced by abandoning cash.
13 Unless we reverse the process and reduce inflation at a temporary cost of less output and employment, which is kind of beside the point.
14 See Nick Rowe (2013).
15 Mario Seccareccia and Marc Lavoie were the prime movers in organizing a letter in support of the dual mandate, signed by over sixty economists, and sent to the Canadian Minister of Finance in 2018.
16 For example, between 1946 and 1975 Canada's unemployment rate averaged 4.7 percent. By contrast, average unemployment was 9.5 percent in the 1980s and 1990s. Although after 2000 the annual national unemployment rate declined to a low point of 5.8 percent in 2018, it was still high compared to a longer-term historical perspective, especially given the favorable demographic trends that have occurred. As far as growth is concerned, GDP growth per capita has slowed considerably during twenty-five years of inflation targeting: averaging 1.4 percent per year, a third less than in the quarter-century before targeting.
17 Estimating the output gap is problematic. There is very little theory to guide estimation of potential output. Currently methods involve using statistical filters that essentially call a projection of past average output levels "potential output." A deep lingering recession will cause estimates of potential output to drop along with actual output. These filter-based estimation techniques for estimating potential output have raised severe criticism. (For example, see Coibion et al. (2018) and Hamilton (2018).) And it turns out the resulting estimates of potential output do not actually add much, if anything, to the accuracy of inflation forecasts. (This finding is true for Canada, the United States, and the OECD countries in general. See Turner (2016) and Osberg (2020: 122) for more references.)
18 Clearly, for policy purposes the width of the unemployment rate band is the crucial issue—one US study has put it at roughly 3.2 percentage points (see Peach, Rich, and Cororaton, 2011). Osberg (2020) points out that even if the full employment level of unemployment could be known to one decimal place, there is still a range of uncertainty of 0.09 percentage points. (Suppose

U^* is 4.5 percent, then the band of uncertainty ranges from 4.45 percent to 4.54 percent.) He points out that "although this is the smallest unemployment rate band one might think of, being at the top or the bottom of that 0.09 percentage point unemployment rate range has non-trivial consequences. In Canada in 2017, this range corresponds to roughly 17.7 thousand jobs, CAN$4.34 billion in GDP and additional tax revenue of CAN$1.3 billion."

19 This is after adjusting for differences in the way unemployment is measured in the two countries.

20 See https://www.rbnz.govt.nz/monetary-policy/policy-targets-agreements/ pta2018.

21 Even more generally, since many climate damaging activities (notably in the energy and agricultural sectors) continue to be incentivized with perverse government subsidies, most financial assets are mispriced to a greater or lesser extent. This poses major challenges for central banks seeking to encourage efficient capital allocation.

Chapter 10

1 Phillips examined inflation in nominal wages rather than prices. For our purposes, the distinction is not important because these two measures of inflation usually move together.

2 In one New Classical approach, unexpected price changes shift labor demand but not labor supply because of an *asymmetry of information requirements* between firms and workers. Firms only need to know their *own product price* in order to put a value on labor's marginal product. Since all firms know this, when we aggregate over all firms, we find that the demand for labor depends on the nominal wage relative to *actual prices*. On the other hand, workers need to know the aggregate price level in order to evaluate the purchasing power of the offered nominal wage, which is not known so workers must form expectations about it. Hence, if the aggregate price level goes up, but the expected aggregate price level does not, the labor supply curve will not shift.

3 All the books authored and coauthored by Gregory Mankiw use this distinction. This is true both for his first year principles books and his intermediate theory books. And it is true for all the national editions of these books. (There's a lot of them!) In addition, the macroeconomics principles book by Stevenson and Wolfers (2020) also has the proper distinction between frictional and structural unemployment. All the rest use the muddled and fuzzy distinction.

4 Another reason to pay above-market wages is to ensure that the firm's better workers don't leave. Workers know better than their employers what their alternative job prospects are. A firm that pays as little as possible risks losing its better workers and retaining more of its lower-quality workers—the ones who wouldn't be able to find better work elsewhere. Furthermore, such firms are likely to have high quit rates and higher costs associated with hiring and training new workers. So paying above-market wages not only increases the average quality of the firm's workers, it also reduces the costs associated with hiring and training new workers.

5 The decision to cut off the data in 2009 is mainly practical—including all the more recent data would make the diagram a tangled mess. Or, if you prefer, even more of a tangled mess!

6 Once the SRPC shifts down, the real money supply begins to increase (since money growth is now greater than inflation), interest rates fall, and the recovery begins.

7 Of course, technically the losses of the debtors are exactly offset by the gains of creditors. But since debtors are likely to have a higher marginal propensity to spend than creditors, aggregate demand for goods will fall.

8 For example, suppose both nominal interest rates and expected deflation are zero, implying the real rate of interest is zero. If people now expect deflation of 2 percent, the real rate of interest increases from zero to 2 percent.

9 This was proposed by Cagan in his 1956 study on hyperinflation and the demand for money.

10 For example, Fortin (2003a) uses this nomenclature.

11 The intermediate textbook by Mankiw and Scarth (2020) is one of the very few that even mentions the possibility of a tail on the LRPC. Our explanation, using temporal dispersion, follows along the lines developed in that text.

12 There is another argument for a tail, known as the "Eckstein–Brinner effect." This suggests that workers tend to ignore inflation when it increases from zero to a small positive value. The cost to ignoring inflation in this context is negligible, making their ignorance "near rational." The key implication is that wages will be set lower relative to prices when inflation is low than they would be when inflation is zero. As a result, there will be a small one-time decline in real wages, permitting an increase in employment and corresponding decrease in unemployment.

13 This is paraphrased from page 331 of Leijonhufvud (1973b).

14 Galbraith notes that the aggregate labor supply function is inappropriate because: first, workers care about relative wages as well as real wages; and second, because the dependence of prices and wages means that workers cannot actually negotiate for their own real wages.

15 Spitz (1989) found little evidence that worker effort is affected by wage differentials when examining a chain of unionized supermarkets in California. Huang et al. (1998) examine whether efficiency wages are paid in US manufacturing. They note that while productivity does respond to wage premia, the effect is very weak. Only 12 percent of the "productivity effect" is associated with wage premia.

16 Mankiw's introductory textbook continues to claim that a 10 percent increase in the minimum wage would decrease employment by 3 percent. Krueger (2001) tracks down this estimate to a survey paper published in 1982. The authors of this survey revised down their estimates the following year. See Krueger (2001) for a discussion.

17 Manning (2003) argues that the dynamic monopsony model would make a better starting point than the competitive model, even for markets where there are many small firms.

18 This is the "segmented labor market hypothesis" (Wilkinson, 1984). Some authors argue that the effect of unions on employment is positive (e.g., Freeman and Medoff (1984) or McDonald and Solow (1985)).

19 In the United States, the Congressional Budget Office publishes estimates of NAIRU, allowing us to identify years when actual unemployment rate was equal to it. Estimates of job vacancies are available from the Bureau of Labor Statistics, and are situated in its JOLTS database. Since these estimates begin in 2000, the only year available to use was 2005, when the job vacancy rate (job openings divided by the labor force) was equal to 2.75 percent. In Canada, Osberg and Lin (2000) use this same methodology to estimate the frictional component at just over 2 percent.

20 McDonald's actual estimate of the full employment level of unemployment was 2.5 percent. Zero long-term unemployment was a necessary but not sufficient condition for full employment.

21 Fortin assumed the NRU was 8.2 percent in 1989 and declined gradually to 6.6 percent in 2000. This implies that the sum of the unemployment gaps cumulated to 19.4 percentage points. Given a SRPC slope of one-half, inflation should have declined by 9.7 percentage points.

22 This "missing deflation puzzle" arose again in many countries after the Great Recession of 2008. Lindé and Trabant (2019) suggest the puzzle can be resolved with a sufficiently convex SRPC. Incidentally, Mankiw and Scarth (2020) make an argument that the missing deflation puzzle can be explained by a depreciating exchange rate, pushing up prices of imported intermediate inputs. While this explanation works for the early 1990s it fails in the early 2000s when Canada's exchange rate went through a long period of appreciation from 2001 to 2012.

23 There are many possible shift factors including demographics, education levels, union coverage, minimum wages, and unemployment insurance benefits. But no combination of influences can explain the gyrations we see. Indeed, their movements suggest that the NRU should have peaked in the 1980s, and then declined back to its value in the 1960s.

24 See, for example, Kalecki (1937).

25 In technical terms, both the first and second derivative of L with respect to w are positive. This is easily shown. Let $\phi = (I+A)/(1-\alpha)$. Then we can write $L = \phi(a-w)^{-1}$. Now the first derivative is: $\partial L / \partial w = (-1)(-1)\phi(a-w)^{-2} > 0$. The second derivative equals $(-2)(-1)\phi(a-w)^{-3} > 0$.

26 I first saw this depiction in Seccareccia (2004). Note that while he correctly identifies both the first and second derivatives of the function as positive, in his article the labor demand curve is incorrectly drawn as concave from below.

27 Myatt (1986) shows how these models can provide Kaleckian micro-underpinnings to a Phillips curve construct that does not involve an NRU.

28 Farmer is quite prolific and actively promotes his ideas using books, speeches, and articles. He has a website (https://www.rogerfarmer.com/) that provides links to his work. Some of his books are aimed at academic audiences, some for the general reader. A good place to begin would be the book *How the Economy Works* written in 2010.

29 One can download Lipsey's curriculum vitae from his homepage. He has recently had three articles published in the *Journal of Evolutionary Economics*. These occurred in 2011, 2012, and 2018.

30 The JG is associated with MMTs such as Randall Wray, Stephanie Kelton, Warren Mosler, Bill Mitchell, and Pavlina Tcherneva. Recently, it was also

endorsed by Mariana Mazzucato and Robert Skidelsky. See the next footnote for several references.

31 The Levy Economics Institute has published several research reports on the JG, for example, Pavlina Tcherneva (2018) and Wray (2018) among others. In addition, the Centre on Budget and Policy Priorities commissioned a paper by Paul, Darity and Hamilton (2018). Bill Mitchell (2013) did a detailed analysis of the resource costs required for a JG.

32 See Lowrey (2018) and the references contained therein.

Postscript

1 See Samuel (2020) for a discussion of both ongoing and past basic income experiments.

2 See Matthews (2020).

3 The money was spent on food (40 percent), merchandise (24 percent), utilities (12 percent), and car repairs (9 percent). See Samuel (2020).

REFERENCES

Ackerman, F. (2002) "Still Dead after All These Years: Interpreting the Failure of General Equilibrium Theory," *Journal of Economic Methodology*, 9(2): 119–39.

Admati, A. (2018) "Ten Years after the Financial Crisis (What Have We Learned?)," June 20 presentation to the Stanford Institute of Economic Policy Research. Posted on YouTube, https://tinyurl.com/y9m2ud5f.

Admati, A., and M. Hellwig (2013) *The Bankers' New Clothes: What's Wrong with Banking and What to Do about It*. Princeton, NJ: Princeton University Press.

Aghion, P., and P. Howitt (1997) *Endogenous Growth Theory*. Cambridge, MA: MIT Press.

Akerlof, G., and P. Romer (1994) "Looting: The Economic Underworld of Bankruptcy for Profit." *NBER Working Paper No. R1869*, https://ssrn.com/abstract=227162. Accessed May 17, 2022.

Akerlof, G., and R. Shiller (2009) *Animal Spirits: How Human Psychology Drives the Economy and Why It Matters for Global Capitalism*. Princeton, NJ: Princeton University Press.

Alesina, A., and S. Ardagna (2010) "Large Changes in Fiscal Policy: Taxes versus Spending," *Tax Policy and the Economy*, Edited by J. Brown, *Volume 24*, National Bureau of Economic Research, University of Chicago Press, 35–68.

Alesina, A., C. Favero, and F. Giavazzi (2019) *Austerity: When It Works and When It Doesn't*. Princeton, NJ: Princeton University Press.

Altavilla, C., L. Burlon, M. Giannetti, and S. Holton (2019) "Is There a Zero Lower Bound? The Effects of Negative Policy Rates on Banks and Firms," The European Central Bank, Working Paper Series, No. 2289, June.

Alvaredo, F., A. Atkinson, T. Piketty, and E. Saez (2013) "The Top 1 Percent in International and Historical Perspective," *Journal of Economic Perspectives*, 27(3): 3–30.

Ando, A., and F. Modigliani (1963) "The 'Life-Cycle' Hypothesis of Saving: Aggregate Implications and Tests," *American Economic Review*, 53(1): 55–84.

Angell, M. (2004) *The Truth about Drug Companies: How They Deceive Us and What to Do about It*. New York: Random House.

Appelbaum, B. (2014) "When She Talks, Banks Shudder," *New York Times*, August 9, https://tinyurl.com/ycexq822. Accessed May 17, 2022.

Arcand, J., E. Berkes, and U. Panizza (2015) "Too Much Finance?" *Journal of Economic Growth*, 20(2): 105–48.

Attanasio, O., P. Levell, H. Low, and V. Marcos (2018) "Aggregating Labour Supply Elasticities: The Importance of Heterogeneity." VOX, CEPR Policy Portal, https://tinyurl.com/yx9udnj7. Accessed May 17, 2022.

Austin, B., E. Glaeser, and L. Summers (2018) "Jobs for the Heartland: Place-Based Policies in 21st Century America," *Brookings Papers on Economic Activity*, Spring: 151–255.

Baker, D. (2014) "Capital in the 21 Century: Still Mired in the 19th," *Huffington Post*, May, https://tinyurl.com/kc44zu4. Accessed May 17, 2022.

Baker, D. (2016) *Rigged: How Globalization and the Rules of the Modern Economy Were Structured to Make the Rich Richer.* Washington, DC: Center for Economic and Policy Research.

Baker, D. (2019) "Trillion Dollar Wall Street Bailouts, Bernie Sanders, and the Washington Post." Centre for Economic and Policy Research, March 19, https://tinyurl.com/4s7v346k.

Bank for International Settlements (2013) "83rd BIS Annual Report," http://www.bis.org/publ/arpdf/ar2013e.htm. Accessed May 17, 2022.

Barro, R. (1974) "Are Government Bonds Net Wealth?" *Journal of Political Economy*, 82(6): 1095–117.

Bathke, B. (2017) "Financial Crisis Bank Fines Hit Record 10 Years after Market Collapse," *Deutsche Welle (DW)*, August 10, https://tinyurl.com/yatkdywn. Accessed May 17, 2022.

Baumol, W., A. Blinder, and J. Solow (2020) *Microeconomics: Principles and Policy*, 14th ed. Boston: Cengage Learning.

Becker, G., and G. N. Becker (1997) *The Economics of Life.* New York: McGraw Hill.

Bell (Kelton), S. (1998) "Can Taxes and Bonds Finance Government Spending?" Levy Economics Institute, Working Paper No. 244, www.levyinstitute.org/pubs/wp244.pdf. Accessed May 17, 2022.

Benes, J., and M. Kumhof (2012) "The Chicago Plan Revisited." *IMF Working Paper*, August, https://www.imf.org/external/pubs/ft/wp/2012/wp12202.pdf. Accessed May 17, 2022.

Berg, A., J. Ostry, and J. Zettelmeyer (2012) "What Makes Growth Sustained?," *Journal of Development Economics*, 98(2): 149–66.

Beveridge, W. (1944) *Full Employment in a Free Society.* London: Routledge.

Black, W. (2005) *The Best Way to Rob a Bank Is to Own One: How Corporate Executives and Politicians Looted the S&L Industry.* Austin: University of Texas Press.

Black, W. (2010) "Why Regulators Must Fight 'Control Fraud' like Public Health Specialists," *SSRN Electronic Journal.* 10.2139/ssrn.1536527, https://tinyurl.com/yacjd262. Accessed May 17, 2022.

Blanchard, O. (2012) "Are We Underestimating Short-Term Fiscal Multipliers?" in *World Economic Outlook*, "Coping with High Debt and Sluggish Growth." October, IMF: 41–3.

Blanchard, O. (2019) "Public Debt and Low Interest Rates," *American Economic Review*, 109(4): 1197–1229.

Blanchard, O., and G. Jordi (2007) "Real Wage Rigidities and the New Keynesian Model," *Journal of Money, Credit and Banking*, 39(1): 35–65.

Blanchard, O., and L. Summers (1988) "Beyond the Natural Rate Hypothesis," *American Economic Review Papers and Proceedings*, 78(2): 182–7.

Blanchard, O., G. Dell'Ariccia, and P. Mauro (2010) "Rethinking Macro Policy," VoxEU.org, February 16, https://voxeu.org/article/rethinking-macro-policy.

Blanchard, O., D. Romer, and J. Stiglitz (2012) *In the Wake of the Crisis: Leading Economists Reassess Economic Policy.* Cambridge, MA: MIT Press.

Blinder, Alan S. (2010) "Quantitative Easing: Entrance and Exit Strategies," *Federal Reserve Bank of St. Louis Review*, 92(6): 465–79.

Blyth, M. (2013) *Austerity: The History of a Dangerous Idea.* Oxford: Oxford University Press.

Bobkoff, D. (2016) "What Just Happened to Apple, Explained," *Business Insider*, August 30, https://www.businessinsider.com/what-just-happened-to-apple-explained-2016-8.

Brulle, R. (2013) "Institutionalizing Delay: Foundation Funding and the Creation of U.S. Climate Change Counter-Movement Organizations," *Climatic Change*, 122(4): 681–94.

Bubonya, M., D. Cobb-Clark, and M. Wooden (2014) "A Family Affair: Job Loss and the Mental Health of Spouses and Adolescents." *IZA Discussion Paper 8588, IZA – Institute of Labor Economics*.

Buell, S. (2016) *Capital Offenses: Business Crime and Punishment in America's Corporate Age*. New York: W. W. Norton.

Buiter, W. H. (2009) "The Unfortunate Uselessness of Most 'State of the Art' Academic Monetary Economics," http://voxeu.org/article/macroeconomics-crisis-irrelevance.

Bullough, O. (2019) "How Britain Can Help You Get Away with Stealing Millions: A Five-Step Guide," *The Guardian*, July 5, https://tinyurl.com/y5e8e7nz.

Burgis, T. (2020) *Kleptopia: How Dirty Money Is Conquering the World*. London: Harper.

Campbell, J., and R. Shiller (1987) "Cointegration and Tests of Present-Value Models," *Journal of Political Economy*, 97(5): 1062–88.

Canada's Office of the Parliamentary Budget Officer (2019) "Closing the Gap: Carbon Pricing for the Paris Target," June 13, https://tinyurl.com/y4otvah6.

Carbon Pricing Leadership Coalition (2017) "Report of the High-Level Commission on Carbon Prices, Executive Summary," May 29, https://tinyurl.com/y5e8saqu.

Cavallo, A., and R. Rigobon (2016) "The Billion Prices Project: Using Online Prices for Measurement and Research," *Journal of Economic Perspectives*, 30(2): 151–78.

Chari, V., and P. Kehoe (2009) "Confronting Models of Financial Frictions with the Data." *Society for Economic Dynamics*, Meeting Papers, https://tinyurl.com/ycgao97z.

Chittum, R. (2014) "Going Easy on Eric Holder's Wal Street Inaction," September 26, *Columbia Journalism Review*, https://tinyurl.com/yclgz2vs.

Cingano, F. (2014) "Trends in Income Inequality and Its Impact on Economic Growth," *OECD Working Paper*, December, https://tinyurl.com/qfgcmfs.

Clark, A., P. Frijters, and M. Shields (2008) "Relative Income, Happiness and Utility: An Explanation for the Easterlin Paradox and Other Puzzles," *Journal of Economic Literature*, 46(1): 95–144.

Cochrane, J. (2009) "Fiscal Stimulus, Fiscal Inflation, or Fiscal Fallacies?" University of Chicago, Booth School of Business, version 2.5, February 27, https://tinyurl.com/y2yy96g2.

Cohan, W. (2015) "How Wall Street's Bankers Stayed Out of Jail," *The Atlantic*, September Issue, https://tinyurl.com/ycesh4ry.

Coibion, O., Y. Gorodnichenko, and M. Ulate (2018) "The Cyclical Sensitivity in Estimates of Potential Output," *Brookings Papers on Economic Activity* (Fall): 343–411.

Colangelo, A., and R. Inklaar (2010) "Banking Sector Output Measurement in the Euro Area—A Modified Approach," *ECB Working Paper Series*, No. 1204.

Colciago, A., A. Samarina, and J. de Haan (2019) "Central Bank Policies and Income and Wealth Inequality: A Survey," *Journal of Economic Surveys*, March, https://tinyurl.com/yy7fbulj.

Dabla-Norris, E., K. Kochhar, N. Suphasphiphat, F. Ricka, and E. Tsounta (2015) "Causes and Consequences of Income Inequality: A Global Perspective." IMF Staff Discussion Note, https://tinyurl.com/2p8aha89.

Darity, W., Jr. (1999) "Who Loses from Unemployment," *Journal of Economic Issues*, 33(2): 491–96.

De Bondt, W., and R. Thaler (1985) "Does the Stock Market Overreact?" *Journal of Finance*, 40(3): 793–805.

Debortoli, Davide, Jinill Kim, Jesper Lindé, and Ricardo Nunes (2017) "Designing a Simple Loss Function for Central Banks: Does a Dual Mandate Make Sense?," *IMF Research Department, Working Paper* WP/17/163, July 2017.

DeLong, B. (2011) "Is Economics a Discipline?" https://tinyurl.com/yxrkxh9s.

Den Haan, W. (2011) "Why Do We Need a Financial Sector," October 24, *VOX CEPR Policy Portal*, https://tinyurl.com/ycczfoxf.

Diener, E., and M. Seligman (2004) "Beyond Money: Toward an Economy of Wellbeing," *Psychological Science in the Public Interest*, 5: 1–31.

Dorman, P. (2012) "The Problem with Microfoundations: Bad Micro." https://tinyurl.com/2xp75xs6. Accessed May 14, 2022.

Easterlin, R. (1974) "Does Economic Growth Improve the Human Lot? Some Empirical Evidence," in *Nations and Households in Economic Growth: Essays in Honor of Moses Abramovitz*, edited by Paul A. David and Melvin W. Reder, New York: Academic Press, 98–125.

Easterly, W. (2007) "Inequality Does Cause Underdevelopment: Insights from a New Instrument," *Journal of Development Economics*, 84(2): 755–76.

Eberstadt, N. (2016) *Men without Work: America's Invisible Crisis*. Pennsylvania: Templeton Press.

Edwards, J. (2019) "Unemployment Is Only Low because involuntary Part-Time Work Is High," *Business Insider*, https://tinyurl.com/j6pa2cdy. Accessed May 14, 2022.

Ehrlich, P. (1968) *The Population Bomb*. New York: Ballantine Books.

Elstein, A. (2019) "Fourth Time's a Charm: Standard Chartered Fined Again for Hiding Illegal Transactions." *Crain's New York*, April 9, https://tinyurl.com/y6u3bakg.

Fama, E. (1965) "Random Walks in Stock Market Prices," *Financial Analysts Journal*, 21(5): 55–9.

Farmer, R. (2009) "Stabilities and Instabilities in the Macroeconomy," Vox CEPR Policy Portal, November 21, https://tinyurl.com/ya5j2u45.

Farmer, R. (2010) *Expectations, Employment and Prices*. Oxford: Oxford University Press.

Farmer, R. (2010) *How the Economy Works: Confidence, Crashes, and Self-Fulfilling Prophecies*. Oxford: Oxford University Press.

Farmer, R. (2013) "The Natural Rate Hypothesis: An Idea Past Its Sell-by Date." *The National Bureau of Economic Research, Working Paper* #19267.

Felipe, J., and J. McCombie (2013) *The Aggregate Production Function and the Measurement of Technical Change: Not Even Wrong*, Cheltenham: Edward Elgar.

Felkerson, J. (2011) "$29,000,000,000,000: A Detailed Look at the Fed's Bailout by Funding Facility and Recipient," *Levy Economics Institute*, Working Paper No. 698, http://www.levyinstitute.org/pubs/wp_698.pdf.

Financial Crisis Inquiry Commission (2011) "Final Report of the National Commission on the Causes of the Financial and Economic Crisis in the United States." Washington, DC: Government.

Fisher, I. (1896) *Appreciation and Interest*. Ithaca, NY: Press of Andrus & Church.

Fisher, I. (1933) "The Debt-Deflation Theory of Great Depressions," *Econometrica*, 1(4): 337–57.

Flegal, K., M. Carroll, B. Kit, and C. Ogden (2012) "Prevalence of Obesity and Trends in the Distribution of Body Mass Index among US Adults, 1999–2010," *Journal of the American Medical Association*, 307: 491–7.

Forget, E. (2011) "The Town with No Poverty: The Health Effects of a Canadian Guaranteed Annual Income Field Experiment," *Canadian Public Policy*, 37(3): 283–305.

Forget, E. (2021) "It's Time to Transform Our Society with a Basic Income," Straight.com, February 19, https://tinyurl.com/yfk3nhx2.

Fortin, P. (2003a) "Can Monetary Policy Make a Difference for Economic Growth and Inequality?" *Canadian Public Policy*, 29, Supplement, S223–S232.

Fortin, P. (2003b) "The Bank of Canada and the Inflation-Unemployment Trade-Off" Bank of Canada Conference entitled "Macroeconomics, Monetary Policy and Financial Stability," https://www.bankofcanada.ca/wp-content/uplo ads/2010/09/inflation.pdf.

Fortin, P. (2020) "What Monetary Policy Framework in 2021?" Paper prepared for the Bank of Canada Conference "*The 2021 Renewal of the Monetary Policy Framework*" held online on August 26, 2020.

Fougére, D., F. Kramarz, and J. Pouget (2009) "Youth Unemployment and Crime in France," *Journal of the European Economic Association*, 7(5): 909–38.

Freeman, R. B. and J. L. Medoff (1984) *What Do Unions Do?* New York: Basic Books.

Frey, B., and A. Stutzer (2002) "What Can Economists Learn from Happiness Research?," *Journal of Economic Literature*, 40(2): 402–35.

Friedman, M. (1957) *The Permanent Income Hypothesis: A Theory of the Consumption Function*. Princeton, NJ: Princeton University Press.

Friedman, M. (1969) *The Optimum Quantity of Money*. London: Macmillan Press.

Friedman, M., and A. Schwartz (1963) *A Monetary History of the United States, 1867–1960*. Princeton, NJ: Princeton University Press.

Frydman, C., and R. Saks (2008) "Executive Compensation: A New View from a Long-Term Perspective, 1936–2005," NBER Working Paper, No. 14145.

Fullwiler, S., R. Grey, and N. Tankus (2019) "An MMT Response on What Causes Inflation" *The Financial Times*, March 1, https://tinyurl.com/y4e638r7.

Furceri, D., and P. Loungani (2016) "Opening Up to Inequity," *Finance & Development*, 53(1): 43–6.

Galbraith, J. (2014) "Kapital for the Twenty-First Century?" *Dissent Magazine*, Spring, https://tinyurl.com/h48nw25.

Galbraith, J. K. (1990) *A Short History of Financial Euphoria*. New York: Viking Penguin.

Galbraith, J. K. (1997) "Time to Ditch the NRU," *Journal of Economic Perspectives*, 11(1): 93–108.

Gans, J., and G. Shepherd (1994) "How Are the Might Fallen: Rejected Classic Articles by Leading Economists," *Journal of Economic Perspectives*, 8(1): 165–79.

Georget, M.-J. (2019) "Did Quantitative Easing Impact Wealth Inequality?" M.A. Thesis submitted to Uppsala University, https://tinyurl.com/y2mrahh9.

Godley, W. (2007) "The U.S. Economy: Is There a Way Out of the Woods?" *The Levy Institute*, November, https://tinyurl.com/y6nkhdvn.

Goldstein, S. (2018) "Here's the Staggering Amount Banks Have Been Fined since the Financial Crisis," *Marketwatch.com*, February 20, https://tinyurl.com/ycqvhdos.

Gomory, R., and W. Baumol (2001) *Global Trade and Conflicting National Interests*. Cambridge, MA: MIT Press.

Gordon, R. (2009) "Is Modern Macro or 1978-Era Macro More Relevant to the Understanding of the Current Economic Crisis?" *Northwestern University, NBER, Working Paper*, http://economics.weinberg.northwestern.edu/robert-gordon/researchPapers.php.

Greenlees, J., and R. McClelland (2008) "Addressing Misconceptions about the Consumer Price Index," *Monthly Labor Review*, August.

Greenspan, A. (2011) "How Dodd-Frank Fails to Meet the Test of Out Times," *Financial Times*, Wednesday, March 30, page 9.

Grossman, G., and A. Krueger (1995) "Economic Growth and the Environment," *Quarterly Journal of Economics*, 110(2): 353–77.

Grossman, S., and J. Stiglitz (1980) "On the Impossibility of Informationally Efficient Markets," *American Economic Review* (70): 393–408.

Hail, S. (2017) "Explainer: What Is Modern Monetary Theory?" https://tinyurl.com/yy3s8a9u.

Haldane, A. (2011) "Control Rights (and Wrongs)," http://www.bankofengland.co.uk/publications/speeches/2011/speech525.pdf.

Haldane, A., and V. Madouros (2011) "What Is the Contribution of the Financial Sector," *VOX CEPR Policy Portal*, November 22, https://tinyurl.com/bvhs2zl.

Hamilton, J. (2018) "Why You Should Never Use the Hodrick-Prescott Filter," *Review of Economics and Statistics*, 100(5): 831–43.

Hansen, J. (2012) "Why I Must Speak Out about Climate Change." Ted talk, https://tinyurl.com/y3lftxv6.

Hatton, T., and M. Thomas (2010) "Labour Market in the Interwar Period and Economic Recovery in the UK and USA," *Oxford Review of Economic Policy*, 26(3): 463–85.

Heilbroner, R. (1999) *The Worldly Philosophers: The Lives, Times and Ideas of the Great Economic Thinkers*, Updated 7th ed. New York: Simon and Schuster.

Helm, S., A. Pollitt, M. Barnett, M. Curran, and Z. Craig (2018) "Differentiating Environmental Concern in the Context of Psychological Adaption to Climate Change," *Global Environmental Change*, 48(January): 158–67.

Herndon, T., M. Ash, and R. Pollin (2013) "Does High Public Debt Consistently Stifle Economic Growth? A Critique of Reinhart and Rogoff," *Political Economy Research Institute, Working Paper #322*.

Hickel, J. (2018) "The Noble Prize for Climate Catastrophe," *Foreign Policy*, December 6, https://tinyurl.com/ycx4vppx.

Hill, R., and T. Myatt (2010) *The Economics Anti-Textbook: A Critical Thinkers Guide to Microeconomics*. London: Zed Books.

Hill, R., and T. Myatt (2021) *The Microeconomics Anti-Textbook: A Critical Thinker's Guide*. London: Bloomsbury Press.

Holland, J. (2013) "Hundreds of Wall Street Execs Went to Prison during the Last Fraud-Fueled Bank Crisis," September 17, *BillMoyers.com*, https://tinyurl.com/ydz8qolt.

Homer-Dixon, T. (2015) "Paris Plan Is Impressive—but Why Peddle Fantasies with Unreachable Targets?" *The Globe and Mail*, December 14, https://tinyurl.com/y7nzpsvf.

Huang, T., A. Hallam, P. Orazem, and E. Paterno (1998) "Empirical Tests of Efficiency Wage Models," *Economica*, 65(257): 125–43.

IPCC (2018) "Global Warming of 1.5° C," October, https://www.ipcc.ch/sr15/.

Ivry, B., B. Keoun, and P. Kuntz (2011) "Secret Fed Loans Gave Banks $13 Billion Undisclosed to Congress," *Bloomberg Markets Magazine*, November 27, https://tinyurl.com/y6c5bd2w.

Ivry, B., B. Keoun, and P. Kuntz (2011) "Secret Fed Loans Gave Banks $13 Billion Undisclosed to Congress," *Bloomberg News*, https://tinyurl.com/y6c5bd2w.

Jacobson, L. (2015) "Donald Trump Says the Unemployment Rate May Be 42 Percent," *Politifact.com*, September 30, https://tinyurl.com/yb5bdezj.

Jaumotte, F., and C. Osorio Buitron (2015) "Inequality and Labour Market Institutions," *IMF Staff Discussion Note No. 15/14*. Washington: International Monetary Fund, https://www.imf.org/external/pubs/ft/sdn/2015/sdn1514.pdf.

Jebb A., L. Tay, E. Diener, and S. Oishi (2018) "Happiness, Income Satiation and Turning Points around the World," *Nature Human Behaviour*, 2(January): 33–8.

Johnson, S. (2009) "The Quiet Coup," *The Atlantic*, May, https://tinyurl.com/yd2t6gl9.

Jones, R. (2019) "The End of a Scandal: Banks Near a Final Release from Their PPI Liabilities," *The Guardian*, August 24, https://tinyurl.com/yxgp237g.

Jung, J., and R. J. Shiller (2005) "Samuelson's Dictum and the Stock Market," *Economic Inquiry*, 43(2): 221–8.

Kahneman, D. (2010) "The Riddle of Experience vs. Memory," TED talk, https://tinyurl.com/pganv4s.

Kahneman, D., and A. B. Krueger (2006) "Developments in the Measurement of Subjective Wellbeing," *Journal of Economic Perspectives*, 20(1): 3–24.

Kahneman, D., and A. Deaton (2010) "High Income Improves Evaluation of Life but Not Emotional Wellbeing," *Proceedings of the National Academy of Sciences of the United States of America*, 107(38): 16489–93.

Kalecki, M. (1937) "A Theory of the Business Cycle," *Review of Economic Studies*, 4(2) : 77–97.

Keen, S. (2011) *Debunking Economics: The Naked Emperor Dethroned*, 2nd ed. London: Zed Books.

Keynes, J. M. (1923) *A Tract on Monetary Reform*. London: Macmillan.

Keynes, J. M. (1931) *Essays in Persuasion*. London: Palgrave Macmillan.

Keynes, J. M. (1936) *The General Theory of Employment, Interest and Money*. London: Palgrave Macmillan.

Keynes, J. M. (1937) "The General Theory of Employment," *Quarterly Journal of Economics*, 51: 209–23.

Kindleberger, C. P. (1973) *The World in Depression, 1929–39*. Orlando: University of California Press.

Kindleberger, C. P. (1978) *Manias, Panics, and Crashes: A History of Financial Crises*. Palgrave-Macmillan.

Klein, M. (2013) "The Best Way to Save Banking Is to Kill It," *Bloomberg News*, March 27, https://tinyurl.com/c6qx9yy.

Koo, R. (2008) *The Holy Grail of Macro Economics: Lessons from Japan's Great Recession*. Singapore: John Wiley.

Koo, R. (2011) "The World in Balance Sheet Recession: Causes, Cure and Politics," *Real-World Economics Review*, (58): 19–37.

Krueger, A. (2001) "Teaching the Minimum Wage in Econ 101 in Light of the New Economics of the Minimum Wage," *Journal of Economic Education*, 32(3): 243–58.

Krugman, P. (1994) *The Age of Diminished Expectations*. Cambridge, MA: MIT Press.

Krugman, P. (2009) 'How Did Economists Get It So Wrong?' *New York Times Magazine*, September 6.

Krugman, P. (2012) "Expectations and the Confidence Fairy," *New York Times Blog*, September 23, https://tinyurl.com/yckvb8b7.

Krugman, P. (2013) "How the Case for Austerity Has Crumbled," *New York Review of Books*, June.

Krugman, P. (2013) "The Four Percent Solution," *New York Times Blog*, May 24, https://tinyurl.com/4henjba4. Accessed May 16, 2022.

Krugman, P. (2014) "Why We're in a New Gilded Age," *New York Review of Books*, May 8, https://tinyurl.com/nbxrlcu.

Krugman, P. (2015) "The Case for Cuts Was a Lie: Why Does Britain still Believe It? The Austerity Delusion," *The Guardian*, UK, Wednesday April 25, https://tinyurl.com/huza4h7.

Krugman, P., and R. Wells (2018) *Macroeconomics*, 5th ed. New York: Worth Publishers, Macmillan Learning.

Lanchester, J. (2013) "Are We Having Fun Yet? On the Banks' Barely Believable Behaviour," *London Review of Books*, 35(13), July 4, https://tinyurl.com/y7bnqnqc.

Lavoie, M. (2014) *Post-Keynesian Economics: New Foundations*. Cheltenham: Edward Elgar.

Lavoie, M. (2016) "Rethinking Macroeconomic Theory before the Next Crisis." Institute for New Economic Thinking, September 23, https://tinyurl.com/y4jl58dj.

Layard, R. (2003) "Happiness: Has Social Science a Clue?," Lionel Robbins Memorial Lectures, London School of Economics, http://eprints.lse.ac.uk/47425/.

Layard, R. (2005) *Happiness: Lessons from a New Science*. New York: Penguin.

Layard, R. (2010) "Measuring Subjective Wellbeing," *Science*, January 29: 534–5.

Leijonhufvud, A. (1968) *On Keynesian Economics and the Economics of Keynes: A Study in Monetary Theory*. New York: Oxford University Press.

Leijonhufvud, A. (1973a) "Effective Demand Failures," *Swedish Journal of Economics*, 75(1): 27–48.

Leijonhufvud, A. (1973b) "Life among the Econ," *Economic Inquiry*, 11(3): 327–37.

Leijonhufvud, A. (2009) "Stabilities and Instabilities in the Macroeconomy," Vox CEPR Policy Portal, https://tinyurl.com/ya5j2u45.

Leon, D., D. Vagero, and P. Otterblad Olausson (1992) "Social Class Differences in Infant Mortality in Sweden: Comparison with England and Wales," *BMJ: British Medical Journal*, 305(6855): 687–91.

Lerner, A. (1943) "Functional Finance and the Federal Debt," *Social Research*, 10(1): 38–51.

Lindé, J., and M. Trabandt (2019) "Resolving the Missing Deflation and Inflation," Voxeu.org, November 12, https://voxeu.org/article/resolving-missing-deflation-and-inflation-puzzles.

Lindo, J. (2011) "Parental Job Loss and Infant Health," *Journal of Health Economics*, 30(5): 869–79.

Lipsey, R. (1960) "The Relation between Unemployment and the Rate of Change of Money Wage Rates in the United Kingdom, 1862–1957: A Further Analysis," *Economica*, 27(105): 1–31.

Lipsey, R., and K. Carlaw (2012) "Does History Matter? Empirical Analysis of Evolutionary versus Stationary Equilibrium Views of the Economy," *Journal of Evolutionary Economics*, 22: 735–66.

Lowrey, A. (2018) "A Promise So Big, Democrats Aren't Sure How to Keep It," *The Atlantic*, May 11, https://tinyurl.com/4wen54nx.

Lucas, R. E. (1973) "Some International Evidence on Output-Inflation Tradeoffs," *American Economic Review*, June 73, 63 (3): 326–34.

Lucas, R. E. (1976) "Econometric Policy Evaluation: A Critique," *Carnegie-Rochester Conference Series on Public Policy*, 1: 19–46.

Lucas, R. E. (1981) "Tobin and Monetarism: A Review Article," *Journal of Economic Literature*, 29(2): 558–85.

Lucas, R. E. (1988) "On the Mechanics of Economic Development," *Journal of Monetary Economics*, 22: 3–42.

Lucas, R.E. (2004) "The Industrial Revolution: Past and Future," *Economic Education Bulletin*, 44(8): 1–8.

Lucas, R. E. (2009a) "In Defence of the Dismal Science," *The Economist*, August 6.

Lucas, R. E. (2009b) "Why a Second Look Matters," *Symposium on a Second Look at the Great Depression and the New Deal, Council on Foreign Relations*, New York, http://tinyurl.com/k8hxjpn.

Lye, J., and I. McDonald (2006) "Union Power and Australia's Inflation Barrier, 1965:4 to 2003:3," *Australian Journal of Labour Economics*, 9(3): 287–304.

MacLean, B. (2015) "Quantitative Easing." In *The Encyclopedia of Central Banking*, edited by L.-P. Rochon and S. Rossi. Cheltenham: Edward Elgar, 414–16.

Malkiel, B., and E. Fama (1970) "Efficient Capital Markets: A Review of Theory and Empirical Work," *Journal of Finance*, 25(2): 383–417.

Malkiel, B. G. (1973) *A Random Walk Down Wall Street: The Time-Tested Strategy for Successful Investing*. New York: W. W. Norton.

Mangan, D. (2019) "Ex-Scotia Capital, Bear Stearns Precious Metals Trader Pleads Guilty, Will Cooperate with Feds in 'Spoofing' Probe," *CNBC*, https://tinyurl.com/y2fdmrcu.

Mankiw, N. G., and W. M. Scarth (2020) *Macroeconomics: Canadian Edition*, 6th ed. New York: Worth Publisher, Macmillan Learning.

Manning, A. (2003) *Monopsony in Motion: Imperfect Competition in Labour Markets*. Princeton, NJ: Princeton University Press.

Manski, C. (2012) "Income Tax and Labour Supply: Let's Acknowledge What We Don't know," VOX, CEPR Policy Portal, https://tinyurl.com/y3zfzqqr.

Marcuzzi, S., and A. Terzi (2019) "Are Multinationals Eclipsing Nation-States?" *Project Syndicate*, February 1, https://tinyurl.com/yxtmzwhb.

Matthews, A. (2020) "Does Finland Show the Way to Universal Basic Income?" Deutsch Welle, May 30, https://tinyurl.com/vrfyzb7h.

Mazzucato, M. (2015) *The Entrepreneurial State: Debunking Public vs. Private Sector Myths*. London: Anthem Press.

Mazzucato, M., and R. Skidelsky (2020) "Toward a New Fiscal Constitution," *Project Syndicate*, July 10, https://tinyurl.com/ydae89l5.

McBride, J. (2016) "Understanding the Libor Scandal," *The Council on Foreign Relations*, October 12, https://tinyurl.com/y9oh8h3z.

McBride, S. (2018) "Eight Things the Crisis Taught Us about Austerity," *Canadian Centre for Policy Alternatives, Monitor*, September.

McDonald, I. (2007) "Where Is Full Employment?" Dept of Economics Working Paper Series #1011, The University of Melbourne, https://mpra.ub.uni-muenchen.de/5404/2/MPRA_paper_5404.pdf.

McDonald, I., and R. M. Solow (1985) "Wages and Employment in a Segmented Labour Market," *Quarterly Journal of Economics*, 100: 1115–41.

Miles, D. (2013) "Bank Capital Requirements: Are They Costly?" *VOX CEPR Policy Portal*, January 17, https://tinyurl.com/ya39jaa3.

Minsky, H. (1986) "*Stabilizing an Unstable Economy*." First edition published by Yale University Press. Second edition published by McGraw-Hill (2008).

Minsky, H. (1986) *Stabilizing an Unstable Economy*. New Haven, CT: Yale University Press.

Mishrafeb, P. (2018) "The Rise of China and the Fall of the 'Free Trade' Myth," *The New York Times Magazine*, February 2, https://tinyurl.com/yb759hvj.

Mitchell, B. (2009) "Inflation Targeting Spells Bad Fiscal Policy," October 15, http://bilbo.economicoutlook.net/blog/?p=5451.

Mitchell, B. (2009) "The Natural Rate of Interest Is Zero!" https://tinyurl.com/ln7rsy.

Mitchell, B. (2013) "Investing in a Job Guarantee—How Much?" May 5, http://bilbo.economicoutlook.net/blog/?p=23728.

Monbiot, G. (2020) "If You Think the UK Isn't Corrupt, You Haven't Looked Hard Enough," *The Guardian*, September 10, https://tinyurl.com/y3w9zql3.

Mullainathan, S., and R. Thaler (2004) "Behavioural Economics," in *International Encyclopaedia of the Social and Behavioural Sciences*, Elsevier: Science Direct, 1094–100.

Myatt, A. (1986) "On the Non-Existence of a Natural Rate of Unemployment and Kaleckian Micro Underpinnings to the Phillips Curve," *Journal of Post Keynesian Economics*, 8(3): 447–62.

Naidu, S. (2017) "A Political Economy Take on W/Y," in *After Piketty: The Agenda for Economics and Inequality*, edited by H. Boushey, J. Bradford Delong, and M. Steinbaum, Cambridge, MA: Harvard University Press.

Nuccitelli, D., R. Way, R. Painting, J. Church, and J. Cook (2012) "Comment on Ocean Heat Content and Earth's Radiation Imbalance. II. Relation to Climate Shifts," *Physics Letters A*, 376 (45): 3466–8.

OECD (2015) "Inequality" https://www.oecd.org/social/inequality.htm.

Osberg, L. (2020) "Full Employment in Canada in the Early 21st Century," in *Aggregate Demand and Employment*, edited by MacLean, Bougrine and Rochon, Edward Elgar: 116–41.

Osberg, L., and X. Lin (2000) "How Much of Canada's Unemployment Rate is Structural?" *Canadian Public Policy*, 26, Supplement: S141–S157.

Ostry, J. D., P. Loungani, and D. Furceri (2016) "Neoliberalism: Oversold?" *Finance & Development*, 53(2): 38–41, http://www.imf.org/external/pubs/ft/fandd/2016/06/ostry.htm.

Ostry, J., A.Berg, and C. Tsangarides (2014) "Redistribution, Inequality, and Growth" IMF Staff Discussion Note, February, SDN1402, https://tinyurl.com/h2r2p2w.

Oxfam (2016) "An Economy for the 1%," Briefing Paper 210, January, https://tinyurl.com/go3q8jl.

Palley, T. (2015) "Money, Fiscal Policy and Interest Rates: A Critique of Modern Money Theory," *Review of Political Economy*, 27: 1–23.

Pannett, R. (2021) "Minimum-Wage Lessons for the U.S. from the Other Side of the World," *Washington Post*, July 26, https://tinyurl.com/5bzarnsp.

Parkin, M. (2018) *Macroeconomics*, 13th ed. New York: Pearson.

Paul, K., and Klaus Moser (2009) "Unemployment Impairs Mental Health: Meta-Analyses," *Journal of Vocational Behavior*, 74(3): 264–82.

Paul, M., W. Darity, and D. Hamilton (2018) |"The Federal Jobs Guarantee—A Policy to Achieve Permanent Full Employment." *Center on Budget and Policy Priorities*, March 9, https://tinyurl.com/ydf34uu7.

Peach, R., R. Rich, and A. Cororaton (2011), "How Does Slack Influence Inflation?," *Current Issues in Economics and Finance*, 17(3): 1–7.

Persson, T., and G. Tabellini (1994) "Is Inequality Harmful for Growth?," *American Economic Review*, 84(3): 600–21.

Philippon, T. (2008) "The Evolution of the Us Financial Industry from 1860 to 2007: Theory and Evidence." *NBER Working Paper*, No. 13405.

Philippon, T. (2011) "Has the Finance Industry Become Less Efficient? Or Where Is Wal-Mart When We Need It?" December 2, *VOX CEPR Policy Portal*, https://tinyurl.com/yb29xnjw.

Phillips, A. W. (1958) "The Relation between Unemployment and the Rate of Change of Money Wage Rates in the United Kingdom, 1861–1957," *Economica*, 25(100): 283–99.

Phillips, K. (2008) "Hard Numbers: The Economy Is Worse Than You Know," *Harper's Magazine*, April 25.

Piketty, T. (2014) *Capital in the Twenty-First Century*, Massachusetts: Belknap Press, Harvard University.

Piketty, T., S. Emmanuel, and S. Stantcheva (2014) "Optimal Taxation of Top Labor Incomes: A Tale of Three Elasticities," *American Economic Journal: Economic Policy*, 6(1): 230–71.

Pitchford, J. (1978) "The Phillips Curve and the Minimum Rate of Inflation." In *Stability and Inflation*, edited by A. R. Bergston, A. J. L. Catt, M. H. Peston and B. Silverstone, Brisbane: John Wiley.

Prasch, R. (2012) "The Obama Administration, the 49 State Mortgage Settlement, and the Spin: A Study in Shamelessness," *Huffington Post*, August 24, https://tinyurl.com/cbs3rc6.

Prasch, R. E. (2008) *How Markets Work: Supply, Demand and the "Real World."* Cheltenham: Edward Elgar, 1–173.

Prescott, E. (2002) "Prosperity and Depression," *American Economic Association, Papers and Proceedings*, 92(2): 1–16.

Prescott, E. (2004) "Why Do Americans Work So Much More than Europeans?" *Federal Reserve Bank of Minneapolis, Quarterly Review*, 28(1): 2–13.

Pullen, J. (2016) "Malthus on Growth, Glut, and Redistribution," *History of Economics Review*, 65(1): 27–48.

Quiggin, J. (2010) *Zombie Economics: How Dead Ideas Still Walk Among Us.* Princeton, NJ: Princeton University Press.

Radelet, S., and J. Sachs (2000) "The Onset of the East Asian Financial Crisis." In *Currency Crises*, Chicago: University of Chicago Press, http://www.nber.org/chapters/c8691.pdf.

Rajan, R. (2010) *Fault Lines: How Hidden Fractures Still Threaten the World Economy.* Princeton, NJ: Princeton University Press.

Raphael, S., and R. Winter-Ebmer (2001) "Identifying the Effect of Unemployment on Crime," *Journal of Law and Economics*, 44(1): 259–83.

Raworth, K. (2017) *Doughnut Economics: Seven Ways to Think Like a 21st-Century Economist.* Vermont: Chelsea Green.

Reeves, R., and K. Howard (2013) "The Glass Floor: Education, Downward Mobility, and Opportunity Hoarding." *The Brookings Center on Children and Families*, November.

Reinhart, C., and K. Rogoff (2010) "Growth in a Time of Debt," *American Economic Review*, Papers and Proceedings, 100: 573–78.

Reinhart, C. M. (2013) "A Letter to PK." http://www.carmenreinhart.com/letter-to-pk/. Accessed October 15, 2019.

Riahi, K., E. Kriegler, and J. Edmonds (2017) "The Shared Socioeconomic Pathways and Their Energy, Land Use, and Greenhouse Gas Emissions Implications: A Overview," *Global Environmental Change*, 42, January: 153–68.

Roberts, D. (2015) "Former Bank of America Executive Pleads Guilty in Bid-Rigging Scheme," February 3, *The Charlotte Observer*, https://tinyurl.com/ybpzbrw4.

Robinson, J. (1955) "*Marx, Keynes, and Marshall,*" Delhi School of Economics, University of Delhi.

Robinson, J. (1976) "Michal Kalecki: A Neglected Prophet," *New York Review of Books*, March 4.

Rodrik, D. (1998) "Who Needs Capital-Account Convertibility?" in *Should the IMF Pursue Capital-Account Convertibility? Essays in International Finance*. Princeton, NJ: Princeton University Press, 207.

Rodrik, D. (2010) "The Return of Industrial Policy," *Project Syndicate*, April 12, https://tinyurl.com/y9r6r49y.

Rodrik, D. (2016) "A Progressive Logic of Trade," *Project Syndicate*, April 13, https://tinyurl.com/ycota8qm.

Rogoff, K. (2017) "Dealing with Monetary Paralysis at the Zero Bound," *Journal of Economic Perspectives*, 31(3): 47–66.

Rogoff, K. (2019) "The Austerity Chronicles,"*Project Syndicate*, April 5,https://tiny url.com/56xksrt6.

Rogoff, K. (2020) "The Case for Deeply Negative Rates," *Project Syndicate*, May 4, https://tinyurl.com/yxekauff.

Romer, C., and J. Bernstein (2009) "The Job Impact of the American Recovery and Investment Plan," *Office of the President Elect*, January 9.

Rosling, H. (2014) "The Overpopulation Myth," https://tinyurl.com/y5g2qfbu.

Roubini, N. (2018) "The Big Blockchain Lie," *Project Syndicate*, https://tinyurl.com/ydfjvtun.

Rowe, N. (2013) "The Bank of Canada's Success and Failure," Worthwhile Canadian Initiative, https://tinyurl.com/yy7u962p.

Runciman, D. (2009) "How Messy It All Is," *London Review of Books*, 31(20), https://tinyurl.com/yavfzur.

Rushe, D. (2011) "Bernard Madoff Says Banks and Funds Were 'Complicit' in $90bn Fraud," *The Guardian*, February, 2011, https://tinyurl.com/y9uuwdvf.

Sacks, D. W., B. Stevenson, and J. Wolfers (2012) "The New Stylized Facts about Income and Subjective Wellbeing," *Emotion*, 12(6): 1181–7.

Samuel, S. (2020) "Everywhere Basic Income Has Been Tried, in One Map," Vox.com, October 20, https://tinyurl.com/2tp3k79j.

Samuelson, P. (2004) "Where Ricardo and Mill Rebut and Confirm Arguments of Mainstream Economists Supporting Globalization," *Journal of Economic Perspectives*, 18(3): 135–46.

Samuelson, P. (1957) "Intertemporal Price Equilibrium: A Prologue to the Theory of Speculation," *Weltwirtschaftliches Archiv*, 79: 181–219.

Sanandaji, N., T. Sanandaji, A. Malm, and C. Snowdon (2010) "Un-Level Ground," *Wall Street Journal*. July 9.

Scarth, W. M. (2014) *Macroeconomics: The Development of Modern Methods for Policy Analysis*. Cheltenham: Edward Elgar.

Schroeder, P. (2012) "NY Regulator: British Bank Helped Iran Evade Sanctions, Hide Billions," *The Hill*, June 8, https://tinyurl.com/ya2mosgq.

Scott, M. (2012) "Former Senior Barclays Executive Faces Scrutiny in Parliament," *The New York Times*, July 16, https://tinyurl.com/yaeqsfzh.

Seccareccia, M. (2004) "What Type of Unemployment? A Critical Evaluation of 'Government as the Employer of Last Resort' Policy Proposal," *Investigación Económica*, LXIII, 247, enero-marzo: 15–43.

Sen, A. K. (1981) *Poverty and Famines: An Essay on Entitlement and Deprivation*. Oxford: Oxford University Press.

Sen, A. K. (1993) "The Economics of Life and Death," *Scientific American*, May: 40–7.

Setterfield, M., D. Gordon, and L. Osberg (1992) "Searching for a Will o' the Wisp: An Empirical Study of the NAIRU in Canada," *European Economic Review*, 36: 119–36.

Shaikh, A. (1974) "Laws of Production and Laws of Algebra: The Humbug Production Function," *Review of Economics and Statistics*, 56(1): 115–20.

Shiller, R. (1981) "Do Stock Prices Move too Much to Be Justified by Subsequent Changes in Dividends?," *American Economic Review*, 7(3): 421–36.

Simon, J. (1981, 1996) *The Ultimate Resource*, Princeton, NJ: Princeton University Press.

Smith, N. (2012) "Why Bother with Microfoundations?" http://noahpinionblog. blogspot.ca/2012/03/why-bother-with-microfoundations.html.

Smith, N. (2017) "Supply-Siders Still Push What Doesn't Work: The Old Recipe of Tax Cuts, Deregulation and Fiscal Austerity Does Little for Growth," Bloomberg, https://tinyurl.com/y3waxx8g.

Snowdon, C. (2010) *The Spirit Level Delusion: Fact-checking the Left's New Theory of Everything*, Democracy Institute/Little Dice.

Solow, R. (1987) "Unemployment: Getting the Questions Right," *Economica*, 53: 23–34.

Solow, R. M. (1957) "Technical Change and the Aggregate Production Function," *Review of Economics and Statistics*, 39(3): 312–20.

Solow, R. M. (2014) "Thomas Piketty Is Right," *The New Republic*, April, https://tiny url.com/y84mlnps.

Son, H., and D. Mangan (2018) "Former JP Morgan Trader Pleads Guilty to Manipulating US Metals Markets for Years." November 6, *cnbc.com*, https://tiny url.com/yyz9jfed.

Spitz, J. (1989) "An Empirical Test of Efficiency Wage Theory," Stanford Graduate School of Business, Working Papers No. 1053.

Staiger, D., J. Stock, and M. Watson (1997) "The NAIRU, Unemployment, and Monetary Policy," *Journal of Economic Perspectives*, 11(1): 33–49.

Stanford, J. (2015) *Economics for Everyone: A Short Guide to the Economics of Capitalism*, 2nd ed. Ottawa: CCPA and Pluto Press.

Stempel, J. (2013) "Ex-GE bankers freed, U.S. too slow to charge bid rigging," *Reuters*, December 9, https://tinyurl.com/yda8jqe6.

Stevenson, B., and J. Wolfers (2008) "Economic Growth and Subjective Wellbeing: Reassessing the Easterlin Paradox," *Brookings Papers on Economic Activity*, Spring: 1–87.

Stiglitz, J. (2003) *The Roaring Nineties: A New History of the World's Most Prosperous Decade*. New York: W. W. Norton.

Stiglitz, J. (2019) "How Can We Tax Footloose Multinationals," Project Syndicate, February 13, https://tinyurl.com/yxhd9ehr.

Stockman, D. (2015) The Warren Buffett Economy – Why Its Day Are Numbered (Part 4), June 15, https://tinyurl.com/y5or2cq9.

Strange, S. (1996) *The Retreat of the State: The Diffusion of Power in the World Economy*. Cambridge: Cambridge University Press.

Stuckler, D., and S. Basu (2013) *The Body Economic: Why Austerity Kills*. New York: Basic Books.

Summers, L. (1985) "On Economics and Finance," *Journal of Finance*, 40(3): 633–5.

Summers, L. (2019) "The Left's Embrace of Modern Monetary Theory Is a Recipe for Disaster," *The Washington Post*, March 4, https://tinyurl.com/3zdj3z8t.

Taibbi, M. (2010) "The Great American Bubble Machine," *Rolling Stone*, April 5, https://tinyurl.com/y3nypuy6.

Taibbi, M. (2012) "The Scam Wall Street Learned from the Mafia," *Rolling Stone*, June 21, https://tinyurl.com/y7wmy9l5.

Taibbi, M. (2013) "Gangster Banks: Too Big to Jail," *Rolling Stone*, February 14, https://tinyurl.com/y74bzmjf.

Taibbi, M. (2019) "Turns Out That Trillion-Dollar Bailout Was, in Fact, Real," *Rolling Stone*, March 18, https://tinyurl.com/y26kdcq2.

Taylor, J. (1993) "Discretion versus Policy Rules in Practice," *Carnegie-Rochester Conference Series on Public Policy*, 39: 195–214.

Tcherneva, P. (2017) "Unemployment: The Silent Epidemic," Levy Economics Institute, Working Paper #895.

Tcherneva, P. (2018) "The Job Guarantee: Design, Jobs, and Implementation," *Levy Economics Institute*, Working Paper No. 902.

Thanassoulis, J. (2009) "Now Is the Right Time to Regulate Bankers' Pay," *The Economists' Voice*, 6 (5): 1–4.

Tobin, J. (1978) "A Proposal for International Monetary Reform," *Eastern Economic Journal*, 4 (3/4): 153–9.

Tobin, J. (1972) "Inflation and Unemployment," *The American Economic Review*, 62, March: 1–18.

Turner, A. (2010) "Economic Growth, Human Welfare and Inequality." The Lionel Robbins Memorial Lectures, https://tinyurl.com/yczuog5e.

Turner, D. (2016) "The Use of Models in Producing OECD Macroeconomic Forecasts," *OECD Economics Department Working Papers*, No. 1336, Paris: OECD Publishing.

Walsh, M. (2014) "Financial Adviser Sidesteps Prison in Bond-Rigging Case," March 12, *New York Times*, https://tinyurl.com/ycx9qjr3.

Weise, K. (2019) "Microsoft Pledges $500 million for Affordable Housing in Seattle Area," *New York Times*, January 16, https://tinyurl.com/yd4xg5p2.

Wilkinson, F. (1984) *The Dynamics of Labour Market Segmentation*. London: Academic Press.

Wilkinson, R., and K. Pickett (2009) *The Spirit Level: Why More Equal Societies Almost Always Do Better*. London: Allen Lane.

Willms, D. (1997) "OECD programme for international student assessment," OECD.

Wolf, M. (2013) "Why Bankers Are Intellectually Naked," *Financial Times*, March 17.

Wolfers, J. (2011) "The Least Radical Case for Happiness Economics," *Freakonomics*, May 21, https://tinyurl.com/y7rl22ws.

Wray, R. (2019) "Everything You Want to Know about Modern Monetary Theory," Bloomberg Business Week Talks, https://tinyurl.com/yy5z7zpr.

Wren-Lewis, S. (2018) *The Lies We Were Told: Politics, Economics, Austerity and Brexit*. Bristol: Bristol University Press.

INDEX

Williams, John 40
Wind, The 17
winner-take-all markets 97–8
Winston, Michael 226
Winterkorn, Martin 226
Wolf, Martin 233
Wolfers, J. 90
Works Progress Administration
    284, 308
World Bank 286

World Business Council for
    Sustainable Development 82
Wray, Randall 193

zero-hours contract work 46
zero inflation 262
zero lower bound and quantitative
    easing 253–4
zero tax rate 177